Since *apologia* refers to a legal argument, it makes perfect sense that defending the faith should find the courtroom a suitable analogy for the specific kind of truth-claim that is the gospel. And no one has ever excelled J. W. Montgomery in articulating this apologetic approach and exhibiting its effectiveness in countless debates for more than a half-century. Although I have had the privilege of teaching alongside Dr. Montgomery on many occasions, there are some essays in this volume that I have not read before. Others I have read many times and will read again and again. This volume is chock-full of some of his best work previously available only to specialists. So make friends with your inner lawyer as you explore the wisdom, wit and immensely practical fruit of a remarkable thinker.

>   Michael Horton, Ph.D., D.D., J. Gresham Machen Professor of Systematic Theology and Apologetics, Westminster Seminary California, co-host of the White Horse Inn and author of *Core Christianity*

In this fascinating collection, the distinguished apologist John Warwick Montgomery shows the relevance of legal reasoning – so often neglected by theologians and philosophers – to the defense of the Gospel and to a wide range of theologically important topics. As always, Montgomery provokes readers to reconsider their prejudices--and to let the evidence have the final word. For a culture distracted by ideology and hearsay, this is a most welcome antidote.

>   Angus Menuge, Ph.D., Professor and Chair of Philosophy, Concordia University Wisconsin; President of the Evangelical Philosophical Society.

For over fifty years the name John Warwick Montgomery has been synonymous with Christian apologetics. He is hands down the leading defender of the faith with regard to legal and evidential apologetics. If you want to experience a genius mind at work in defending the gospel in legal style, read this book!

>   Chad Meister is Professor of Philosophy and Theology at Bethel College, USA

John Warwick Montgomery is the founder of the modern-day legal apologetic. What a privilege to have this new book featuring some of his finest argumentation! His apologetic method, with its focus on the resurrection of Jesus, draws people to faith. Its appeal is the common use of the legal paradigm. People daily encounter the juridical process. Now we have a collection of essays from the leading exponent of how to use legal reasoning to defend classic Christianity. The chapter in defense of Christ's resurrection "by way of Wigmore's juridical analysis of evidence" is alone worth the price of this book. The book also explores the application of the legal paradigm to theological issues beyond the strictly apologetical. As always, Montgomery's writing is accessible to all. A "must read" and essential resource for all who take the scriptural command in 1 Peter 3:15 seriously.

> Dr Ross Clifford, Principal, Morling Theological College, Sydney, Australia; former lawyer and barrister; graduate of the University of Sydney, the Australian College of Theology, the Simon Greenleaf School of Law; President of the Asia Pacific Baptist Federation, past President Baptist Union of Australia; author of 10 books including, Leading Lawyers Case for the Resurrection.

One might think that after writing more than 60 books in six languages and obtaining 11 earned degrees (including three doctorates), John Warwick Montgomery might be tempted to take a short literary holiday. Thankfully, not so! This volume is Montgomery at his controversial, hard-hitting and often politically-incorrect best as he brilliantly defends both the truth claims and resulting societal impact of Christianity, establishing that Christian belief and practice are positions of maximum relevancy in addressing the major secular challenges of our day. The field of legal apologetics would simply not exist in its current robust form absent the tireless efforts of Dr. Montgomery and the International Academy of Apologetics in Strasbourg (www.apologeticsacademy.eu) where, for over two decades, he has taught that St. Luke's "many infallible proofs" supporting the Christian proclamation are overwhelmingly sufficient to persuade any reasonable secular juror. There is simply no other thinker in Christendom who combines the professional expertise of a lawyer, historian, philosopher and theologian with the panache of an internationally regarded trial lawyer.

> Craig Parton, A.B., M.A., J.D., (Chairman of the Litigation Department of Price, Postel & Parma LLP of Santa Barbara, California)

This book brings together a wide range of essays – insightful, provocative work from one who is both an eminent scholar of legal apologetics and its greatest living practitioner. It is hard to imagine a reader who would not learn much from these pages.

> Dr. Timothy McGrew, Professor and Chairman, Department of Philosophy, Western Michigan University

Dr Montgomery is a trail-blazing creative scholar who has devoted his life's work to defending and commending the gospel message that God was in Jesus Christ reconciling the world to himself. In *Defending the Gospel in Legal Style* we quickly appreciate his gifted and creative thoughts which are expressed in a series of crisply written essays. He acts as a venerable teacher and guide to help non-lawyers understand how the lawyer's craft may be applied in testing both the documentary and eyewitness evidence for Jesus' resurrection. He also discusses crucial questions about the standard of proofs and the evidential criteria that is needed to assemble a case and reach a verdict on the resurrection. In part two he show cases how to think like a lawyer about theological matters such as doctrinal fidelity as well as highlighting the relevance of Christian apologetics in the church's heritage. He also teases out the heartfelt tensions between religious and secular values by illustrating the problems that arise when socially and politically conservative values are narrowly interpreted as being synonymous with a biblical understanding of life in the public square. Other controversial questions he discusses include the problem of religious fraud and the tensions generated about immigration in the midst of the terrorist crisis. The final part of the book contains brief articles where Montgomery's razor sharp logic cuts through matters under discussion. I enjoyed reading and re-reading all the essays which I found challenging and rewarding. I warmly commend it as a text that is rich in thought, incisive in observations, very witty in delivery, as well as frequently ruffling feathers in its no-nonsense arguments. You may discover that you do not have to become a credentialled lawyer in order to think like one about ultimate questions.

> Philip Johnson, Visiting lecturer in apologetics, Morling Theological College, Sydney Australia, and co-author of *Taboo or To Do* and *The Cross is not Enough: Living as witnesses to the resurrection*.

This new collection of essays by John Warwick Montgomery is a must read for anyone who wants to do serious apologetics in the modern age. Montgomery is still the *maestro* of the legal-evidential approach to defending the faith and *Defending the Gospel in Legal Style* is a brilliant presentation of this effective, creative, and biblical methodology. This is vintage Montgomery – not only erudite and educational, but always delightfully entertaining. I have been a fan of his work for forty years and this collection is a great way to get a grand introduction and survey of some of JWM's best thinking on key theological, cultural, and apologetic issues.

> Craig J. Hazen, Ph.D., Founder and Director, Graduate Program in Christian Apologetics, Biola University; Editor of the Journal, *Philosophia Christi*

In the specified field of legal apologetics, my good friend John Warwick Montgomery is without peer – he is at the head of the class! For many years I have enjoyed thoroughly his apologetic forays across the evidential spectrum, covering such a wonderfully wide range of crucial topics. Once again, I was delighted to see this new volume and its wealth of evidences and interactive critiques. His works have always held treasured places on my book shelves and this one will take its place alongside the many others. Kudos once again, John! Highly recommended!

> Gary R. Habermas, Distinguished Research Professor & Chair, Dept. of Philosophy, Liberty University

In today's culture, the Gospel is in need of defense and sadly, the church is not doing a great job. When it does venture into apologetics, it often resorts to presuppositionalism, which is unhelpful or its focus is on personal experience or holiness, neither of which provide concrete evidence to get the unbeliever to the cross. Dr. Montgomery reminds us of the need to provide a legal defense as directed by the apostle Peter (I Peter 3:15). This book presents the evidence for the gospel in a persuasive manner and the arguments are skillfully made by a well trained barrister. It is a must read for those interested in defending the faith and getting people to reach a verdict! It should be a required text for college and seminary courses on apologetics.

> The Honourable Dallas K. Miller, Justice of the Alberta Supreme Court, Lethbridge, Alberta, Canada

John Warwick Montgomery

**Defending the Gospel in Legal Style**

# Christliche Philosophie heute – Christian Philosophy Today – Quomodo Philosophia Christianorum Hodie Estimatur

## Volume 19

Vol. 1: John Warwick Montgomery. Tractatus Logico-Theologicus.

Vol. 2: John W. Montgomery. Hat die Weltgeschichte einen Sinn? Geschichtsphilosophien auf dem Prüfstand.

Vol. 3: John W. Montgomery. Jésus: La raison rejoint l'histoire.

Vol. 4: Horst Waldemar Beck. Marken dieses Äons: Wissenschaftskritische und theologische Diagnosen.

Vol. 5: Ross Clifford. John Warwick Montgomery's Legal Apologetic: An Apologetic for All Seasons.

Vol. 6: Thomas K. Johnson. Natural Law Ethics: An Evangelical Proposal.

Vol. 7: Lydia Jaeger. Wissenschaft ohne Gott? Zum Verhältnis zwischen christlichem Glauben und Wissenschaft.

Vol. 8: Herman Bavinck. Christliche Weltanschauung. hrsg. von Thomas K. Johnson und Ron Kubsch.

Vol. 9: John W. Montgomery. La Mort de Dieu: Exposé et critique du plus récent mouvement théologique en Amérique: Réimpression de l'édition 1971.

Vol. 10: David Andersen. Martin Luther – The Problem of Faith and Reason: A Reexamination in Light of the Epistemological and Christological Issues.

Vol. 11: Wim Rietkerk. In dubio: Handbuch für Zweifler.

Vol. 12: Patrick Werder: Wenig niedriger als Gott: Der Mensch als Person von der Antike bis zur Gegenwart.

Vol. 13: John Warwick Montgomery: Christ As Centre and Circumference: Essays Theological, Cultural and Polemic.

Vol. 14: Lydia Jaeger. Als Mensch in Gottes Welt: Im Licht der Schöpfung leben.

Vol. 15: Frederik Herzberg. Theo-Logik: Über den Beitrag des Jansenismus zur formalen Methode in Theologie und Religionsphilosophie.

Vol. 16: Hanniel Strebel. Eine Theologie des Lernens: Systematisch-theologische Beiträge aus dem Werk von Herman Bavinck.

Vol. 17: John Warwick Montgomery. Fighting the Good Fight – A Life in Defense of the Faith.

Vol. 18: Henry Hock Guan Teh. Principles of the Law of Evidence and Rationality Applied in the Johannine Christology: An Argument for the Legal Evidential Apologetics.

John Warwick Montgomery

# Defending the Gospel in Legal Style
## Essays on Legal Apologetics & the Justification of Classical Christian Faith

WIPF & STOCK · Eugene, Oregon

Wipf and Stock Publishers
199 W 8th Ave, Suite 3
Eugene, OR 97401

Defending the Gospel in Legal Style
Essays on Legal Apologetics & the Justification of Classical Christian Faith
By Montgomery, John Warwick
Copyright©2017 by Montgomery, John Warwick
ISBN 13: 978-1-4982-9875-9
Publication date 10/10/2017
Previously published by Verlag für Kultur und Wissenschaft, 2017

To

**Professor Dr Dr Dr Thomas Schirrmacher**

Faithful Theologian and Friend

# Contents

Foreword (by Thomas Schirrmacher) .......................................................... 13
Preface ........................................................................................................... 15
Acknowledgments ....................................................................................... 17

PART ONE: LEGAL APOLOGETICS *PER SE* ................................................... 19
1. How Much Evidence to Justify Religious Conversion? ...................... 21
2. The Criminal Standard of Proof ........................................................... 35
3. Legal Evidence for the Truth of the Faith ........................................... 47
4. A New Approach to the Apologetic for Christ's Resurrection by Way of Wigmore's Juridical Analysis of Evidence ............................. 55
5. Legal Hermeneutics and the Interpretation of Scripture .................. 69
6. Higher Criticism and the Legal Standard for Expert Testimony ...... 81
7. Law and Justice ...................................................................................... 93
8. Why Human Rights Are Impossible Without Religion ..................... 129

PART TWO: THINKING LIKE A LAWYER IN THE THEOLOGICAL REALM ....................... 145
9. Artificial Intelligence and Societal Transformation .......................... 147
10. The Last Meow: An Indeterminacy Argument for God's Existence, with a Further Glance at Schrödinger's Cat ................... 155
11. Apologetics Insights from the Thought of I. J. Good ....................... 161
12. Miracle Evidence: How Philosophers Go Wrong ............................. 171
13. The Heritage of the Reformation – and Why It Should Be Defended ............................................................................................. 177
14. The Apologetic Thrust of Lutheran Theology .................................. 191
15. Christian Apologetics in the Light of the Lutheran Confessions .... 209
16. The Kloha Catastrophe ....................................................................... 227
17. Christian Concern UK: Evangelicals contra Irreligion in an Increasingly Secular Britain .............................................................. 273
18. A Non-Politically-Correct Remedy to Muslim Terrorist Immigration ........................................................................................ 281
19. Religious Fraud: Its Etiology and Prevention .................................. 293
20. Doctrinal Fidelity in the Light of Comparative Professional Negligence .......................................................................................... 303

PART THREE: SHORT ESSAYS ON CRITICAL TOPICS ............................................ 313
21. Lesser-of-Evils ...................................................................................... 315
22. Reflections on John 7:53-8:11 ............................................................. 319
23. Secularism and Stupidity in the Fast Lane ........................................ 321

24. "Intolerant Religion" As Threat To "Tolerant-Liberal Democracy"? ..................................................................................... 323
25. The New Age of Christian Martyrdom ................................................ 327
26. "Ararat," the Armenians, and Missionary Doctor Clarence Ussher ..................................................................................................... 329
27. Martin Scorsese's *Silence* ...................................................................... 333
28. Evangelical Chauvinism ......................................................................... 337
29. American Law and Freedom of Expression ....................................... 341
30. Hate Speech ............................................................................................. 345
31. Check Your References ......................................................................... 349
32. Beliefs Have Consequences – in Spades! ........................................... 353
33. Why English Theology and Churchmanship Are Hopelessly Weak ......................................................................................................... 357
34. Parabolic Interpretation ........................................................................ 361
35. Two Mathematical Excursions ............................................................. 367
36. Regeneration: Biological, Computational, Theological .................. 373

**INDEX OF NAMES** ........................................................................................ 383

# Foreword

*By Thomas Schirrmacher*

In recent years, we have published several new books by John Warwick Montgomery (*Tractatus Logico-Theologicus*, 2002, fifth ed. 2012, *Heraldic Aspects of the German Reformation*. 2003, *Homeschooling in America and in Europe: A Litmus Test of Democracy*, 2014; *The Libraries of France at the Ascendancy of Mazarin*, 2015; *Fighting the Good Figth: A Life in Defense of the Faith*, 2105), and also reprinted some of his earlier books in German (on China: *China zur Zeit des Massakers auf dem Tiananmenplatz*, 2011; on history: *Hat die Weltgeschichte einen Sinn?* 2003) and in French (*Jésus: La raison rejoint l'histoire*, 2003; *La Mort de Dieu*, 2009). We also published Ross Clifford's work, *John Warwick Montgomery's Legal Apologetic: An Apologetic for All Seasons*, 2004.

In 2002 we began gathering older articles and essays as well as unpublished studies so as to make them available to a wider public (*Christ our Advocate: Studies in Polemical Theology, Jurisprudence and Canon Law*, 2002; *Christ As Centre and Circumference: Essays Theological, Cultural and Polemic*, 2012). And still there were more, as this present volume shows! Reactions from all over the world demonstrate how highly Christians from very different cultures and conditions value the thoughts of this giant of biblical and Reformation theology.

Montgomery, to be sure, is first of all a son of Luther, not of Calvin. He is not an ascetic like Calvin; he praises Luther and his heirs for their influence on music, art, culture and even good food and wine. Yet, what he has in common with Calvin is obvious: 1. His love for the French language and culture, 2. theology as apologetics and the conviction that apologetics follows legal rules. So his having been trained as lawyer has added mightily to his defense of revealed truth.

In common was Luther and Calvin, Montgomery's writings continually display his conviction that theology, even systematic theology, is not produced in an ivory tower but in the very life and conflicts of the church. Here we have an explanation for his many, many superb shorter and longer contributions on a remarkable variety of contemporary issues and in amazingly different genres – all of them worthy of preservation for the future. For Montgomery, truth mandates struggle in the everyday life of the church and society; and the fact that a defense of truth mirrors the original situation is not something militating against its later use – just the opposite.

Five hundred years after the Reformation it should be obvious: If justification by faith is the central doctrine of the Christian faith, legal matters play a central role in our relation to God. God and his Holy Word are trustworthy – and that is not just a moral statement. It is also at its very heart a legal statement, for true justification will carry believers through the Last Judgment, surely the apex of all genuinely legal affairs. When we all stand before that final tribunal, only the absolute judgments by the Creator and the sacrificial advocacy by his Son will validate our poor human attempts at judgment and grace.

*Prof. Dr. Dr. Thomas Schirrmacher, publisher,*
*Associate Secretary General for Theological Concerns, World Evangelical Alliance*

# Preface

A decade ago – during April of 2007, to be exact – I received an e-mail from an unknown sender; he wrote, *inter alia*:

> I have been reading a bit of apologetics and especially your writings dealing with law and apologetics. Although there are a few other authors/lawyers writing on legal methods in apologetics, I find that you are the most qualified.
>
> Since [your] writings on legal apologetics are "scattered." I was thinking whether it would be a good idea for you to compile (systematically) [such] articles.
>
> The aim might be to come out with a new field of apologetics dealing with the evidential approach used by the law courts.

Since that time, legal apologetics has been recognized as an important branch of study in the defense of historic Christian faith – witness, as a single example, William P. Broughton's *The Historical Development of Legal Apologetics, with an Emphasis on the Resurrection* (Xulon, 2009). The American issue of Australian lawyer and theologian Dr Ross Clifford's *John Warwick Montgomery's Legal Apologetic: An Apologetic for All Seasons* (Wipf & Stock, 2016), following its original publication in Germany by the Verlag für Kultur und Wissenschaft, has given additional impetus to the arguments of the legal apologists.

It has therefore seemed fitting to pull together a number of my essays that deal, directly or indirectly, with the legal defense of historic Christian faith.

The reader will note that, unlike most legal advice, what is offered here (1) touches not just this world but eternity, and (2) will not be billed at an hourly rate to the client.

*John Warwick Montgomery*
*31 October 2017*
*All Saints Eve: the 500th Anniversary of the Reformation*

# Acknowledgments

A number of the essays comprising the present volume have appeared elsewhere in journals or other publications. Their prior appearances are listed below – with thanks from the author for permission to reprint (occasionally with slight revisions). Asterisked essays were also included in my book, *Christ As Centre and Circumference* (VKW, 2012). Many of the papers in this book – including those previously unpublished – were delivered at a variety of international conferences, details of which are given in the first footnote to each of those essays.

"How Much Evidence to Justify Religious Conversion?": *Philosophia Christi,* Vol. 13, No. 2 (2011).

"The Criminal Standard of Proof": 148 *New Law Journal* 582 (1998).

"Legal Evidence for the Truth of the Faith": revised version and conflation of *Law and Gospel: A Study Integrating Faith and Practice* (2d ed.; Calgary, Alberta, Canada: Canadian Institute for Law, Theology and Public Policy, 1994), chap. 16 (in article form in *Modern Reformation,* March/April, 2006), and "Witnesses, Criteria for," *New Dictionary of Christian Apologetics,* ed. C. Campbell-Jack and G. J. McGrath (Leicester, England: Inter-Varsity Press, 2006). A shorter version of this article appeared in *Border Crossings: Festschrift for Irving Hexham,* ed. Ulrich van der Heyden and Andreas Feldtkeller (Stuttgart, Germany: Franz Steiner Verlag, 2008).*

"A New Approach to the Apologetic for Christ's Resurrection": *Journal of the International Society of Christian Apologetics,* Vol. 3, No. 1 (2010).*

"Legal Hermeneutics and the Interpretation of Scripture": *Evangelical Hermeneutics: Selected Essays from the 1994 Evangelical Theological Society Convention,* ed. M. Bauman and D. Hall (Camp Hill, PA: Christian Publications, 1995).*

"Law and Justice": *Applying the Scriptures: Papers from ICBI Summit III,* ed. Kenneth S. Kantzer (Grand Rapids, MI: Zondervan Academie Books, 1987).

"Why Human Rights Are Impossible Without Religion": *A Place for Truth*, ed. Dallas Willard (Downers Grove, IL: IVP Books, 2010).

"Artificial Intelligence and Societal Transformation": 16/1 *Acta Systematica: Journal of the International Institute for Advanced Studies in Systems Research and Cybernetics* (2016).

"Apologetics Insights from the Thought of I. J. Good": 13/1 *Philosophia Christi* (2011).

"Miracle Evidence: How Philosophers Go Wrong": 17/1 *Philosophia Christi* (2015).

"The Apologetic Thrust of Lutheran Theology": *Lutheran Synod Quarterly*, Fall, 1970; *Ditt Ord är Sanning: En handbok om Bibeln*, ed. S. Erlandsson (Uppsala: Stiftelsen Biblicum, 1971) [in Swedish]; *Modern Reformation*, January/February, 1998 [abridged]; *Theologia et Apologia*, ed. A. S. Francisco, K. D. Maas, and S. P. Mueller (Eugene: OR: Wipf & Stock, 2007).

"Christian Apologetics in the Light of the Lutheran Confessions": *Concordia Theological Quarterly*, July, 1978.*

"The Kloha Catastrophe": *Christian News* (multiple issues and in pamphlet format), 2015-2016.

"Doctrinal Fidelity in the Light of Comparative Professional Negligence": *Christian News*, January 16, 2017.

Previously-published essays in Part Three of this book first appeared as editorial introductions to issues of the *Global Journal of Classical Theology* (www.globaljournalct.com), with the exception of "Why English Theology and Churchmanship Are Hopelessly Weak," which was published in *Anglican Way: the Magazine of the Prayer Book Society*, Vol. 37, No. 1 (March, 2014), with responses and author's rejoinder; and "Martin Scorsese's *Silence*," which first appeared in *Christian News* (27 February 2017).

# Part One:

# Legal Apologetics *Per Se*

# 1. How Much Evidence to Justify Religious Conversion?

## Some Thoughts on Burden and Standard of Proof vis-à-vis Christian Commitment

A simple answer to the question posed in the title of this essay would be: "None" – since it is perfectly possible to make a genuine religious commitment, even to Christianity, without troubling oneself with matters of proof. One thinks of John Wesley, appropriately to become one of the fathers of 18th-century revivalism and the Great Awakening, who, at a little Moravian meeting in Aldersgate, found his heart "strangely warmed."[1] Since the essence of Christian commitment is personal recognition that one has fallen short of God's perfect standards and that restoration to fellowship with him is available only through the redemption Christ accomplished on the Cross, that commitment can occur without agonies over evidential considerations.

However, in a secular age highly critical of Christian claims and offering a plethora of religious and philosophical options, many seeking persons hesitate to commit to the Christian gospel on the ground of their doubts as to what would constitute a reasonable decision. Having heard, pondered, and seen the value of what the New Testament describes as the "many infallible proofs"[2] of Christian truth, they are still deeply troubled as what whether any such evidences would really justify a life commitment. Example: a participant at the July, 2011, session of our annual International Academy of Apologetics, Evangelism and Human Rights,[3] wrote to us on registering: "I think Christianity hasn't met its burden of proof. I'm pretty familiar with the standard apologetic arguments, and I don't find

---

[1] "In the evening I went very unwillingly to a society in Aldersgate Street, where one was reading Luther's preface to the Epistle to the Romans. About a quarter before nine, while the leader was describing the change which God works in the heart through faith in Christ, I felt my heart strangely warmed. I felt I did trust in Christ alone for salvation; and an assurance was given me that He had taken away **my** sins, even **mine**, and saved **me** from the law of sin and death" (*Journal* of John Wesley, May 24, 1738).

[2] Acts 1:3.

[3] http://www.apologeticsacademy.eu

them compelling. They strike me as useful only if someone has a preconception that needs to be supported."

This paper will deal only incidentally with specific Christian evidences as such, since these have been set out in great detail elsewhere.[4] Our purpose here is simply to pose the question: *given that evidence for a religious position does exist,* what in principle would constitute adequate ground for committing oneself to the truth of the faith to which that evidence points?

The Academy participant just quoted uses the expression "burden of proof." This is quite natural, since evidential questions are particularly within the province of the law. We shall therefore begin in that realm – where the most intransigent conflicts of society are arbitrated by the refined standards of legal evidence. Any aid offered from a jurisprudential standpoint should therefore be of more than routine utility as we go on to treat the religious issue as such.[5]

## Burden of Proof

What does "burden of proof" mean? In the Anglo-American common law tradition, it refers to one of two interrelated notions: the burden of producing evidence and the burden of persuasion.

> The burden of producing evidence on an issue means the liability to an adverse ruling (generally a finding or directed verdict) if evidence on the issue has not been produced. It is usually cast first upon the party who has pleaded the existence of the fact ...
>
> In most cases, the party who has the burden of pleading a fact will have the burdens of producing evidence and of persuading the jury of its existence as well.[6]

---

[4] For example, in such works by the present author as: *Tractatus Logico-Theologicus* (5th ed.; Bonn, Germany: Verlag für Kultur und Wissenschaft, 2012); available from Wipf and Stock publishers in the western hemisphere. See also: Montgomery, *The Law Above the Law* (rev. ed.; Irvine, CA: NRP Books/1517. The Legacy Project, 2015).

[5] "If sceptics admit that the law courts are reliable instruments of justice, then they should also admit that the cognitive faculties, given adequate development and attentiveness, are reliable instruments for apprehending the world" (William C. Davis, *Thomas Reid's Ethics: Moral Epistemology on Legal Foundations* [London and New York: Continuum, 2006], p. 62). For more detail on the value of legal evidence to the defence of Christian truth, see Montgomery, *History, Law and Christianity* (3d ed.; Irvine, CA: NRP/1517.Legacy Project, 2014).

[6] *McCormick on Evidence,* ed. John William Strong (4th ed., 2 vols.; St. Paul, MN: West Publishing Co., 1992), II, 425, 427 (sec. 336, 337).

One should not conclude that the plaintiff (or the prosecutor in criminal cases) always retains the burden of producing evidence. If the defendant offers an affirmative defense (insanity, for example), that defendant has the burden of providing evidence to support his or her contention.

As for the burden of persuasion, it

> becomes a critical factor only if the parties have sustained their burdens of producing evidence and only when all of the evidence has been introduced ... The jury must be told that if the party having the burden of persuasion has failed to satisfy that burden, the issue is to be decided against that party.[7]

The interlocking of the two legal meanings of burden of proof should be obvious. In the most general terms, "traditional legal commentary has been comfortable placing burdens on the party seeking the law's intervention: on the plaintiff in civil cases and on the prosecution in criminal trials."[8] This is based on common sense, as the great 20th century authority on the law of evidence, John Henry Wigmore, argued: the principle is but a special case of "the situation common to all cases of attempted persuasion, whether in the market, the home, or the forum ... It is the *desire to have actions taken* that is important. In the affairs of life there is a penalty for not sustaining the burden of proof."[9]

What, then, of the oft-heard claim by religious believers – especially those of dogmatic or pietistic persuasion – that "the burden rests on the unbeliever to show that the faith is *not* true"? This argument is sometimes buttressed by Scripture passages such as "The fool hath said in his heart, there is no God" (and thus – the passage is said to mean – since all people other than fools believe in God, it must be the non-believer's responsibility to demonstrate his or her atheism/unbelief). But (1) the text here refers specifically to the "heart," not the "head" (there may well be non-foolish arguments against the faith even though the heart longs for God), and (2) in a pluralistic world there are numerous conflicting religious options available, so it seems silly and unproductive to expect the unbeliever to refute them all, and (3) considering the contingent nature of the universe, a cosmic negative can never be proven anyway – so attempts along this

---

[7] *Ibid.* p. 426 (sec. 336).
[8] Richard H. Gaskins, *Burdens of Proof in Modern Discourse* (New Haven, CT: Yale University Press, 1992), p. 23.
[9] John Henry Wigmore, *Evidence in Trials at Common Law,* ed. James H. Chadbourn (rev. ed., 11 vols.; Boston, MA: Little, Brown, 1981-1985), IX, 285-86 (sec. 2485); italics Wigmore's.

line hardly establish the validity of all or any positive propositions (such that a given Deity exists).

Against this effort to place the burden of proof on the unbeliever, philosopher Antony Flew argued that it should rest on the one advocating a religious position:

> If it is to be established that there is a God, then we have to have good grounds for believing that this is indeed so. Until and unless some such grounds are produced we have literally no reason at all for believing; and in that situation the only reasonable posture must be that of either the negative atheist or the agnostic. So the onus of proof has to rest on the proposition [of theism].[10]

We must concur. And we view with grave suspicion the level of spirituality of believers who try to cast the burden of proof on the non-Christian. Have they never understood St Paul's missionary principle that it is the believer who has the burden – the burden to become "all things to all men, that by all means some may be saved; and this for the gospel's sake."[11]

## Standard of Proof

It should now be plain that even though our objector writes, "I think Christianity hasn't met its burden of proof," what he is really concerned about is not the *burden* (which Christianity properly should assume) but the *standard* of proof – i.e., the degree of evidential force proffered in behalf of the faith.

What are the common-law legal principles relating to the standard of proof?

First, proof depends on *probability* – not on absolute certainty or on mere possibility. The Federal Rules of Evidence put this is very clear terms: relevant evidence is "evidence having any tendency to make the existence of any fact that is of consequence to the determination of the action more probable or less probable than it would be without the evidence."[12] This reliance on probability, rather than on absolute certainty or possibility, is

---

[10] Antony Flew, *The Presumption of Atheism: God, Freedom and Immortality* (Buffalo, NY: Prometheus Press, 1984), p. 22. Before his death in 2010, Flew moved from atheism to deism, primarily as a result of the evidence for intelligent design in the universe.

[11] Paul's entire argument is worth contemplating: 1 Corinthians 9: 19-23.

[12] Fed. R. Evid. 401. Cf. Montgomery, *Law and Gospel* (2d. ed.; Calgary, Alberta: Canadian Institute for Law, Theology and Public Policy, 1994), sec. 16 ("The Law of Evidence"), pp. 34-37.

fully in accord with the conclusions of modern analytical epistemology: the only absolute certainties are those created by definition (conformity to the primitives – chiefly the law of non-contradiction – in formal logic, conformity to the axiom set in pure mathematics, self-referential assertions such as the tautology); and these operate only in the realm of the purely *formal*. Where matters of fact are concerned – as in legal disputes, but also in the religious assertions of historic Christianity – claims can be vindicated only by way of evidential probability. As to possibilities, they can hardly be the basis of decision-making, since, in a contingent universe, *anything* is theoretically possible, so possibility reasoning can yield an infinite number of results, no one of which is necessarily compelling.

But the law does not rest with a general category of probability; it endeavours to distinguish varieties, or standards, of probability decisions. In classic English law, two such standards exist: the higher standard applicable to criminal trials (which are the most serious, since penalties can involve incarceration, and, in America, execution) and a lesser standard for civil actions. The former standard is that of "moral certainty, beyond reasonable doubt"; the latter, "preponderance of evidence." The civil standard, applicable where only money or property is usually at stake, is a mere weighing of evidence: the party able to show 51% versus the other party's 49% prevails. In criminal trials, *moral* certainty (note that the standard is not *absolute* certainty) is required before judging the defendant guilty, and "beyond reasonable doubt" is understood generally to mean that the jury, to find the defendant guilty, must be able to exclude any and all other "reasonable" explanations of the crime (i.e., explanations which would fit the admissible evidence in the case) other than that the defendant committed the crime.[13]

To be sure, these two standards are not the only ones possible. "Three standards of proof appear to be recognized in the United States, proof by 'clear, strong and cogent' evidence lying midway between proof on a preponderance of probability and proof beyond reasonable doubt."[14]

At which of these levels should evidence be required for religious commitment? The best analogy would seem to be with the criminal standard, since a religious decision, like verdicts and judgments in criminal trials,

---

[13] In modern English law, however, the judge is not permitted to define "moral certainty, beyond reasonable doubt" beyond telling the jury that they must be "certain" or "sure" of the defendant's guilt. We have suggested in a scholarly legal article on the subject that this reticence may stem at least in part from the endemic fear of the English to offend through speaking with too much precision; see Montgomery, "The Criminal Standard of Proof," *New Law Journal*, April 24, 1998.

[14] Rupert Cross, *Evidence* (5th ed.; London: Butterworths, 1979), p. 118.

entail the most serious of consequences, touching life itself. Defenders of historic Christianity have been at pains to show, for example, that (1) the prophecies of the Old Testament fulfilled in the earthly life of Jesus rise to a level of statistical significance making naturalistic explanations utterly inadequate[15]; and (2) the case for the *de facto,* physical resurrection of Christ from the dead is so powerful that all attempts to explain it away simply do not wash: they fly in the face of the relevant (and overwhelming) historical evidence.[16]

## "Extraordinary Claims Require Extraordinary Proof"?

But when one passes into the realm of religious commitment, does one not face insuperable problems not to be found in the legal realm – since religious decisions are of an eternal dimension? Can the unbeliever not argue that it is simply impossible in principle for evidence – any evidence – to justify religious commitment?

Historically, this style of argument has been presented in different guises. Going back to late classical times is the axiom, "the finite is not capable of the infinite"[17]: the world is incapable of the presence of the absolute, so no amount of evidence could ever demonstrate the presence of the infinite in our finite world. The fallacy of this argument (applicable not only to a divine Incarnation and an infallible Bible, but also to the real presence of Christ in the Holy Eucharist) is simply that, *qua* human beings, we have no idea what God is or is not capable of, so we have no business ruling out events *a priori.* It may well be that the reverse of the aphorism is true: *infinitum capax finiti!*[18] Only a factual investigation of the world to see if God has entered it will ever answer the question.

Then there is Lessing's "ditch": the claim that the accidental facts of history can never attain or justify the absolute truths of reason. Here, a

---

[15] Montgomery, "Prophecy, Eschatology and Apologetics," in his *Christ Our Advocate* (Bonn, Germany: Verlag für Kultur und Wissenschaft, 2002), pp. 255-265, also in David W. Baker (ed.), *Looking Into the Future* (Grand Rapids, MI: Baker Academic, 2001), pp. 362-70.

[16] Montgomery, *Tractatus Logico-theologicus (op. cit.),* prop. 3.1 - 3.7; Montgomery, *Christ As Centre and Circumference* (Bonn, Germany: Verlag für Kultur und Wissenschaft, 2011), Pt. 4, chap. 2.

[17] Cf. Peter Bruns, "Finitum non capax infiniti: Ein antiochenisches Axiom in der Inkarnationslehre Babais des Grossen (nach 628)," 83 *Oriens christianus* (1999), 46-71.

[18] Cf. the angel to the Virgin Mary: "With God nothing will be impossible" (Luke 1:37; see also Luke 18:24-27).

serious category mistake has been made. If the "absolute truths of reason" are purely formal, lacking entirely in content, then they have nothing to do with Christian religious claims at all. If, however, they are factual in nature, then only factual investigation and probability reasoning could justify them. But this is exactly what historical proof consists of: probable evidence for historical occurrences. If, for example, God became man in Jesus Christ, that contention is as capable of historical investigation as are any other purported occurrences.

David Hume argued that no miracle could ever be demonstrated, since (on the basis of "uniform experience") it would always be more miraculous that one claiming a miracle or providing evidence for it were not deceiving or deceived than that the miracle actually happened. Miracle arguments (such as the case for the resurrection of Christ) are therefore impossible from the outset. But Hume's position has been thoroughly refuted – and not just by Christian philosophers.[19] The intractable problem with the Humean argument is that it is perfectly circular: *to be sure,* if nature is completely uniform (i.e., if natural laws are never broken), miracles do not occur. *But that is precisely the question requiring an answer!* And the only way properly to respond is by engaging in serious factual investigation of given miracle claims. One cannot short-circuit the miracles issue by *a priori* pontifications about the nature of the universe. Indeed, as noted earlier, in an Einsteinian, relativistic universe, no event can be excluded on principle: everything is subject to empirical investigation.[20]

But the most influential current argument against the effectiveness of religious claims based on historical evidence is that represented by the adage, "Extraordinary claims require extraordinary proof" – a saying popularized by the late Carl Sagan but which apparently originated with sociologist Marcello Truzzi.[21] Does not this declaration constitute an obvious truth militating against all miracle claims – and in particular the resurrection of Christ? Since a miracle is maximally "extraordinary," would not the

---

[19] John Earman, *Hume's Abject Failure: The Argument Against Miracles* (New York: Oxford University Press, 2000).

[20] Antony Flew's preference for a "psychological miracle" (the disciples proclaiming the resurrection and dying for it whilst knowing that it never occurred) to a factual, physical "biological miracle" (Christ's resurrection) is but a variation on the Humean argument, and suffers from exactly the same aprioristic fallacy. See Montgomery, *Faith Founded on Fact* (Nashville, TN: Thomas Nelson, 1978), pp. 52-58.

[21] See Montgomery, "Apologetics Insights from the Thought of I. J. Good," 13/1 *Philosophia Christi* (2011), 203 ff.

evidence required to demonstrate it have to be maximally extraordinary as well?

In a word, the answer is No! Why? In line with what we have noted above, the Truzzi-Sagan tag would have meaning if, and only if, one knew the fabric of the universe – its cosmic laws and what therefore can and cannot happen; but in Einsteinian, relativistic terms, no one has such knowledge, so no one can rationally determine the probabilities for or against a given event: only factual investigation permits one to conclude that event *x* did or event *y* did not occur.

Does not the law, however, recognise a difference in the weight to be afforded to evidence in the case of less probable events? In an oft-quoted judgment, Lord Denning spoke of "degrees of proof" within both the criminal and the civil standards of proof:

> The degree depends on the subject-matter. A civil court, when considering a charge of fraud, will naturally require for itself a higher degree of probability than that which it would require when asking if negligence is established. It does not adopt so high a degree as a criminal court, even when it is considering a charge of a criminal nature; but still it does require a degree of probability which is commensurate with the occasion.[22]

Here we must distinguish the descriptive from the normative. Though the variation described by Denning, L. J. doubtless occurs in practice, especially when lay juries are the triers of fact, the notion that the "subject-matter" should be allowed to cause a relaxation or an augmentation of the standard of proof is a very dangerous idea. For example, ought a court take an easy view of the proof required if only £100 is fraudulently converted, but a very tough approach to the evidence if the amount is £5,000? No one would rationally agree to a sliding evidence scale dependant on the monetary sum involved – nor should such a scale be created in relation to the type of offense (little evidence to show shoplifting, much evidence to show carjacking, etc.). Thus, in discussing the standard of proof in tort actions for libel, Professor Kiralfy quite rightly observes: "The defendant who pleads justification does not have to discharge a heavier burden of proof of [the] truth of an imputation just because the imputation is a very damaging one."[23]

---

[22] *Bater v. Bater*, [1951] P. 35, at pp. 36-37.
[23] Albert Kiralfy, *The Burden of Proof* (Abingdon, Oxon., UK: Professional Books, 1987), p. 89. Professor Kiralfy refers to the case of *Lawrence v. Chester Chronicle*, [1986] 2 C.L. 329.

The application to religious arguments based on the factuality of historical events should be obvious. Of course, the resurrection of Christ is of immensely more significance than Caesar's crossing of the Rubicon, but the standards required to show that the one occurred are no different from those employed in establishing the other. If "importance" were to be allowed as a criterion for the sufficiency of evidence, it would follow that a Frenchman could legitimately require far more evidence to show that Napoleon lost at Waterloo than would be demanded by a Japanese – since the battle and its outcome are far less important to a Japanese than to a Frenchman.

But what about the very concept of a "miracle"? Is not the notion in itself so extraordinary that no amount of evidence could properly count to prove it? Here we must distinguish *mechanism* from *factuality*. The mechanism of a miracle is indeed beyond our ken – but that is irrelevant to whether or not such an event occurs. As long ago as the 18th century, Thomas Sherlock, Master of London's Temple Church and pastor to barristers, noted that the case for the resurrection of Jesus Christ does not depend on our comprehension of how resurrections occur but squarely on whether there is sufficient evidence that Jesus died on the Cross and that following his death he showed himself physically alive to sound witnesses.[24] There is thus nothing "extraordinary" about determining that Jesus rose from the dead: one need only show (a) that he died and (b) that later he was physically alive – determinations which we make every day (though in reverse order).

Are we saying that miracle evidence should be accepted as readily as non-miracle evidence? The visions of Fatima and the appearance of the Angel Moroni to Joseph Smith on the same basis as Lincoln's assassination and Hitler's *Anschluss*? We are saying simply that the standard of proof does not depend on the frequency of the event (since *all* historical events are unique) nor on the characterisation of the event as "miraculous" or "non-miraculous." The standard of proof depends, in *all* instances, on the quality of the evidence in behalf of the claimed event – that and *nothing more*; that and *nothing less*. If one were to claim that a peach can be miraculously turned into a cumquat, he or she would have to show, by ordinary scientific means, that there is a peach present at the outset, and, then, afterwards, a cumquat. For a resurrection from the dead: the same kind of

---

[24] Thomas Sherlock's *Tryal of the Witnesses of the Resurrection of Jesus* (London: J. Roberts, 1729); Sherlock's book is photolithographically reproduced in Montgomery (ed.), *Jurisprudence: A Book of Readings* (rev. ed.; Strasbourg: International Scholarly Publishers, 1980).

testimony is required as for any other historical event – in this instance, that the object of the miracle was in fact dead and then, afterwards, physically alive. The issue of proof is not in any way metaphysical: one relies on sound historical investigation of the testimony to miracle claims of past events (or sound contemporary scientific investigation, in the case of the peach). The nature of the claim determines the method of proof, and the standard will be that appropriate to parallel determinations in the same realm.

## The Existential Factor

There is, however, a further consideration worthy of treatment where religious commitment is in question. The following discussion may seem to be a variation on Pascal's Wager, but in fact it differs considerably from it. Pascal's Wager (as Pascal intended it) was an attention-focusing argument along the following line: even if there were no evidence for Christianity – or if the evidence were equally balanced *pro* and *con* – you should still accept Christ.[25] What we shall be suggesting here is that if (as is the case) there is good evidence for Christ's claims and therefore for commitment to him, hesitation should be considerably lessened by the very nature of the Christian claim itself.

Suppose one is offered an internet deal with considerable solid backup (but by no means 100% certainty). If one must provide a non-returnable sum of, say, $500, one can and should be wary. But suppose there is no requirement of a deposit: one need only send in one's address (to be on the safe side, one's post office box address) and the indicated amount will be mailed in the form of a cheque. In the latter case, any misgivings as to the standard of proof would be resolved by the nature of the offer. One would, of course, have to have sufficient confidence in the offeror to cash the cheque when it arrived, but that would involve no loss to the offeree, and therefore the reasonable solution would be to enter into the transaction.

Religions differ greatly in character. The word "religion" derives from the Latin *religio* – which is a "binding." All the religions of the world other than Christianity "bind": they involve a plethora of moral, ceremonial, and social obligations. The Christian gospel, however, is – as someone has put

---

[25] Note – as is seldom recognised – Pascal, having set forth the Wager, then proceeded to show that there are in fact powerful arguments in favour of Christian truth. See the classic edition of Pascal's *Pensées* (*Pascal's Apology for Religion*, ed. H. F. Stewart [Cambridge: Cambridge University Press, 1942]) and the recent analysis of the Wager by Jeff Jordan (*Pascal's Wager: Pragmatic Arguments and Belief in God* [New York: Oxford University Press, 2006]).

it – the *easiest* and the *hardest* religion in the world – easiest because everything for salvation has been done by God himself through Christ, so one need only accept the free gift, but hardest since this requires that one recognise one's self-centredness, and thus one's incapacity to save oneself. The hard part does not consist of having to satisfy an onerous lifestyle; it merely demands giving up one's unrealistic egocentrism – the root source of one's problems in the first place.[26]

If one considers committing oneself to the religion of Islam, questions of proof or standards of proof are of no consequence: the belief system is predestinarian and deterministic; one must simply accept the revelational authority of the Qur'an without question or evidence. On acceptance, one is saddled with a social and legal code embracing all aspects of life. Even if a proper standard of proof were minimally satisfied, one would need to consider commitment most seriously in light of the obligations following on acceptance.[27]

To become a Jehovah's Witness requires a refusal to salute the flag, to engage in military service, or to employ blood transfusions even in the case of life-threatening illness. Thus, even if there were strong evidence in behalf of the Watchtower Society's Arian view of Jesus and odd exegesis of Biblical passages (which there is not[28]), one might well hesitate to commit to that religious position.

In the case of historic Christianity, however, the burden of proof is properly assumed by the adherent, not passed off on the unbeliever, and the standard of proof is the highest: to a moral certainty. If one still hesitates becoming a Christian, perhaps one should consider that *nothing* is demanded but the recognition of one's self-centred condition (attested not just by Biblical teaching but by secular psychoanalysis, the great literature of the world, and one's own degree of self-knowledge), and a concomitant admission that one cannot pull oneself up to heaven by one's own bootstraps.

---

[26] But what about the inevitable, post-conversion "conformity to Christ"? This occurs naturally, not onerously, since (1) the Holy Spirit, who enters the heart on regeneration, is the active agent in achieving a holy life, and (2) one's value system and desires change owing to the new love relationship with Christ – just as, after an ideal marital union, the husband will prefer to spend time with his wife rather than drink at the club with his old cronies.

[27] Cf. William F. Campbell, *The Qur'an and the Bible in the Light of History and Science* (Upper Darby, PA: Middle East Resources, 1986).

[28] See, *inter alia,* Walter R. Martin, *The Kingdom of the Cults* (rev. ed.; Minneapolis: Bethany, 1985); we recommend that readers use the editions of this classic prepared by the author before his death.

Moreover, suppose that the potential and demonstrable benefits of a religious commitment are of the highest. This would then provide a further reason to commit where a properly high standard of proof is satisfied. In Islam, a paradise with virgins is offered, but this kind of "eschatological verification"[29] is hardly persuasive in this world. As for life in this world, it is ruled by a strict, predestinarian deity, whose decisions are unfathomable and to which one must submit in all instances (the word "Islam" means "submission"). As for biblical Christianity, the contrast could not be greater: there is the unqualified promise to believers in Romans 8:28 that "all things work for good" on the basis of God's character as a loving Father – a promise that has been experientially and personally verified again and again in the lives of believers.[30]

Let us express this point in formulaic as well as in diagrammatic fashion.

*Assuming that the standard of proof is satisfied* (and *only* if that is the case):

If one still hesitates in making a religious commitment, then

Where C = legitimate commitment, B = concrete, empirical benefits promised by the faith, and E = entrance requirements to the faith,

$$C = B / E$$

Ergo: *The less the entrance requirements and the higher the benefits, the more reason exists to commit to the evidence for a faith position already satisfying a high standard of proof.*

---

[29] Liberal theologian John Hick coined the term and seriously advocated it as an argument for Christianity; its silliness is reflected in Hick's later departure from the faith.

[30] And it is worth noting that the biblical promise of eternal life, unlike eschatological hopes in other religions, is grounded in the evidence for the *de facto* conquest of death by Jesus Christ. Said he: "Because I live, you shall live also" (John 14:19).

Or,

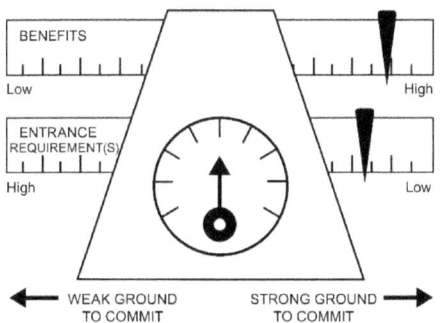

We are arguing that, in contrast with competing religious claims, acceptance of the gospel is a win-win situation. Any doubts as to satisfying the standard of proof (and can this really be a problem, since the evidence level accords with the highest legal standard?) should be resolved in favour of the gospel, not against it. To argue in any other fashion is simply to declare: *regardless of the evidence – and regardless of the maximal potential benefits available with minimal demands upon me*[31] – I prefer to remain the centre – the god – of my own life and universe. But that, as C. S. Lewis rightly observed, is the very definition of hell.

Conclusion: in light of the weight of the evidence, the only reasonable course of action is that of St Augustine in the 5th century, followed by a host of converts to Christianity across the centuries. After years of intellectual struggle, Augustine saw that Christian faith deserved his commitment. Only a moral problem remained: a lifestyle incompatible with the love of Christ. Finally, as he heard the Scriptural message, "Put ye on the Lord Jesus Christ and make not provision for the flesh" (Romans 13:13-14), "by a light as it were of serenity infused into my heart, all the darkness of doubt vanished away."[32]

---

[31] In the words of the gospel song: "Just as I am, without one plea, but that thy blood was shed for me, and that thou bidd'st me come to thee, O Lamb of God, I come, I come."

[32] Augustine, *Confessions*, VIII, sec. 12.

## 2. The Criminal Standard of Proof

When, more years ago than I like to remember, I served my pupillage with a Rumpole-like criminal barrister, I was interested to observe the reaction of juries to the judge's instruction concerning proof beyond reasonable doubt. The judge would say something like, "Members of the jury, to convict, you need to be satisfied so that you are sure of the defendant's guilt. If not, you must bring in a verdict of not guilty." When a mystified jury asked for clarification, the judge invariably (to accord with the House of Lords' approach and, more important perhaps to the judge personally, to reduce the chances of reversal on appeal) repeated himself – offering no further assistance whatsoever.

I contrasted this with my experience as a practising lawyer in the United States. There, in a fair proportion of jurisdictions, owing to the influence of the Federal constitution and state-mandated or statutory jury instructions (and, doubtless, to the American penchant for explicitness), juries are often provided with careful definitions of the "beyond reasonable doubt" standard.

A year ago, therefore, we endeavoured to test the two approaches on potential English jury members. The results are most interesting. But before describing the survey and its conclusions, let us look a bit more closely at the English and the American law relative to defining the criminal standard of proof. (The most careful study of the ideological – philosophical and theological – origins of the criminal standard of proof in Anglo-American law is B J Shapiro, *"Beyond Reasonable Doubt" and "Probable Cause"* (Berkeley: University of California Press, 1991).)

### The English Law

Lord Goddard CJ, in Kritz ([1950] 1 KB 82, 89-90.) and in Summers, ([1952] 1 All ER 1059, 1060.) set forth obiter the "satisfied so that they are sure" language most commonly used today to assist a jury with the meaning of the criminal standard of proof. That direction received the approval of the Privy Council in Walters. ([1969] 2 AC 26, 30.) Following Walters and Gray ([1973] 58 Cr App R 177, 183 (CA).), Archbold declares (at para 4-395): "It is submitted that the judge should not volunteer an explanation of the expression 'reasonable doubt.' If, however, the jury asks for an explanation, they should be told that a reasonable doubt is the sort of doubt that might affect the mind of a person in dealing with matters of importance in his own affairs."

Interestingly, when it was argued that in a circumstantial evidence case the judge should direct the jury to convict only if the evidence is inconsistent with any rational conclusion other than the accused's guilt, the House of Lords held that there is in fact no rule of law requiring this, and discouraged any explanation beyond the usual one. (McGreevy v DPP, (1973] 1 WLR 276; cf Blackstone Criminal Practice, F3.14.)

Thus the current English practice, as exemplified in the Crown Court Bench Book. For the purposes of our survey, we used the accepted formulation of Lord Scarman in Ferguson: "You must be satisfied beyond reasonable doubt so that you feel sure of the defendant's guilt." ([1979] 1 WLR 94, 99.)

## The American Approaches

Since American criminal law is largely a matter for the individual states (taking into account, to be sure, the protections afforded to the criminal defendant by the Federal Constitution), there is diversity both in statute or code and in case law. A few jurisdictions take the English line and shy away from defining the reasonable doubt standard, for example, Illinois, where the judge in People v Cagle declared: "This court has repeatedly held that the legal concept of 'reasonable doubt' needs no definition." (244 NE 2d 200, 204 (1969). Cf McCormick on Evidence, 3d ed, 963, para. 341.) But, in general, owing to the protections guaranteed to the accused by the Bill of Rights, the states have gone the route of providing juries with specific assistance as to the meaning of the criminal standard of proof.

One might classify these definitional approaches in six categories, from least to most specific.

1) "Beyond reasonable doubt": an "abiding conviction or belief" in the guilt of the accused (Washington State, Guam, etc). This seems very close to the English use of "satisfied so that you are sure."
2) "Reasonable doubt": you must be able to give a "valid reason" for convicting rather than finding innocent (Rhode Island, Indiana, etc). The problem here, as pointed out in Victor v Nebraska (114 SCt 1239, 1252 (1994).), the most comprehensive recent review of the problem by the United States Supreme Court, is that such definitions are in fact tautologous: they entail "uninstructive circularity."
3) "Reasonable doubt": absence of speculation (Alabama, New York, etc.). But, one is forced to ask, what is "speculation"?

4) The preceding three approaches combined (California, Louisiana, North Dakota, Texas, etc). For example, Louisiana: "Reasonable doubt is doubt based on reason and common sense and is present when, after you have carefully considered all the evidence, you cannot say that you are firmly convinced of the truth of the charge." One might point out that three weak explanations, taken together, do not make one strong explanation.
5) "Reasonable doubt": doubt similar to what one might experience in making important decisions in one's own life. Thus the Federal instruction: "Proof beyond a reasonable doubt must, therefore, be proof of such a convincing character that a reasonable person would not hesitate to rely and act upon it in the most important of his or her own affairs." But a committee of Federal judges has commented critically: "Decisions we make in the most important affairs of our lives – choosing a spouse, a job, a place to live, and the like – generally involve a very heavy element of uncertainty and risk-taking. They are wholly unlike the decisions jurors ought to make in criminal cases." (Federal Judicial Center, Pattern Criminal Jury Instructions 18-19 (1987) (commentary on instruction 21).)
6) Instructions that define proof "beyond reasonable doubt" as, in the words of the Corpus Juris Secundum, "such proof as precludes every reasonable hypothesis except that which it tends to support, and is proof which is wholly consistent with the guilt of the accused, and inconsistent with any other rational conclusion." (23 CJS 1108.)

This, the most explicit of all the definitional approaches, can be illustrated from a welter of leading cases from a variety of US jurisdictions, for example, State v Stevenson (504 A2d 1029 (Connecticut).), State v Newcomb (78 A2d 787 (Maine.), State v Kaster (300 NW 897 (Minnesota).), Commonwealth v Albert (30 A2d 184 (Pennsylvania).), State v Manns (37 SE 613 (West Virginia).), Jenkins v State. (134 P 260 (Wyoming).). In the Georgia case of Yearwood, the Court of Appeals affirmed the lower court's ruling in these words: "The trial court gave correct jury instructions on the presumption of innocence, the state's burden of proof, reasonable doubt, and on the law regarding circumstantial evidence and the exclusion of every reasonable hypothesis save the guilt of the accused." (401 SE 2d 558, 559 (Ga App 1991).)

The American concern for explicitness may superficially appear to be an attempt to pin down the unpinnable – reminding one of the forensic expert in Richard North Patterson's *Silent Witness*, who asks ironically, "So what's the ratio on reasonable doubt these days?" But the rationale for careful definition is clear enough; American legal scholar H A Diamond concludes his study of the question thus:

"Because the meaning of reasonable doubt is not self-evident to the lay juror and definition of the term is possible, it logically follows that jurors do derive a benefit from instructions that properly define the term. Such instructions are necessary to ensure consistent, rational application of the standard of proof. Therefore, instructions defining reasonable doubt should always be given in criminal trials and are constitutionally required upon request by the defendant or jury.

"It is impossible to judge reliably what effect an erroneous refusal to define reasonable doubt had on the outcome of the trial and such refusals prejudice the trial process itself. They are, therefore, not subject to harmless error review; instead, these errors require the automatic reversal of the conviction." (H A Diamond, "Reasonable Doubt: To Define, or Not To Define," 90 Columbia L Rev 1716, 1736 (1990).)

## Earlier Research

Hastie has provided a useful summary of jury research to date on the standard of proof. (R Hastie (ed), *Inside the Juror: The Psychology of Juror Decision Making* (Cambridge: Cambridge University Press, 1993), pp 100-106.) Depending on the type of survey, subjects have set the evidential percentage at which they would convict anywhere from 51% to 92% – and the percentage required to meet the lower civil standard (preponderance of evidence) from 48% to 92%! Three prior research studies provide useful background for our purposes here.

Kagehiro (summarised in 1990) attempted to determine the effect on jury decision-making of variations in the form of the judge's instructions. (D K Kagehiro, "Defining the Standard of Proof in Jury Instructions," 113 Psychological Science 194 (May 1990).) "The theme that emerges from her research is that verbal instructions expressing alternate standards of proof (eg, the 'preponderance' instruction contrasted with a 'reasonable doubt' instruction) have surprisingly small effects on the decision criterion." (Hastie, op cit, p 108.) But Kagehiro was concerned solely with the civil versus the criminal standard, not with our question as to the impact of the American over against the English approach to defining what the criminal standard means.

More directly pertinent to our topic were earlier studies by Sealy (English, 1973) and Kerr (American, 1976). Sealy (A P Sealy et al, "Juries and the Rules of Evidence," [1973] Crim L Rev 208.) endeavoured to test the effect of three standard of proof variations ([A] "reasonable doubt" = "a doubt that might affect you in daily business or domestic decisions" and "for which reasons can be given" [B] "reasonable doubt" = you do not "feel sure and certain" of guilt; [C] "reasonable doubt" = you do not "feel satisfied that it is more likely than not that the accused is guilty"). In spite of obvious weaknesses in these formulations (for example, [A] speaks only of ordinary affairs, whereas in the English practice if one uses this analogy at all, it must refer to "matters of importance in one's own affairs"; and the rather muddy statement of the civil standard in [C]), the interesting result was that the "sure and certain" direction [B], being the most subjective, produced a significantly higher proportion of acquittals.

Kerr (N L Kerr et al, "Guilt Beyond a Reasonable Doubt: Effects of Concept Definition . . .," 34/2 J Personality and Social Psychology 282 (1976).) also employed three variants of the standard of proof instruction; in his research, these were: [A] no definition of "beyond reasonable doubt" at all – merely the bald use of the expression itself; [B] an explanation of "beyond reasonable doubt" corresponding roughly to our American category four above (convinced, able to give a valid reason, and absence of speculation), and [C] "beyond reasonable doubt" defined as in our American category six above: the strictest definition, where, in order to convict, one must eliminate all reasonable alternative explanations of the crime other than that the defendant did it. Kerr used students, not representative venirepersons, for his experiments, and focused solely on the American legal context (the subjects saw videotapes of an American trial). Kerr's conclusion was even more clean-cut than that of the Sealy study: the weaker the definition or explanation of the criminal standard of proof given to the subject, the less likely he or she was willing to convict.

## The Present Study

Our research project was devoted to the straightforward question as to whether the standard, House of Lords approved, English approach (defining the standard of proof, if at all, only in terms of "satisfied so that you feel sure") or the strictest of the American approaches (American category six above) would produce a more satisfactory result.

We designed a questionnaire (see Addendum at the end of the chapter) with the personal advice of the foremost American specialist in the jury-research field, Dr Amiram Elwork, director of the Law-Psychology Program at Widener University in Pennsylvania. (Cf A Elwork et al, *Making Jury Instructions Understandable* (Charlottesville, Va: Michie, 1982).) A first-run questionnaire was tested and non-significant questions thrown out, thereby refining the product for the actual survey.

The final questionnaire was prepared in two variants. Each set out briefly the facts in the same criminal case and asked for a correct legal verdict (here: not guilty, owing to the presence of genuine "reasonable doubt"). Half the recipients were given the English instruction concerning reasonable doubt, based on the Crown Court Bench Book; the other half received the strongest of the American jury instructions on the criminal standard of proof. All respondents were then given the same five possible interpretations of what the judge's standard of proof instruction meant and asked to choose one or more of these explanations; here the object was to determine the subjects' understanding of the application of the given standard to the verdict arrived at. Finally, an open-ended opportunity was provided for respondents to clarify their views on the subject. A personal (but anonymous) biographical addendum made it possible to weed out subjects who would not have been able to join a jury pool, and also to observe individual differences within the sample.

Our original expectation (naive, as it turned out) was to survey members of actual jury pools or just-served jurors at the Luton Crown Court: Resident Judge His Honour Daniel Rodwell QC could not have been more gracious and accommodating to the project. However, after a delay of more than nine months, our request was denied by the Lord Chancellor's Office, in line with the senior judiciary's (oft-criticised) antipathy to jury research of any kind. (Cf Viscount Runciman of Doxford (The Royal Commission on Criminal Justice Report [London: HMSO, 1993], p 2): "We were barred by s 8 of the Contempt of Court Act 1981 from conducting research into juries' reasons for their verdicts. We recommend, however, that such research should be made possible for the future by an amendment to the Act so that informed debate can take place rather than argument based only on surmise and anecdote.") We therefore substituted adult next-of-kin of Luton University students (the names having been required as references on current student registration forms), a fair proportion of whom live in and around the Luton area. 750 "English" and 750 "American" questionnaires were sent out, and the overall response rate was 36%. We then vetted the results against a random sample of the Chester electoral roll, sending forth 100 "English" and 100 "American" questionnaires, thus mirroring the process by which real jurors are selected. Here, the response rate was 14%. The Chester and Luton results were virtually identical, indicating that the Luton next-of-kin were also representative of potential or actual jurors. The Luton and Chester results have been merged in the analysis to follow.

## Confidence of Guilt needed to Convict

– % of confidence of guilt needed to convict on the part of those finding the defendant ("George") not guilty (the "correct" verdict):

English: 73.5% of the sample said 100%
US: 18.4% of the sample said 100%

Ie, on the basis of the English instruction, only 26.5% would convict on less than 100% certainty of guilt, whereas on the US instruction 81.6% would convict on less than 100% certainty.

– % of confidence of guilt needed to convict on the part of those finding George guilty (the "incorrect" verdict):

English: 35.7% of the sample said 100%
US: 18.7% of the sample said 100%

Ie, on the basis of the English instruction, almost twice as many potential jurors would convict only if 100% certain of guilt than would do so on the basis of the US instruction.

In both instances (US and English instructions), very few, whether they in fact found George guilty or innocent, would convict on the basis of less than 75% certainty (3.3% of the total respondents).

Conclusion: Neither standard results in "civil" verdicts – decisions equivalent to what the civil standard of proof would produce. However, the vagueness of the English explanation of the criminal standard encourages a disproportionate number of potential jurors to refuse convictions on less than an (impossible!) requirement of 100% certainty. (The percentage of wrongful convictions in our sample was very low: an overall 5.3%. It was slightly higher in the case of the American instruction, and this may suggest that whereas the English instruction clearly errs on the side of making convictions exceedingly difficult, the strongest form of the American instruction is capable of being misread in the opposite direction. Additional research on the relative effects in this regard of the varieties of language in the American instructions is surely called for.) It is noteworthy that this result confirms the conclusions of both Sealy and Kerr (supra) that the more subjective and undefined the instruction concerning the standard of proof, the harder it is to obtain convictions.

## Reactions to the Five Interpretations of the Standard Offered

1) "If the evidence against the accused is entirely certain, then and only then, should he be found guilty."

English: 64%     US: 54.5%

Confirms the above results: the English instruction appears to lead to fewer convictions.

2) "If my conscience tells me the accused is guilty, I should convict him."

 English: 12%  US: 16.85%

"Conscience" appears to be assimilated to more objective considerations in the case of the American instruction and thus stands as a more reliable indicator. Here again, the English instruction seems to lead to fewer guilty verdicts.

3) "If I would find a friend guilty on the evidence presented against the accused I should find the accused guilty."

 English: 15.5%  US: 4.6%

It appears evident that three times the respondents using the English explanation of the criminal standard would convict or acquit on the basis of subjective/experiential/existential considerations ("friendship") rather than looking to more objective factors. And, as we have already seen, this seems particularly to result in acquittals, since 100% subjective certainty of guilt would be insisted upon for friend or stranger by most of the respondents using the English interpretation of the standard.

4) "Greater evidence is required to find a person accused of murder guilty than a person accused of shoplifting."

 English: 20.4%  US: 18.3%

This result is particularly troubling when we note that nothing whatsoever was said – in either set of instructions – on the matter. It is painfully evident that jury instructions should clarify the issue – not leave it undiscussed. Jurors need to know that the "seriousness" of the crime is not a factor in determining the application of the standard of proof. Note that in neither English nor American jurisdictions is such specific assistance offered to the juror! It is of more than passing interest, moreover, that those in both groups who (incorrectly) found George guilty were more than twice as likely as those who found him innocent to hold this viewpoint (26.8% vs 11.9%).

5) "If after all the evidence is in, I feel entirely confident of the accused's guilt, I need have no reservations in convicting him."

English: 69.5%    US: 68.1%

As expected, a higher percentage of those following the English style would convict on the basis of "confidence" (a subjective standard). The problem is, as we have seen, that on the basis of the English instruction a level of confidence sufficient to convict is very difficult for many jurors to arrive at. It would seem to follow that those who have heard the American instruction may well place less stress on subjective considerations when determining whether to convict or acquit.

## Conclusion

The present survey may well be criticised methodologically for its small size and for its restrictive geographical focus; but it is certainly representative of venirepersons in two ethnically and sociologically different parts of England, each well removed geographically from the other. Granted, we provided no opportunity for jury group interaction or the existential tensions of an actual trial setting, as would have been the case in a mock courtroom atmosphere; but our purpose was to test individual understanding of the standard of proof directions, not how individual perceptions might change in a group or courtroom context. To determine the latter, mock trials or mock juries would have had to be created and surveyed – since there seems little chance that the existing prohibition against research on actual juries in England will be relaxed in the immediate future. (Letter of April, 1996, from John Briden, Policy Group Secretariat, Lord Chancellor's Department, to the author (letter actually mailed July 24, 1996).)

What do we conclude from the present study, granting its necessary limitations? Beyond the need for additional research already alluded to, it seems clear that, in the realm of jury instructions at least, the traditional English view that less is more is simply incorrect. By not making it clear that the standard of proof does not vary with the seriousness of the crime, potential jurors can assume that it does, thus wrongly acquitting defendants charged with more serious offences and wrongly convicting those charged with petty crimes.

The subjectivistic "satisfied so that one feels sure" approach can result in the near impossibility of getting a conviction, since if 100% certainty is required to convict, convictions disappear from the realm of the metaphysically possible. As has frequently been emphasised by zealous advocates, to be 100% certain that the defendant did it, the juror would have had to be present at the scene of the crime and observed the criminal act: but then he or she would be a witness and could not serve on the jury at all! Juries need help in these areas, and the American efforts to provide more explicit instructions on the standard of proof, even when we find them less than ideal, should encourage us to move forward to better clarifications ourselves.

Judge Jon O Newman is surely correct when he says wryly, "I find it rather unsettling that we are using a formulation ['beyond reasonable doubt'] that we believe will become less clear the more we explain it." (J O Newman, "Beyond 'Reasonable Doubt'," 68 New York University L Rev 979, 984 (1993).) Such a paradoxical notion not infrequently appears, however, to be an obvious truth to the English mind. In 1859, Benjamin Jowett wrote approvingly: "It seems to be an opinion which is gaining ground among thoughtful and religious men, that in theology, the less we define the better." (B Jowett, *Select Passages*, ed L Campbell (London: John Murray, 1908), p 93.) Such an approach has done little for English theology (ineffability leaves one with no criteria to distinguish truth from error, right from wrong). In law, the result is catastrophic, for whatever else it may be, the law needs to be clear – particularly where, as in criminal jurisprudence, the freedom of the individual and the protection of the society at large depend upon it.

(NOTE: This project was approved for funding by the University Research Committee of Luton University (now the University of Bedfordshire). It benefited greatly from the labours of Alan Robinson, formerly my teaching assistant, now research student and doctoral candidate, Department of History, University College, Chester. Also helping in the project was Mrs Sylvia Elwes, lecturer, Department of Law, University of Luton. I am solely responsible for the interpretations placed upon the data and for the judgments in the present article.)

## Addendum: The Questionnaire

### Part One

Imagine you are serving on a jury.

The prosecution say that George murdered Kevin. They prove that George owed Kevin a lot of money and that Kevin was threatening him with ruin if he did not pay. They also show that George had no alibi for the time when the crime was committed. The murder weapon was an old knife with no fingerprints on it but with the letter "G" faintly visible on the handle.

The defence prove that Kevin was a loan shark and had many irate debtors who were also being threatened if they did not pay up. Five of them have a surname beginning with "G"; of the five, two do not have good alibis for the time of the murder. When questioned under oath, George is aggressive, surly and evasive. He is a thoroughly unattractive person and appears entirely capable of committing murder.

The English version: The judge summarises the evidence, directs you to the law applicable to this case and in particular explains that the defence does not have to prove that George is innocent, but that the prosecution must prove George guilty. The judge continues: "Before you can convict any defendant of any offence you have to be satisfied of his guilt on that offence so that you are sure."

The American version: Suppose the judge gives the American form of direction, viz, "You must find George innocent unless you are convinced to a moral certainty, beyond reasonable doubt that George is guilty." He then explains that "beyond reasonable doubt" means the following: "Though you do not have to be one hundred percent certain of guilt (since absolute certainty is not possible in ordinary human affairs), you can only find the accused guilty when you are able to exclude every other reasonable hypothesis or explanation of the crime than that the accused did it; and your decision must not be based on mere guesses, surmises or vague possibilities, but solely on the evidence admitted in the trial of this case."

Tick the box to show if you would find George Not Guilty? or Guilty?

*Part Two*
Considering the instructions given by the judge (above in italics), how confident do you have to be of the accused's guilt before convicting?
51%-55%-75%-90%-95%-99%-100%

*Part Three*
What do you consider the instructions given by the judge, in Part One, to mean? (Tick one or more of the following boxes.) [For the text of the five possibilities, see above, the section entitled, "Reactions to the Five Interpretations"].

*Part Four*
Please explain briefly the differences, if any, you see between being convinced to a moral certainty, beyond reasonable doubt and being more than 50% certain that the accused is guilty.

# 3. Legal Evidence for the Truth of the Faith

The Apostle exhorts Christians to "be ready always to give an answer to everyone who asks you a reason for the hope that is in you" (1 Peter 3:15). The word translated "answer" here is the Greek *apologia*, "defense," and from it comes the name of the theological discipline concerned with defending Christian truth-claims: Apologetics.

Through church history apologists for the faith have often relied on philosophical styles of reasoning to bolster their efforts; thus Augustine depended heavily on Plato, and Aquinas borrowed extensively from Aristotle. With the decline of these classical philosophies and particularly since the rise of modern rationalism in the eighteenth century (Kant, Lessing, Hume), non-Christians have generally presumed that no meaningful defense of Christian faith is possible – that religion is, in the final analysis, only a question of personal feeling – and Christians themselves (the so-called presuppositionalists, existentialists, and pietists) have often unwittingly aided and abetted such a presumption by declaring that Christianity starts from its own presuppositional faith-experience and cannot be either proved or disproved by factual evidence.[1]

Worth emphasizing is the legal flavor of the Greek word *apologia*: the Apostle consciously employed a technical term of ancient Greek law, having reference to the answer given by a defendant before a tribunal. One should not therefore be surprised to discover that the Law of Evidence offers innumerable valuable insights for the defense of historic Christian faith. Our expectations in this regard are particularly heightened when we consider that the evidential machinery of the law has been developed, as the 1975 *Federal Rules of Evidence* state, "to the end that the truth may be ascertained."[2] All societies, whether civilized or primitive, require legal techniques for getting at the truth when disputes arise, and these techniques are refined through experience until they reach a level of sophistication satisfying to litigants who otherwise would breach the peace to settle their conflicts. Small wonder that philosopher Stephen Toulmin argues

---

[1] J. W. Montgomery, *Christianity for the Toughminded* (1973); J. W. Montgomery, *Faith Founded on Fact* (1978).

[2] Fed. R. Evid. 102; on the **Rules** in general, see **ALI-ABA** *Federal Rules of Evidence Resource Materials, with October 1975 Supplement* (1975).

that philosophical inquiry itself could be considerably improved if it would look to legal reasoning as a model.[3]

Early Christianity based its case for divine truth on the deity of Jesus Christ, and its claim to His deity on His resurrection from the dead (1 Corinthians 15). The Law of Evidence well sustains this argumentation as will be seen from the application of several specific evidential rules.

1) Decisions on questions of fact must be made by the trier of fact on the basis of the weight of relevant evidence, defined by the *Federal Rules* as "evidence having any tendency to make the existence of any fact that is of consequence to the determination of the action more probable or less probable than it would be without the evidence."[4] Christians are therefore precisely on the right track when they defend their position in terms of the weight of factual evidence for Christ's deity. A disputed question of religious truth must not be prejudged in a presuppositional manner: no one can expect that judicial notice will be taken for or against Christian truth, since "a judicially noticed fact must be one not subject to reasonable dispute."[5] The outcome of the case will depend, rather, on evidential probability.[6] And probability has to do with the weight of evidence for the particular claim at issue, without reference to general or collateral considerations. Thus just as "evidence of a person's character or a trait of his character is not admissible for the purpose of proving that he acted in conformity therewith on a particular occasion,"[7] so the non-Christian will be prevented from arguing against Christ's resurrection on the ground that regular events in general make a particular miracle too "improbable" to consider. The law refuses to obscure concrete evidence of the particular by the introduction of collateral generalities, for it recognizes that "there are too many differences to insure that what holds true in one case will apply in the other."[8]

---

[3] S. E. Toulmin, *The Uses of Argument* (1958); cf. J. W. Montgomery, *The Law above the Law* 84-90 (1975).

[4] *Fed. R. Evid.* 401. This definition of relevant evidence derives from Professor Thayer's classic *Preliminary Treatise on Evidence* (1898).

[5] *Fed. R. Evid.* 201. Indeed, statutes undertaking to establish conclusive presumptions with respect to material facts are held unconstitutional – on the ground that they deprive the accused of due process of law (Caroline Products Co. v. McLaughlin, 365 Ill. 62).

[6] Cf. V. C. Ball, "The Moment of Truth: Probability Theory and Standards of Proof," in *Essays on Procedure and Evidence* 84-107 (T. G. Roady and R. N. Covington ed. 1961).

[7] *Fed. R. Evid.* 404.

[8] H. P. Chandler and S. D. Hirschl, "Evidence," 11 *American Law and Procedure* 21 (1910, rev. ed. 1955).

2) "The common law system of proof," writes McCormick in his standard treatise on Evidence, "is exacting in its insistence upon the most reliable sources of information. This policy is apparent in the Opinion rule, the Hearsay rule, and the Documentary Originals rule. One of the earliest and most pervasive manifestations of this attitude is the rule requiring that a witness who testifies to a fact which can be perceived by the senses must have had an opportunity to observe, and must have actually observed the fact." In strict conformity to these requirements, the Christian properly focuses attention on the New Testament documents relating to the life of Christ as the best evidence concerning Him, since these can be shown to be primary sources – either written by those, such as Matthew and John who had immediate, firsthand, eyewitness contact with Jesus, or by others (Mark, Luke, Paul) who were intimately acquainted with the original apostolic circle. Moreover, as Simon Greenleaf of Harvard, author of the nineteenth century classic on Evidence stressed, any common-law court would favor the New Testament writings with a presumption of authenticity as ancient documents regular on their face and preserved through the centuries in a place of natural custody. The burden of proof thus rests upon the unbeliever to disprove the testimonial value of these apostolic books, not upon the Christian to build up support for documents already having prima facie legal authenticity.[9]

3) Where direct evidence is not available, the law allows circumstantial evidence, and also proof by *res ipsa loquitur*. The latter is often resorted to in negligence cases where no one directly observed the act in question but where, by process of elimination, only the defendant was in a position to have done it.[10] Likewise, no one was present at the moment of Christ's resurrection, but the events surrounding it were testified to by careful eyewitnesses (Jesus was in fact put to death by crucifixion; Jesus afterwards made numerous, physical post-resurrection appearances over a forty-day period).

*Res ipsa loquitur* in a typical negligence case

1) Accident does not normally occur in the absence of negligence.
2) Instrumentality causing injury was under the defendant's exclusive control.
3) Plaintiff did not himself contribute to the injury.

---

[9] Professor Greenleaf makes this important point in his *Testimony of the Evangelists*, now reprinted in J. W. Montgomery, *The Law above the Law* 91-140, 149-63 (1975). On the historical soundness of the New Testament writings, see F. F. Bruce, *The New Testament Documents: Are They Reliable?* (5th ed. 1960), and cf. J. A. T. Robinson, *Redating the New Testament* (1977).

[10] M. Shain, *Res Ipsa Loquitur, Presumptions and Burden of Proof* (1945).

*Therefore*, defendant negligent: "The event speaks for itself."

*Res ipsa loquitur* as applied to Christ's resurrection

1) Dead bodies do not leave tombs in the absence of some agency effecting the removal.
2) The tomb was under God's exclusive control, for it had been sealed, and Jesus, the sole occupant of it, was dead.
3) The Romans and the Jewish religious leaders did not contribute to the removal of the body (they had been responsible for sealing and guarding the tomb to prevent anyone from stealing the body), and the disciples would not have stolen it, then prevaricated, and finally died for what they knew to be untrue.

**Therefore**, only God was in a position to empty the tomb, which He did, as Jesus Himself had predicted, by raising Him from the dead: "The event speaks for itself."

This reasoning process has close affinities with the method of *reductio ad absurdum*, which Professor Daube has shown to have been common in Greek and Roman law: supporting a case "by shewing the alternative to be in striking contrast to the declared specific objective of the enterprise."[11] If the object of examining the primary-source documentary evidence for Christian claims is to determine what in fact happened, one cannot arrive at an "explanation" of the resurrection which contradicts what these documents have to say about the historical circumstances and about the personalities and motivations of the people involved in them.[12]

And here, in contact with Greco-Roman jurisprudence, we see that the Law of Evidence is not a self-serving technique developed by common-law jurists in subtle support of Christian theology! The fundamental canons of evidence which we have employed in defense of biblical faith are found with remarkable consistency in all legal systems – from primitive to civilized, from ancient to modern. Max Gluckman writes of the Lozi people of Northern Rhodesia: "The Lozi distinguish between different kinds of evidence as hearsay, circumstantial, and direct, and attach different degrees of cogency to these and different degrees of credibility to various witnesses."[13] The ancient Persian *Digest of a Thousand Points of Law* begins with a detailed chapter on the Law of Evidence, insisting, as does the common law, on "independent and convincing proof" to support allegations, and

---

[11] D. Daube, *Roman Law: Linguistic, Social and Philosophical Aspects* 180 (1969).
[12] J. W. Montgomery, *History, Law and Christianity* (2014).
[13] M. Gluckman, *The Judicial Process among the Barotse of Northern Rhodesia* 82 (1955).

setting forth detailed criteria for distinguishing reliable from unreliable testimony (declarations against interest as opposed to self-serving declarations, etc.).[14] In Roman law,

> When the witnesses for the parties gave conflicting testimony on any point, it was the duty of the judge, not to count the number on each side, but to consider which of them were entitled to the greatest credit, according to the well-known rule, *"Testimonia ponderanda sunt, non numeranda."* It rarely happens that the evidence is so nicely balanced as not to preponderate on one side or the other. But questions of fact may be supported and opposed by every degree of evidence, and sometimes by that degree of evidence of which the proper effect is to leave the mind in a state of doubt, or in an equipoise between two conclusions. Where such a case occurred, the Roman law provided that the benefit of the doubt should be given to the defendant rather than to the plantiff.[15]

Jewish evidential standards were, if anything, even more rigorous than those of Roman law at the time of Christ. For Jewish tribunals of the first century, "all evidence must be direct, and not circumstantial or presumptive. Be the chain of evidence every so strong, if not all links are forged by direct eye-testimony, and that of at least two competent witnesses, the accused cannot be adjudged guilty".[16]

Where unsatisfactory or bizarre evidential standards have been developed in a society, these have generally been due to religious influences of an unfortunate kind. Thus among the Muslims one finds not only severe deficiencies in substantive law (e.g., the inferior legal position of women) but also sad procedural standards:

> One of the most serious limitations upon the practical efficiency of the Shari'a courts lay in the rigid system of procedure and evidence, applicable both in civil and criminal cases, by which they were bound. The burden of proof was strict, and the party who bore it, usually the plaintiff, was obliged to produce two male, adult, Muslim witnesses, whose moral integrity and religious probity were unimpeachable, to testify orally to their direct knowledge of the truth of his claim. If the plaintiff or prosecution failed to

---

[14] 1 *The Laws of the Ancient Persians* pt. 1, 12, 26-27 (S. J. Bulsara ed. 1937).
[15] Lord Mackenzie, *Studies in Roman Law, with Comparative Views of the Laws of France, England and Scotland* 382 (7th ed. J. Kirkpatrick 1911). Cf. H. F. Jolowicz, *Roman Foundations of Modern Law* 102 (1957).
[16] S. Mendelsohn, *The Criminal Jurisprudence of the Ancient Hebrews, Compiled from the Talmud and Other Rabbinical Writings, and Compared with Roman and English Penal Jurisprudence*, para. 82 (1891).

discharge this burden of proof the defendant or accused was offered the oath of denial. Properly sworn on the Qur'an, such an oath secured judgment in his favour; if he failed to take it, judgment would be given for the plaintiff or prosecution, provided, in some circumstances, this side in turn took the oath. Such a system of procedure and evidence may have reflected the religious idealism of the scholars: but it was largely because of the often impractical burden of proof that was imposed upon a plaintiff, and the corresponding ease with which unscrupulous defendants might avoid a civil or criminal liability which reason declared to exist, that the Shari'a courts proved an unsatisfactory organ for the administration of certain spheres of the law.[17]

What, then, are the evidential standards pertinent to the question of the reliability of the testimonies to Jesus Christ as found in the primary documents of the New Testament?

In courts of law, admissible testimony is considered truthful unless impeached or otherwise rendered doubtful. This is in accord with ordinary life, where only the paranoic goes about with the bias that everyone is lying. The burden, then, is on those who would show that the New Testament testimony to Jesus is not worthy of belief.

In their standard work on the subject, McCloskey and Schoenberg offer a fourfold test for exposing perjury, involving the determination of *internal* and *external* defects in the *witness himself or herself* on the one hand and in the *testimony itself* on the other.[18] Can the New Testament witness to Jesus be impeached by way of these standard criteria?

(1) Internal defects in the witness refer to any personal characteristics or past history tending to show that the witness is inherently untrustworthy, unreliable or undependable. There is no reason whatsoever to conclude that the apostolic witnesses to Jesus were tainted with criminal records or suffered from pathological lying. If anything, their simple literalness and directness is almost painful. Nor do they have any of the characteristics of mythomanes (2 Pet. 1:16-18).

(2) Did the apostolic witnesses suffer from external defects, that is, motives to falsify? Surely no sensible person would argue that they would have lied about Jesus for monetary gain or as a result of societal pressure. After all, they lost the possibility both of worldly wealth and of social acceptability among their Jewish peers because of their commitment to Jesus. But might that very affection for and attachment to Jesus serve as a

---

[17] N. J. Coulson, "Islamic Law," in *An Introduction to Legal Systems* 67-68 (J. D. M. Derrett ed. 1968). For an expanded treatment of the same subject, see N. J. Coulson, *A History of Islamic Law* 124-27 (1964).

[18] McCloskey and Schoenberg, 5 *Criminal Law Advocacy*, para. 12.01-12.03 (1984).

motive to falsify? Not when we remember that their Master expressly taught them that lying was of the devil (John 8:44).

(3) Turning to the testimony itself, we ask if the New Testament writings are internally consistent or self-contradictory. Certainly, the four Gospels do not give identical, verbatim accounts of the words or acts of Jesus. But if they did, that fact alone would make them highly suspect, for it would point to collusion. The several accounts are complementary, not contradictory. To use New Testament translator J. B. Phillips' expression, the internal content of the New Testament records has "the ring of truth."

(4) Finally, what about external defects in the testimony itself, i.e., inconsistencies between the New Testament accounts and what we know from archaeology or extra-biblical historical records? Unlike typical sacred literature, myth and fairytale ("once upon a time ..."), the gospel story begins and ends in history (Luke 3:1-3). Modern archaeological research has confirmed again and again the reliability of New Testament geography, chronology and general history.

Thus, no one of the four elements of the McCloskey-Schoenberg construct for attacking perjury allows us to impugn the veracity of the New Testament witnesses to Jesus.

Furthermore, a point well understood by trial lawyers but seldom by laymen needs to be stressed, namely, the extreme difficulty of successful lying in the presence of a cross-examiner. As the late F. F. Bruce declared:

> It was not only friendly eyewitnesses that the early preachers had to reckon with; there were others less well disposed who were also conversant with the main facts of the ministry and death of Jesus. The disciples could not afford to risk inaccuracies (not to speak of wilful manipulation of the facts), which would at once be exposed by those who would be only too glad to do so. On the contrary, one of the strong points in the original apostolic preaching is the confident appeal to the knowledge of the hearers: ... Acts 2:22. Had there been any tendency to depart from the facts in any material respect, the possible presence of hostile witnesses in the audience would have served as a further corrective.[19]

In short, even if the New Testament witnesses to Jesus were the kind of people to engage in deception (which they surely were not), *had* they attempted it, they could not have gotten away with it. Admittedly, they were never put on a literal witness stand, but they concentrated their preaching on synagogue audiences, thus putting their testimony at the mercy of the hostile Jewish religious leadership. That audience had the *means, motive*

---

[19] F. F. Bruce, *The New Testament Documents: Are They Reliable?* 45-46 (5th ed. 1960).

*and opportunity* to expose the apostolic witness as inaccurate and deceptive if it had been such, and the fact that they did not can only be effectively explained on the ground that they *could not.*

Legal standards of evidence, such as have here been applied to the New Testament witnesses to Jesus Christ, must not be ignored by believers or unbelievers: since courts of law exist to decide the most intractable conflicts in society, to jettison legal methodology is to melt the very glue that holds society together.

Simon Greenleaf, the greatest of the 19th century common-law experts in legal evidence, summarises in the following terms:

> Let the [Gospel] witnesses be compared with themselves, with each other, and with surrounding facts and circumstances; and let their testimony be sifted, as if it were given in a court of justice, on the side of the adverse party. ... The result, it is confidently believed, will be an undoubting conviction of their integrity, ability, and truth.

It is almost universally agreed that to solve disputes over truth questions in society, factual evidence – not mere sincerity – must carry the day. In the words of the pre-Christian Roman dramatist Plautus,

> *Pluris est oculatus testis unus, quam auriti decem: Qui audiunt, audita dicunt, qui vident, plane sciunt.*
> One eyewitness is worth more than ten purveyors of hearsay;
> Those who only hear about things say what they've heard, but those who see, know the score![20]

Christian faith, alone among the religious claims of history, is able to stand in the dock and be vindicated evidentially.[21] For only Christianity rests its case on the divine life, sacrificial death, and miraculous resurrection of the Incarnate God – events witnessed to by those who had direct contact with them and who in consequence "knew the score" (Acts 1:1-3; 2 Pet. 1:16-18). May serious Christian believers – those concerned to bring the secularists of our day to the Cross of Christ – therefore employ the solid canons of evidence by which this truth can be effectively shown. May we never lose an opportunity to serve as advocate for the One who has Himself promised to plead our cause before His heavenly Father.

---

[20] Plautus, *Truculentus* Act ii, sc. 6, 11.8-9 (our translation).
[21] Cf. C. S. Lewis, *God in the Dock* (W. Hooper ed. 1970).

## 4. A New Approach to the Apologetic for Christ's Resurrection by Way of Wigmore's Juridical Analysis of Evidence

**Synopsis**

*Philosophical and theological arguments for Christ's deity based on his miracles have not always had the convincing force expected of them. As epistemological efforts in general move more and more in a juridical direction, we apply for the first time the most sophisticated of these – Wigmorean analysis – to the central apologetic for the resurrection of Jesus from the dead.*

– – –

In my books, Human Rights and Human Dignity and Tractatus Logico-Theologicus,[1] I emphasised the shift on the part of distinguished philosophers such as Mortimer Adler and Stephen Toulmin toward a juridical approach to the solving of epistemological problems. At a recent conference at the Institute of Advanced Legal Studies at the University of London, Professor David Schum of George Mason University, who instructs at the U.S. Joint Military Intelligence College, pointed to the same phenomenon in the field of military strategy: juridical argument, particularly Wigmorean argument construction, is now being employed in the analysis of potential insurgency operations and analogous tactical themes.[2]

The prime reason for the move toward juridical thinking in these fields is the sophistication with which lawyers must deal with evidence questions. Decisions of law can only be made once facts have been established, so lawyers and legal scholars must employ the most effective techniques possible in arriving at factual conclusions on which life or death may depend – and these must be sufficiently persuasive to convince the "triars of fact" (juries and judges) to arrive at just verdicts.

Moreover, the factual decisions to be reached in the courts are seldom of a single-issue character; they generally involve a great number of fac-

---

[1] John Warwick Montgomery, *Human Rights and Human Dignity* (2d ed.; Calgary, Alberta, Canada: Canadian Institute for Law, Theology and Public Policy, 1995), pp. 134-36; *Tractatus Logico-Theologicus* (3d ed; Bonn, Germany: Verlag für Kultur und Wissenschaft, 2004), para. 3.126.
[2] "Teaching Evidence and Fact Analysis," 9 June 2006.

tual particulars and the interlacing of numerous sub-arguments. Even Toulmin, who argued so eloquently in his classic, *The Uses of Argument*, for replacing the epistemological models of "psychology, sociology, technology and mathematics" with "the discipline of jurisprudence,"[3] when he produced his highly useful text, *An Introduction to Reasoning*, never went beyond two levels of analysis.[4]

In diametric contrast, John Henry Wigmore (1863–1943), the greatest common-law specialist on the law of evidence after Harvard's Simon Greenleaf,[5] endeavoured to treat what he termed "the ultimate and most difficult aspect of the principles of Proof; namely, the method of solving a complex mass of evidence in contentious litigation."

> Nobody yet seems to have ventured to offer a method. ... The logicians have furnished us in plenty with canons of reasoning for specific single inferences; but for a total mass of contentious evidence, they have offered no system. ...
>
> The problem of collating a mass of evidence, so as to determine the net effect which it should have on one's belief, is an everyday problem in courts of justice. Nevertheless, no one hitherto seems to have published any logical scheme on a scale large enough to aid this purpose.[6]

Wigmore produced what is still the most comprehensive work in the field of legal evidence, his *Evidence in Trials at Common Law*; the 4th edition (1985) runs to eleven volumes,[7] plus a massive 1999 supplementary volume.[8] Even Wigmore's sharpest critic, one Edmund Morgan, called it "the best work ever produced on any comparable division of American Law."[9]

We therefore have every good reason to examine Wigmore's method of proof, and, having done so, to discover its relevance to the question of the facticity of the resurrection of Jesus Christ.

---

[3] Stephen E. Toulmin, *The Uses of Argument* (Cambridge: Cambridge University Press, 1958), p. 7.

[4] Stephen E. Toulmin, Richard Rieke, and Allan Janik, *An Introduction to Reasoning* (New York: Macmillan, 1978). An apparently unchanged "second edition" was issued in 1984 by the same publisher.

[5] See Greenleaf's "Testimony of the Evangelists," reprinted in Montgomery, *The Law Above the Law* (rev. ed.; Irvine, CA: NRP/1517.Legacy Project, 2015), pp. 91 ff.

[6] John Henry Wigmore, *The Principles of Judicial Proof: As Given by Logic, Psychology, and General Experience, And Illustrated in Judicial Trials* (Boston: Little, Brown, 1913), pp. 3-4, 747.

[7] Published by Little, Brown, with various editors following Wigmore's death.

[8] Published by Aspen Law & Business; edited by Professor Arthur Best.

[9] Quoted by William L. Twining, "Wigmore, John Henry," in A. W. B. Simpson (ed.), *Biographical Dictionary of the Common Law* (London: Butterworths, 1984), p. 533.

## Wigmorean Chart Analysis

In his biographical sketch of Wigmore, Professor William Twining comments that Wigmore's *Principles of Judicial Proof* "remains largely forgotten, perhaps because it placed too much emphasis on an ingenious system of analysing masses of evidence through elaborate charts that involved resort to unfamiliar symbols."[10] Yet Twining himself, in his own publications in field of reasoning and legal evidence, has seen the tremendous value of this complex analytical technique and has endeavoured to explain it to the *non cognoscenti*.[11] In the explanations to follow, we rely heavily on Twining's materials, developed largely to present the Wigmorean method to law students unacquainted with it.

One begins with an overall analysis of the problem. Here is Twining's seven-step summary of the methodology:

1) Clarification of standpoint, purpose, and role;
2) Formulation of potential ultimate *probandum* [that which is to be proven] or *probanda* [those things which are to be proven];
3) Formulation of potential penultimate *probanda*;[12]
4) Formulation of theory and themes of the case: choice of strategic ultimate, penultimate, and intermediate *probanda*;[13]
5) Compilation of a key-list;
6) Preparation of the chart(s); and
7) Completion of the analysis.

Twining illustrates by way of a simple criminal case. The *ultimate probandum* is that "X murdered Y," or, stated more formally, that "(A) Y is dead;

---

[10] Twining, *op. cit.*, p. 534.
[11] Twining, *Theories of Evidence: Bentham and Wigmore* (London: Weidenfeld & Nicolson, 1985), pp. 125 ff.; *Rethinking Evidence* (2d ed.; Cambridge: Cambridge University Press, 2006), pp. 426-28 *et passim*; Terence Andreson, David Schum, and William Twining, *Analysis of Evidence* (2d ed.; Cambridge: Cambridge University Press, 2005), pp. 123-44 *et passim*.
[12] The "penultimate *probanda*" remind one of mathematical philosopher Imre Lakatos' use of the term *proof* for "a thought-experiment - or 'quasi-experiment' - which suggests a decomposition of the original conjecture into subconjectures or lemmas" (Imre Lakatos, *Proofs and Refutations: The Logic of Mathematical Discovery*, ed. John Worrall and Elia Zahar [Cambridge: Cambridge University Press, 1977], pp. 9, 13-14). On Lakatos, see John Worrall's article in the *Concise Routledge Encyclopedia of Philosophy* (London: Routledge, 2000), pp. 449-50.
[13] Step 4 is clearly unique to advocacy and persuasion: choosing the strategy most likely to convince the trier of fact and win the case; it would presumably not figure into a straight investigation of a factual issue.

(B) Y died as a result of an unlawful act; (C) it was X who committed the unlawful act that caused Y's death; and (D) X intended (i) to commit the act and (ii) thereby to cause Y's death." The coroner's report and observations at the scene satisfy all concerned that "Y died at approximately 4:45 p.m. on 1 January in his house as the result of an unlawful act committed by another." We thus develop a key-list and corresponding chart involving some five testimonial assertions and related inferences that appear relevant to the *penultimate probandum* (C) that "It was X who committed the unlawful act that caused Y's death."

We do not need to go into the details of this illustration. Just a few basic points require clarification.

The chart symbols vary somewhat from one Wigmorean analysis to another. In general, a *circle* represents evidence; more explicitly (and not used in this chart), a *filled-in circle* is used to depict factual, empirical data – what Sherlock Holmes called the "trifles" which are capable ultimately of deciding issues[14] – as contrasted with *unfilled-in circles*, representing circumstantial evidence or mere inferences; a *square* depicts testimonial assertions (it does not have to be used when the entire case is a matter of testimony or conflicting testimony); a *triangle* identifies an argument that corroborates a fact or inference to which it is related; an *open angle* represents an alternative explanation for an argument given by the other side; *arrows* show the direction of an inferential relationship between one fact or fact to be proven and another; and the letter *G* is used for generalisations which are taken (correctly or incorrectly) as not requiring proof because they are accepted as such and would supposedly be received by a tribunal as worthy of judicial notice.

It will be observed that in the illustration one single chart has been used to show both the "prosecution" and the "defense" arguments (thus, for example, items 1 and 8 are mutually contradictory and cannot both be true). A clearer picture and a more effective analysis is usually possible by separating the pro- and the con- streams of argument by the use of separate, parallel charts. Either way, it is vital to chart the strongest arguments both *for* and *against* the ultimate *probandum*.

Here, in an unpublished chart which avoids the use of symbols, Twining separates pro- and con- lines of argumentation, designating the opposition case with the term "infirmative":

---

[14] "You know my method. It is founded upon the observation of trifles" (*The Boscombe Valley Mystery*). "It is, of course, a trifle, but there is nothing so important as trifles" (*The Man with the Twisted Lip*). Cf. John Warwick Montgomery, *The Transcendent Holmes* (Ashcroft, British Columbia, Canada: Calabash Press, 2000), especially pp. 97–139.

## 4. A New Approach to the Apologetic for Christ's Resurrection ...

### The Key-List

1. X was in Y's house at 4:45 P.M. on January 1.
2. X entered Y's house at 4:30 P.M. on January 1.
3. $W_1$ saw X enter Y's house at 4:30 P.M. on January 1.
4. $W_1$: I saw X enter Y's house at 4:30 P.M. on January 1 as I was walking on the sidewalk across the street.
5. X left Y's house at 5:00 P.M. on January 1.
6. $W_2$ saw X leave Y's house at 5:00 P.M. on January 1.
7. $W_2$: I saw X leave Y's house at 5:00 P.M. on January 1.
8. X was not at Y's house on January 1.
9. X did not enter or leave Y's house on January 1.
10. X: I never went to Y's house on January 1.
11. X was at her office at 4:45 P.M. on January 1.
12. X was working at her office from 9:00 A.M. to 5:00 P.M. on January 1.
13. X: I was working at my office from 9:00 A.M. to 5:00 P.M. on January 1.
14. A claimed eyewitness identification by a pedestrian walking on the other side of the street is doubtful.
15. It may be someone other than X whom $W_1$ saw enter Y's house.
16. The sun had set before 5:00 P.M. on January 1.
17. A claimed eyewitness identification made after the sun has set is doubtful.
18. It may have been someone other than X whom $W_2$ saw leave Y's house.
19. $W_3$ saw X enter Y's house at 4:30 P.M. on January 1.
20. $W_3$: I saw X enter Y's house at 4:30 P.M. on January 1.
21. X's testimony should not be accepted.
22. X is lying about her actions and whereabouts on January 1.
23. A person accused of a crime has a strong motive to fabricate testimony that might exonerate her.
24. X is the accused in this case.
25. X was probably not in her office on January 1.
26. January 1 is New Year's Day and a legal holiday in this jurisdiction.
27. Few people go to their office and work all day on New Year's Day in this area.

### The Chart

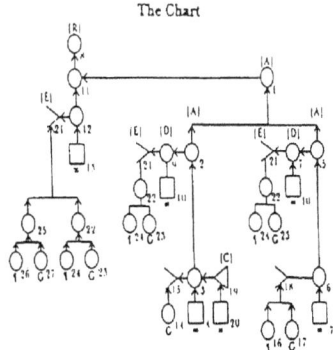

A = assertion; E = explanation; R = rival; and D = denial. Note that a defendant becomes a "proponent" of rival and denial assertions, and thus the prosecutor may use the process of "opponent's" explanation to undermine these assertions.

**Inference upon inference** (source: Twining, unpublished)

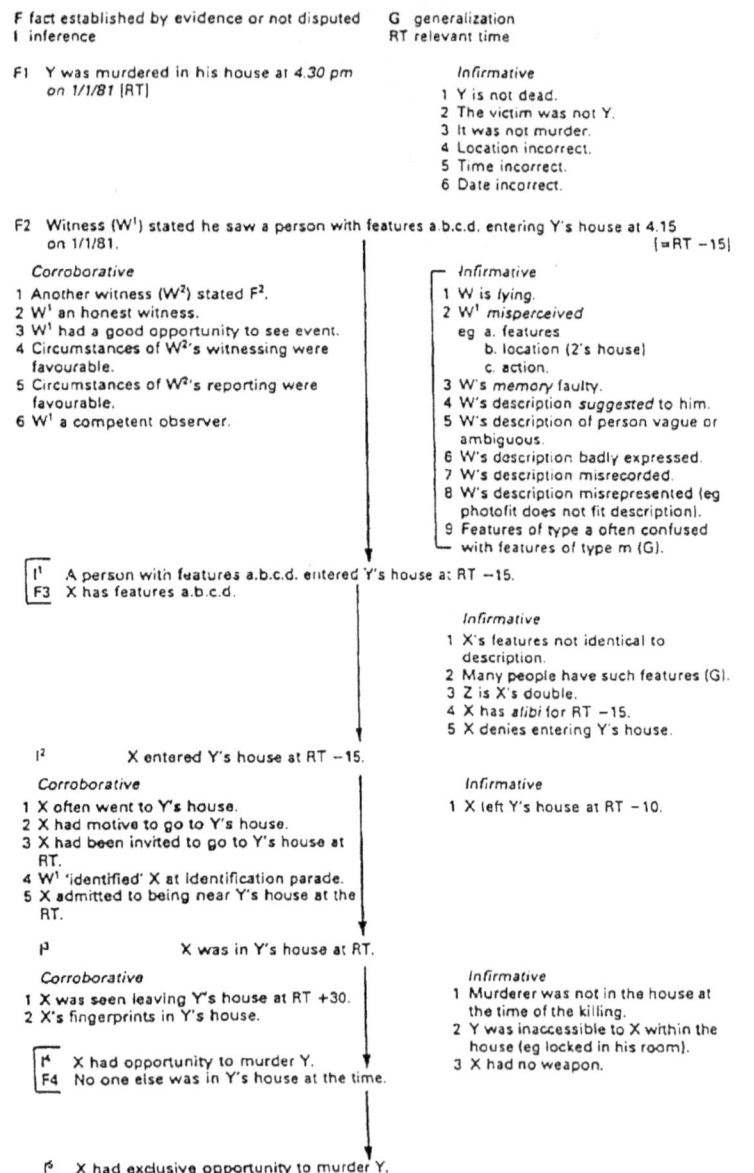

Note that the "RT" (relevant time) category would be employed only when the issue in question turned on a matter of chronology.

## Application to the Claim That Jesus Christ Was Resurrected

We are now in a position to use the foregoing style of analysis to evaluate the evidence for Christ's resurrection.

Before we do, however, it may be well to observe the desirability of employing this approach rather than the Bayesian probability calculus. Bayes' theorem, in essence, asserts that the probability of an event can be calculated by multiplying posterior odds by prior odds to obtain a likelihood ratio. But as Earman (the secular author of a devastating critique of Hume's argument against the miraculous[15]) observes:

> Attempts to objectify priors run into notorious difficulties. ... The anomalous advance of the perihelion of Mercury was known to astronomers long before Einstein formulated his general theory of relativity. A naïve application of Bayes's theorem would seem to imply that no incremental confirmation takes place, despite the fact that physicists uniformly claim that general relativity receives strong confirmation from the explanation of the perihelion advance.[16]

True, the Bayesian approach has been usefully employed by Richard Swinburne in his book, *The Resurrection of God Incarnate*.[17] But a particular problem with using it in arguing for the resurrection of Christ (or any miracle, for that matter) is the number of prior events which do not have a miraculous character. Wigmore's approach, based solidly in historical and testimonial evidence for events themselves rather than in philosophical speculation or probabilistic calculation involving prior events, bypasses this problem.

In arguing for the resurrection of Christ, our terms are as follow:

**Ultimate probandum [UP]:** "God raised Jesus from the dead as Saviour of the world."
**Penultimate probandum [PP]:** "Jesus rose from the dead."

---

[15] John Earman, *Hume's Abject Failure: The Argument Against Miracles* (New York: Oxford University Press, 2000).
[16] John Earman, "Bayesiansim," *The Encyclopedia of Philosophy Supplement*, ed. Donald M. Borchert (New York: Macmillan Reference, 1996), p. 52. Cf. Earman's book-length treatment of the problem: *Bayes or Bust? A Critical Examination of Bayesian Confirmation Theory* (Cambridge, Mass.: MIT Press, 1992).
[17] Richard Swinburne, *The Resurrection of God Incarnate* (Oxford: Clarendon Press, 2003), especially pp. 206 ff. I have cited Swinburne's conclusions positively in my *Tractatus Logico-Theologicus (op.cit.)*, para. 3.8732.

Stated more formally:

**[PP(A)]:** "Jesus died on the Cross."
**[PP(B)]:** "On and after the first Easter morning, Jesus was physically alive."
**[PP(C)]:** "Jesus' transition from death to life occurred miraculously - without third-party human agency."

## The Positive Key-list:

1) All events related to Christ's death and resurrection were reported by eyewitnesses or associates of eyewitnesses.
2) Jesus is said by these witnesses to have been born miraculously and performed numerous impressive miracles, including the raising of Lazarus, during his public ministry.
3) On several occasions, Jesus predicted his resurrection.
4) Jesus was tried publicly by Jewish and by Roman leaders, given a death sentence, and executed by crucifixion.
5) On the cross, a sword was driven into his side to assure the soldiers in charge that he was indeed dead.
6) Jesus' crucifixion occurred publicly in Jerusalem at the high season of the Jewish religious year.
7) Jesus' body was then placed in a well-known tomb belonging to a prominent Jewish religious personality.
8) Efforts were made by the Jewish religious leaders to prevent a stealing of Jesus' body and to surpress any rumours of resurrection.
9) On the first Easter morning, Jesus' disciples encountered a Jesus who was alive.
10) Jesus appearsed subsequently to his followers over a 40-day period, followed by his public ascension into heaven.
11) Jesus' disciples did not believe that he would rise prior to the event having occurred - as evidenced, for example, by "doubting Thomas."
12) Jesus' resurrection appearances were physical in nature (Jesus eating fish, Thomas able to touch wounds in Jesus' hands and side).
13) Paul testified to having seen and spoken to the risen Christ on the Damascus road.
14) Paul provided a list of named witnesses to the risen Christ and claimed that over 500 were still alive to testify to it in A.D. 56 (1 Cor. 15) - as well as claiming when on trial before the Roman governor that Christ's death and resurrection were "not done in a corner" (Acts 26:26).

## 4. A New Approach to the Apologetic for Christ's Resurrection ...

15) Absence of motive to steal Jesus' body on the part of the Romans or the Jewish religious leaders, and every reason on their part not to do so.
16) Irrationalism of any argument that Jesus' disciples or followers would have stolen his body and then claimed he rose from the dead – thus inviting persecution and death.
17) Irrationality of any unnamed third parties stealing the body or inventing such a story.
18) No contemporary refutations or attempted refutations of the fact of the resurrection by those with means, motive, and opportunity to do so.
19) Explanations of the event other than that by Jesus and the firsthand witnesses have no cogency and should be rejected.
20) Jesus claimed to be God incarnate, raised up by his Father, and the unique Saviour through his death and resurrection.

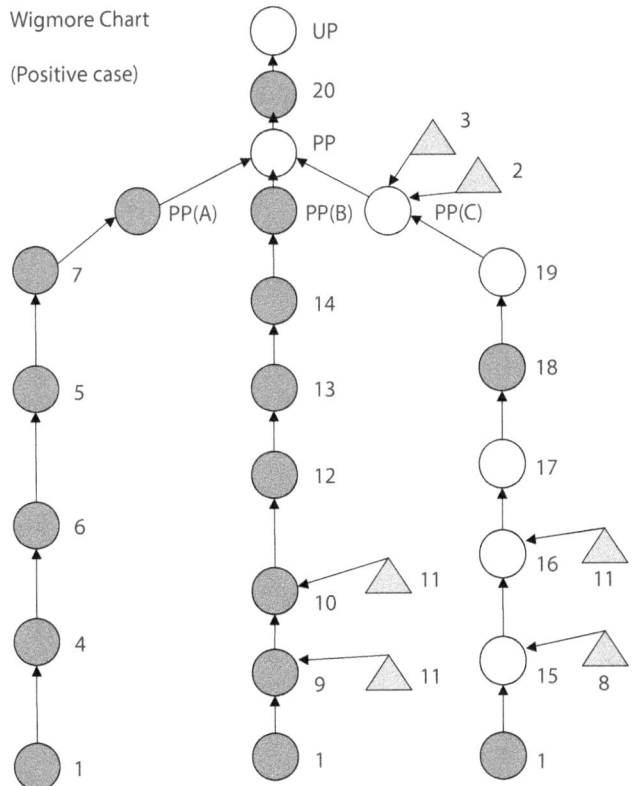

**Note:** In the positive Chart (above), red filled-in circles (facts) and white unfilled-in circles (circumstantial evidence or inferences) need to be distinguished, and it is important also to observe the difference between the circles and the pink triangles (=corroborations).

## The Negative Key-list (based on Twining analysis):

F Fact established by evidence
I Inference

### Infirmative

**F-1 [PP(A)]**
Jesus died on the cross

1) He did not die on the cross (**2**)
2) Victim was someone else (**3**)
3) He died later under other circumstances (**4**)
4) One cannot trust the documents/witnesses (**1**)

**F-2 [PP(B)]**
On and after the first Easter morning, Jesus was physically alive

1) Disciples mistook someone else for Jesus (**5**)
2) Disciples had a mystical vision (**6**)
3) Disciples suffered from a collective hallucination (**7**)
4) Disciples stole the body (**8**)
5) Unnamed persons stole the body (**9**)
6) Jesus rose "spiritually" but not physically (**10**)
7) One cannot trust the documents/witnesses (**1**)

**I-1 [PP(C)]**
Jesus' transition from death to life occurred miraculously – without third-party human agency

1) Miracles simply do not happen: people who die stay dead (**11**)
2) To prove an extraordinary event, you would need extraordinary evidence – which we don't have (**12**)

## 4. A New Approach to the Apologetic for Christ's Resurrection ...  65

**I-2 [UP]**

God raised Jesus from the dead as Saviour of the world

3) Any natural explanation is preferable to a supernatural, miraculous explanation (**13**)

4) One cannot trust the documents/witnesses (**1**)

1) Jesus was lying or lacking in self-knowledge/knowledge of the true explanation of his resurrection (**14**)[18]

2) One cannot logically move from a miracle – even a resurrection – to divine truth; cf. Lessing's ditch & the naturalistic fallacy (**15**)

3) One cannot trust the documents/witnesses (**1**)

---

[18] It is worth stressing that (1) he who rises from the dead is in a far better position to explain how this happened than are those who have not (cf. Montgomery, *Tractatus Logico-Theologicus* [*op. cit.*], para. 3.72 – 3.7321), and (2) Jesus' factual claim can be accepted without prior proof of God's existence – *pace* Norman Geisler, R. C. Sproul, William Lane Craig and the so-called "classical" apologists (see Gary R. Habermas, *The Risen Jesus & Future Hope* (Lanham, Maryland: Rowman & Littlefield, 2003), especially chaps 2-3; also Habermas's contribution to *Five Views on Apologetics*, ed. Steven B. Cowan (Grand Rapids, Michigan: Zondervan, 2000), pp. 91 ff.).

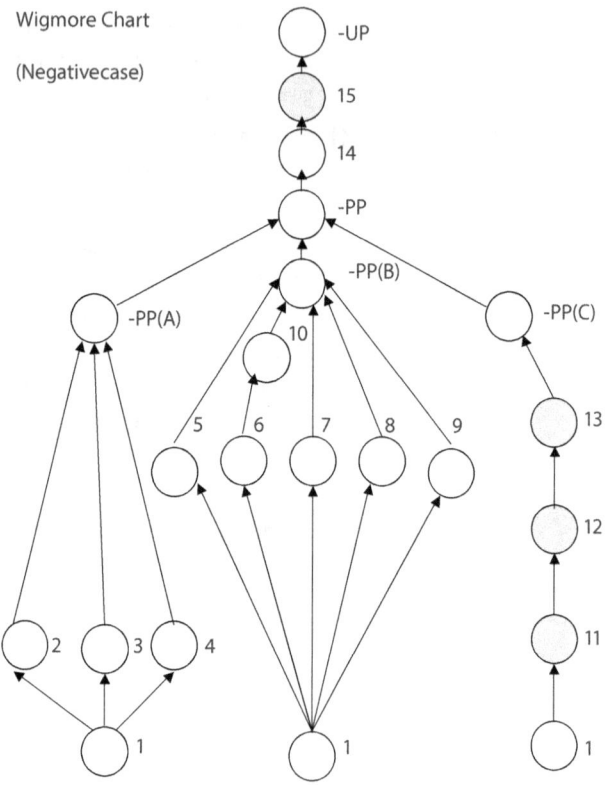

**Note:** In the Chart of the negative case (below), numbers correspond to the *italicised* figures in parentheses which appear at the end of each **Infirmative** in the corresponding Key-list. Yellow filled-in circles represent generalisations (G) – items which the proponent assumes to be universally accepted without requiring proof.

## Conclusion: What This Evidential Approach Reveals

It would be inappropriate here to present the data underlying each of the items in the Key-lists. Such data can readily be obtained elsewhere, and I myself have devoted a fair number of my writings to this very purpose.[19] What we wish to do instead is note how the Wigmorean method assists in

---

[19] Montgomery, *Tractatus Logico-Theologicus* (op. cit.); *Human Rights and Human Dignity* (op. cit.): *The Law Above the Law* (op. cit.); *History, Law and Christianity* (3d ed.; Irvine, CA: NRP/1517.Legacy Project, 2014); *Faith Founded on Fact* (Nashville: Thomas Nelson, 1978); etc., etc.

## 4. A New Approach to the Apologetic for Christ's Resurrection ...

revealing the core issues at stake in reaching a proper decision on a vital factual issue – here, the central epistemological question of Jesus' resurrection and divine claims.

First, as we compare the negative with the positive Key-lists by way of the Charts, we observe that the objector to the facticity of the resurrection relies entirely, not on factual data, but on conjecture, inference, and supposed universal generalisations. This in itself places the negative case in the worst possible light.

Secondly, it is plain that in the final analysis the issue of the truth of the resurrection and of Christ's claims depends squarely on the reliability of the New Testament records – not on philosophical, presuppositional, or sociological argument. It follows that the apologetic task is best carried on in an evidential context, and that any and all dehistoricising and higher critical dismembering of the New Testament documents must be shown as erroneous methodologically – as bad scholarship – rather than being somehow baptised as theologically legitimate.

Finally, the Wigmorean approach keeps the resurrection question focused on those considerations which are truly determinative: a genuine death, a subsequent living, physical presence, the absence of human third-party agency, and the Subject's (Christ's own) explanation as to the Divine source of this miraculous event – an event on which depended nothing less than the salvation of the human race.

# 5. Legal Hermeneutics and the Interpretation of Scripture

## The Hermeneutical Impasse

What divides Christian theology and turns the theological landscape into a battlefield today is not so much confessional differences as hermeneutical perspectives. On the one side, regardless of denominational commitment, are those who insist on interpreting the biblical text in its natural (not necessarily literal) sense; on the other, those who flatly deny that any such objective interpretation is possible and who therefore see the text as a reflection of its original environment and in dialectic interaction with the contemporary interpreter. The conflict may almost be reduced to: Billy Graham ("The Bible says ...") vs. Robert Funk's Jesus Seminar.

One might even go so far as to claim that biblical hermeneutics constitutes the great gulf dividing the church at the end of the twentieth century. As illustrated by Robert Campbell, O.P.'s companion volumes, *Spectrum of Protestant Beliefs* and *Spectrum of Catholic Attitudes*,[1] far more basic than Protestant-Catholic doctrinal differences today is the cleavage between those who take revelational sources as objectively true and those who relativize and subjectivize them. The conservative-liberal split on how to read the Bible cuts across all denominational lines, and directly or indirectly colors the theology and church life of every church person. Clearly, if the Bible does not mean what it appears to mean and does not teach what it seems to teach, the door opens wide for an infinite number of new interpretations, teachings, and styles of church life.

The essential difference between historical-grammatical interpretation and the new hermeneutic is not difficult to describe. The former, set out in such classic treatises as Milton S. Terry's *Biblical Hermeneutics*, maintains that the scriptural text can be objectively known, that it has a clear, perspicuous meaning, and that that meaning can be discovered if the text is allowed to interpret itself, without the adulteration of the interpreter's personal prejudices. Professor Eugene F. A. Klug summarizes this approach, which dominated the field of scriptural interpretation at least from the Reformation to the rise of modern biblical criticism, as follows:

---

[1] The present writer was one of the five contributors to *Spectrum of Protestant Beliefs* (Milwaukee: Bruce, 1968).

It is a fundamental principle to assume that there is one intended, literal, proper sense to any given passage in Scripture ("sensus literalis unus est"); also that the Scripture is its own best interpreter ("Scriptura Scripturam interpretat" or "Scriptura sui ipsius interpres"). ... The literal sense thus always stands first and each interpreter must guard against cluttering that which is being communicated with his own ideas, lest the meaning be lost.²

In diametric contrast to this classic hermeneutic is the so-called "hermeneutical circle" of Rudolf Bultmann and the contemporary followers of *formgeschichtliche Methode* and related higher-critical philosophies. Here, the text and the interpreter are locked together in such a way that a purely objective, "presuppositionless" understanding of the text is out of the question. The interpreter always brings his own understanding to the text, and interpretation is the product *both* of the text working on the interpreter *and* the interpreter working on the text.³ And this will be true not only of the current interpreter vis-à-vis the text but also of the original writer or editor of it: neither the events described in the text nor the resulting description of them can ever represent objective truth in any absolute sense. A text is ultimately inseparable from its *Sitz im Leben* in the widest sense of that term.

Philosopher Roy J. Howard thus sets forth "three important aspects of contemporary hermeneutics": (1) "There is no such thing as presuppositionless knowing." (2) "Just as there is no uniform stance from which to begin thinking, so there is no uniform term in which to end it. Hermeneutics is willing to rethink the dialectical logic of Hegel but not to accept his conclusion of an absolute mind." (3) "Hermeneutics' recognition that intentionality is present and operative and effective on both sides ... and in a dialectical way. This effectiveness might be resident in the social condition of the researcher (cf. Haber-mas and Winch) or in the very logic of his research activity (cf. von Wright), or in the choice and manner of the questions he addresses to experience (cf. Gadamer)."⁴

---

[2] Eugene F. A. Klug, "'Sensus Literalis' – das Wort in den Wörtern, eine hermeneutische Meditation vom Verstehen der Bibel," 12/5 *Evangelium* (December, 1985), 165-75.

[3] Cf. Bultmann's seminal essay, "Is Exegesis Without Presuppositions Possible?," conveniently available in English translation in Kurt Mueller-Vollmer, ed., *The Hermeneutics Reader: Texts of the German Tradition from the Enlightenment to the Present* (Oxford: Basil Blackwell, 1986), 241-48.

[4] Roy J. Howard, *Three Faces of Hermeneutics: An Introduction to Current Theories of Understanding* (Berkeley: University of California Press, 1982), 165-66. On the varieties of contemporary higher criticism, see Steven L. McKenzie and Stephen R. Haynes,

The impasse between classical and contemporary hermeneutic approaches is well illustrated by the current controversy engendered by Adrian Desmond's and James Moore's biography, *Darwin* (1991). The authors set Darwin in his 19<sup>th</sup> century context, relating the development of his theory of organic evolution to the social influences that played upon him. Evangelical reaction has been mixed: on the one hand, there is joy that evolutionary theory is now less able to be regarded as scientific fact than as "the contingent product of complex inferences between the Victorian natural and social orders"; on the other, there is much disquiet that such sociological reductionism is the very thing that has characterized the treatment of the Bible by the modern critics! Moore, in responding to the evangelicals on the latter point, puts it bluntly: "Can texts interpret themselves? If the Bible's don't, why *a fortiori* should Darwin's?"[5]

To determine whether or not texts such as Scripture can or cannot interpret themselves, we may perhaps benefit from a perspective other than that afforded by theology or even the liberal arts. Theological discussions of the hermeneutical impasse tend to become mired in dogmatic considerations; and philosophical, historical, and literary treatments of the question are often highly abstruse and far removed from the practicalities.

In the present essay we shall offer assistance by way of legal hermeneutics – and that for two reasons. First: Lawyers – perceived through the centuries as motivated by filthy lucre and woefully deficient in moral character and spirituality – can hardly be thought to be offering surreptitious theological solutions to the hermeneutic dilemma! Secondly, and far more important: As I have pointed out elsewhere,[6] law is necessitarian, coloring all aspects of societal life; so its solutions to fundamental problems carry powerful weight. On the interpretation of contracts, wills, statutes, and constitutions hang the lives and property of all of us. A legal hermeneutic will not represent mere academic theory: it will have developed a necessary response to resolving peaceably the otherwise intractable conflicts within society. A legal hermeneutic, in short, constitutes the interpretive cement by which society is kept from fragmenting.[7] The plain consequence

---

    eds., *To Each Its Own Meaning: An Introduction to Biblical Criticisms and Their Application* (London: Geoffrey Chapman, 1993).

[5]  James Moore, "Cutting Both Ways – *Darwin* Among the Devout: A Response to David Livingstone, Sara Miles, and Mark Noll," 46/3 *Perspectives on Science and Christian Faith: Journal of the American Scientific Affiliation* (September, 1994), 169-72.

[6]  John Warwick Montgomery, *Human Rights and Human Dignity*, 2<sup>d</sup> ed. (Calgary, Alberta: Canadian Institute for Law, Theology and Public Policy, 1995), 134-36.

[7]  In legal literature there are occasional references to possible connections between legal hermeneutics and theological interpretation – for example, Per Olof Ekelöf,

is that the theologian has every reason to observe law's hermeneutic methodology with care.

## How Lawyers Construe Documents

It is a truism that written instruments have played and continue to play a central role in legal activity. Legal historian Frederic William Maitland argued that the "forms of action" – the documentary writs – were the most important single factor in the development of the Anglo-American common law tradition.[8] As early as the 17th century, written evidence of contractual relations, as compared with purely oral contracts, was deemed so important that in certain key areas only contracts in writing or evidenced by written memoranda could any longer be enforced.[9] Written instruments such as contracts, deeds, wills and trusts, legislative statutes, and constitutions represent the very essence of the law, and their proper interpretation is a *sine qua non* for the effective operation of the machinery of justice.

Not surprisingly, therefore, canons for the proper construction of legal documents were developed early in the history of the law and remain with us to this day. The Oxford *Concise Dictionary of Law* lists the six "principal rules of statutory interpretation" as follows.

1) An Act must be construed as a whole, so that internal inconsistencies are avoided.
2) Words that are reasonably capable of only one meaning must be given that meaning whatever the result. This is called the *literal rule*.
3) Ordinary words must be given their ordinary meanings and technical words their technical meanings, unless absurdity would result. This is the *golden rule*.
4) When an Act aims at curing a defect in the law any ambiguity is to be resolved in such a way as to favor that aim (the *mischief rule*).

---

"Teleological Construction of Statutes," 2 *Scandinavian Studies in Law* (1958), 88-89 – but the subject remains undeveloped. Moises Silva, in his brief work, *Has the Church Misread the Bible? The History of Interpretation in the Light of Current Issues* (Grand Rapids: Zondervan Academic Books, 1987), includes as fields creating "Today's Hermeneutical Challenge" (chap. 1): Philosophy, Literary Criticism, Linguistics, History, Science, and Theology. Law is conspicuous by its absence!

[8] Frederic William Maitland, *The Forms of Action at Common Law* (Cambridge: Cambridge University Press, 1936).

[9] The so-called Statute of Frauds, 29 Car. II, c.3, s.17 (1676). Though modified in various particulars, sections of this historic Statute remain in force today in all common law jurisdictions.

# Legal Hermeneutics and the Interpretation of Scripture

5) The *ujusdem generis rule* (of the same kind): when a list of specific items belonging to the same class is followed by general words (as in "cats, dogs, and other animals"), the general words are to be treated as confined to other items of the same class (in this example, to other *domestic animals*).

6) The rule *expressio unius est exclusio alterius* (the inclusion of the one is the exclusion of the other): when a list of specific items is not followed by general words it is to be taken as exhaustive. For example, "weekends and public holidays" excludes ordinary weekdays.[10]

In the law of contracts, the *parol evidence rule* sets forth the same hermeneutic philosophy: Integrated writings cannot be added to, subtracted from, or varied by the admission of extrinsic evidence of prior or contemporaneous oral or written agreements; extrinsic evidence is admissible to *clarify* or *explain* the integrated writing, but never when it would *contradict* the writing.[11] The construction of deeds follows the same approach: the parties "are presumed to have intended to say that which they have in fact said, so their words as they stand must be construed."[12] And at the loftiest point of American constitutional interpretation the identical philosophy prevails; thus Chief Justice John Marshall in *Gibbons v. Ogden*:

> As men whose intentions require no concealment, generally employ the words which most directly and aptly express the ideas they intend to convey, the enlightened patriots who framed our Constitution, and the people who adopted it, must be understood to have employed words in their natural sense, and to have intended what they have said. If, from the imperfection of human language, there should be serious doubts respecting the extent of any given power, it is a well-settled rule that the objects for which it was given, especially when those objects are expressed in the instrument itself, should have great influence in the construction. ... We know of no rule

---

[10] Elizabeth A. Martin, ed., *A Concise Dictionary of Law* (Oxford: Oxford University Press, 1987), 189. For a fuller discussion of these canons, see, *inter alia*: Herbert Broom, *Legal Maxims*, ed. W. J. Byrne, 9th ed. (London: Sweet & Maxwell, 1924), chap. 8 ("The Interpretation of Deeds and Written Instruments"), 342-444; P.B. Maxwell, *The Interpretation of Statutes*, ed. G. Granville Sharp and Brian Galpin, 10th ed. (London: Sweet & Maxwell, 1953); Rupert Cross, *Statutory Interpretation*, ed. John Bell and George Engle, 2d ed. (London: Butterworths, 1987).

[11] Cf. *Uniform Commercial Code*, sec. 2-202.

[12] Charles E. Odgers, *The Construction of Deeds and Statutes*, 4th ed. (London: Sweet & Maxwell, 1956), 21. The cited statement offers a direct challenge to and refutation of the so-called "intentional fallacy" as commonly practiced in contemporary biblical interpretation; see John Warwick Montgomery, ed., *God's Inerrant Word* (Minneapolis: Bethany, 1974), 30-31, 41.

for construing the extent of such powers, other than is given by the language of the instrument which confers them, taken in connection with the purposes for which they were conferred.[13]

Concerning the interpretation of legal documents in general, Lord Bacon summed up aphoristically.[14]

> Non est interpretatio, sed divinatio, quae recedit a litera. (Interpretation that departs from the letter of the text is not interpretation but divination.) Cum reciditur a litera, judex transit in legislatorum. (When the judge departs from the letter, he turns into a legislator.)

More recently, Sir Roland Burrows drives the same point home with admirable clarity:

> The Court has to take care that evidence is not used to complete a document which the party has left incomplete or to contradict what he has said, or to substitute some other wording for that actually used, or to raise doubts, which otherwise would not exist, as to the intention. When evidence is admitted in connection with interpretation, it is always restricted to such as will assist the Court to arrive at the meaning of the words used, and thus to give effect to the intention so expressed.[15]

Now it is certainly true that among contemporary thinkers in the fields of political theory and jurisprudence (philosophy of law) the classical hermeneutic approach just described has not received uniform approbation. The most radical of today's legal philosophies, the Critical Legal Studies (CLS) movement, which reached its high water mark in the 1970s in the work of Roberto Unger and Duncan Kennedy, argues in deconstructionist fashion against the face-value of virtually all legal instruments. Carrying American Legal Realism's doubts about the objectivity of legal operations virtually to the point of existential solipsism, CLS regards the legal interpreter as all-important and the text as infinitely malleable grist for the mill of political activism.[16] But CLS has been decisively shown to be incapable of practical application in the legal field, since its position undercuts the very Rule of

---

[13] "*Gibbons v. Ogden*, 9 Wheaton, 187-89 (1824).
[14] Francis Bacon, *The Advancement of Learning*, II. 20. viii.
[15] Roland Burrows, *Interpretation of Documents*, 2ᵈ ed. (London: Butterworth, 1946), 13.
[16] Roberto Unger, *The Critical Legal Studies Movement* (Cambridge: Harvard University Press, 1986); Mark Kelman, *A Guide to Critical Legal Studies* (Cambridge: Harvard University Press, 1987); Peter Fitzpatrick and Alan Hunt, eds., *Critical Legal Studies* (Oxford: Basil Blackwell, 1987).

Law.[17] The impact of CLS on day-to-day judicial activity has been virtually nil.

Professor Ronald Dworkin, H. L. A. Hart's successor in the chair of jurisprudence at Oxford, maintains that interpretation, in law and other fields, is essentially concerned with *purpose*: "but the purposes in play are not fundamentally those of some author but of the interpreter. Roughly, constructive interpretation is a matter of imposing purpose on an object or practice."[18] On the surface, this suggests that Dworkin is prepared to sacrifice the text to the interpreter, but he insists that "constructive interpretation" does not mean that "an interpreter can make of a practice or work of art anything he would have wanted it to be."[19] The text or object of interpretation is a residual given which limits what the interpreter can do to it.

Moreover, Dworkin is so unhappy with American Legal Realism and so horrified by Critical Legal Studies – and quite rightly, in our view – that he has set forth his "one right answer" thesis: the view that, in deciding cases, judges can indeed arrive at a single correct answer, based objectively on the existing legal tradition.[20] Such a view, inconsistent though it may be with Dworkin's concept of "constructive interpretation," nonetheless shows that he is at heart an objectivist who refuses to sacrifice the integrity of the legal documentary tradition to the subjective whims of the interpreter.

The most powerful contemporary theoreticians of legal hermeneutics are certainly those in the "original intent" camp – thinkers who argue (as did Chief Justice John Marshall) that texts must be understood in their original sense, not twisted to fit the interpreter's agenda. Robert Bork, for example, admits to the difficulty of psychoanalyzing the Founding Fathers to discover what they really "intended" in framing the American Constitution (the dilemma thrown up by liberal constitutionalists such as Laurence Tribe), and so prefers the expression "original understanding": "What we're really talking about [is] not what the authors of the Bill of

---

[17] See especially J. W. Harris, "Legal Doctrine and Interests in Land," in *Oxford Essays in Jurisprudence, Third Series*, ed. John Eekelaar and John Bell (Oxford: Clarendon Press, 1987), 167-97.
[18] Ronald Dworkin, *Law's Empire* (Cambridge: Harvard University Press, 1986), 52.
[19] Ibid.
[20] Ronald Dworkin, in *Law, Morality and Society: Essays in Honour of H. L. A. Hart*, ed. Hacker and Raz (Oxford: Oxford University Press, 1977), 58-83.

Rights had in the backs of their minds, but what people who voted for this thing understood themselves to be voting for."[21]

If, however, trying to determine the "original intent" of the author over and above his text poses extreme problems (Sibelius, for example, was hopeless at explaining the true intent and significance of his *Finlandia!*), the same dilemma attaches to the original audience of the text: they, too, may have misunderstood it – for any number of personal, societal or cultural reasons.

Thus the most sophisticated academic analysis of legal interpretation would appear to focus on the Wittgenstein-Popper approach: the analogy of the shoe and the foot. Interpretation is like a shoe and the text like the foot. One endeavours to find the interpretation that best fits the text (allowing the text itself to determine this). Here, "intent" or "understanding" is decided by the text itself.[22]

Such an approach fully supports the principle that the text must be allowed to interpret itself – in the sense that when different or contradictory interpretations of it are offered, each will be brought to the bar of the text to see which fits best. Interpretations therefore function like scientific theories which are arbitrated by the facts they endeavour to explain: the facts ultimately decide the value of our attempts to understand them.[23]

In the Wittgenstein-Popper model, the interpreter of course brings his prejudices (*aprioris*, presuppositions, biases) to the text, but it is the text that judges them also. And the meaning of the text is not to be established by extrinsic considerations, for that would yield an infinite regress. (If the given fact or text has no inherent meaning and one must appeal beyond it for its true signification, then that must *also* be true of the extrinsic facts to which one appeals. "Bigger bugs have littler bugs upon their backs to bite them/And littler bugs have littler bugs/And so – *ad infinitum*.") Of

---

[21] Robert Bork, interview in "Bork v. Tribe on Natural Law, the Ninth Amendment, the Role of the Court," *Life* (Fall Special, 1991): 96-99. For his position in detail, see Bork, "Neutral Principles and Some First Amendment Problems," 47/1 *Indiana Law Journal* (Fall, 1971); Bork, *The Tempting of America* (New York: The Free Press, 1990); and cf. Ethan Bronner, *Battle for Justice: How the Bork Nomination Shook America* (New York: W.W. Norton, 1989).

[22] For examples of the contribution of Wittgensteinian analysis to legal hermeneutics, though centering more on the *Philosophical Investigations* than on the *Tractatus Logico-Philosophicus*, see Jim Evans, *Statutory Interpretation: Problems of Communication*, corrected ed. (Auckland, New Zealand: Oxford University Press, 1989), 16-19, 25-26, 29-30, 188.

[23] See John Warwick Montgomery, "The Theologian's Craft," in his *The Suicide of Christian Theology* (Minneapolis: Bethany, 1970), 267-313, and above, Part Two, chap. 1, in the present volume.

course, extrinsic considerations can be used to clarify ambiguity, but never to contradict the clear meaning of a text.[24]

## Free Legal Advice for Theologians

What has our discussion of legal hermeneutics to do with the interpretation of Scripture? Could it not be argued that Christian faith is a matter of grace and not law and that therefore the preceding analysis, interesting as it may be for the history of ideas, is irrelevant to the Bible interpreter?

Hardly, for (1) the Bible – as a matter of fact – presents *both* gospel *and* law, and, as Luther stressed, the theologian's task is not to eliminate either one for the sake of the other, but properly to distinguish them;[25] and (2) a confusion of categories occurs when we do not recognize that Scripture, which indeed centers on grace and salvation, is first of all a collection of *writings*. If we do not employ a proper hermeneutic to discover what the Bible says, we cannot be sure of its message at all, whether it deals with grace or law.

Legal hermeneutics offers the most powerful reinforcement for traditional, grammatical-historical interpretation of Holy Writ. And why is such

---

[24] The corresponding principle of classical biblical hermeneutics is that extra-biblical materials may be used *ministerially*, but never *magisterially*, in the interpretation of the sacred text. On the English legal scene, the opinion prevails in some quarters that the recent House of Lords decision in *Pepper (Inspector of Taxes) v. Hart and Others* (*Times* Law Report, 30 November 1992) erodes the fundamental hermeneutic principle that statutes must interpret themselves, since it allows the record of Parliamentary debate ("Hansard") to assist in interpreting them. However, *Pepper* emphatically does not displace the classic rule, for the decision expressly makes "a limited modification to the existing rule, subject to strict safeguards." These are: (1) use of Hansard is allowed only "as an aid to construing legislation which [is] ambiguous or obscure or the literal meaning of which led to absurdity" and only "where such material clearly discloses the mischief aimed at" by the legislation; and (2) even in such instances, it is highly unlikely that any use can legitimately be made of a Parliamentary statement "other than that of the minister or other promoter of a Bill." Thus *Pepper* is little more than a gloss on the *golden rule* and the *mischief rule* of the classic canons of legal hermeneutics (see rules 3. and 4. in the list corresponding to note 10, *supra*).

[25] See C. F. W. Walther, *The Proper Distinction Between Law and Gospel*, ed. W. H. T. Dau (St. Louis, Mo.: Concordia, 1928); John Warwick Montgomery, "Luther's Hermeneutic vs. the New Hermeneutic," in his *Crisis in Lutheran Theology*, I, 2$^d$ ed. (Minneapolis: Bethany, 1973), 45-77 – also in his *In Defense of Martin Luther* (Milwaukee: Northwestern Publishing House, 1970), pp. 40-85; and John Warwick Montgomery, *Law & Gospel: A Study for Integrating Faith and Practice*, 2$^d$ ed. (Calgary, Alberta: Canadian Institute for Law, Theology and Public Policy, 1994), especially 5-10, 23-26.

reinforcement important? Because of the tragic departure from such standards of literal, textual interpretation of the Bible in the church today. Modern theology has done perhaps its greatest harm to classical Christian faith through the new hermeneutic. In general, modern interpreters refuse to be held to the fundamental rule of classical biblical hermeneutics that "Scripture must interpret itself." Because the contemporary theologian does not regard the Bible as a qualitatively unique divine revelation, he constantly employs extra-biblical materials (ancient non-biblical Near Eastern documents, modern scientific and social theories, etc.) to structure and recast the scriptural data.

Thus the Creation account in Genesis is construed – on the basis of extrinsic evolutionary considerations – not to intend to teach *how* the world came about (but only *that* God created it), in spite of its clear and repeated stress on the creation of each species "after its kind"; alleged scientific "impossibilities" transmute the account of Noah and the Flood – which could hardly teach more plainly a universal deluge – into a minor Near Eastern drizzle; ancient extra-biblical literary parallels are allowed (by fallacious *post hoc, ergo propter hoc* reasoning) to contradict the veracity of Jesus' own affirmations of the Mosaic and Davidic authorship of Old Testament books; and modern rationalistic antipathies to the supernatural provide hermeneutic justification for construing our Lord's miraculous ministry as little more than a morality play. These are but illustrations of the fact that practitioners of the new hermeneutic operate on the general assumption that no biblical text is capable of objective interpretation but must be construed in a "dynamic life-relation" with extra-biblical materials of the past and present and with the presuppositions of the contemporary interpreter.[26]

Here indeed we have the "divination" – as opposed to interpretation – Lord Bacon warned against. Such an approach is the death of all meaningful understanding of Scripture – as it would be in reference to legal documents too, were jurists to enter on the same suicidal hermeneutic course. They do not, of course, since if they did they would be disbarred or removed from the bench; our courts would crumble. And the society which

---

[26] On the scholarly problems with form- and redaction-criticism, see the references in John Warwick Montgomery, Letter to the Editor, 3/12 *Ecclesiastical Law Journal* 45-46 (January, 1993); and John Warwick Montgomery, "Why Has God Incarnate Suddenly Become Mythical?," in *Perspectives on Evangelical Theology: Papers from the 30th Annual Meeting of the Evangelical Theological Society*, ed. K. S. Kantzer and S. N. Gundry (Grand Rapids: Baker Book House, 1979), 57-65.

depends on the Rule of Law would collapse with them – or be transformed into something closer to barbarism and anarchy than to civilization.

In theology, however, defrocking is virtually impossible today (witness the late Bishop James Pike and the just-retired Bishop of Durham); and the effects of textual destruction are far less visible. Apathy and invisibility, however, have never prevented fatal diseases from spreading or reduced the numbers of their victims. We conclude, therefore, with two words of advice for the theologian interpreting Scripture today: *Gardez bien!*[27]

---

[27] The Montgomery clan motto.

# 6. Higher Criticism and the Legal Standard for Expert Testimony

## Introduction

The standard rejoinder to attempts to present the classic view that the biblical record in general is a work purporting to offer statements of objective historical fact is a confident (and often supercilious) reference to "the assured results of the higher criticism." One is told that theological faculties of mainline denominations and secular universities simply accept higher critical methodologies as normative. The implication is that true expertise in the field is thereby established beyond question and that anyone still accepting biblical accounts on their face value and employing the classic hermeneutic rule that the text should function as its own interpreter is operating in a hopelessly pre-modern fashion.

Procedural law offers a new perspective on this key issue. Recent years have seen a vital change in the way in which American courts, both federal and state, have come to treat expert testimony. In this short essay, we shall discuss that change and its implications for "assured results of higher criticism."

## The Modern American Law of Expert Testimony

The importance of expert testimony in both civil and criminal trials is simply immense. Writes a recent commentator in this area:

> A judge's decision whether to admit expert testimony can determine the outcome of a trial. If, for example, in a pharmaceutical liability lawsuit, the plaintiff cannot proffer an expert's opinion causally linking the drug at issue to her infirmity, she is unlikely to get the case to the jury. In a criminal trial, the admission of expert testimony questioning the reliability of eyewitness identifications may mean the difference between creating reasonable doubt or not. The standard, therefore, by which courts assess whether to admit expert testimony can be a crucial filter.[1]

Until quite recently, American courts accepted expert testimony on the basis of a leading case: *Frye v U.S.*, 293 F. 1013-1014 (D.C. Cir. 1923). The

---

[1] Patrick McGlone, "Time To Retire the *Frye* Test," *Washington [D.C.] Lawyer*, June, 2015, p. 27.

Court declared "... while courts will go a long way in admitting expert testimony deduced from a well-recognized scientific principle or discovery, the thing from which the deduction is made must be sufficiently established to have gained general acceptance in the particular field in which it belongs."

This "general acceptance" test to recognizing expert testimony came under more and more criticism over the years. The test focuses on "counting scientists' votes, rather than verifying the soundness of a scientific conclusion."[2] The advantage to the judge was that he did not have to evaluate the scientific evidence himself; his task was essentially to count noses – determining concurrence or non-concurrence of the scientific community on the matter.

Twenty-two years ago, the U.S. Supreme Court substituted a new test for recognizing expert evidence. The *Daubert* test – named from the leading case of *Daubert v Merrill Dow Pharmaceuticals*, 509 U.S. 579 (1993) – substituted a far more rational and sophisticated approach, consisting of an examination of four non-exclusive factors: (1) whether the theory on which the presumed expert is being called on to testify has been or can be tested, (2) whether the theory has been submitted to peer review and publication, (3) the method's known or potential rate of error, and (4) whether the theory finds general acceptance in the relevant scientific community. The *Frye* test may still be relevant, but it stands in fourth place and is entirely subordinated to questions as to the *de facto* scientific value of the expert's opinion. *Daubert* became the required standard in the federal courts, for the U.S. Supreme Court construed Rule 702 of the Federal Rules of Evidence as mandating the *Daubert* approach. Most State courts in the intervening years have come to follow *Daubert*. The result has been that judges now have a more serious task before them: they must themselves evaluate the scientific (or non-scientific) basis of the proposed expert testimony; they can no longer simply play statistician with the numbers of scientists in favour of or against a particular theory.[3]

The great advantage of the Daubert approach is that it moves determination of expertise from a war of numbers to an examination of the *evidence* for or against a theory. In a recent case, Associate Judge Frederick H.

---

[2] *Jones v U.S.*, 27 A.3d. 113, 1136 (D.C. 2011), cited in *Pettus v U.S.*, 37 A.3d. 213, 217 (D.C. 2012).

[3] To be sure, there has been resistance in some quarters to the additional burden on judges created by the *Daubert* decision – but its positive merit is now almost universally recognized; cf. "Daubert v. Merrell Dow Pharmaceuticals," in Joseph B. Kadane (ed.), *Statistics in the Law* (New York: Oxford University Press, 2008), pp. 52-65.

Weisberg effectively compared *Frye* with *Daubert*, pointing up the vast superiority of the latter:

> ... if a reliable, but not yet generally accepted, methodology produces "good science," *Daubert* will let it in, and if an accepted methodology produces "bad science," *Daubert* will keep it out; conversely, under *Frye*, as applied in this jurisdiction, even if a new methodology produces "good science," it will usually be excluded, but if an accepted methodology produces "bad science," it is likely to be admitted.[4]

## Application to the Higher Criticism of the Bible

Now let us see the value of applying *Daubert* analysis to "the assured results of the higher criticism" of the Holy Scriptures.

There is no doubt that a majority of faculty members at mainline denominational theological seminaries and in secular university and college departments of religion accept – religiously – the higher criticism. For them, it is indeed possible to reconstruct biblical materials by a literary analysis of the alleged sub-documents used editorially to create them as we have them today. The biblical critics would have no problem whatever passing the *Frye* test of "general acceptance" in their specific domain. (We leave aside here the pertinent question of why the views of faculty at conservative theological seminaries, Bible colleges, and Christian universities would be snubbed in such a nose count, but self-styled "liberals" have never been famous for their toleration of views to the right of their own.[5])

The *Daubert* formulation, however, insists that the judge *examine the underlying evidence for the given theory and its actual or potential negative effects*. It will never suffice merely to determine how many specialists agree or disagree with the theory.

So let us examine the rationality of the higher criticism. A convenient way to do this is to survey the propositional analysis of New and Old Testament higher criticism in the author's *Tractatus Logico-Theologicus*.[6] This we shall do in the following pages.

---

[4] *Murray v Motorola*, Case No. 2001 CA 008479 B, 2014 WI. 5817891, at *26 (D.C. Super. 8 August 2014).

[5] Cf. John Warwick Montgomery, "Bibliographical Bigotry, in his *Suicide of Christian Theology* (Minneapolis: Bethany, 1970), pp. 180-83

[6] Montgomery, *Tractatus Logico-Theologicus* (5th ed.; Bonn, Germany: Verlag für Kultur und Wissenschaft, 2012), propositions 3.3-3.394 and 4.63-4.633.

| | |
|---|---|
| 3.3 | Do not "assured results of modern biblical criticism" destroy the force of the foregoing argument for the soundness of the New Testament documents? |
| 3.31 | Even the most radical of the biblical critics has to accept the results of the bibliographical test which establishes the transmissional reliability of the New Testament documents. |
| 3.32 | Moreover, even after the most extreme criticism has been exercised, the critics themselves have not been able to excise central, miraculous elements from the narratives (G. Habermas). |
| 3.321 | For example, the discovery of the empty tomb on Easter morning – accepted by the great majority of critics because that discovery by women would have been so unlikely a fabrication in the context of male-dominated 1$^{st}$ century Judaism. |
| 3.33 | How, then, in spite of having to agree with the textual (lower) critics as to the value of the New Testament texts, do the higher (form- and redaction-) critics conclude that the life of Jesus, as set forth therein, is not – regardless of the asseverations of the writers – an accurate, historically reliable account, but is instead a theological product of "the faith experiences of the early church"? |
| 3.331 | The higher critics analyse the texts, identifying what they believe to be irregularities and inconsistencies in style and content; these are explained as the result of multiple authorship and the later editing and redacting of the materials by diverse faithorientations within the early Christian community. |
| 3.34 | This hypothesis faces the following insuperable objections: |
| 3.341 | No documentary evidence whatsoever exists to show the multiple authorship of New Testament books, i.e., no manuscripts of "pre-edited" material have ever been found; nor have any accounts been discovered which describe the redaction of the books by churchmen or by early Christian communities. |
| 3.3411 | Indeed, the early church and its spokesmen are uniform in their affirmations of respect for the Apostolic writings and the need to follow them without question. |
| 3.3412 | The conclusion seems inescapable that the methodology of the higher critic is a subjective one, dependent on the critic's views as to what constitutes a consistent literary product. |
| 3.34121 | It appears that what the critic is actually saying is that, were she to have written the book in question, she would not have |

written it that way; but perhaps that is why, in the ways of Providence, higher critics were not chosen as biblical authors.

3.342 Higher critical method has been weighed in the balance and found wanting when used to establish the authenticity of writings in other scholarly fields.

3.3421 Ugaritic scholarship discarded prior efforts to find multiple authorship on the basis of variation in the use of divine names (Cyrus Gordon).

3.34211 "If we applied the criterion of 'Divine names' to Ugaritic, Egyptian, or Arabic texts, we should see that the principle was not valid. I could multiply examples for all other criteria of the documentary hypothesis" (E. Yamauchi).

3.3422 Classical scholars, having attempted to locate multiple authors and establish the redaction of the Homeric poems, now conclude that "if the Iliad and the Odyssey were not written by Homer, they were written by someone of the same name who lived about the same time" (H. Caplan).

3.34221 "The chief weapon of the separatists has always been literary criticism, and of this it is not too much to say that such niggling word-baiting, such microscopic hunting of minute inconsistencies and flaws in logic, has hardly been seen, outside of the Homeric field, since Rymar and John Dennis died" (H. J. Rose, *Handbook of Greek Literature from Homer to the Age of Lucian*).

3.3423 Efforts to show the redaction of the English ballads were given up because the time span was considered too short for such a process (John Drinkwater, *English Poetry*); yet "no Gospel section passed through such a long period of oral tradition as did any genuine ballad" (McNeile and Williams, *Introduction to the Study of the New Testament*).

3.3424 C. S. Lewis (essay on "Modern Theology and Biblical Criticism") pointed out that interpreters of his Narnian Chronicles had not in a single instance been successful in isolating his sources, even though they were his contemporaries, employing the same language he used; Lewis then wondered why biblical critics, working with material two thousand years old and in ancient languages, think that they can succeed in a parallel endeavour.

3.3425 "The game of applying the methods of the 'Higher Criticism' to the Sherlock Holmes canon was begun, many years ago, by Monsignor Ronald Knox, with the aim of showing that, by

|     |     |
| --- | --- |
|     | those methods, one could disintegrate a modern classic as speciously as a certain school of critics have endeavoured to disintegrate the Bible" (Dorothy Sayers, *Unpopular Opinions*). |
| 3.343 | Forgeries of sculptures (Scopas) and paintings (Mondrian) have been purchased – at staggering cost – by major museums, such as the Getty and the Centre Pompidou, as a result of relying on experts who have employed stylistic arguments for attribution, rather than objective, scientific analysis of paint and compositional material. |
| 3.35 | Legal scholarship, with no literary axe to grind, has found the work of the biblical higher critics "curious": |
| 3.351 | "It is astonishing that while Graeco-Roman historians have been growing in confidence, the twentieth-century study of the Gospel narratives, starting from no less promising material, has taken so gloomy a turn in the development of form-criticism that the more advanced exponents of it apparently maintain – so far as an amateur can understand the matter – that the historical Christ is unknowable and the history of his mission cannot be written. This seems very curious when one compares the case for the best-known contemporary of Christ, who like Christ is a well-documented figure – Tiberius Caesar. The story of his reign is known from four sources, the *Annals* of Tacitus and the biography of Suetonius, written some eighty or ninety years later, the brief contemporary record of Velleius Paterculus, and the third century history of Cassius Dio. These disagree amongst themselves in the wildest possible fashion, both in major matters of political action or motive and in specific details of minor events. Everyone would admit that Tacitus is the best of all the sources, and yet no serious modern historian would accept at face value the majority of the statements of Tacitus about the motives of Tiberius. But this does not prevent the belief that the material of Tacitus can be used to write a history of Tiberius" (A. N. Sherwin-White, *Roman Society and Roman Law in the New Testament*). |
| 3.36 | What of the mediating scholars, generally of evangelical persuasion (Gundry, Osborne), and particularly found in the British Isles (Tyndale House, N. T. Wright), who believe that a mild, chastened, baptised higher criticism can be productively employed in New Testament scholarship? |

| | |
|---|---|
| 3.361 | This viewpoint partakes of the classic failing of "the curate's egg": the fact that a minute portion may not be bad does not warrant eating it. |
| 3.362 | If a methodology is fundamentally flawed – as is higher criticism by the inherent subjectivity of its analysis – it must be rejected per se and not employed selectively (G. Maier; E. Linnemann). |
| 3.363 | If, on occasion, the results of a bad methodology are not themselves bad, that hardly vindicates the method. |
| 3.37 | Even if it were possible to remove the anti-supernaturalistic bias from higher criticism – which is by no means certain – this would not correct its subjectivism. |
| 3.371 | We have already seen how a bias against veridical prophecy leads the higher critics to postdate Gospel materials after A.D. 70 – against the full weight of evidence in favour of their having been written within a generation of the events in the life of Jesus. |
| 3.372 | The subjectivity of higher critical method is particularly evident from the fact that the critics cannot agree among themselves as to the particular "sources" behind biblical materials – much less as to where one source leaves off and another begins. |
| 3.3721 | Probative is the very short history of the once projected "Polychrome Bible," which was to show in colours the different alleged strands underlying the received text and employed by the "redactors" to arrive at it; but the Polychrome Bible was never published, owing to the fact that the critics could not agree amongst themselves as to the sources. |
| 3.3722 | To bypass this difficulty, the end-of-the-20th-century "Jesus Seminar" (Robert W. Funk, Gerd Luedemann, *et al.*) has resorted to *voting* on the reliability of Gospel pericopes, thus avoiding the need for unanimity – surely a damning admission as to the inadequacy of the higher critical method itself. |
| 3.373 | Computer-assisted efforts to establish the "true," underlying authorship and provenance of New Testament writings have led to most unsatisfactory results. |
| 3.3731 | MacGregor and Morton fed the "literary style" of Romans and Galatians into a computer, so as to compare them with the other New Testament letters claiming to be Pauline; their conclusion: none of these other works were written by Paul. Then |

| | |
|---|---|
| | the MacGregor and Morton book on the subject was itself subjected to computer analysis using parallel criteria, proving that their work was actually a product of multiple authorship. |
| 3.374 | Style and vocabulary are not sufficiently stable criteria for determining questions of authorship. |
| 3.3741 | Parts one and two of Goethe's *Faust* would never be considered the work of a single author on the application of such criteria – but Goethe in fact wrote both; compare John's Gospel and the Revelation of St. John. |
| 3.3742 | Would the single authorship of one's love letters and academic productions survive higher critical analysis? |
| 3.3743 | "Many measures are extremely sensitive to a text's length (measured in number of words) and to its subject content. Longer texts and specialist texts prepared for expert audiences, for example, may have larger vocabularies than shorter texts and those written for general audiences. Genre, too, has an impact. A collection of newspaper articles and an autobiographical account all by the same author may differ considerably in their measurable style. Clearly, then, stylistic analyses are fallible and cannot provide positive identification of a text's authorship or literary heritage" (D. I. Greenstein, *A Historian's Guide to Computing*). |
| 3.38 | As for the anti-supernaturalism of the critics, it is worth noting that since the New Testament materials are thoroughly impregnated with miraculous occurrences, from the Virgin Birth of Jesus to his resurrection from the dead, the rejection of such material makes it logically impossible to retain the non-miraculous as representing an accurate record of his life and work. |
| 3.381 | Thus, the illogic of such efforts as the so-called *Jefferson Bible,* in which the third American president (a Deistic rationalist) included only Jesus' moral teachings after excising all the miraculous elements from the Gospel accounts. |
| 3.382 | Thus also (to take but a single current example), the critics' oftrepeated comment that, after all, the Virgin Birth accounts appear only in two Gospels (Matthew and Luke) and so, presumably, can be rejected; *but* they disregard the fact that this is equally the case with the teachings of the Sermon on the Mount (a favourite of those liberal critics themselves). |
| 3.383 | One cannot have it both ways: either none of the material is of historical value or all of it must be taken seriously, since the |

authorship and dating issues are identical for the material in its totality.

3.3831 As in the legal construction of documents, integrated texts are to be viewed as a whole: "Lord Justice Peter Gibson said it was possible for a court to find that part of a will did have the knowledge and approval of the deceased and that another part did not. But the circumstances in which it would be proper to find such a curate's egg would be rare" (*Fuller* v *Strum*, Times Law Report, 22 January 2002, finding that the will, in its entirety, was valid).

3.39 Do not the alleged "contradictions" in the New Testament material support the need for a higher critical analysis of the texts? Not at all, for:

3.391 The burden falls on the critic to show the existence of contradictions, and she cannot discharge that burden.

3.392 In most instances, the critic is not aware of the definition of a logical contradiction, namely, two incompatible states of affairs, one of which cannot logically exist at the same time or place, or under the same conditions, as the other.

3.393 Is it a "contradiction" when the Gospel of John records that Jesus cleansed the Temple early in his ministry, whilst the Synoptic Gospels speak of a cleansing of the Temple at the end of his ministry? *Only* if one assumes that there was one, and only one, cleansing; but that is not required by the language of the texts.

3.3931 Considering the condition of the Temple at the time, might we wonder why Jesus did not clean it out every Sabbath?

3.394 We have already noted that it is a fundamental principle of responsible literary criticism always to give the benefit of doubt to the writing; this principle is honoured only in the breach by the higher critics of the New Testament documents.

4.63 ... One must reject the documentary criticism of the Old Testament, which modifies the plain meaning of the text by recourse to hypothesised underlying sources and supposed editorial revisions of the text.

4.631 Thus, the Graf-Kuenen-Wellhausen J-E-P-D theory, which held that the Pentateuch was not written by Moses, as Jesus thought, but was a 10th century B.C. paste-up created from four major sources (one using *Yahweh/Jehovah* as the name for God, one using *Elohim* for the name of God, one a priestly, sacrifice-

| | |
|---|---|
| | orientated source, and one a deuteronomic or law-focused source). |
| 4.6311 | What we have said previously as to the hopelessly subjective, and therefore unscholarly, character of New Testament form- and redaction-criticism applies equally here. |
| 4.63111 | No manuscripts have ever been discovered which represent any one of the supposed underlying sources of Old Testament books. |
| 4.63112 | The critics have by no means stopped with J-E-P-D; Morgenstern of Hebrew Union College endeavoured to divide a K source into K and $K_1$. |
| 4.63113 | "Review of activity in the field of Old Testament criticism during the last quarter century has revealed a chaos of conflicting trends, ending in contradictory results, which create an impression of ineffectiveness in this type of research. The conclusion seems to be unavoidable that the higher criticism has long since passed the age of constructive achievement" (H. F. Hahn). |
| 4.6312 | The attempt to rearrange the Old Testament material by way of alleged sources has been deeply influenced by extrinsic, ideological considerations; thus, the naïve progressive-evolutionary thinking of the 19$^{th}$ century led critics to assert that "primitive" blood-sacrifice passages must have come earlier than "advanced" moral-prophetic passages (thereby allegedly showing the evolution of Old Testament religion from "lower" to "higher" monotheism). |
| 4.632 | Higher critics of the Old Testament almost universally maintain that the Book of Isaiah is actually two books, one earlier, the other (Deutero-Isaiah) later. |
| 4.6321 | One of the chief reasons for this supposition is the critic's antimiraculous bias: if the book is a unity, written at the time claimed for it, it must contain de facto fulfilled prophecy (cf. E. B. Pusey's powerful refutation of antimiraculous postdating [*Daniel the Prophet*]). |
| 4.6322 | Our earliest manuscript of an Old Testament book, a Dead Sea scroll Isaiah (*ca.* 125 B.C.), has the same text as in Bibles today, and shows no break whatsoever at the point where Deutero-Isaiah is supposed to commence. |
| 4.633 | Such examples make plain that rejection of Old Testament criticism has only one scholarly disadvantage: one will not be asked to deliver papers at the conferences of the critics. |

## Conclusion

If contemporary biblical scholarship were to follow the latest and best legal reasoning in the determination of valid expert testimony, it would reject *in toto* the subjectivistic methodology of the higher criticism. "General acceptance" of higher criticism by its advocates would be seen as an entirely inadequate ground for admitting its exegetical conclusions. Higher criticism as an interpretive methodology has been tested in other scholarly realms (Greco-Roman literature, Ugaritic, the English ballads, contemporary literature, computer studies) and found wanting; and its "known or potential rate of error" is gigantic. If one assesses whether the "reasoning or methodology underlying [its] testimony is scientifically valid,"[7] the only possible conclusion is a resounding negative. It is time for the mainline theological community to go beyond its myopic confines and listen to the judgment of the jurisprudents – on whose reasoning in the courtroom (unlike the subjective opinions of liberal theologians) societal health squarely depends.

---

[7] *Daubert,* 509 U.S. at 592-93.

# 7. Law and Justice

## With Contributions by Dr Gleason L. Archer and William N. Garrison, Esq.

In his discussion of "Law As the Will of God: The Heritage of the Old Testament," Carl Joachim Friedrich observed that "Yahweh, the God without name of Israel, was clearly distinguished from surrounding gods of other peoples by His preoccupation with law."[1] If the Bible is what it claims to be – not a collection of fallible ancient New Eastern opinion but the inerrant written revelation of the God of the universe – what does this scriptural "preoccupation with law" mean in the sphere of human jurisprudence? It is the contention of the present essay that a divinely given, biblical philosophy of law offers two overarching contributions to the human search for justice: explicit eternal norms against which positive law can and must be judged and a redemptive perspective for all juridical activity.

## I. Biblical Jurisprudence and the Quest for Norms

Is human law no more than a sociological product of the *Zeitgeist*, the spirit of the age? If so, the truly clever man is the one who can "get away" with violating it in order to achieve his purposes; after all, law observance is then only a question of the values of some over against the values of others. In W. H. Auden's words,

> ... Law-abiding scholars write:
> Law is neither wrong nor right,
> Law is only crimes
> Punished by places and by times,
> Law is the clothes men wear
> Anytime, anywhere,
> Law is Good-morning and Good-night.[2]

---

[1] Carl Joachim Friedrich, *The Philosophy of Law in Historical Perspective*, 2d ed. (Chicago: University of Chicago Press, 1963), p. 8.
[2] W. H. Auden, "Law Like Love" (From *The Collected Poetry of W. H. Auden*), reprinted in John Warwick Montgomery, ed., *Jurisprudence: A Book of Readings*, 2d ed. (Strasbourg, France: International Scholarly Publishers; Anaheim, Calif.: The Simon Greenleaf School of Law, 1980), pp. 4-5.

These lines point to the single most important conceptual battle in modern philosophy of law: the struggle between natural law theorists on the one hand and the legal positivists or realists on the other.

The most influential contemporary representative of legal positivism or realism is H. L. A. Hart, a thinker schooled in the best traditions of the analytical philosophy movement. Hart has raised to a level of considerable sophistication the rather simplistic nineteenth-century view that law and rights are no more than products of the commands of a sovereign (John Austin) or the results of judicial decision (John Chipman Gray). In Hart's view, law requires a social dimension (rules have an "internal aspect") and can only function by way of "shared morality."[3]

But, as Rosenbaum well observes, Hart's "community" approach to rights does not tell us "how to obtain universal agreement on the essentials of a community" or "how it is possible to experience the sense of community when the competing views around the world on the nature of community seem to thwart the development of a unified concept of human rights."[4] The force of these criticisms becomes particularly evident when we note that for Hart the ultimate "rule of recognition" on which any given legal system is founded is *unjustifiable* outside of the system itself.

> We only need the word "validity," and commonly only use it, to answer questions which arise *within* a system of rules where the status of a rule as a member of the system depends on its satisfying certain criteria provided by the rule of recognition. No such question can arise as to the validity of the very rule of recognition which provides the criteria; it can neither be valid nor invalid but is simply accepted as appropriate for use in this way. To express this simple fact by saying darkly that its validity is "assumed but cannot be demonstrated," is like saying that we assume, but can never demonstrate, that the standard meter bar in Paris which is the ultimate test of the correctness of all measure in meters, is itself correct.[5]

---

[3] Hart has presented his philosophy of law systematically in *The Concept of Law* (Oxford: Clarendon, 1961). J. W. Harris offers a helpful interpretation of Hart's ideas with a good bibliography (*Legal Philosophies* [London: Butterworths, 1980], pp. 105-14).

[4] Alan S. Rosenbaum, "Introduction," in his *The Philosophy of Human Rights: International Perspectives* (Westport, Conn.: Greenwood, 1980), p. 33.

[5] Hart, *The Concept of Law*, pp. 105-6.

We are thus left – as in the case of sociological and anthropological relativism – with no single, unified, justifiable legal standard.[6]

The single gravest problem with all forms of legal realism or positivism is their restriction of the idea of justice to the confines of particular legal systems or jurisprudential orientations. No overriding standard of law and justice is brought to bear on the human situation. As the great Belgian philosopher of law, Ch. Perelman, succinctly puts it:

> This conception of juridical positivism collapses before the abuses of Hitlerism, like any scientific theory irreconcilable with the facts. The universal reaction to the Nazi crimes forced the Allied chiefs of state to institute the Nuremberg trials and to interpret the adage *nullum crimen sine lege* in a nonpositivistic sense because the law violated in the case did not derive from a system of positive law but from the conscience of all civilized men. The conviction that it was impossible to leave these horrible crimes unpunished, although they fell outside a system of positive law, has prevailed over the positivistic conception of the grounding of the law.[7]

In the nineteenth century, legal positivism or realism replaced a much older juridical philosophy, the theory of natural law. And today, the overwhelming difficulties with all varieties of realism are producing still another pendulum-swing in the history of ideas – a swing back to natural law thinking.[8] But the most influential representatives of the current natural law revival do not operate theologically as did their medieval predecessors; rather, they attempt philosophically to establish a ground within human nature for absolute legal norms, a ground allegedly surpassing positive law and cultural relativity.

The most impressive contemporary effort to rehabilitate natural law is provided by John Finnis, fellow of University College, Oxford. Finnis is Roman Catholic and much concerned with the interpretation of Thomas Aquinas vis-a-vis the arguments he presents, but Finnis's great work, *Natural Law and Natural Rights*, is not disguised theologizing. He is thoroughly trained in analytical philosophy and attempts to show in the most general sense that "practical reasonableness" in ordering human affairs requires

---

[6] For a more detailed treatment of legal positivism with an examination of the views of Hans Kelsen, Ronald Dworkin, et al., see my *Human Rights and Human Dignity* (Dallas: Probe; Grand Rapids: Zondervan, 1986), ch. 4.
[7] Ch. Perelman, "Can the Rights of Man Be Founded?" in *The Philosophy of Human Rights*, ed. Rosenbaum, p. 47. See also M. J. Detmold, *The Unity of Law and Morality: A Refutation of Legal Positivism* (London: Routledge & Kegan Paul, 1984).
[8] Cf. C. G. Haines, *The Revival of Natural Law Concepts* (Cambridge: Harvard University Press, 1958).

an approach to the state, law, and justice that will preserve and extend human goods (specifically: life, knowledge, play, aesthetic experience, friendship or sociability, religion, etc.). "There are human goods," he writes, "that can be secured only through the institutions of human law, and requirements of practical reasonableness that only those institutions can satisfy."[9]

> What Finnis is trying to show is how any common enterprise of human beings aims at achieving a common good, and hence demands something which can only be called political or governmental authority. Nor is the function of such authority to be understood exclusively, or even primarily, in terms of any mere exercise of coercive force. No, it is rather for the necessary and indispensable coordination of the efforts of the different agents of the community that the authority is instituted in the first place; and it is only through the exercise of such a directing and coordinating authority that the common good of the community can even be concretely determined, much less achieved. And as for law – human law or positive law – it is nothing if not the indispensable instrument of such a public or governmental authority, aimed at the attainment of the good of the community. Moreover, since the good of the community is not any literally collective good, or even an addictive good, but simply the well-being of each and all of the members of the community individually, the law needs to be so constituted as to respect the rights of the individual members of the community. And here again, in his discussion of the rights, i.e. the natural rights, of citizens, Finnis is very careful to construe such rights – e.g. common law rights, such as the right to property, to a fair trial, to protection against self-incrimination, to safeguards against violence – not as absolute rights, in the way in which this term is so often understood nowadays, but rather as rights that are justified in terms of the natural needs and requirements of the individual, if he is ever to be able to live the life of a truly moral and autonomous human person.[10]

Finnis's commendable attempt to establish standards of justice in terms of practical reasonableness and the common good of the community suffers from great difficulties, however. Bankowski has pointed out that, of the several "human goods" Finnis sets forth, only "knowledge" is effectively

---

[9] John Finnis, *Natural Law and Natural Rights* (Oxford: Clarendon, 1980), p. 3. Finnis's list of human goods is based upon Germain Grisez, "The First Principle of Practical Reason," *Natural Law Forum* 10 (1965): 168-96.

[10] Henry B. Veatch, review of *Natural Law and Natural Rights* by John Finnis, *American Journal of Jurisprudence* 26 (1981): 253.

justified by his retorsive argument that one cannot argue against it without cutting the ground out beneath one's own feet. And even in the case of knowledge the vital question is still left open: "what items of knowledge we should seek."[11] Indeed, Finnis "is better at showing how law needs to be grounded in ethics, than he is at showing how the principles of ethics are discoverable right in the very facts of nature and reality."[12]

Like every natural law thinker, Finnis must solve the problem of defining what man's nature really is. As Aristotle well observed: "In order to find what is natural we must look among those things which according to nature are in a sound condition, not among those that are corrupt."[13] Granted, man frequently desires knowledge, life, and friendship; but it is equally the case empirically that human beings have often sought to deceive, kill and subjugate their fellows. After all, Hobbes – and Machiavelli before him – built his totalitarian social theory strictly on the natural law basis that human life is "nasty, brutish and short"! A successful natural law theory must be able to say whether the good or the bad in human life is truly "natural" and to what degree – for otherwise no one can determine what values are justly to receive legal sanction in society.

And this dilemma connects with the related quandary for natural law thinkers as to how, even if we know what human nature actually consists of, we can justify deriving an "ought" from the "is." The great analytical ethicist G. E. Moore termed this difficulty the "naturalistic fallacy": the false idea that once you know what is natural you will have justified it as a positive value.[14] In reality, even as the natural fact of murder or torture *does not* justify killing or inhuman punishment, so the natural fact of self-preservation or truth-seeking does not vindicate the alleged right to life or civil liberties.

A fatal error is therefore committed when well-meaning religionists (not excluding some Evangelicals) try to solve the root problems of legal philosophy by rejecting positivism in favor of a return to natural law thinking. In reality – though this is almost never recognized – jusnaturalism and legal positivism have correlative strengths and weaknesses which

---

[11] Z. K. Bankowski, review of *Natural Law and Natural Rights* by John Finnis, *Law Quarterly Review* 98 (July 1982): 474.

[12] Veatch, Review of *Natural Law and Natural Rights* by Finnis, p. 250.

[13] Aristotle, *Politics*, 1.5.

[14] G. E. Moore, *Principia Ethica* (Cambridge: Cambridge University Press, 1903), ch. 1. For a more extended discussion and critique of contemporary natural-law theories, including the Neo-Kantian approaches of Rawls and Gewirth, see my *Human Rights and Human Dignity*.

point directly to the need for *biblical jurisprudence*. Consider the two essential defining elements of all natural law theories with their corresponding advantage and disadvantage, and the parallel defining elements and strength/weakness of legal positivism or realism:

|  | | **Defining Elements** | | **Advantages / Disadvantages** |
|---|---|---|---|---|
| **Natural Law Theory** | N-1. | Insistence on an ideal standard of judgment above positive legislation or case law | a. | *Advantage:* Ethical judgment is brought to bear on existing positive law |
| | N-2. | The conviction that only law which conforms to this ideal is truly law | b. | *Disadvantage:* Bad law is not recognized as law at all, thus opening the doors to anarchy |
| **Legal Positivism or Realism** | P-1. | Absence of any ideal standard of judgment above positive legislation or case law | a. | *Disadvantage:* No standard of ethical judgment is brought to bear on existing positive law, thus leaving demonic legal systems (e.g., National Socialism) untouched |
| | P-2. | The conviction that all societal rules with the formal, official sanction of the body politic are law | b. | *Advantage:* Even bad law is seen to be law, thus preserving the rule of law |

What is needed for a sound jurisprudence is a *combination of defining element (N-1a) of jusnaturalism with defining element (P-2b) of legal positivism* – and the rejection of the corresponding disadvantageous elements of the two positions ([N-2b] and [P-1a]). *This is precisely what the biblical jurisprudence offers.*

Thus Romans 13 plainly asserts that "the powers that be are ordained of God," that "whosoever resisteth the power, resisteth the ordinance of God," and that we are to be subject to constituted authority "not only for wrath, but also for conscience sake." Scripture clearly holds that even bad law is nonetheless law and that there is something worse even than bad law – namely anarchy. The positivist concern with the preservation of the rule of law (P-2b) is thus vindicated.

Even more important, Holy Writ provides from cover to cover innumerable declarations of God's normative standards for human life. These norms are exactly what natural law theory gropes for (N-1a) but is unsuccessful in defining apart from a clear and unambiguous Word from God. In the Genesis-versus-evolution area of evangelical discussion, where the noninerrantists have claimed that the "law of nature" must be placed on an equal footing with Scripture (since, admittedly, God is the source of both), consistent believers in the inerrancy of the Bible have rightly pointed out that Holy Scripture, being already in verbal, propositional form, has a tremendous advantage in clarity and perspicuity over "nature." The same point applies jurisprudentially: God has unambiguously set forth his normative standards in the pages of Scripture, and the "natural law" cannot hope to compete with, much less contradict, its asseverations. As Sir William Blackstone well put it: "Man, considered as a creature, must necessarily be subject to the laws of his Creator ... No human laws should be suffered to contradict these."[15] It is Scripture that has the final word on what the eternal laws in fact are, thereby preserving us from moral and jurisprudential chaos and relativism.

How does biblically revealed law relate to the laws "written in men's hearts" (Heb. 8:10; *et al.*)? Principally on the basis of Romans 1 and 2 (in particular, 1:20 and 2:14-15), the Reformers maintained that even after man's fall into sin, a limited general knowledge of the universal principles of morality remained, indelibly inscribed on man's heart. This was Luther's position and Calvin's also.[16] In the twentieth century, following the col-

---

[15] Sir William Blackstone, *Commentaries on the Laws of England*, ed. Stanley N. Katz, et al.; 4 vols., facsimile ed. (Chicago: University of Chicago Press, 1979), 1:39, 42.

[16] On Luther, see Philip S. Watson, *Let God Be God! An Interpretation of the Theology of Martin Luther* (London: Epworth Press, 1947), pp. 73-85, 105-16; and Marc Lienhard, "Luther et les droits de l'homme," *Revue d'Histoire et de Philosophie Religieuses* 54/1 (1974): 15-29 (English translation in *A Lutheran Reader on Human Rights*, eds. Jorgen Lissner and Arne Sovik: *LWF Report* 1-2 [September 1978]: 66-80). Paul Helm of the

lapse of the old modernism or religious liberalism which in effect jettisoned biblical revelation in favor of a saving view of general revelation, a powerful reaction set in. Karl Barth in particular cried *nein* to Emil Brunner's relatively mild endeavor to maintain natural revelation (as in the case of the Reformers, not as a means of salvation, but only as a partial and imperfect knowledge of divine standards for human life and thus an objective judgment on man's sinful conduct toward his fellows).[17] Brunner's position was in fact little more than a restatement of the classic Reformation doctrine of the *Schöpfungsordnungen* (Orders of Creation), declaring on the basis of Scripture that even after the Fall, God in his grace structured human life through government, the family, education, etc., to prevent sinful man from destroying himself through unrestrained selfishness.[18] The weight of evangelical scholarship has concluded that Barth's total rejection of natural theology – and, with it, natural law theory – is scripturally unwarranted.[19]

But even if a biblical natural law theory is accepted, does it provide the necessary grounding for human jurisprudence? Norwegian theologian Einar Molland contends that:

---

University of Liverpool's Department of Philosophy, in delivering the third Finlayson lecture, provides an excellent overview of "Calvin and Natural Law": *The Scottish Bulletin of Evangelical Theology* 2 (1984): 5-22.

[17] See the celebrated debate between Barth and Brunner, *Natural Theology: Comprising "Nature and Grace" by Professor Dr. Emil Brunner and the Reply "No!" by Dr. Karl Barth*, trans. Peter Fraenkel (London: Geoffrey Bies, 1946).

[18] John Warwick Montgomery, "Karl Barth and Contemporary Theology of History," in his *Where Is History Going? Essays in Support of the Historical Truth of the Christian Revelation*, reprint ed. (Minneapolis: Bethany, 1972), pp. 104-5; and Montgomery, "A Critical Examination of Emil Brunner's *The Divine Imperative*, Bk. III," in his *The Shape of the Past*, rev. ed. (Minneapolis; Bethany, 1975), pp. 358-74.

[19] See, for example, Alan F. Johnson, "Is There a Biblical Warrant for Natural-Law Theories?" *Evangelical Theological Society Journal* 25/2 (June 1982): 185-99; and Bruce A. Demarest, *General Revelation* (Grand Rapids: Zondervan, 1982). Professor Demarest (p. 244) rejects on biblical grounds the entire – predominately Dutch hyper-Calvinist – tradition which maintains that "no knowledge is mediated by general revelation in nature and providence" (Demarest refers specifically to Abraham Kuyper, G. C. Berkouwer, Cornelius Van Til, Gordon Oark, T. F. Torrance, and Donald Bloesch – as well as Karl Barth). Jacques Ellul, as one would expect, follows Barth in unqualifiedly rejecting natural theology: see his *The Theological Foundation of Law*, trans. Marguerite Wieser (New York: Seabury, 1969); and cf. John Warwick Montgomery, "Technology and Eschatology," in his *Faith Founded on Fact* (Nashville: Thomas Nelson, 1978), pp. 155-59.

It is enough to believe in the value of man and in a written law which is valid for all mankind at all times, that is, in the law which ancient thinkers called the natural law. This is not what the natural sciences understand by natural law, since the law they refer to raises us above nature. The law in question here is concerned with man and corresponds to man's nature. For human coexistence, it is enough to believe that such a natural law exists and that we can all more or less clearly discern it.[20]

We doubt very much that this is "enough for human co-existence." The problem is not that formal natural-rights structures or orders are absent from human society. The trouble is that, though ubiquitously present, they *are* "formal," lacking in universal or justifiable substantive content. Perrott's theory of fundamental rights highlights the root difficulty when he concludes that "there are what may be called Natural Areas of Legal Concern rather than Natural Law principles with a specific content," and that "the precise content of the rules, within limits, does not matter very much; what does matter is that legal discriminations should be drawn and then generally adhered to. We *do* need to decide which side of the road to drive on; the choice of sides is, within limits, arbitrary."[21]

With respect, this is simply inadequate. In a footnote to the quoted passage, Perrott states that "of course, it [the choice of substantive legal content] matters enormously from an evaluative or emotional point of view." Does it only matter emotionally? Is it just an arbitrary question of which side of the road one drives on? A little earlier in his essay, Perrott declares that "a number of different definitions of murder may be equally acceptable"! In point of fact, the substantive definition of legal standards is all-important, and it is these clear definitions which natural law fails to provide. Carl Joachim Friedrich noted that the formula of the Justinian Code is so "imprecise" that it does little more than to underscore the need for "some kind of equity."[22] I observed at the Buchenwald death camp in East Germany that the *Digest's* vague expression, "Give to each his own" was inscribed in German translation (*Jedem das Seine*) on the metal doors leading into that place of horror.

---

[20] Quoted in Marc Lienhard, "Protestantism and Human Rights," *Human Rights Teaching* [UNESCO] 2/1 (1981): 30.
[21] D. L. Perrott, "The Logic of Fundamental Rights," in *Fundamental Rights*, eds. J. W. Bridge, D. Lasok, *et al.* (London: Sweet & Maxwell, 1973), pp. 13-15.
[22] Friedrich, *Philosophy of Law in Historical Perspective*, p. 33. See also John Warwick Montgomery, *The Law Above the Law*, rev. ed. (Irvine, CA: NRP Books/1517. The Legacy Project, 2015), pp. 38-40.

This is not in any sense to deny the reality of natural rights: it is only to say that their content is left undefined by natural law thinking, and it is precisely their content which is essential to solve the jurisprudential dilemma. C. S. Lewis is correct that all human societies operate – and must operate – with ethical values;[23] but in order effectively to oppose the myriad variations of man's inhumanity to man, we must be able to determine *which* ethical values are good, bad and indifferent. (Is torture wrong? What about cannibal environmentalists cleaning their plates?) The Orders of Creation are a reality; but it is not enough to know that the family has been instituted by God: one must be able to determine whether polygamy and polyandry are an asset or a liability to human dignity.

The best that can be said of religious natural law theories is that, like John the Baptist, they point beyond themselves. They point to God's special revelation of himself in the living Word (Jesus Christ) and the written Word (the Bible). God's inerrant special revelation yields concrete eternal norms of divine law by which human laws can and must be evaluated and judged.[24] This is the first of the two great contributions of biblical religion to man's quest for law and justice. The second is no less important, and we now turn our attention to it.

## II. Biblical Jurisprudence and the Centrality of Redemption

An inerrant catalog of divine norms for jurisprudence is of incalculable value, for it makes fundamentally impossible the reduction of human law to mere sociological consensus – to

> ... the clothes men wear
> Anytime, anywhere.

But revealed norms are not enough, for the profoundly practical question remains: granting that we know or are in a position to learn God's will in the sphere of normative jurisprudence, *what is law supposed to accomplish?* What are its proper functions? What is it supposed to do, and what is it incapable of doing? Without an answer to this basic functional question, we are like workers who have been given a perfect tool but are unclear as to what the tool should properly be used for.

---

[23] C. S. Lewis, *The Case for Christianity* (New York: Macmillan, 1943), reprinted in his *Mere Christianity* (New York: Macmillan, 1953); and cf. his *Abolition of Man* (New York: Macmillan, 1947).

[24] For a systematic presentation of the scriptural norms governing positive law, see, for example, H. B. Clark, *Biblical Law*, 2d ed. (Portland, Ore.: Binfords & Mort, 1944).

The God of the Bible has not left us in such a quandary. The Scriptures make clear what the law's proper functions are and what they are not. Here is a summary expression of biblical teaching on the subject in terms of the classic doctrine of the "three uses of the law":

> The Law has three uses, the Political, the Elenchtico-pedagogical and the Didactic. By the Political use is meant the use of the law as a curb to hold in check wicked men, and to protect society against their aggressions. By the Elenchtico-pedagogical use is meant its use to convict men of sin and thus indirectly to lead them to Christ (Gal. 3:24). This use of the Law refers primarily to the unconverted. But there is an Elenchtico-pedagogical use of the Law even for the regenerate, inasmuch as the Christian's life should be a daily repentance, and the Law enables him to see his daily shortcomings and his need for Christ more and more clearly. The Didactic use of the Law is its use as a guide for the Christian mind and conduct.[25]

Politically, the law is regarded as a restraint for the wicked, not as a means of building the "perfect society." Christian faith has no illusions about man: "there is none that doeth good, no, not one" (Ps. 14:1, 3 KJV; 53:1; Rom. 3:12). To be sure, the Christian should strive to maximize good through the existing legal system and employ all legitimate efforts to change that system for the better where it falls short; but no legal system will be perfect, for it is administered by imperfect men, and even if it were perfect, it could not make men good. Is the lawyer's task therefore an unimportant one, viewed politically? Hardly, for without it society would literally explode, since the conflicts of self-interest among sinful men will be resolved either within an ordered, legal framework or in an anarchical conflict. But the attorney or judge must see his work in this respect as more analogous to that of the policeman (ponder the double meaning of the term "lawman") than to the endeavors of the social reformer.

At the same time, the Christian in the legal sphere has a positive role of the most powerful nature – one far more significant than the (often naive) role of the social activist. The pedagogical use of the law, which Luther regarded as its primary function, is that of "schoolmaster [Greek, *paidagogos*: the slave who took the schoolchild to his master] to bring us to Christ." The law shows us where we fall short and therefore continually reminds us of our need for Christ's redemptive work on the cross. Lawyers

---

[25] Joseph Stump, *The Christian Faith* (Philadelphia: Muhlenberg, 1942), pp. 309-10. This basic conceptualization is found in all the standard works of classical dogmatics.

and those who administer the law have, not so incidentally, an ideal vantage point from which to drive home to others this central truth of the gospel. They are constantly in contact with those in trouble – whether because the latter have personally displayed a *mens rea* or because they are caught in the machinery of a sinful world. What better time or opportunity to help them to see that Christ is the only ultimate answer?[26]

As for the third, or didactic, use of the law, the most important thing to note about it is that, unlike the political and pedagogical uses which apply to non-Christian and Christian alike, it has meaning solely for the believer. Only those who have experienced the forgiveness of sin in Jesus Christ can look at the law (revelational or civil) as something more than a threat. Only the Christian believer can say *ex corde*: "O how I love thy law" (Ps. 119:97, 113 KJV) and "Thy law is my delight" (vv. 77, 92, 174 KJV). Christ's presence alone is capable of transmuting law from a terror (*lex semper accusat*) into an expression of God's loving will.[27]

Having seen what law is from the standpoint of biblical revelation, we must now state with equal precision what it is *not*. As noted in our comments on the political and pedagogical uses of the law, law is *not gospel*. Indeed, the proper distinction between law and gospel can be regarded as the key to all sound theology and Christian life.[28] In his great New Year's sermon of 1532 on Galatians 3:24-25, Luther – who had read law for a year before taking up theological studies – declared:

> The difference between the Law and the Gospel is the height of knowledge in Christendom. Every person and all persons who assume or glory in the name of Christ should know and be able to state this difference ...
>
> ... To be sure, both are God's Word: the Law, or the Ten Commandments, and the Gospel; the latter first given by God in Paradise, the former on Mount Sinai. But everything depends on the proper differentiation of these two messages and on not mixing them together ...
>
> Therefore place the man who is able nicely to distinguish the Law from the Gospel at the head of the list and call him a Doctor of the Holy Scripture, for without the Holy Spirit the attainment of this ability to differentiate is impossible ...

---

[26] This theme is further developed in my book, *Law & Gospel: A Study in Jurisprudence* (Oak Park, Ill.: Christian Legal Society, 1978 – now available from NRP Books/1517. The Legacy Project, Irvine, CA).

[27] See John Warwick Montgomery, "The Law's Third Use: Sanctification," in his *Crisis in Lutheran Theology*, 2 vols., rev. ed. (Minneapolis: Bethany, 1973), 1:124-27.

[28] C. F. W. Walther, *The Proper Distinction Between Law and Gospel*, ed. W. Dau (St. Louis: Concordia, 1928).

> ... By "Law" we should understand nothing but God's Word and command by which He tells us what we are to do and not to do and demands our obedience or work ...
>
> The Gospel is such a doctrine or Word of God as does not demand our works or command us to do anything but bids us simply receive the offered grace of the forgiveness of sins and eternal salvation and be satisfied to have it given to us as a free gift.[29]

The essential difference between law and gospel is not that gospel comes from God while law comes from man; both have their origin in the Divine will. The distinction between them is not genetic but functional: law *commands*, while gospel (Old English *godspel*, "good news") *bestows a gift*. Law and gospel are differentiated on this basis throughout the length and breadth of Scripture, but the distinction can be seen with particular clarity when the Bible speaks of the way of salvation or provides salvatory examples. When the people asked our Lord, "What shall we *do*, that we might *work the works* of God?" (thereby confusing gospel with law in thinking that salvation comes by fulfilling the law), Jesus answered in terms of pure gospel: "This is the work of God, that ye believe on him *whom he hath sent*" (John 6:28-29 KJV, italics mine). Similarly, Jesus with the rich young ruler (Matt. 19:16-22), and Paul with the Philippian jailer (Acts 17:29-34).

The apostle states this principle in formal terms again and again; indeed, it constitutes the very theme of his epistles to the Romans and to the Galatians. For example, in Romans 3:20-22 he draws the line between law and gospel with surgical precision:

> By the deeds of the law there shall no flesh be justified in his sight: for by the law is the knowledge of sin. But now the righteousness of God without the law is manifested, being witnessed by the law and the prophets: even the righteousness of God which is by faith of Jesus Christ unto all and upon all them that believe ... (KJV).

Why is this distinction between law and gospel so vital? Simply because the whole message of salvation turns on it. A sinful human race wants above all to prove its worth by saving itself – by demonstrating that it can create and maintain ideal legal and ethical structures and thereby satisfy the most exacting cosmic demands. But Scripture depicts such activity as a Tower of Babel – an impossible effort to scale the heights of heaven. "The fear of the Lord is the beginning of wisdom": man needs to recognize that the first step in salvation is to admit that he cannot save himself by the

---

[29] WA (the standard, critical Weimar edition of Luther's writings), 36:25, 29-31.

deeds of the law – however impressive the deeds or however commendable the law. "No man hath ascended up to heaven, but he that came down from heaven, even the Son of man" (John 3:13).

This endemic fallacy of egotistic fallen man – turning law into gospel – is evident whether one looks back into history or gazes across the expanse of the present. Contemporary political theorist Eric Voegelin, in his epochal series, *Order and History*, has identified the theme of "metastatic gnosis" in the human drama: the Promethean urge to create on earth a millennial perfection which only God is in fact capable of achieving. Voegelin charts the appalling evils produced by this Nietzschean transvaluation of all proper value, and correctly stresses that its result is always the very opposite of true order.[30]

In the Marxist East, one observes a religious conviction (a genuine opiate of the people?) to the effect that if the structures of society are altered, human perfection is attainable: eliminate by revolutionary action the inequities in the ownership of the means of production, recast law so that it no longer favors a ruling caste of capitalists, and a millennial "classless society" will arise.[31] In the capitalist West the means of social engineering are different, but the theory is the same: change the structures, and you will save mankind. Somehow no one asks the painfully obvious question: How can a self-centered Skinner build a Skinner box that will provide an environment capable of yielding non-self-centered future generations? Our craze for environmental works-righteousness disregards C. S. Lewis's perceptive observation that "man's power over Nature is really the power of some men over other men, with Nature as their instrument."[32] And in the Third World, whether we observe the lamination of a modern Euro-

---

[30] See Montgomery, *Shape of the Past*, pp. 131-37. Norman L. Geisler has recently pointed out similarly disquieting tendencies in the Calvinist "Reconstructionist" camp ("A Premillennial View of Law and Government," *Bibliotheca Sacra*, July-September 1985, pp. 250-66), though the true source of the Reconstructionist error would appear to lie not in their rejection of premillennialism or dispensationalism but in their acceptance of the Calvinist view that the pedagogical use of the law is to be subordinated to the third or didactic use. Such triumphalism opens the door to postmillennial naïveté.

[31] See John Warwick Montgomery, "The Marxist Approach to Human Rights: Analysis & Critique," *The Simon Greenleaf Law Review*, vol. 3 (1983-84), passim.

[32] Quoted in P. H. Sand, "The Socialist Response: Environmental Protection Law in the German Democratic Republic," *Ecology Law Quarterly* 3 (1973): 485.

pean civil code on a medieval Ethiopia or seek to comprehend mystical socialism in Tanzania, it becomes plain that law is regarded as a prime weapon of social change.[33]

No Christian, much less the Christian lawyer, can justify otherworldly indifference to social amelioration or to the importance of law revision in achieving worthwhile societal goals. But the way of salvation does not lie along that path. Law must be rigorously distinguished from gospel. "The law was given through Moses; grace and truth came through Jesus Christ" (John 1:17 KJV).

Confusion of law and gospel is possible in two directions. Law may be invested with the quality of gospel, thereby deceiving men into thinking that they can save themselves through personal or societal efforts. But gospel may also try to replace law, producing what Bonhoeffer has classically phrased "cheap grace." In the one case, law swallows up gospel, and the result is *legalism*; in the other, gospel absorbs law, yielding *antinomianism*. The gravity of dispensing with law for any reason – even on the alleged ground that grace renders it no longer necessary – is suggested by the New Testament use of the Greek word *anomos* ("lawless one") for the Antichrist (2 Thess. 2:8).

In contemporary theology the antinomian error is rife. Among modern theologians Paul Lehmann argues that not law or moral rules but rather "believing contexts" should guide our actions; what we should do will be discovered dynamically as we participate in the believing community.[34] A more radical variation on this new morality is Joseph Fletcher's "situation ethics," where we learn that "only one thing is intrinsically good, namely love," and that "love's decisions are made situationally, not prescriptively."[35] Such views fail to recognize that law and principle are unavoidably present – implicitly if not explicitly – in personal and societal decision-making and are far more dangerous when implicit; that love is a motive, incapable of charting specific action apart from a structure of values; and that to depend on situations to yield their own answers is to engage in a

---

[33] H. C. Dunning, "Land Reform in Ethiopia: A Case Study in Non-Development," *UCLA Law Review* 18 (1970): 271; R. B. Seidman, "Law and Stagnation in Africa," *Zambia Law Journal* 5 (1973): 39.

[34] Paul Lehmann, *Ethics in a Christian Context* (New York: Harper and Row, 1963), pp. 159-61.

[35] Joseph Fletcher, *Situation Ethics: The New Morality* (Philadelphia: Westminster, 1966).

most perilous form of magic, since what bubbles up from the caldron of sinful situations has no guarantee whatever of ethical purity.[36]

The late James A. Pike, a lawyer before he entered the Episcopal priesthood, declared in his 1962 Rosenthal Lectures at the Northwestern University School of Law that though the Ten Commandments "give us a very good rule of thumb as to standard situations," they are "pregnable to the assault of a higher claim:" "rules, whether they be traffic regulations or commandments from Mount Sinai, do not exhaust the full moral dimensions of things." And where is the "higher claim" to be found? In the dynamics of the existential situation. "In these pages," wrote Pike, "it will become apparent that I am an existentialist." As an illustration, he commends the heroine of the apocryphal Book of Judith for her willingness to operate with a "higher claim" than the sixth commandment in being willing to commit adultery so as to kill a political enemy of her people.[37] Here, as in situation ethics, the sinful human existential moment is invested with revelatory quality: immediate, individual situations are naively supposed to be able to "reveal" what neither human law – the product of far wider and deeper reflection – or even Holy Scripture – which claims to be and is the very Word of God – can adequately provide.[38]

The belief that the world of law is capable of being humanistically replaced by a climate of love, peace, and joy has been expressed by Charles Reich, formerly of the Yale law faculty, in *The Greening of America*. There he declares that the hippie exuberance – turning on and dropping out – of the 1960s heralded the dawn of a new consciousness: "Consciousness III," representing no less than "the beginning of the development of new capacities in man" and positing "a community of a very different sort, based upon love and trust." The conquest of scarcity has made literally possible a "change in human nature," since "man no longer needs to base his society on the assumption that all men are antagonistic to one another." As for legal structures, Reich grudgingly concedes that "perhaps democracy, law, and constitutional rights will still be wanted in a new society"; but he quickly adds that, if so, "they cannot be based or justified any longer on assumptions" such as that "man is a wolf to man."[39]

---

[36] Joseph Fletcher and John Warwick Montgomery, *Situation Ethics-True or False; A Dialogue* (Minneapolis: Bethany, 1972), pp. 25-48.
[37] James A. Pike, *Beyond the Law* (New York: Doubleday, 1963), pp. xii, 14-16.
[38] For my critiques of Pike's theology, in dialogue with him and in print, see John Warwick Montgomery, *The Suicide of Christian Theology* (Minneapolis: Bethany, 1971), pp. 17-61, 231-32.
[39] Charles A. Reich, *The Greening of America* (New York: Bantam, 1971), pp. 379-430.

And yet that is precisely what man continues to be. The Christian must never make the mistake of thinking that in his personal life or in the life of his society law is dispensable. If he does, the wolf within him and others will gnaw away his very soul and that of society. Concretely, the Christian will recognize that Romans 13 makes any violation of positive law an evil, even if in particular instances the law is not wise or just, and even if the subject matter prohibited by it is not *malum in se*. (Thus revolution is always an evil – though in some instances it may admittedly be a lesser of evils – and alcohol or marijuana, even if not inherently harmful to the body, cannot be used with moral impunity where prohibited by law.)

In sum, the Christian will test all positive law by the pronouncements of Holy Scripture, endeavoring by every legitimate means at his disposal to bring man's temporal law into conformity with God's eternal law.[40] Such a practical recognition that law is indispensable will serve the highest purpose of all: It will remind the individual and the society how far short of God's standards of justice they fall and will, as a schoolmaster, point them to Christ's perfect salvation.[41]

---

[40] For guidelines in those difficult situations where the implementation of divine norms in a secular legal climate conflicts with the Christian's primary evangelistic task, see John Warwick Montgomery, *The Shaping of America* (Minneapolis: Bethany, 1976), pp. 152-58.

[41] Noteworthy as contemporary illustrations are Charles Colson and Jeb Magruder, who came to Christ as a direct result of seeing their lives in shambles because of their participation in the Watergate illegalities.

# A Response to "Law and Justice"

*Gleason L. Archer*

John Montgomery's discussion of the proper relationship between human law enacted by men and the law of God set forth in Holy Scripture serves to bring out very clearly the basic principle that human legislation must ultimately rest on those concepts of right and wrong which are set forth in the Bible. This paper comes as a solemn reminder to the courts and legislative bodies established by mankind that they are finally responsible to the Lord of Justice himself for a faithful administration of their trust. In his opening section, "Biblical Jurisprudence and the Quest for Norms," he points out that valid human law must rest on a firmer foundation than the spirit of the age, a mere sociological product of the *Zeitgeist* that happens to prevail in modem times. The now popular view of the legal positivists, that human governments are answerable to no higher power than their own, fails to take stock of the operative principle upheld by the Nuremberg trials conducted against the leaders of the Nazi Reich. What seemed warranted and proper within Hitler's Germany between 1935 and 1945 with its unbridled tyranny and systematic genocide was completely rejected as an unpardonable offense against the human race. The condemnation of those surviving members of Hitler's high command were not condemned on the basis of the disapproval of the victorious allied nations themselves but on a much higher authority than that of men. The underlying assumption behind these judicial proceedings was that mankind as a whole is answerable to a standard of right and wrong imposed on the human race by the Author of creation.

We must, therefore, recognize from the outset that the very basis of commitment to a moral order, to which we all as human beings are answerable, stems from the understanding set forth in the very first chapter of the Bible, that man has been created in the moral and spiritual image of God. After the destruction of the great Flood, when Noah and his family are given the assignment of beginning a new race of men governed by a sense of responsibility toward God, the Lord himself is quoted as charging Noah with governmental authority on this basis: "From every man, from every man's brother, I will require the life of man. Whoever sheds man's blood, by man his blood shall be shed, for in the image of God he made man." This can only mean that he who transgresses against his fellow man or unjustly takes his life must pay for that murder with his own life, precisely because he has transgressed against God himself. It further implies that human courts are finally answerable to Almighty God if they fail to carry out capital punishment for justifiable homicide. This is a mandate which cannot be altered to a term of years in jail or the payment of monetary damages or be altogether forgiven on the basis of a spurious plea of insanity.[42] The divine mandate is one of justice, of recognizing the worth of the victim who has been slain, acknowledging him as one born in the image of God.

Montgomery rightly observes, concerning John Finnis, that his attempt to find a secure base for the "natural" rights of man on the inherent worth of man as a created species, even apart from his status as a son of God under the covenant that God made with Adam, turns out to be less than compelling. A view of man such as reflected in the Declaration of Independence, with an inherent right to "life, liberty and the pursuit of happiness," may be taken as a mere self-flattering delusion on the part of the human species – unless it is based on the presupposition expressed in the Declaration itself. The context affirms that man has "by his Creator" been endowed with these inalienable rights. Without the decree of God the human race has no objective foundation for claiming any such status at all. Apart from the revealed decree of the Lord Almighty in Genesis 1 and 2, there is no solid basis for asserting such natural rights, as over against the rights of the rat or the tiger or of any other animal with aims and goals quite contrary to the good of mankind. For the human race to proclaim any kind of inherent worth or set of privileges over against the rest of the animal world is unjustified arrogance incapable of logical justification.

From the foregoing considerations concerning the divine image decreed by the personal God who first created man, it inevitably follows that the human race is not at liberty to spell out the implications of life, liberty, and happiness according to its preferences or desires. These so-called natural rights, bestowed on us by God, must be exercised only in accordance with the will of God as revealed in his written Word, the Bible. This has been almost universally acknowledged by various races of mankind from the beginning of recorded history. Even the most idolatrous nations, like

---

[42] [Though I of course agree with Dr Archer on the biblical requirement that human government should carry our God's revealed will in the legal and political realms, I am not convinced that this mandates capital punishment. The European Convention, indeed, sees capital punishment as a violation of human rights. I understand the Noahic pronouncement as requiring, in all cases, just punishment – punishment that fits the crime, the criminal, the victim, and the totality of surrounding circumstances. Cf. my essay, "Some Remarks on Punishment and Freewill in Legal Theory & Classical Christian Theology," in my *Christ As Centre and Circumference* (Bonn, Germany: Verlag für Kultur und Wissenschaft, 2012), pp. 278-85. – JWM]

the ancient Egyptians, understood that their entire pantheon sponsored and enforced the moral law as represented by Ma'at, the goddess of "truth," against whom the heart of each deceased person had to be weighed on the scales of judgment in the presence of Osiris, the king of the dead. They understood full well that this moral order was divinely ordained rather than being manufactured by any sort of organized human government or human authority. The inherent rights of men had been given them by the gods themselves rather than by human legislation based on some sort of "social contract." Even the Pharaoh, though regarded as a divine son of Re', the sun god, was subject to the guidelines and the penalties of Ma'at, no matter how much he would have had it otherwise.

From this standpoint, then, the humanistic assumptions which seem to underlie some of the recent decisions of the United States Supreme Court, which understands the mandates of basic morality to depend on the majority opinion of contemporary culture, are altogether unsound. While public opinion must be taken into consideration in the making of legal decisions, it must be clearly understood that popular sentiment is altogether incompetent to abrogate or set aside the basic principles embodied in the Ten Commandments. What God has established, man may not validly annul. As we read in Isaiah 5:20-23:

> Woe to those who call evil good, and good evil;
> Who substitute darkness for light and light for darkness; ...
> Woe to those who are wise in their own eyes,
> And clever in their own sight! ...
> Who justify the wicked for a bribe,
> And take away the rights of the ones who are in the right!
>    (NASB)

These pronouncements from the God of Isaiah make clear the wickedness and the folly of human judges and human teachers in our public schools who advocate the right of any mother-to-be to have her unborn child butchered in an abortion clinic, the right of all murderers to escape the penalty of death even though they have snuffed out the life of another who has been created in the image of God. Those who have given themselves over to the depravity of homosexual pollution or who brutally abuse their wives and defile their children by incest, those who make a business of prostitution or who indulge in the sordid practice of fornication and adultery-all of these stand under the judgment of God. No changing values in modern society, no new approaches to sexual morality or to the stewardship of the human body, have the slightest validity to overturn the standards of the past which were derived from the guidelines of Holy Scripture.

The tragic history of the northern kingdom of Israel, which failed to honor even the most basic moral principles of God's law (Hos. 8-10; Amos 3-4) and was completely destroyed and exiled by Assyria in 721 B.C. serves to demonstrate that divine retribution ultimately overtakes any nation that settles for a man-made set of values in preference to the standards appointed by the Lord. The judgment imposed on the heathen neighbors of Israel for disregarding the basic requirements of humanity and justice is similarly declared against Damascus, Gaza, Tyre, Edom, Ammon, and Moab in Amos 1-2. The surrender of Judah to crass materialism and brutal disregard of the rights of God and man led to the total destruction of Jerusalem and its temple in 587 B.C. There can be no reasonable doubt that a similar fate awaits the nations of Christendom, Islam, and the Marxist powers of our present day unless their people repent of their wicked folly in abandoning the standards of the moral law and return to moral sanity.

Dr. Montgomery suggests that biblical jurisprudence combines the emphasis on an ideal standard of judgment over against positive legislation or mere case law (characteristic of the natural law theory) together with the stress of legal positivism on the duty of obedience even to laws or regulations which seem to be defective or ill-conceived. It should perhaps be added that the cultural framework of the Old Testament, reflecting a divinely appointed body of law intended for the guidance of the entire nation of Israel, presented a clearer case for unquestioning obedience (apart from tyrannical decrees by wicked Hebrew kings), than would have been true for the New Testament age when the Gentile power of Rome was in control with Nero at its head, for example. But whether the government was in the hands of Jews or Gentiles, the duty of obedience to God over against the evil mandates of unjust rulers is clearly maintained by the refusal of Daniel's three Hebrew comrades to bow down to Nebuchadnezzar's golden image (Dan. 3:16-18) and by the firm insistence of the apostles before the Sanhedrin in Acts 5:29: "We ought to obey God rather than men" (KJV). It might be profitable to comb carefully through the specific instances in the record of both Testaments in order to establish a clear definition of when such a conflict arises. But in general it may be observed that there is a qualitative difference between modern perceptions of the advocates of "social justice" (so called), who identify their policies of radical activism with the will of God; and those clear-cut confrontations between the divinely established moral law and the decrees of brutal opponents of the Lord such as Pharaoh in the time of Moses, or of Ahab and Jezebel in the time of Elijah, and of Nebuchadnezzar in the time of Daniel. The courageous stand of the Hebrew midwives against infant abortion, of Lot against the Sodomites who tried to attack his angelic visitors, of General Obadiah in shielding the prophets of Jehovah against the bloody persecution of Queen Jezebel, the absolute refusal of Nebuchadnezzar's Jewish civil servants to join in an act of idolatry – all of these examples serve as guidelines of a far different character from that of the sitdown strikes and the harboring of illegal aliens in the present-day sanctuary movement espoused by certain liberal churches in open defiance of the duly-enacted legislation of our national Congress.

Another important area that needs to be explored with greater precision is the feasibility in injecting factors of Christian compassion into the theory of criminology. A dangerous element of confusion has been introduced into the administration of justice in such a way as to favor and protect the wrongdoer as against his victims. A false sentimentalism which injects primary concern into psychological or environmental factors which led the criminal to commit his crime tends to obscure the just and proper rights of those whose lives he has unjustly taken or ruined, has made a travesty of much of American criminology.

It is doubtful how long any nation can endure that devotes its courts and legal process to the grossest miscarriages of justice, often upheld by a Supreme Court that feels free to manipulate and profoundly alter the Constitution of the United States away from the intention of the framers of that document and the congresses and state legislatures that enacted the subsequent amendments. We live in an age when the judicial branch of our government usurps the functions of the legislative, handing down decisions tantamount to new law, in which the voting public and the legislative bodies elected by them have not the slightest say. The benevolent endorsement of any expectant mother to have her baby murdered by an abortionist has rendered our Supreme Court indirectly responsible for the execution of well over 13 million totally innocent American citizens. The only higher tribunal left to bring such heinous guilt to a proper trial is that of the Lord God Almighty before whom each of those justices who voted with the majority in *Roe v. Wade* will some day have to give account.

A closely related misconception implicit in the present-day sentimentalism is the completely unfounded and unbiblical notion that the primary purpose of imprisonment is psychological rehabilitation. The futile expectation implied in the heart-wringing appeal of the defense attorney is that his unfortunate client should be viewed not as an enemy of society deserving of punishment but as a misguided victim of his environment or heredity who needs psychological counseling and a brief term in prison in order to straighten out his thinking and emerge from incarceration as a newly productive and exemplary citizen. It is, of course, most blatant in the typical humiliation and sneering innuendoes leveled against the women who are victims of forcible rape that the criminal is to be justified in our American courts, and the objects of their brutality are subjected to public shame without the achieving of any kind of justice. But in general it should be pointed out that all too often the compassion of judge and jury is directed toward the rapist or the robber or the perpetrator of incest who has psychologically ruined his children for the rest of their lives. Little or no concern is shown toward the objects of their brutality or lust, and no provision is made to help them through the consequences of the injustice perpetrated against them. It is high time that these grave abuses are called to the full attention of our American electorate while there is still time to replace the present breed of judges and justices with those who believe that the real purpose of our courts is to administer justice rather than injustice.

Dr. Montgomery is to be commended for his sturdy Lutheran emphasis on the need of distinguishing between law and gospel. This is, of course, a specifically religious concern that pertains more particularly to our churches rather than to our citizenry as a whole. But it is of utmost importance to make clear that there is no necessary connection between moral living and a state of redemption. It is safe to say that no class of sinners is so hard to convert to a saving knowledge of Christ as those who are religiously uncommitted but who maintain a high moral standard in their actual lifestyle. They are the hardest to convince that they are still nothing but guilty sinners worthy of eternal hell. They fail to comprehend that only the righteousness of Jesus Christ and the blood he has shed for their atonement can avail before God. In this sense the law has no redemptive value at all but only serves to demonstrate that they too have "come short of the glory of God" (Rom. 3:23 KJV). But this emphasis on the second use of the law, the pedagogical, must not obscure the first use of the law, the political, which has a binding force on all men, whether believers or not.

There remains only one other observation to make in regard to the Montgomery paper. The closest and most careful attention needs to be devoted to the distinction between the general and universally binding provisions of the moral law of God and those of a ceremonial or ritual character, which served to train and prepare God's ancient people for the coming of Christ. Helpful guidelines may be found in Acts 10:9-15 (Peter's vision of the great sheet), Acts 15:22-29 (the Gentiles excused from circumcision and the ceremonial law), Colossians 2:16-23 (matters of diet and the observance of Jewish feasts), Hebrews 8:7-13 (the New Covenant by which the law is written on the hearts of true believers) and Hebrews 9:9-10. Passages of this sort should be studied with great care in order to bring out those guidelines of holy and morally responsible living which are contained in the Hebrew Scriptures and are applicable to the context of the present world. Admittedly there may arise highly defensible differences of interpretation in this whole investigation, but surely there will be many a principle or standard of justice or equity that can be appropriated in our modern jurisprudence. All of this process must be carried on with a solemn sense of responsibility before the Author of liberty whose gracious providence made possible the kind of life and polity which we presently enjoy in this favored land. Legislators, judges, and lawyers are responsible not only to their human electorate but also to their divine Sovereign before whose tribunal all men shall some day stand in order to give an account of the deeds done in the body, whether good or bad. "It is appointed unto men once to die, and after this the judgment" (Heb. 9:27).

# A Response to "Law and Justice"

*William N. Garrison*

Dr. Montgomery has set before us well a foundation for our discussion on the Christian and his relationship to law and justice. He has demonstrated that neither the theory of natural law nor positivism can, in and of itself, provide a sufficient basis for law. His development of this brings to mind the wistful words of James M. Wall, editor of the *Christian Century*, as he writes concerning his encounter with an intellectual fundamentalist, "It is the curse of liberalism that we have to start over again with each issue, searching for right and wrong and defending our conclusions against a *backdrop of relativity*. The fundamentalist who is also an intellectual (and there are some) continues to probe the nature of evil, but always within the perimeters of a moral universe." All of us here are in editor Wall's frame of reference "Fundamentalist," and we are here probing the nature of evil within the perimeters of a moral universe. We are also here in a common conviction that God has revealed himself in a divinely superintended written account of his intervention in the affairs of creation and mankind, culminating in the incarnation, death, resurrection, and ascension of his Son, Jesus Christ; and we believe that that written Word is inerrant, subject to the caveats and qualifications of understanding which are included in the 1978 Chicago Statement. We are also here in substantial agreement that that inerrant document can be understood sufficiently well so that its message is clear. Our task on this occasion is to address the "So What?" which is unavoidable in that line of thought. If this be the Word of God, and we are in agreement as to how it should be understood, what impact should, and shall, it make on our lives? Our subject is the Christian and his relationship to law and justice, and in that connection I would like to ask for discussion under three headings.

## 1. Secular Law, or the Law of Nations

We think it is essential to recognize and distinguish the Mosaic law from the secular law, that is, the law of Romans 13. When the theologian speaks of the law he instinctively thinks of Sinai and the elaborate commands and instructions which were there given to Israel in connection with worship, with diet, and with the relationships between men. We believe that Sinai was and is a distinctive in history, an event when God brings into existence the nation which he has ordained in a unique way as a portion of his program of self-manifestation. Albright has commented on the uniqueness of the recorded origins of that nation, beginning as it does with a lowly sheepherder, passing through a protracted family experience, then through the nomadic and tribal multitude of descendants of that family and finally being transformed into a nation with its elaborate laws and with its distinctive ownership and possession of the land. This sequence of events is so unique that we must be careful lest we attempt to extrapolate it into something normative for all men for all ages and for all societies. We do not know of any biblical authority commanding us to impose the Sinai law on any nation other than Israel, nor are we aware of any statement that any other nation will be judged according to that law.

To speak to the application of law and justice insofar as the Christian is concerned requires that we address secular law in the same way that the apostles Peter and Paul encountered it and learn from their and other illustrations in the Scriptures. It is the Roman secular law, which exclusively benefited its citizens, that Paul appealed to in Acts 16 and 21; and that his appeal was utilitarian is obvious. He sought the protections accorded him by that law for his life and safety. But I am certain that he had no illusions that it was "holy and righteous and good" in the sense that he spoke of in Romans 7:12. Nevertheless, that is the law to which he referred in Romans 13, declaring that it is of God. It is particularly significant that by the time of his writing, the Roman Empire had begun to take notice of the Christian sect within Judaism and was responding with an accelerating degree of persecution.

It is interesting to note that when the Jews set out to destroy Jesus they were scrupulous in their recognition of their limitations in the carrying out of capital punishment. They were careful in the fabrication of the stories concerning Jesus and presented him as a threat to the Roman Empire, thereby attempting to incite Pilate and Herod to view him as an insurrectionist, posing great danger to the empire for which he could be executed. This attitude on the Jews' part seems to have been unique for this one occasion, and beyond their knowing, important in the eternal scheme to bring to pass the insidious religious hatred joining forces with Gentile indifference and callousness for the execution of the Son of God. A short time later the Jews were not nearly so fastidious in the stoning of Stephen, nor is there any evidence that the Romans were at all disturbed about this happening. Nowhere else in the Book of Acts does the Gentile power take offense at the Jewish excesses of this nature, the attitude of Gallio in Acts 18:17 being a case in point. In Acts 21 the Jews would have killed Paul but for intervention by the Roman commander upon learning that Paul was a Roman citizen.

Paul enjoins Timothy from prison that prayers are to be offered for the people in power in government, and the reason is given that it facilitates godly living and the spread of the gospel. The question of application is just as relevant for us today as it was for Peter in Acts 4 and later in Acts 12 after the execution of James by the Romans; and the history of the church is, in large measure, a record of the believer's struggle with secular law.

## 2. Making of Law and its Administration

There has been debate recently about the evangelical commitment of the fathers of our country. There is no doubt, however, that their frame of reference was greatly shaped by the philosophy of the Protestant Reformation, which acknowledged the sinfulness of man, the accountability to a sovereign God, all of which resulted in a respect for government and our need for it. The making of our early laws, however, was not spontaneous, nor was it a consensus of all of those involved. The following quote concerning the Massachusetts Bay Colony illustrates the diversity expressed.

> It must also be remembered that the principal leaders of early Massachusetts – Cotton, Winthrop, Dudley, and Endicott in particular, were overly zealous in their efforts to prevent and suppress any manifestation of independence in religious or political matters. They considered democracy in any form to be at variance with the will of God and the good of man and hence were violently opposed to any democratic innovations. Suspicious of a common people and distrustful of the motives and intentions of ordinary men, they inaugurated a stringent policy, which in some instances, amounted to spiritual, intellectual and political repression.

By contrast today the function of law making, that is government service, has been abdicated by the Christian community until very recent efforts to reinvolve the Evangelical. In the early part of this century the Evangelicals retreated, for reasons which are too complicated to speculate here, and they did not train and encourage their children with a view to public service. How we love to discover evangelical Christians in government, but all too often we discover that they are converts in later life. Since politics and government are viewed as essentially dirty and suspect, this is a convenient attitude because we are spared the process of political advancement and only have to deal with people who are already "winners" in that arena – that is, already in office.

There probably is a lack of awareness that law in the secular sense has developed dramatically over the years, and that development is a response to the needs of society. A simple tribal society has a simple set of laws. Commerce and financial activity carry with them the necessity for a sophistication of law. The early English common law was simple in the extreme by comparison with our laws today. An expanding economy inevitably leads to an expanding sophistication of the law. It is also essential to notice that an expanded view, or an enlightened view, of human rights and the protection of those rights by the law best occurs in an expanding and dynamic economy. Political power that exists in a poor and deprived economy will very seldom produce significant human rights advancement except superficially.

British common law was a development of law based on the doctrine of *stare decisis*, meaning law is an accumulation of all the opinions which have been rendered by the courts down through the years and decades. This law in England tended to be arbitrary, and it functioned on the proposition that all wrongs which a person experienced could be compensated for in a pecuniary sense. This law is the "legal" system of thought, but as the economy of Britain expanded, it became apparent to the Crown that monetary judgments were not sufficient in all cases. There developed from this an expression of the king's conscience, through his chancellor, a whole new body of law which came to be known as "equity." In the first instance equity knew no tradition, and the chancellor simply looked at each situation and made a determination as to what was right. The subjectivity was without bounds, and there developed a series of statements characterizing this new form of relief. The courts of equity were separate from the courts of law, and in them a man who "seeks equity" must "do equity." It was further said that a man "must seek equity with clean hands." "Equity is the King's conscience." After a good many years equity began to build its own volume of reported cases, and when jurists held the post of chancellor there began to be more system in the matter. In the American courts today, both federal and state, the courts sit at law and in equity without advertising to the public the distinction. In Deuteronomy 19:14 is the command "You shall not move your neighbor's boundary mark, which the ancestors have set, in your inheritance which you shall inherit in the land that the Lord your God gives you to possess" (NASB). There is no penalty prescribed, but presumably the remedy would be equitable – that is, forcing the offender to move the boundary mark back to its rightful place. The legal remedy would simply be monetary damages for the offense. That the concept of equity in England took shape as late as the sixteenth century illustrates that the law of the land, the secular law, is a developing, evolutionary thing which reflects the complexity of civilization and is an indicator of the economic dynamics of the sovereign as well as its concern for the protection of individual rights.

The last several decades have witnessed a phenomenon in American law which is unprecedented in previous history, and that is the concept of affirmative action. You will notice in the Decalogue that the commandment "Honor thy father and mother" (Exod. 20:12) is an affirmative commandment, while the others are negative. Think if you will the difficulty of monitoring and measuring obedience to an affirmative commandment. If the question were asked here today, "Do you honor your father and your mother?" the answer will be "Yes," but in your mind, "Compared to what?" None of us is completely comfortable that we have done all we could in the honoring of our parents, and we will look instinctively to relative standards to which we can compare ourselves. The American jurisprudence system has entered an era of almost overwhelming complexity as the legislatures have commanded us not only to refrain from evil in regard to our relationships to our fellow man, but also to pursue and do what is right. As a result, we have burgeoning federal and state agencies to make employers be reasonable and kind to their employees. We have agencies to make us be kind to our environment. We have agencies that monitor our biases so that we will not engage in subjective hiring practices and thereby discriminate against anyone because of age, sex, race, or religious persuasion. The businessman knows today the demands which are placed on him to make sure that he "does right" in all matters. Those of us who are white, Protestant males in middle America sometimes wish for an agency that would attend to our own selfperceived suffering as we comply with all these mandatory requirements that we "be nice." In our treatment of the application of the Christian in his relationship to law and justice, we must take into account the enormous complexity of life and business in a world which has gone mad in the creation of paper and computer memory storage.

The question before us is: "How do John Q. and Mary C. Christian live for Jesus Christ in this environment of the Western world?" The spiritual prosperity of religious freedom has dulled our Christian sensibility to the fact that true spirituality has always been in conflict with secular government insofar as ultimate goals are concerned. The biblical records of men of God living in hostile environments are Daniel in the Babylonian/Persian captivity and Joseph in the patriarchal days of Israel in Egypt. What can be learned from these men is that they functioned in an exemplary manner in environments completely hostile to the Jewish way of life. Their advancement in offices is not a direct product of their spirituality but of their efficiency and competence in performing the tasks which were placed before them. We have little but imagination to tell us the nature of these tasks, but it can be safely assumed that on a daily basis over the period of years involved, these were not tasks that were dear to their Jewish hearts. It cannot be assumed that the democratic experiment is a given for all time; and as secularization occurs, it will be increasingly incumbent upon church leadership to prepare people for the task of significant and authentic Christian living in a society which may elect to become more and more secularized.

In this section we have dealt with the involvement of the individual Evangelical in the making of law and its administration, but there is another aspect to be considered, and this is the role of the institutional church in government. Perhaps a brief overview of the church and its relationship to the state in New Testament times would be helpful. In the instances which have already been noted in Acts, particularly in Acts 4, 12, and 16, it can be seen that politically the church is perceived as powerless, and the state is indifferent to it. Organized religion – that is, Judaism – constantly appeals to the state for power and authority to make the early church conform to religion's view of society, under the guise that the religious view was also the state's view. This did not continue indefinitely. Whereas the early church was, in the words of British historian Paul Johnson, "charismatic and eschatological," after the elapse of several centuries it became institutional, political, and confrontational.

After the Edict of Milan and in the fourth century Augustine made his presence felt in many ways, including his view of the church. Under him the church took on the ways of the state. It became institutional, it became confrontational, and the ministry was defined by the clergy. Note the evaluation by Peter Brown, biographer of Augustine:

> The Catholicism of Augustine, by contrast, reflects the attitude of a group confident of its powers to absorb the world without losing its identity. This identity existed independently of the quality of the human agents of the Church: it rested on "objective" promises of God, working out magnificently in history, and on the "objective" efficacy of its sacraments. This Church was hungry for souls: let it eat, indiscriminately if needs be. It is a group no longer committed to defend itself against society; but rather, poised, ready to fulfill what is considered its historic mission, to dominate, to absorb, to lead a whole Empire. "Ask me, and I shall give the uttermost parts of the earth to Thy possession." It is not surprising, therefore, that Africa, which had always been the home of articulate and extreme views on the nature of

the Church as a group in society, should, once again, in the age of Augustine, become the "cockpit of Europe," for this, the last great debate, whose outcome would determine the form taken by the Catholic domination of the Latin world until the Reformation.

The church, having found its expression in Augustine, that the Catholic church in its empirical form was the kingdom of Christ, from that time forward found itself in interaction and conflict for power with the state wherever they coexisted. The lives of Luther, Calvin, Knox, Cromwell, and Kuyper all have their dimension of theonomy as the church has as its goal the imposition of God's law as it understands it on the state.[43] Nevertheless, with the exception of the United States, all of the Western countries have the continuing experience of a state church inextricably bound up with the secular system itself.

The American system is a unique experiment in history, and after slightly over two hundred years it can still not be considered too much more than an experiment. The early settlers came to the thirteen colonies primarily from Britain but all from Northern Europe, and they brought with them varying reactions to the church they had experienced in their homelands. In some colonies, such as Massachusetts, there were strong expressions which we would recognize as theonomic today and which are cited by current theonomists as normative for where the church and state should be in their relationships. While the attitude varied in the thirteen states when the Constitution was finally hammered out, a unique concept of separation of church and state had been incorporated. This we know today as the establishment clause of the First Amendment which states simply that "Congress shall make no law respecting an establishment of religion, or prohibiting the free exercise thereof." In reading the writings and statements of the men who drafted that document and considering the deliberation that attended it, it is highly unlikely that any of them would conceive that religion, of all forms, would be relegated completely in the minds of the secular government to a matter only of private concern. The statement that the state would create no church has in two hundred years of interpretation by the courts created polarization, a secularization which is exceeded by no other nation of Northern European extraction. Whereas the United States experiment has furnished a matrix for a very virile and expansive form of evangelical Christianity, it has dismayed itself with its capacity for fracturing the unity of the church and its

---

[43] [It is doubtful that Luther should be included in this list, even though he certainly functioned within a state-church system. JWM]

ability in this century to assert itself through the conscience of men on the government itself. The current politics of the New Right are an expression of frustration on the part of millions of American citizens who are weary of the extremes of that secularization process.

In our first section we stated our persuasion that Christians are, by the examples of both Testaments and the expressed commandments, to be subject to the secular laws of their environment. In this section it is our conclusion that Christians must be responsible citizens wherever they live; and this consists, at a minimum, of obeying the law, paying taxes, and exercising the privileges of vote to the extent that that is possible. In addition, the vocational call of politics and government service is just as valid as any other vocational call; and the evangelical world should treat it accordingly. Such a call to the making of law and its administration in society must be respected as much as any other, and it will be to a pattern of day-by-day activities of government in the same spirit which motivated Daniel and Joseph. They both functioned as sojourners in the eschatological sense but were exemplary in their day-to-day performance. Too often the Christian thinks of involvement in government as exclusively being a concern over single issues. God has left his people, those whom he has redeemed, in the world to interface with society; and we believe it is to be a pervasive, persistent, patient encounter with all of legitimate society, including participation in the making of law and its administration.

Insofar as the individual Christian is concerned, we would conclude that his command is to represent a pervasive influence of redemption in the society in which he lives. On the other hand, we are not persuaded that the Bible, either Testament of it, furnishes any basis for a theonomic mandate to the institutional church. There is no evidence of that mind-set in the first-century church, and the above quotation concerning Augustine places the origin of that theological view in the fourth century, long after the biblical canon was completed.

## 3. Bad Law, Justice, and Revolution

Dr. Montgomery pointed out in his paper that bad law is still law and must be obeyed by the Christian, although he would, I think, by rationalization conclude that the American Revolution was God ordained.[44] From the Romans passage in chapter 13 it is evident when seen in the context of Paul's

---

[44] [My position is that the American Revolution can be regarded as a lesser-of-evils, but hardly a moral good, since it – like all revolutions – entailed a refusal to be "subject to the higher powers." JWM]

own experience that he would concur that bad law is nevertheless the law. Although there is bad law in connection with business and commerce which usually fails to give proper redress for wrongs which have been perpetrated, we normally think of bad law as it provokes criminal injustice. Injustice, in fact, occurs when the law is bad and when good laws are not properly administered.

A cursory review of slavery provides a good insight on man's inhumanity to man. The idea of ownership of the person and all the rights of another individual goes so far back in history that its roots are uncertain. It prevailed in Greek and Roman cultures, to say nothing of the Assyrians, Persians, and the Egyptians before them. In considering this matter, one must give pause to the fact that Jesus never spoke out on this particular form of brutish behavior, nor did the apostle Paul condemn it in his letter to Philemon. And yet we know that the dignity afforded the individual by the message of the Gospels, the divine fiat that man is created in the image of God, is ultimately the basis on which slavery has come to an end in history.

In eighteenth-century England there appeared a popular Wedgwood ceramic cameo which depicted a black man on his knees with the prayer, "Am I not a man and a brother?" The literature defending the slave trade in those days reveals the horrible fact that men, for mercantile and commercial reasons, convinced themselves that the blacks of Africa were subhuman if they were human at all. Wilberforce offered his first resolution in Parliament in 1792 for the abolition of the slave trade, and it was finally in 1833 when Parliament abolished the practice of slavery throughout the empire. Wilberforce's resolutions enjoyed parliamentary support from Pitt, Burke, and many others of great stature in the British government; yet it required more than forty years to answer affirmatively the question "Am I not a man and a brother?"[45]

How do Christians respond to injustice from bad law or from improperly administered law? It would seem that they must register their protest, and there is shame for all of us as we realize those great issues of our day in which we were absent or late in arriving on the scene to make our expression. God makes it abundantly clear that true religion works itself out in care and compassion in the pursuit of justice. Fortunately, the "law of widows and orphans" is tacitly recognized in most of our courts, which

---

[45] [Cf. Montgomery, "Slavery, Human Dignity and Human Rights," in his *Christ As Centre and Circumference* (Bonn, Germany: Verlag für Kultur und Wissenschaft, 2012), pp. 420-39.]

guard their rights with a diligence not shown in other matters. The prophets of the Old Testament are pointed in their indictments that a true and proper relationship with God will work itself out in the doing of justice.

What of revolution? Is it ever appropriate? Those of us who are beneficiaries of the American Revolution wish desperately for a biblical rationale to justify that great event in the course of our country's history. Dr. Montgomery infers that he has that all worked out, but the question persists. Is it different from any other revolution which at best is an expression of rebellion against the law, even though it is a bad law? Perhaps the most sobering thing about revolution is that it rarely achieves what it promises to the masses, and it depends a great deal on demagoguery. That they get out of control is amply illustrated by the French Revolution in the death on the guillotine of Robespierre, an event which terrified the British aristocracy to move toward a democratic procedure that avoided a civil war of a like kind in Britain. In this century we have long debated the role of the church and the ministry in the fascist state of Nazi Germany. It is to the embarrassment of many of the clergy and the church leaders that no outcry was made on the awful destruction of society which was being conducted in Germany on the rise of the Third Reich. Out of that era came Bonhoeffer, who posthumously became a hero to much of the Christian world. On the occasion of his impending death he stated beautifully for all of us the ambiguities inherent in the decision to resist or acquiesce. In his *Letters and Papers from Prison* we read, "It is therefore impossible to define the boundary between resistance and submission on abstract principles, but both of them must exist and both must be practiced. Faith demands elasticity of behavior."

To those of us in this country, our forefathers assumed by implication a formidable task when they wrote that *all* men everywhere are created equal and have the right to the pursuit of happiness. We have yet in this society to translate that into reality even within our own borders. Our efforts to export our principles by which the stated goal can be achieved have met with more failures than successes. The test of our own relationships to these issues will be in terms of our obedience to the will of Jesus Christ for our lives. The history of the development of law, the dealings of mankind with its own injustices to the rest of mankind, are warnings to us of our ultimate inability properly to self-govern and our inability to create any sort of utopian state of affairs. The kingdom that we profess to long for will only be established under the personal reign of Jesus Christ when he makes his appearance for that purpose on this earth. The task for every Christian in the meantime is to be obedient to all of the implications of the incarnation of Jesus Christ and the revealed and stated will of God. There is nothing in history to encourage us to believe that we are upon any final solution in this matter, and, in fact, we can know that our perception of our failings and shortcomings will be as imperfect as our forefathers were imperfect in their evaluation of their own days and times. But of this we can be sure, that God has redeemed us and called us to be his own and has decreed that we are to interface with the society, in time and space if you will, in real and meaningful terms. And in our relationship to him, he has scripturally furnished us with sufficient eschatological data that we should serve him as sojourners in the here and now with an eye on the eternity which he has prepared for us.

# 8. Why Human Rights Are Impossible Without Religion[1]

Everyone is in favor of human rights. Human rights in many ways parallel motherhood, apple pie and the flag. No matter where we go in the world, we will find that the political leaders in power – including some of the very worst dictators – are nevertheless in favor of human rights. Human rights, as my head of school in England remarks, is a "sexy" subject. It's a subject which immediately elicits interest, and everyone presumably favors human rights.

And yet.

And yet a decade ago Claude Lelouch, the famous French film director, did a movie based on George Orwell's *Animal Farm*, the title of which, *Les uns et les autres,* was taken from Orwell's celebrated line: "All the animals are equal, but some are more equal than others." And the point of the film is that in reality – in practice – though everyone favors human rights, they favor human rights in their own terms. That is to say, human rights are employed as a device, very often, to justify what one's own nation is doing, to ensure that one's own nation receives favorable treatment, but other nations are not looked at in the same light.

The most important question in the area of human rights is certainly how rights can be justified. Very often in the field of human rights there is a confusion between rights, on the one hand, and wants and needs on the other. The fact that we want something, the fact that our life would be immensely better were we to have something, or the fact that we genuinely need something – do those matters equate with a right to have such?

How do we define rights? And after we've defined them, how do we justify them? That's what we have to address. And in order to do this I will take you on a little journey back in time to the nineteenth century.

## Human Rights: From Natural Law to Legal Positivism

In the nineteenth century the prevailing legal philosophy of the West was replaced by another legal philosophy. For some fifteen hundred years the prevailing legal philosophy in the West was known as *legal naturalism* or *natural law theory or juris naturalism*. That philosophy held that there is a

---

[1] Transcription of a public lecture delivered in 1999 at the University of California, Santa Barbara, under the auspices of the Veritas Forum.

higher or deeper standard, outside of the law, on the basis of which the law needs to be judged. When the positive law sets forth a particular statute or a particular series of a case decisions, it is nonetheless necessary to judge all of that from the outside by a higher ethical or moral standard.

In the middle of the nineteenth century that legal philosophy was replaced very largely in the West by a philosophy known as *legal positivism* or *legal realism*. (There's a slight difference between the two, but we won't worry about it.) In general, that philosophy came to prevail in legal instruction in the common law world, England and America, and also in the civil law world, the European continent.

According to the legal philosophy of legal positivism, law is the command of the sovereign. It is not to be judged by any standard outside of itself. It is impossible for such standards to operate within the law per se, and one must go to the positive law, to the law of the land, in order to find out what the law is. If it looks like law, tastes like law and smells like law, *it's law*, and we don't ask subsequent ethical questions in regard to it. If we are asking such questions, we're not asking them within the area of law at all.

**Jeremy Bentham.** Now this philosophy was developed by two English scholars. One of them is well known: Jeremy Bentham, the utilitarian philosopher. (The other is John Austin, whose work was solely within the area of jurisprudence, and he died quite young.)

The problem is that Bentham had diarrhea of the pen. He could not stop writing. He wrote a great deal, and most of it was not published during his own lifetime. Bentham, a utilitarian, had various ideas on social improvement, ideas that influenced the law, penal reform and the like.

(Parenthetically, one of his ideas was that it would be useful, utilitarian that he was, if great men were not buried. It would be better for them to be embalmed and set up in public places as models for the next generation. Fortunately, this idea was not carried out, except in the case of Bentham himself. If you would like to see Bentham, you can – he is stuffed in University College London. The embalming was not entirely successful, however; the original skull is between his legs and the head is wax, but in any case, this is quite something to see. And we understand that he is rolled out for certain board meetings at the University of London. His vote is not known, but that's true of the other members of the board as well.)

Anyway, the fundamental philosophy of the law set forth by these gentlemen is that once we have identified the political system in operation, and we've determined how law is made within that particular culture, whatever it happens to be, we cannot raise higher issues as to the legitimacy of the whole thing. The thing is legitimate by virtue of the fact that it follows from the commands of the sovereign. This doesn't require a monarchial system or an autocratic system. If we have, for example, a constitutional democracy and those procedures are employed, and we end up with a certain law, then that law is law. Period.

This, of course, means as a philosophy that there will be different legal systems with contradictory laws, as compared to other Systems, and there is no ultimate way to resolve this, because though we can criticize the laws within a system as to their consistency, we cannot criticize the system per se. The system stands beyond that.

**H. L. A. Hart and Hans Kelsen.** And this carries us to the two most influential representatives of this position in the twentieth century, namely H. L. A. Hart, professor of jurisprudence at Oxford (who dicd just a few years ago) and Hans Kelsen. Kelsen, who was an Austrian fortunate enough to immigrate to the United States before he could be persecuted under the Hitler regime, spent his last years in California. He taught at the University of California at Los Angeles and also in the north, in the San Francisco area.

These two gentlemen refined legal positivism. We can't go into their positions here since that would carry us too far afield, but their positions, in spite of the refinements presented, are nonetheless classical positivism. They will not allow the law to be judged by an extrinsic ethic. Let me read you a fairly dense paragraph from H. L. A. Hart, and then I will translate from English into English:

> We only need the word "validity," and commonly only use it to answer questions which arise within a system of rules, where the status of a rulc as a member of the system depends on its satisfying certain criteria provided by a rule of recognition. No such question can arise as to the validity of the very rule of recognition, which provides the criteria. It can neither be valid nor invalid, but is simply accepted as appropriate for use in this way.[2]

He employs the analogy of the meter bar in Paris. Let's say we're in Strasbourg, France, during the summer, and we go into a hardware store and buy a meter stick. But we suspect the owner of the hardware store is selling meter sticks that are not accurate. So we get on the train to Paris, clutching our meter stick in our hand, and we go to the Bureau of Standards, and there in a case is a Standard meter bar. Now we can go up to that case and compare the length of your meter stick with the standard meter bar. But suppose the thought occurs: *How do I know that the standard meter bar is the right length?* So we ask the guard there, "Is the meter bar the right length?" And he says, "You can't ask that question! The meter bar is an arbitrary

---

[2] H. L. A. Hart, *The Concept of Law* (Oxford: Oxford University Press, 1960).

measure. You can compare other meter sticks with it, but you can't meaningfully ask the question as to whether the meter bar is the right length."

Says Hart, that's the way it is in legal Systems. We can determine whether the individual elements in the system properly fit the system, but we can't ask whether the total legal system is valid or invalid, right or wrong, genuine or not. That kind of a question can't be answered. Thus, H. L. A. Hart is indeed a legal positivist.

In an unpublished but recorded lecture given at the University of California at Los Angeles, Hans Kelsen says this:

> It is of the greatest importance to be aware of the fact that there is not only one moral or political system, but at different times and within different societies several different moral and political systems are considered to be valid by those living under these normative systems. The systems come into existence by custom, or by the commands of outstanding personalities like Moses, Jesus, or Mohammed. If men believe that these personalities are inspired by a transcendental, supernatural (that is a divine) authority, the moral or political system has a religious character. It is, especially in this case, when the moral or political system is supposed to be of divine origin that the values constituted by it are considered to be absolute.
>
> However, if the fact is taken into consideration that there are, there were, and probably always will be several different moral and political systems actually presupposed to be valid within different societies, the values constituted by these systems can be considered to be only relative. Then the judgment that a definite government or a definite legal order is just can be pronounced only with reference to *one* of the several different political and moral systems, and then the same behavior or the same governmental activity or the same legal order made with reference to another moral or political system be considered as morally bad or politically unjust.

What Kelsen is saying is that total legal systems are like trains passing in the night. There is no vantage point on the basis of which we can judge them, except from the standpoint of another system. And if system A makes nasty statements about the immorality of system B, they don't mean anything, because system B can turn around and make nasty statements about system A. The systems stand by themselves. We can tinker with the systems internally, but what we cannot meaningfully do is to criticize the systems per se. Law is the command of the sovereign.

This did not worry nineteenth-century thinkers at all. It particularly didn't worry the English. Why? Because the nineteenth century was the great century of English imperial expansionism and it was a firm conviction, an unquestioned position, of those in England during the Victorian period that the world would eventually become English! And of course under those conditions, different legal systems wouldn't make any significant difference, because ultimately everything would be English.

## Problem of the Positivist View of the Nineteenth Century

The end result of the expansion of the empire in the nineteenth century was of course the disintegration of that empire early in the twentieth century. And what was the general situation in the twentieth century? Well, we managed to have two perfectly horrendous world wars and several perfectly ghastly totalitarianisms. And at the end of World War II it was discovered that the rumors concerning Nazi activity were underestimated. The Third Reich had attempted systematically to destroy the Jewish population of Europe and all political dissidents. And they had done this by techniques almost too horrible to describe.

So the Nuremberg war crimes trials took place, and at those trials the Nazi leaders of course attempted to defend themselves. How? By virtue of the philosophy of legal positivism!

They said, "Granted, our legal system is not the same as yours. Our fundamental values are not the same as yours – and we simply made our system reflect our own values. Our rule involved Aryan supremacy; we did not regard Jews as human beings on the same level as Aryans. From our standpoint, then, Jews certainly did not deserve to benefit from Aryan rights. And the only reason that we find ourselves on trial here is that you won and we lost"

On the basis of legal positivism, of course it's impossible for one legal system to judge another legal system. And the Nazis argued at Nuremberg, among other things, that they therefore did not deserve to be judged by the Allied victors.

Now this put the prosecution at Nuremberg into a very interesting position. In order for the prosecution to justify the criminal prosecution of the Nazi war criminals, it was necessary for them to move beyond legal positivism. They had absolutely no choice. At Nuremberg the American chief prosecutor was Robert H. Jackson, an associate justice of the Supreme Court of the United States, and in his summing up he said: "It is common to think of our own time as standing at the apex of civilization, from which the deficiencies of preceding ages may patronizingly be viewed in the light of what is assumed to be 'progress.'" Note that he put the word *progress* in quotation marks. *No one* put the word *progress* in quotation marks in the nineteenth century. It was simply assumed that civilization was rising to higher and higher levels, and that therefore a cultural millennium was before us and we didn't need to worry about questions such as justifying legal systems. Jackson continues, "The reality is that in the long perspective of history the present century will not hold an admirable position, unless its second half is to redeem its first."³

Well, we're now looking back on the second half of the twentieth century, and it surely has not done that. We've discovered, for example, that under Stalin there was even more evidence of atrocities than under Hitler! And then there have been Pol Pot and Idi Amin Dada and a whole succession of miserable tyrants who have hurt, maimed and killed their fellow human beings.

> These two score years in this twentieth century will be recorded in the book of years as one of the most bloody in all annals. Two World Wars have left a legacy of dead, which number more than all the armies engaged in any war that made ancient or medieval history. No half-century ever witnessed slaughter on such a scale, such cruelties and inhumanities, such wholesale deportations of peoples into slavery, such annihilations of minorities. The terror of Torquemada pales before the Nazi inquisition. These deeds are the overshadowing historical facts by which generations to come will remember this decade. If we cannot eliminate the causes and prevent the repetition of these barbaric events, it is not an irresponsible prophesy to say that this twentieth century may yet succeed in bringing the doom of civilization.
>
> Goaded by these facts, we have moved to redress the blight on the record of our era ... At this stage of the proceedings, I shall rest upon the law of these crimes as laid down in the Charter [the Charter of the International Military Tribunal, the vehicle by which the war criminals were being judged]. In interpreting this Charter, however, we should not overlook the unique and emergent character of this body ... It is no part of the constitutional mechanism of internal justice of any of the signatory nations ... As an International Military Tribunal it rises above the provincial and transient, and seeks guidance not only from international law, but also from the basic principles of jurisprudence, which are the assumptions of civilization.⁴

Jackson is saying: Agreed, the law used against the Nazi war criminals is not part of English law, American law, French law, Russian law – not at all. It takes itself from the guidance available in international law, but also from the basic principles of jurisprudence, which are the assumptions of civilization.

---

³ *Trial of the Major War Criminals Before the International Military Tribunal, Nuremberg, 14 November 1945-1 October 1946* (Nuremberg, 1947).
⁴ Ibid.

He's saying that we must go to a law that is higher or deeper than national law. We can't simply rest with the law of a nation, because the law of a nation can be damnable, as it was in the ease of Nazi jurisprudence.

A book published in France, *Les lois du Vichy* (The Vichy Laws), exposes a rigorously systematic code modeled on the French civil and criminal codes that provided the Pétain regime with the equivalent of the Nazi laws of the time. And as a result of this, Jews in France could not hold any public positions, couldn't be teachers, and were eventually deported to the death camps, just as Jews were throughout Europe.

Human rights violations demand a higher law. Human rights violations, in order to be dealt with, require our being able to find some rights that human beings have that must not be taken away by any government, no matter what the government or legal system. But where can we possibly find that sort of thing?

## Conscience as a Guide

Let's look at the natural law position, which existed for centuries, and which was moved to the wings by legal positivism. Is the answer to go back to natural law? The essence of natural law theory is that we have inherent within us an understanding of human value and an ethic, a morality, an understanding of human rights, which we can use to judge positive law. This approach was first set forth by Aristotle, and then it was baptized, as it were, by Thomas Aquinas and other medieval theologians, and brought within the framework of the medieval West. It continued on by way of the Declaration of the Rights of Man at the time of the French Revolution, and to be sure, the American founding documents. The fundamental idea here is that people really know what's right, and they should use that to judge the positive law.

Why did that viewpoint disappear? Why was it supplanted by legal positivism? In criticizing William Blackstone (an English jurist), Bentham declared that the whole natural law idea was "nonsense on stilts," meaning that human beings maintaining that viewpoint think that their personal consciences can be elevated to the point of criticizing the law of the land. But how can they prove that their conscience represents anything that is capable of doing such?

Bentham had a point. One of the biggest difficulties with natural law theory, and one of the reasons that it disappeared from prominence in the nineteenth century, is the ambiguity and subjectivity of it. In a way, we might say that this is the "Jiminy *Cricket*" approach to law of human rights.

Do you remember Jiminy Cricket in Walt Disney? He sings a little song, "Let your conscience be your guide."

What's the trouble with this? The trouble is, of course, that conscience is culturally conditioned, and often culturally determined. When you were a little shaver and you took cookies out of the cookie jar when you shouldn't, Mommy came along and whacked your little hand, and as a result of this you began to feel guilty when you stole cookies. As a result, you stole fewer and fewer cookies.

But that's not the only kind of conditioning of conscience possible. Remember Fagin in *Oliver Twist*? He teaches the street children to steal, to engage in the activity of a cut purse or a pickpocket. Fagin shows them how to do it and makes them feel guilty if they don't bring back valuable watches. So, when the kid gets back at the end of the day and he hasn't stolen a good watch, he's blamed for it and he feels guilty. The next day he's going to work harder to steal something of greater value.

Conscience is culturally conditioned, and therefore it isn't capable of providing the needed objective standard. It's also ambiguous. I'll give you a horrifying example.

One of the greatest statements of natural law theory appears in the Justinian Code, the great sixth-century law code of antiquity. A section of that law code is called the Digest, and at the beginning of the Digest there is a definition of natural law: *Honeste vivere, alterum non laedere, suum cuique tribuere,* which translated means "To live honesty, to harm no one, and to make sure that each one has what he deserves." That's the essence of a natural law.

Surely, no one would disagree with this. But what exactly does it mean? Shortly after World War II, I took friends to the death camp at Buchenwald, just outside the Enlightenment city of Weimar, Germany. The metal gates leading into Buchenwald have a German inscription on them, *Jedem das Seine.* That means, "Each person gets what he properly deserves." It is the German translation of the third element in the Justinian Code's definition of the natural law.

See what's going on here? The fact of the matter is that the natural law is so vague, so ill-defined, that it can be moved into any context we wish, and it can be employed to create hideous injustice, because it doesn't define what is meant by what each person properly deserves. It doesn't tell what harm actually consists of, and it certainly doesn't define honesty.

Natural law theory may not be as bad as nonsense on stilts, but it certainly isn't going to provide the kind of solid foundation that we need for human rights and for judging inhumanities within legal systems. Where, then, can we go for an answer? Where could we possibly go?

## A Universal Rule Approach

Some attempts have been made in recent years to rehabilitate another kind of natural law approach. It isn't called natural law; it actually goes back to the philosopher Immanuel Kant in the eighteenth century. Kant said, "You can't prove God's existence or anything theological, but you can prove an ethic. You can establish an ethic that stands beyond any and all argument."

This ethic was based on a particular kind of principle, and the principle goes like this: act so that your action can become a universal rule. He termed this *the categorical imperative.* It's an imperative – it tells us what we're supposed to be doing. It's categorical, meaning we can't argue against it. Said Kant, "Everyone must rationally see the value of this kind of principle."

**Rawls and a neo-Kantian ethic.** Today there are political scientists and legal theorists who have used Kant's fundamental notion in order to try to justify human rights. For example, John Rawls, probably the greatest twentieth-century American political theorist, says that if we can take, hypothetically, human beings in a state of ignorance, so that they don't know anything about any particular advantages that they have over others, then they will necessarily have to form governments that embrace his two principles.

1. Each person is to have an equal right to the most extensive system of equal basic liberties, compatible with a similar system of liberty for all. In other words, there will need to be civil liberties, and people will *logically* have to agree to those civil liberties if they are removed from any understanding of the special advantages that they have over others.

2. Social and economic inequalities are to be arranged so that they are both to the greatest benefit of the least advantaged, consistent with what Rawls calls "the just savings principle" (that is, keeping in mind future generations) and attached to offices and positions open to all, under conditions of equality and opportunity.

These two principles are the equivalent of the first and second generations of human rights, as they are termed in contemporary parlance. In a lecture at Oxford, Rawls applied his analysis to the issue of international human rights. He said, in effect, "If you take nations and you can abstract from them their special advantages, nations would also have to agree to these same first- and second-generation human rights." In other words, nations would have to ratify the civil and political covenant of the United Nations, in line with principle number one, and the economic and social covenant of the United Nations in terms of principle number two.

Well, what is the problem with this sort of thing?

First, the problem is simply that there is no way that we can get people to forget their special advantages. We can't put them in that kind of an isolated situation. And there's no point in doing it in theory if in practice people will always operate in terms of their special advantages and privileges.

Second, even if you got individuals and nations to agree that they should always act so that their action could be universalized or generalized, that's no guarantee that they're going to follow it.

Third, the worst of the dictators in human history, those we've had the worst amount of difficulty with, are not going to agree to this at all. They know their personal power and are convinced that they can effectively grind down on other people, and they see no reason why they should stop. For example, let's try to present a neo-Kantian ethic to Genghis Khan.

I say, "Genghis, you've been out raping and pillaging again, haven't you?" And Genghis says, "Yes, I have."

And I say, "Genghis, Genghis, you have got to operate with a principle of universalization. You don't want other people to rape and pillage you, do you? Well, under those circumstances you surely cannot justify raping and pillaging others. So act that your action could become a universal rule."

Genghis grabs me by the throat and says, "Listen, you little pipsqueak. I am Genghis and I am powerful. I can rape and pillage, and the others are not going to be able to do this to me. Moreover, I enjoy raping and pillaging. Some people collect stamps. I rape and pillage."

And he thereupon inverts me and pounds me into the ground, and the discussion ends.

A neo-Kantian ethic is simply incapable of solving fundamental human rights problems. So, where can a solution be found?

## Need for a Transcendental Solution: Wittgenstein

We need to do a little bit of epistemology, a little bit of work in the philosophical area of truth claims. And probably the best place to start is with Ludwig Wittgenstein, the great analytical philosopher of the twentieth century. Wittgenstein wrote a work titled the **Tractatus**. It is not good bedtime reading, frankly. It is in numbered propositions and is a very difficult work, but in it Wittgenstein helps us to determine how one can verify propositions that are not formal in character – factual propositions and ethical propositions.

And when Wittgenstein gets to issues of ethics in proposition 6 and following, he summarizes the situation very simply in a three-word proposition, "Ethics is transcendental."

Ethics is transcendental. What did he mean? Well, he explains it in a lecture he delivered at Oxford, which was posthumously published. He said,

> If a man could write a book on Ethics which really was a book on Ethics, this book would, as with an explosion, destroy all the other books in the world.

Wittgenstein is saying that any ethic arising from the human situation is limited by the human situation. It's culturally conditioned. It can't possibly be absolute because its source isn't absolute. So the only true ethic would be an ethic that doesn't arise from the human situation, that breaks in from the outside. A transcendental, transcendent ethic.

Wittgenstein didn't think there was any such book. One of my professors of philosophy at Cornell University, when I was an undergraduate, was Norman Malcolm. Malcolm was a great friend of Wittgenstein's and wrote a memoir of Wittgenstein. At one point in the memoir he says, "Often Wittgenstein would say, 'Oh my God,' as if imploring a divine intervention." He apparently didn't think there was such an intervention, but he saw perfectly well what the human condition is like without one.[5]

## Archimedes: Need for a Fulcrum

Or we can go to Archimedes. Said Archimedes, "Give me a lever long enough and a fulcrum outside the world, and I can move it." The point being that no matter how great the world is, if he had a lever long enough and a fulcrum properly placed, with his little finger, with his pinky, it would have been possible for Archimedes to move the world.

But the essential condition is that the fulcrum be outside the world. If the fulcrum is in the world, you cannot move it. It would be like trying to pull ourselves up by our own bootstraps. One falls on his own *derrière*! That's painful and accomplishes nothing. The fulcrum's got to be outside the world in order to move it.

Here's a much simpler illustration: water doesn't rise above its own level; that is, we can't get absolute principles from a non-absolute source. Human beings are finite and self-centered, and the ethics they produce

---

[5] Cf. John Warwick Montgomery, *Tractatus Logico-Theologicus,* 5th ed. (Bonn, Germany: Verlag für Kultur und Wissenschaft, 2012).

will be limited in precisely those ways. Or to quote Thomas Hobbes, "Human life is nasty, brutish and short," and human rights deriving from the human condition will therefore not reach anything like the needed absolute standards.

The American founding fathers talked about "inalienable" rights. What are they? The rights that cannot be taken away by governments, and which the individual cannot even take away from himself or herself.

Where could we possibly get that sort of thing? If human beings create the rights, of course human beings can take away those rights. Epistemologically, the only way we are ever going to be able to get absolute human rights standards is to go outside the human situation to a nonhuman source. And incredibly, Jean-Jacques Rousseau, the eighteenth-century political philosopher, understood this. (It is very difficult to find profundity in Rousseau. In this case he actually managed it.) I am not suggesting that Rousseau is a guide in general matters of philosophy, but in the section on law, in the social contract, the *Contrat Social*, Rousseau says:

> In order to discover the rules of society best suited to nations, a superior intelligence beholding all the passions of men without experiencing any of them would be needed. This intelligence would have to be wholly unrelated to our nature, while knowing it through and through. Its happiness would have to be independent of us, and yet ready to occupy itself with ours. And lastly, it would, in the march of time, have to look forward to a distant glory, and working in one century be able to enjoy in the next. It would take gods to give men laws.

The point being: in order to get laws that are going to apply under all conditions, everywhere, we've got to be able to have a perspective that can see into the human condition, past, present and future. And it must be sufficiently independent of the human situation that it will not be locked into a particular viewpoint so as to bias the laws being set forth. Thus, "it would take gods to give men laws."

**Religion as Basis for Transcendent Claims**

This inevitably takes us into the realm of religion. It's in the realm of religion that transcendent claims have been made to deity and to revelation. That is to say, religions have claimed that there is a transcendent source, and that the transcendent source has spoken.

The problem here, of course, is that the religious claims of the world through history have been inconsistent with each other in most instances.

And the religious positions themselves have sometimes not been at all attractive, for example, the Aztec religion, which I intend to revive when I have particular difficulty with my neighbors. The Aztec solution to the problem of salvation is to sacrifice your neighbor. You simply create a pyre, cut your neighbor open and burn him or her. Instances like this have not encouraged people to look for religious solutions.

And there are not only the obnoxious religious options like that, but there are also religious solutions that are technically meaningless. For example, there is the claim in Hinduism that "Brahman is all." No one can really dispute this. The problem is, what does it mean? Does it mean that everything is God? If everything is God, then I suppose in a sense nothing is God, because our world often displays an appalling absence of human dignity and rights. Or is this an attempted definition? If it is, it doesn't seem to distinguish the transcendent in any way from the immanent. And therefore we find ourselves unable to do very much with it.

If we look at the spread of religions across the centuries, what we really should be looking for is a religion that can demonstrate the truth of its claims, because making claims is easy. Surely those living in California understand this: if people don't like a religion, by next weekend they've started their own. So the number of religions increases. The real issue is not that of making religious claims but of offering some justification for a given claim.

I have a little illustration that may be helpful. This is also a true story. At the time of the French Revolution, an attempt was made to substitute various "rational religions" for historic Christianity, and one of these attempts, a deistic attempt, was created by the French philosopher La Revellière. La Revellière invented a religion he called "Theanthropy," Man Is Godism. He did tracts, booklets and social programs, and worked very hard on this, but it didn't take, and he was very discouraged.

So he went to fellow philosophers for advice. One of them was the French sceptical philosopher Talleyrand. Talleyrand, who had a wonderful sense of humor, said to him, "It seems to me that Jesus Christ, in order to found His religion, first died and rose again on the third day. You could at least do that much."

This suggests that there may be a considerable difference among religious positions, not necessarily in their claims, but in their ability to back them up.

## Christianity's Claims and Bases

I gave a talk previously at this university pointing out how many distinguished lawyers have become Christians on the basis of checking out the evidence for the resurrection of Jesus Christ. Sir Norman Anderson, the head of the School of Advanced Legal Studies at the University of London, for example, the greatest authority on Muslim law outside the Muslim world, became a Christian on the basis of the evidence for the resurrection of Christ, and wrote several books on that subject.

One can engage in historical investigation and discover that the Christian claims are based solidly in empirical, observational fact – and they lead in one direction: Jesus – not as a Jewish boy scout helping little old ladies across the Sea of Galilee, but a person who claimed to be no less than God Almighty come to earth to die for the sins of the world. And he rose again from the dead in order to demonstrate the truth of those affirmations.

Furthermore, Jesus put a stamp of approval on the Bible. As a result of this, the Christian claim is that God was in Christ, reconciling the world unto himself, providing a specific revelation of principles that are inalienable. These principles hold under all circumstances, owing to the fact that they do not derive from a merely human source. They derive from the transcendent. They fulfill Wittgenstein's description of the book, "which with an explosion would destroy all the other books in the world." Now this is a perfectly staggering kind of claim, but it's a claim backed up by solid historical evidence.

In Boston I gave a paper dealing with the specific prophesies in the Old Testament concerning the coming of the Messiah. I used the so-called product rule in statistics. If the Old Testament prophecies are independent of each other (which they are), we can use the product rule to calculate the probabilities against, say, twenty-five of the most specific being fulfilled by pure chance. If the probability of any one of them being valid is taken as only 25 percent, then the likelihood of twenty-five coming to pass by sheer chance would be one in a thousand trillion. **One in a thousand trillion!**

Statistics don't establish cause and effect, obviously. But what are you going to do with a situation like this? The Old Testament was written before the New. So the prophecies can't have been written after their fulfillments. And there is no way that the life of Christ could have been fudged to make it fit the prophesies, because the records of his life were in circulation while hostile religious witnesses were still alive. They would surely have blown the whistle on it. My goodness, the Jewish religious leaders knew their Old Testaments, and if Jesus had not been born in Bethlehem but in Detroit, they would have been the first to raise an objection. We've got a combination of powerful prophetic evidence and solid resurrection evidence that Jesus was the very person he claimed to be.

## A Christian Basis for Human Rights

Now if this turns out to be the case, notice what we get in the human rights realm.

First, we get that book Wittgenstein talked about. We get the principles, and not in the vague sense of natural law. We get definitive principles, not just the Ten Commandments, but the principles that are running all through Scripture. In my book **Human Rights and Human Dignity**, I've correlated these principles to various human rights conventions today. They are highly specific. And the principles have a solid, transcendent basis.

But we get more than this. We get something more important than the principles. I began by pointing out that everybody is in favor of human rights. The most greasy dictators are always saying nice things about human rights – meanwhile they're boiling someone in oil. What does this say? That the real problem with human rights is something beyond the question of the principles – it's the motivation to follow the principle.

Genghis may very well know that it's not nice to rape and pillage, but he enjoys it. The fact of the matter is that the human race is self-centered, and therefore nations are self-centered. It follows that they skew human rights in their own direction to protect themselves, and they don't worry about the next person. **Some are more equal than others.**

In the area of human rights, what is really needed is some device by which human rights can be interiorized, made a part of the human being, so the human being really wants to treat the other person decently. No human rights philosophy, other than the gospel of Jesus Christ, can change people's hearts, and until hearts are changed we can plaster proper human rights principles on every wall everywhere but the results will not be appreciably different from the current ones. Somebody has said, "What we need is not more good advice. What we need is good news." The Christian message not only makes it possible to know what the principles are and to ground these principles transcendentally, but also opens the avenue – for you and me – to be changed inside. How does this happen? A physician can't force a medicine down someone's gullet if the person doesn't believe he or she has a disease. To do so happens to be a tort against the person in law. We can't do that. People have to recognize they're sick before they're going to take the medicine.

So, the first step is to recognize just how radically self-centered we are. And if we see this, then the question is, What's to be done about it? Well, we can't pull ourselves up to heaven by our own bootstraps anymore than it's possible to make the world rise when the fulcrum is on it. We need help from outside. We need a fulcrum outside, and that's exactly why Jesus entered our world as Savior.

Jesus came to earth to die for us on the cross, to take the punishment we deserve and to expiate it, and make it possible for us to enter in to God's presence forever. If we believe this, if we enter into a relationship with him on that basis, then he comes into our heart by way of the Holy Spirit and our life is changed.

"If anyone is in Christ, there is a new creation: everything old has passed away; see, everything has become new!" (2 Corinthians 5:17). Those who have accepted Christ as Lord of their life are the living proof of this. They are not engaged in some kind of subjective religiosity, working themselves up into a mystic state. Not at all. They have accepted God's revelation of himself, based on the historical fact that God was in Christ, reconciling the world to himself.

The objective evidence of the resurrection of Christ and the solidity of the Scriptures offer the basis for entering into that relationship. And when people do that, they really do become more interested in other people than in themselves. They really do go along with Augustine's principle, "Love God and do as you please," because if we love God, what we want to do is what pleases God, and the Scriptures tell us what pleases him. This is precisely the basis we so desperately need for a solid understanding of human rights.

# PART TWO:

# THINKING LIKE A LAWYER IN THE THEOLOGICAL REALM

# 9. Artificial Intelligence and Societal Transformation

*Keynote Address at the 27<sup>th</sup> IIAS International Conference, Baden-Baden, Germany, 1-5 August 2016*

**Abstract:** The IIAS has two particular foci: AI and the need to raise ethical levels in today's materialistic society. This paper addresses these two concerns. Firstly, we ask whether advances in cybernetics can in principle solve the ethical woes of society. This entails a discussion of freewill. Secondly, we deal with the nature of human nature, analyzing the complex notion of natural law. We shall discover that an inadequate understanding of natural law has produced naïveté in scholarly solutions (Rawls) and in political orientations (the Soviet "new man"). A more rigorous, transcendental approach will then be offered.

## A Sobering Introduction

"Not many years ago it was reported from France that a man had made a statue that could play various pieces on the *Fleuttraversière,* placed the flute to his lips and took it down again, rolled its eyes, etc. But no one has yet invented an image that thinks, or wills, or composes, or even does anything at all similar. Let anyone who wishes to be convinced look carefully at the last fugal work of the above-praised Bach [or] the Chorale which he dictated in his blindness to the pen of another: *Wenn wir in höchsten Nöthen seyn* ["Lord, when we are in direst need," BWV 668] ... Everything that the champions of Materialism put forward must fall to the ground in view of this single example" – J. M. Schmidt [1754] (David and Mendel, 1966).

## AI: The Solution to Mankind's Ethical Dilemmas?

In diametric contrast with the above-quoted sentiment, much popular contemporary thinking – and not a few scholarly judgments – see robotics as the answer to the multifarious problems of our society, beset by injustice and terrorism. Dr Robert Jastrow of NASA opined: "It is entirely possible that man has evolved as far as he can and that a new form of life, based on silicon, will replace the carbon-based human life form as the dominant species" (Davies, 1983).

And, assuming that this will occur, "Twenty-first century machines – based on the design of human thinking – will do as their human progenitors have done – going to real and virtual houses of worship, meditating, praying, and transcending – to connect with their spiritual dimension" (Kurzweil, 1999).

There are, however, overwhelming problems connected with such projections. Tallis, for example, has offered arguments against the blending of artificial with human intelligence that cannot be easily dismissed: "It should be unnecessary to have to point out that (unconscious) automata do not have goals; and if they execute plans, it is our plans (of which they are quite unaware) that they execute, not their own" (Tallis, 1994, 2004). But the definitive refutation of the assumption of robotic intelligence is surely that of John Searle, in his refinement of his classic "Chinese Room Argument": Anything "that caused minds would have to have causal powers at least equivalent to those of the brain ... For any artifact that we might build which had mental states equivalent to human mental states, the implementation of a computer program by itself would not be sufficient. Rather, the artifact would have to have powers equivalent to the powers of the human brain" (Searle, 1984).

The essential reason for not regarding a product of AI as human is its lack of freewill, and therefore its inability to make conscious decisions, create meaningful personal goals, or develop a genuine ethic. Arguments to the contrary generally endeavour to show that human beings are themselves "programmed" – that their biological makeup determines their actions. The insurmountable difficulty here is, of course, that the determinist must assume his or her own freewill (if only in setting forth the determinist claim); otherwise, that argument could have no potential truth-value: it would be no more than the consequence of materialistic necessity.

To be sure, humans are *influenced* by their genes and by their environment, but anyone who speaks of freewill as *caused* by such factors does not understand the meaning of freewill. By definition, freewill is uncaused. And it must be presupposed in human society; otherwise, neither praise for loving, caring, self-sacrificial acts in behalf of others nor any form of retribution for unethical conduct could be justified. A criminal sentence (for example, at the Nuremberg War Crimes Trials) would be purely sociological, since the defendant's anti-social or inhumane action could be logically attributable to nothing other than heredity and/or environment, not to wilful and therefore culpable choice on his or her part (Montgomery, 2010).

Responsible advances in AI are to be encouraged, and their value in modern society has been incalculable. But it is hardly Luddite obscurantism to recognise that their worth is as a tool, not as a master or a substitute for human personality and human values. The biblical command to "subdue the earth" (Genesis 1:28) applies not only to the physical environment but also to the tools we develop in the course of achieving this.

## Human Nature and the Necessity of Transcendence

The need to appeal to the concept of freewill in order to recognize the impossibility of a cybernetic solution to the problems of human society reminds us that, without a satisfactory understanding of human nature, we shall hardly be in a position to ameliorate human ills, individual or societal.

The natural law tradition in western thought – from the Stoics, through medieval theology, to the modern human rights movement – has often been appealed to as a solution to man's inhumanity to man. However, there is not just one "human nature" – that represented by high moral ideals, allegedly held in common by all decent human beings. In point of fact, there is another, darker side to the human person – well known to psycho-analysts, great *littérateurs* (Dante, Kierkegaard, Kafka, Sartre, Camus, *et al.*), and the political tradition represented by Machiavelli's *Il Principe,* Hobbes' *Leviathan,* and Realpolitik. This is the radical selfishness that is concerned solely or predominately with *Looking Out for #1* and *Winning through Intimidation* – to cite the titles of Robert Ringer's popular treatises on achieving success (Ringer, 1975, 2013). Individuals and nations have manifested this side of human nature throughout recorded history.

When this aspect of the human drama is ignored, the result – inevitably – is the offering of naïve solutions to individual and societal problems. A prominent example is the neo-Kantian political philosophy of John Rawls. In his influential work, *A Theory of Justice,* Rawls attempts to justify a humane society by showing that all human beings, if placed under a hypothetical "veil of ignorance" (without a knowledge of their special advantages or disadvantages) would by logical necessity arrive at a society manifesting both civil liberties and socio-economic rights – and would even take into account the needs of future generations by following a "just savings" principle in their use of environmental resources (Rawls, 1999).

Rawls' final book was titled, *The Law of Peoples* (Rawls, 2001), and a collection of essays treating it, published five years later, carried the subtitle, "A Realistic Utopia" (Martin and Reidy, 2006). But that is the key question: how realistic is the Rawlsian theory? For one thing, human beings cannot be expected to make moral or political decision under a "veil of ignorance." In reality, all of the decisions of a self-centred human race are made with full appreciation of the special advantages one person – or one nation – has over against the others. And one's ethics, individually, collectively, and nationally, will be directed more often than not to achieve and maximise personal and national advantage. Example: not even the worst dictators argue against human rights; they simply refuse to accept criticisms of their own human rights violations and, at the same time, scream foul the moment *their own* rights are being trampled (Montgomery, 1986).

The existence of both a positive and a negative side to human nature means that (1) the specific moral values espoused by the natural law tradition will need to be independently justified (versus pseudo- and deceptive principles and goals masking as true moral values) and (2) independent evidence will have to be marshalled to show which aspect of human personality and society (the positive or the negative) is the more fundamental. If Machiavellian man is primary, then the Robert Ringers are correct: one must "do others before they do us." If the positive side of humanity is its true essence, then Jesus was right that we should "do unto others as we would have them to do unto us" (Matthew 7:12; Luke 6:31).

But how can we determine primacy? Not from observing the human situation from within, since we are finite and, even worse, part of the problem. We would need a perspective from outside the human situation. As Archimedes put it, to move the world one needs a lever whose fulcrum is outside the world. Water doesn't rise about its own level. Or consider Wittgenstein's apodictic judgement in his *Tractatus:* "Ethics is transcendental" (Wittgenstein, 1961; cf. Montgomery, 2012b). Thus, we arrive at the logical necessity of relying upon a divine revelation from the One who created the human race and who therefore knows it more intimately than humans know themselves.

A transcendent revelation would likewise be required to discover which human ethical principles are genuinely moral – as opposed to principles (and practices) that are presented as ethical but which are really little more than techniques for justifying self-interest.

We are therefore compelled – in order to see if in fact a justifiable divine revelation does exist – to enter the religious realm, and, more specifically, the related areas of epistemology and apologetics

Before speaking to the issue of evidence vis-à-vis a divine revelation, let us suppose, for the sake of argument, that the Christian claim to divine revelation in the person of Jesus Christ and in the Bible he declared to be divinely revelatory is indeed valid. What would this offer? First, it would establish the primacy of positive human nature: the *imago Dei* as the defining mark of the human being. God's existence and fundamental morality are imprinted on the human heart (Romans 1). But, secondly, Christian revelation is no less definitive as to the fallen nature of the human race – humanity "dead in trespasses and sins" and without the ability to save itself (Romans 3). Human nature needs to be transformed from within. As Jesus put it, 'There is nothing from outside a man, that entering into him can defile him: but the things which come out of him, those are they that defile the man' (Matthew 15:11; Mark 7:15). Our problem is internal – within ourselves.

The only solution, therefore, is to be saved – transformed – so that we come to the point of loving God first, our neighbour second, and ourselves in last place. That can occur only after Christ becomes the centre and the circumference of individual and societal life.

Fascinatingly, even atheistic Marxism realised that the only solution to human egotism – the only way people would ever agree to a redistribution of wealth – would be a change in human motivation and values: the creation of a Marxist or Soviet "new man" (Montgomery, 1994). Sadly, however, without a transcendent Saviour (and such was entirely lacking in the Marxist system), no such transformation ever did or could occur. Indeed, as with atheistic systems in general, uncontrolled selfishness led to totalitarianism, and totalitarianism to massive human rights violations.

How different with Christianity (Schmidt, 2004)! A single example: the abolition of the slave trade was directly and uniquely due to the massive efforts of Christian believers (Montgomery, 2012a).

But why accept the Christian revelational claim? Answer: because, unlike its religious competitors, it is backed by the most solid evidence that "God was in Christ, reconciling the world unto himself" (2 Corinthians 5:19; see Montgomery, 2014). Here we have space for but one parabolic – but thoroughly historical – anecdote. We shall conclude with it.

"On one occasion this Director [Larevellière-Lépaux] read a long paper explaining his religious system to his ministerial colleagues. After most of them had offered their congratulations, the Minister for Foreign Affairs, Talleyrand, remarked: 'For my part, I have only one observation to make. Jesus Christ, in order to found His religion, was crucified and rose again. You should have tried to do something of the kind'" (Toynbee, 1987).

But, of course, no one but Jesus Christ ever has. And in doing so, he offers the only solid basis for individual and societal transformation. What we do with this, however, depends squarely on our willingness to recognize the true nature our problem and our incapacity to resolve it unaided.

## References

David, H. T. and Mendel, A. (1966); The Bach Reader; Norton (pp. 255-56)

Davies, O. (1983); The Omni Book of Computers & Robots; Zebra (quoted by R. Ballad)

Kurzweil, R. (1999); The Age of Spiritual Machines: When Computers Exceed Human Intelligence; Viking (p. 153)

Martin, R. and Reidy, D. (2006); Rawls' Law of Peoples: A Realistic Utopia; Wiley-Blackwell

Montgomery, J. (1986); Human Rights and Human Dignity; Zondervan

Montgomery, J. (1994); Giant in Chains; Nelson Word [U.K.] (pp. 83-85)

Montgomery, J. (2010): Proceedings of the 23$^{rd}$ and 24$^{th}$ IVR World Congress Kraków 2007 and Beijing 2009, ed. F. Toepel; Franz Steiner Verlag [Also included in Montgomery, 2012a]

Montgomery, J. (2012a); Christ As Centre and Circumference; Verlag für Kultur und Wissenschaft (pp. 420-439)

Montgomery, J. (2012b); Tractatus Logico-Theologicus, 5$^{th}$ ed.; Verlag für Kultur und Wissenschaft

Montgomery, J. (2014); History, Law and Christianity, 3$^{rd}$ ed.; 1517 Legacy Project/NRP Books

Rawls, J. (1999); A Theory of Justice; Belknap

Rawls, J. (2001); The Law of Peoples; Harvard

Ringer, R. (1975); Winning Through Intimidation; Funk & Wagnalls

Ringer, R. (2013); Looking Out for Number #1: How to Get from Where You Are Now to Where You Want to Be in Life; Skyhorse

Schmidt, A. (2004); How Christianity Changed the World; Zondervan

Searle, J. (1984); Minds, Brains, and Science; Harvard Cf. A. Turing, Computing Machinery and Intelligence, Mind (October, 1950)

Tallis, R. (1994, 2004); Why the Mind Is Not a Computer; Imprint Academic (p. 48)

Toynbee, A. (1987); A Study of History: Abridgment of Vols. I-VI; Oxford (Vol. 1, pp. 493-494)

Wittgenstein, L. (1961); Tractatus Logico-Philosophicus, ed. D. Pears and B. McGuinness; Routledge (proposition 6.421)

# 10. The Last Meow: An Indeterminacy Argument for God's Existence, with a Further Glance at Schrödinger's Cat

Heisenberg's "indeterminacy principle" has posed a number of problems for classical theology. This brief paper will suggest that, when they are not pseudo-problems, they have a remarkably positive bearing on the case for the objective value of Christian evidences and the existence of God.

## 1. The Principle

Heisenberg determined that, on the subatomic level, one cannot objectively determine both the position and the momentum of an electron or other elementary particle; only when the observer tests the situation is the quantification known. This does not mean that it was always there: it means that the observer is essential to the establishment of the data.

The formula for this is: $\Delta x \Delta p \geq h/4\pi$, where x is the position of the object, p is the momentum, and h is Plank's constant. This means that the product of position and momentum uncertainty is always greater than, if not equal to, the (finite) number $h/4\pi$, i.e., either the position or the momentum will be known – but never both. As the one declines, the other compensates by rising so as to maintain the product of the two ($h/4\pi$).

Niels Bohr understood this extraordinary situation to mean that the ontological reality of the electron comes about only when it is observed; prior to observation, the electron is objectively in a state of non-being. This view, termed the "Copenhagen interpretation," was "abhorrent to Einstein,"[1] who preferred a "hidden variable" theory: we must postulate the existence of variables the measurement of such would eliminate the irrationality of indeterminacy – even though we have no evidence for their existence.[2] Another interpretation of the phenomenon to commend attention is the so-called "many worlds" argument: that, on measurement, the quantum system splits into possible states, one of which (the one observed) remains in our world whilst the other states pass into other worlds,

---

[1] Roger Penrose, *The Emperor's New Mind: Concerning Computers, Minds, and the Laws of Physics* (London: Vintage, 1989), p. 362.
[2] Ian G. Barbour, *Religion in an Age of Science* ("Gifford Lectures, 1989-1991, Vol. I"; London: SCM, 1990), p. 142.

creating ontological enlargements of the universe as a whole.³ The "hidden variable" and the "many worlds" hypotheses suffer from the same overwhelming problem: an entire lack of empirical evidence supporting them.⁴

## 2. Consequence for arriving at objective knowledge

Should one conclude from the uncertainty principle that the subject-object distinction has been broken and objective knowledge is therefore not possible – that the observer is a necessary factor in establishing knowledge? Surely not.

> 2.322 Empirical method assumes a distinction between myself as empirical investigator (the subject) and the empirical world I am investigating (the object).
>
> 2.32201 "Bohr has emphasized the fact that the observer and his instruments must be presupposed in any investigation, so that the instruments are not part of the phenomenon described but are used " (Lenzen).
>
> 2.3221 Neither Einsteinian relativity nor the Heisenberg indeterminacy principle destroys the subject-object distinction; indeed, relativity and indeterminacy could not even have been discovered if Einstein and Heisenberg had lost the distinction between themselves and what they were investigating
>
> 2.32211 How sad Robert Benchley's account of his college biology course, where he spent the term meticulously drawing the reflection of his own eyelash as it fell across the microscopic field.
>
> 2.32212 How unfortunate also if, as has been suggested, Schiaparelli's Martian "canals" were in part the result of incipient cataract in his own eye.⁵

---

[3] F. Tipler, "The Many-Worlds Interpretation of Quantum Mechanics in Quantum Cosmology," in Roger Penrose and C. J. Isham (eds.), *Quantum Concepts in Space and Time* (reprint ed.; Oxford: Clarendon Press, 1986), pp. 206-207.

[4] This is, to be sure, the difficulty with all "multiverse" cosmologies, *pace* Stephen Hawking; see Montgomery, "Speculation vs. Factuality," in his *Christ As Centre and Circumference* (Bonn, Germany: Verlag für Kultur und Wissenschaft, 2011), Pt. 1.

[5] Montgomery, *Tractatus Logico-theologicus* (4th ed.; Bonn, Germany: Verlag für Kultur und Wissenschaft, 2009).

## 3. Schrödinger's Cat

The standard illustration of indeterminacy has been offered by way of a cat placed in a closed container with a toxic gas inlet that can be triggered from within. The cat can only be known to be dead or alive *when the observer lifts the lid on the container*. It is important to note that the observer does not cause the cat to live or die; whilst the container is closed, the cat is *neither* dead *nor* alive; it is the observation that establishes the cat's otherwise indeterminate state. So with the position/momentum of the electron.

In Douglas Adams' striking novel, *Dirk Gently's Holistic Detective Agency*, Gently speculates whether a psychic could see into the box without opening it. But his interlocutor rightly notes that "the whole thing turns on what happens inside the box before it's observed. It doesn't matter how you observe it, whether you look into the box with your eyes or – well, with your mind, if you insist. If clairvoyance works, then it's just another way of looking into the box, and if it doesn't then of course it's irrelevant."[6]

The point is simply this: no observer, no specificity for subatomic events.

## 4. The Macro-world

Of course – unless we are alcoholics in an advanced state of inebriation – we do not experience this problem in our day-to-day existence. Owing to probabilities, we find our world subject to the ordinary laws of Newtonian physics and regular testability. At levels above the subatomic, the act of observational measurement, having collapsed the probability waveform wherein electrons have an infinite number of possible courses of action, produces a resolution into actual events. The cumulative result is indistinguishable from the outworking of classical, Newtonian physical law. Though this is our daily experience, we must not forget that underlying our everyday world the subatomic realm operates in the absence of observation without any definitive objective existence or specifiable character.

---

[6] Douglas Adams, *The Dirk Gently Omnibus* (London: William Heinemann, 2001), p. 124.

## 5. Solution

For the cosmos to have objective existence and be subject to objective investigation, only three realistic explanations are possible[7]: (1) the cosmos has its objective existence due to human observation; (2) the cosmos has its objective existence due to non-human observation – by other finite creatures; (3) the objective existence of the cosmos is due to its observation by a transcendent God who created it. Option (1) appears hopelessly anthropocentric (was there no universe before we began to observe it? Does the subatomic tree falling in the forest not exist unless someone is there to see it fall?). Option (2) is entirely gratuitous, since we know of no extraterrestrials, much less extraterrestrials engaged in observing the universe. Option (3) is thus the reasonable answer – requiring a God who has observed the cosmos from its creation and whose observations of it have elevated its content to a state of determinate factuality.

Alastair Reynolds science-fiction novelet, "Understanding Space and Time," eliminates the inadequate solutions most effectively:

> And ... how did this universe manage for fifteen billion years before we dropped by and provided an intelligent observer? Are you seriously telling me it was all fuzzy and indeterminate until the instant one anonymous caveman had a moment of cosmic epiphany? That suddenly the entire quantum history of every particle in the visible universe – right out to the furthest quasar – suddenly jumped to one state, and all because some thicko in a bearskin had his brain wired up slightly differently to has ancestor?
>
> ... "No ... I'm not saying that. There were other observers before us. We're just the latest."
>
> "And those other observers – they were there all along, were they? An unbroken chain right back to the first instant of creation?"[8]

And Ronald Knox made the same point poetically (*God in the Quad*) vis-à-vis Bishop Berkeley:

---

[7] We ignore unrealistic – and fantastic – ones, such as that the universe created itself out of nothing (Daniel Dennett; physicist Lawrence Krauss). Maria – in Richard Rodgers' and Oscar Hammerstein's *Sound of Music* – provides a sufficient reply: "Nothing comes from nothing, nothing ever could." As to why God needs no creator to explain Him, see Montgomery, *Tractatus Logico-theologicus (op. cit.)*, sec. 3.85.

[8] Alastair Reynolds, "Understanding Space and Time," in *Science Fiction: The Best of the Year, 2006 Edition*, ed. Rich Horton (Rockville, MD: Prime Books, 2006), pp. 298-99.

*There was a young man who said, "God*
*Must think it exceedingly odd*
*If he finds that this tree*
*Continues to be*
*When there's no one about in the Quad."*

REPLY

*Dear Sir:*
*Your astonishment's odd:*
*I am always about in the Quad.*
*And that's why the tree*
*Will continue to be,*
*Since observed by*
*Yours faithfully,*
*GOD.*[9]

## 6. Theological Commentary

"Truth" in biblical terms is conceived normally in terms of factual accuracy – as the correspondence between an affirmation and objective reality.

> 2.38412 "It really ought to go without saying that with all its different genres and figures of speech, Scripture, like all cognitive discourse, operates under the rubrics of a correspondence idea of truth: see John 8:46; Eph. 4:25; I Ki. 8:26; 22:16, 22 ff.; Gen. 42:16, 20; Deut. 18:22; Ps. 119:163; Dan. 2:9; Prov. 14:25; Zech. 8:16; John 5:21-32 ff.; Acts 24:8-11; I Tim. 1:15; note, too, the forensic picture which haunts all of Scripture – for example, such concepts as witness, testimony, judge, the Eighth Commandment, etc.; John 21:24" (Robert Preus).[10]

But, since "the devils also believe and tremble," mere acknowledgement of factual truth does not save: one must enter into a personal, living relationship with Jesus Christ, the Son of God who died on the cross for us, to inherit eternal life. And, on the most fundamental level, personal relationships constitute the nature of truth: the Holy Spirit – "the Spirit of truth" – "guides into all truth," for he speaks not of himself but of the Son and glorifies him, just as the Son speaks of and glorifies his Father (John 16:13-15).

---

[9] Cf. Colossians 1:16-17.
[10] Montgomery, *Tractatus Logico-theologicus* (op. cit.). Cf. Montgomery, *Crisis in Lutheran Theology* (2d ed., 2 vols.; Minneapolis: Bethany, 1973), II, 24.

And, as we have argued elsewhere, it is only because God is not "unitarian" that from eternity love has existed (as among the persons of the Holy Trinity) owing to their interrelationships.

> 3.747 The philosophical importance of Trinitarian doctrine (three Persons in one Godhead) is often overlooked: if God is indeed love, and has always been so (even before he created other persons), he would have to be more than monopersonal.

> 3.7471 The only alternatives for a unitarian God would be (1) in his essential nature he is not love, or (2) his "love" was first and most fundamentally manifested in self-centredness – for prior to creating other persons it could only have been directed at himself.

> 3.74711 Aristotle's Deity was of the latter sort, spending eternity loving himself, since no other object of love could be equally worthy of his attention.

> 3.74712 "Even if God exists, yet is of such a nature that he feels no benevolence or affection towards men, good-bye to him, say I. Why should I say 'God be gracious to me'? – since he cannot be gracious to anybody" (Cicero, *De natura deorum*).[11]

It is no less true that God's observation of – interaction with – his universe is the only explanation as to why its subatomic non-specificity has been transformed into the objective solidity we experience every day of our lives. No God necessarily means no concretisation of the subatomic into the reality of everyday experience. But the world of our experience is patently there; *ergo*, so is its Creator and Sustainer. Is this perhaps the point of Colossians 1:17 (God in Christ "is before all things, and by him all things consist")?[12]

---

[11] Montgomery, *Tractatus Logico-theologicus* (op. cit.).
[12] καὶ αὐτός ἐστιν πρὸ πάντων καὶ τὰ πάντα ἐν αὐτῷ συνέστηκεν.

# 11. Apologetics Insights from the Thought of I. J. Good

**Introduction**

Who, the reader may well ask, was I. J. Good? Irving John – "Jack" – Good (1916-2009) was a British mathematician, educated at Cambridge, who taught at the University of Manchester, later immigrating to the United States, where he served as University Distinguished Professor of Statistics at Virginia Polytechnic Institute. His concept of "technological singularity" and speculations concerning ultraintelligent machines led to his becoming a technical consultant on supercomputers to Stanley Kubrick in the filming of *2001: A Space Odyssey*. But the most celebrated phase in Good's career was surely his time at the great World War II cryptography centre of Bletchley Park, where the German Enigma code was broken; there he acted as the chief statistical assistant to Alan Turing and contributed mightily to the Allied victory against Hitler.[1] Here is an account of one of his successes:

> Jack Good ... had been baffled by his failure to break a doubly enciphered *Offizier* message. This was one of the messages which was supposed to be enciphered initially with the Enigma set up in accordance with the *Offizier* settings, subsequently with the general Enigma settings in place. However, while he was sleeping before returning to another shift, he dreamed that the order had been reversed; the general settings had been applied before the *Offizier* settings. Next day he found that the message had yet to be read, so he applied the theory which had come to him during the night. It worked; he had broken the code in his sleep.[2]

---

[1] On Bletchley Park, Turing, and Good, see, *inter alia*, Gordon Weichman, *The Hut Six Story: Breaking the Enigma Codes* (2d rev. ed.; Kidderminster, U.K.: M. & M. Baldwin, 1997); Michael Smith, *Station X: The Code Breakers of Bletchley Park* (rev. ed.; London: Pan, 2004); F. H. Hinsley and Alan Stripp (eds.), *Codebreakers: The Inside Story of Bletchley Park* (Oxford: Oxford University Press, 1993)—chap. 19 (pp. 149-66) contributed by I. J. Good.

[2] Hugh Sebag-Montefiore, *Enigma: The Battle for the Code* ("Cassell Military"; London: W&N/Orion, 2000), p. 189.

Good produced a considerable number of papers, many of which are unpublished. As for his published material, it is often as stylistically cryptic as one would expect of one who spent much energy on enigmas.

Having, as a reference librarian at the University of California at Berkeley, broken the (admittedly simple) substitution code used by Sinclair Lewis in his diaries, and, years later, having visited the Bletchley Park museum and built and toyed with a model of the Enigma machine, I have a special interest in the cryptological activities that went on there. This short paper will apply a few of Good's insights to central issues in Christian apologetics.[3]

## Religion and the Paranormal

Good's book-length collection of essays consists of twenty-three articles – followed by a bibliography of hundreds of items not included in the book (numbered from 1 to 1517, with many numbers inexplicably omitted).[4] All of these entries are, however, provided with an extensive subject index! Under the entry for "Religion" one is led in particular to papers by Good published in the off-the-wall periodical *Zetetic Scholar* – a journal founded by sociologist Marcello Truzzi of Eastern Michigan University; this skeptical journal, devoted to research in parapsychology and the occult, lasted for only some thirteen issues (1978-1987). It was Truzzi who was apparently the source of Carl Sagan's well-known tag, "extraordinary claims require extraordinary proof."

Good recognizes that evidence for religious claims will not reach 100% certainty, and, indeed, should not do so, since were that the case subjective commitment (i.e., what theology refers to as "faith") would not be neces-

---

[3] This is not to imply that Good was a Christian believer; he was born Isadore Jacob Gudak to a Polish-Jewish family; obituaries: *Times* [London], 16 April 2009; *Guardian* [U.K.], 29 April 2009; *Independent* [U.K], 14 May 2009.

[4] I. J. Good, *Good Thinking: The Foundations of Probability and Its Applications* (reprint ed.; Mineola, NY: Dover Publications, 2009). This is one of only four books written by Good. As the title suggests, he had a "good" sense of humour. We refer in the present article to only two of Good's books; the others are not directly relevant to our purposes: *The Estimation of Probabilities: An Essay on Modern Bayesian Methods* (Cambridge, Mass.: M.I.T. Press, 1965), and *Information, Weight of Evidence, the Singularity between Probability Measures and Signal Detection*, coauthored with D. B. Osteyee (Berlin, Heidelberg, New York: Springer Verlag, 1974). Good was also editor of a fun collection—*The Scientist Speculates: An Anthology of Partly-Baked Ideas* (London: Heinemann, 1962), which was translated into German and French—and several encyclopedia articles.

# Apologetics Insights from the Thought of I. J. Good

sary. He also recognizes that one's worldview ("presuppositions") will impact the weight one gives to the evidence. In discussing the case for ESP, Good writes:

> I do not know whether there is any known case of spontaneous ESP that can overcome thoroughly stringent criteria. And if there have been lots of coincidences of the order $10^{-18}$, why haven't there been some much more decisive ones of the order such as $10^{-50}$? If there is good evidence, why isn't there some overwhelming evidence also? Could it be that paranormal phenomena are miracles intended by some power to encourage us to become religious, and which reveal themselves only "through a glass darkly" or are "shy" as it is sometimes expressed? It is a well known theological thesis that one's faith is not supposed to be forced upon one. That is, one's subjective probability of the truth of the religion must not be forcibly increased much. If this is so, a miracle can occur only to people whose degree of belief is already close to 1. When, on rare occasions, miracles are presented to people whose degrees of belief are not close to 1, they will suspect trickery so they will not be forced into complete belief. It is certainly rational to suspect trickery in this imperfect world. Jim Jones performed fraudulent miracles, so perhaps other religious leaders did so too.[5]

Much the same point is made by Good in his statistical discussion of the evidence for astrology as presented by Gauquelin[6]:

> The rational judgement of an initial probability depends on how a hypothesis fits in with one's previous knowledge or preconceptions. If you believe in the existence of ancient Greek gods, in which case you may as well stop reading, then your value of x ["the odds that there is some personal attribute associated with some planet"] will be appreciable. To parody Voltaire, although the Greek gods did not exist men invented them. But if you think that the great ancient religions were twaddle, humbug, and balderdash, then you might feel that the best way to enhance x is by de-astrologization.[7]

But Good's arguments are not all of a negative sort. He clearly sees the difficulty with the argument that the stuff of the universe arose from nothing:

---

[5] I. J. Good, "Scientific Speculations on the Paranormal and the Parasciences," *Zetetic Scholar,* No. 7 (December, 1980), p. 11.
[6] On Gauquelin and astrology, see Montgomery, *Principalities and Powers: The World of the Occult* (Calgary, Alberta: Canadian Institute for Law, Theology and Public Policy, 2001), chap. 4.
[7] I. J. Good, "Is the Mars Effect an Artifact?", *Zetetic Scholar,* No. 9 (1982), p. 67.

> To assume that our universe came from another universe is like assuming that people came from people. To assume that it suddenly came from nothing, on the other hand, is like assuming that fruit flies are spontaneously generated by bananas.[8]

In general, Good may be said to agree with Truzzi that claims – religious or otherwise – need to be backed up by sufficient evidence, and that the one making the claim (or attempting to refute a claim) has the burden of demonstrating what is being proposed. Here is Truzzi's credo, as set out in the final issue of the *Zetetic Scholar*:

> In science the burden of proof falls upon the claimant ... But if a critic asserts that there is evidence for disproof, that he has a negative hypothesis – saying, for instance, that a seeming psi result was actually due to an artifact – he is making a claim and therefore also has to bear a burden of proof.[9]

## Probability

But how does one marshal evidence to demonstrate one's contentions? Good's answer is: by way of probability and the weighing of evidence. Probability theory was one of Good's prime interests – along with the Bayesian calculus. We shall not deal with the latter, for we agree with John Earman, author of *Hume's Abject Failure: The Argument Against Miracles*[10] that its value is frequently overestimated.[11] We shall, however, very definitely want to hear from Good on the importance of probability reasoning.

In his earliest book, *Probability and the Weighing of Evidence* – which he describes elsewhere as "succinct ... although I knew that large books look more impressive"[12] – Good deals with a most fundamental epistemological question:

---

[8] Good, "Scientific Speculations on the Paranormal and the Parasciences," *op. cit.*, p. 17.
[9] Marcello Truzzi, "On Pseudo-Skepticism," *Zetetic Scholar*, No. 12/13 (1987), pp. 3-4.
[10] New York: Oxford University Press, 2000.
[11] See "A New Approach to the Apologetic for Christ's Resurrection by way of Wigmore's Juridical Analysis of Evidence," in Montgomery, *Christ As Centre and Circumference* (Bonn, Germany: Verlag für Kultur und Wissenschaft, 2011), Part 4, chap. 2 (and *supra* in the present volume). Earman's fullest treatment of Bayesianism is: *Bayes or Bust? A Critical Examination of Bayesian Confirmation Theory* (Cambridge, Mass.: M.I.T. Press, 1992).
[12] *Good Thinking* (*op. cit.*), p. xii.

The question arises how to select a suitable theory. It must be logically consistent and, more generally, it must never force you into a position that after mature consideration you regard as untenable. (This would happen if a body of beliefs became classified as "unreasonable" while not containing any judgments that could be conscientiously removed.) The theory should be applicable to most of the practical problems concerning degrees of belief, and it would be convenient for it to apply also to idealized problems.[13]

Christian believers will note that classic biblical faith satisfies this criterion: the totality of scriptural doctrine comprises an internally consistent whole – as distinct from what operates in the other world's religions and the cults. The contrast could not be greater with (for example) Buddhism, whose systemic irrationality is inherent – since the religion could not survive the removal of central teachings such as the notion that the source of all cosmic suffering is *desire* (not *evil* desire, but desire *as such*).[14] Thus also the diametric contrast between biblical Christianity and the irrationality of Christian Science, whose belief that sickness is an illusion cannot be removed without destroying that entire cultic belief-system.

Later in *Probability and the Weighing of Evidence*, Good comments briefly on "legal applications" of his approach. Unfortunately, doubtless owing to a lack of background in the niceties of legal evidence, he does not treat the vital common-law distinction between the civil evidence standard (preponderance of evidence) and the criminal standard (moral certainty, beyond reasonable doubt).[15] However, he properly observes the Sherlockian dimension of probability reasoning in legal and scientific decision-making:

> It is convenient to refer here to a principle stated by Sherlock Holmes. *If a hypothesis is initially very improbable but is the only one that explains the facts, then it must be accepted.* From the present point of view this is because the

---

[13] I. J. Good, *Probability and the Weighing of Evidence* (London: Charles Griffin; New York: Hafner, 1950), p. 5. This has now become a very rare book; having foregone a copy at $600 at Second Story Books in Washington, D.C., I obtained one through Abebooks.com for a mere $300.

[14] Montgomery, *Giant in Chains: China Today and Tomorrow* (Milton Keynes, U.K.: Nelson Word, 1994), especially pp. 127-36. (In German: *Wohin marschiert China?* [Neuhausen-Stuttgart: Haenssler-Verlag, 1991].)

[15] See Montgomery, *Human Rights and Human Dignity* (Calgary, Alberta: Canadian Institute for Law, Theology and Public Policy, 1995), chap. 6; *Tractatus Logico-Theologicus* (4th ed.; Bonn, Germany: Verlag für Kultur und Wissenschaft, 2009), proposition 3.1 ff.

hypothesis receives an infinite factor from the evidence. The principle is often used in scientific work.[16]

The application of this principle to the factuality of the miracles in the life of Christ (and particularly to his resurrection from the dead) should be obvious. And here, two brief comments on the Truzzi/Sagan aphorism, "extraordinary claims require extraordinary proof," are in order. (1) That assertion would be true if, and only if, one knew the fabric of the universe – its cosmic laws and what therefore can and cannot happen; but in Einsteinian, relativistic terms, no one has such knowledge, so no one can rationally determine the probabilities for or against a given event: only factual investigation permits one to conclude that event $x$ did or event $y$ did not occur. (2) There is nothing extraordinary about determining, for example, that Jesus rose from the dead: one need only show (a) that he died and (b) that later he was physically alive – determinations which we make every day (though in reverse order).

Good is much concerned with the need to evaluate the specific evidence pertinent to a given claim – as opposed to reaching conclusions by generalization: "Seeing a black crow does not necessarily confirm the hypothesis that all crows are black."[17] He also recognizes the danger of letting one's preconceptions create a prejudice against the actual force of the evidence:

> In elementary textbooks the advice is often given to decide on one's tests of significance before taking a sample ... But consider the following example. A sample of 100 readings is taken from some distribution for which the null hypothesis is that the readings are independently distributed with a normal distribution of zero mean and unit variance. It is decided in advance of sampling to divide this normal distribution up into ten equal areas, and to apply the $\chi^2$ test to the ten-category equiprobable multinomial distribution of frequencies with which the readings fall into the ten areas. This would appear to be a very reasonable statistic. But what if it leads to a non-significant result even though one of the 100 readings was 20 standard deviations above the mean?[18]

---

[16] Good, *Probability and the Weighing of Evidence* (op. cit.), p. 67. Though his argument does not require it, Good goes on unnecessarily to qualify what he says here by an appeal to Bayesian reasoning.

[17] Good, *Good Thinking* (op. cit.), p. xv.

[18] *Ibid.*, pp. 60-61. Apropos statistics and the defense of the faith, see David J. Bartholomew's devastating refutation of "Victor Stenger's Scientific Critique of Christian Belief," 22/2 *Science and Christian Belief* [U.K.] (October 2010), 117-31.

The answer, of course, is to pay attention to that one reading which is 20 standard deviations above the mean! Likewise, the issue as to the accounts of Christ's resurrection is not how many other people have died and stayed dead – but how strong is the testimonial evidence in behalf of One who died and did *not* stay dead. We have illustrated elsewhere how essential it is to investigate particulars without the prejudice of generalizations: as in the case of the successful chemical combination of noble gases, long considered "inert" because that conceptualization fitted the general structure of the Periodic table. Particular facts must determine generalizations, *not* the reverse.[19]

In discussing "kinds of probability," Good makes clear that "degree of belief (intensity of conviction), belonging to a highly self-contradictory body of beliefs ... hardly deserves to be called a probability."[20] Indeed, this should remind us that mere "intensity of conviction," whether in the secular or in the religious realm, is no guarantor of truth whatsoever. How many terribly wrong, and dangerous, belief-systems have been held with fanatical conviction!

So what is sound probability thinking? Good describes his view as a "black box theory of probability and rationality." The concept of the "black box" has been extensively employed in computer science[21] and cryptanalysis; in essence, it refers to anything (an algorithm or even the human mind) which is viewed in terms of input and output without knowledge of the internal workings – or where those inner components are unavailable for inspection. "Black box" analysis is in effect a species of "opaque" implementation.[22] Says Good:

> The black box is supposed to contain ... a "body of beliefs." The output consists of *discernments.* By a "discernment" I mean a judgment that becomes compulsory once it has been deduced. The inside of the black box is sup-

---

[19] Montgomery, *Faith Founded on Fact* (Nashville, Tenn.: Thomas Nelson, 1978), pp. 70-73.
[20] Good, *Good Thinking (op. cit.),* p. 70.
[21] On the connections between computer science and apologetics, see Montgomery, "Computer Origins and the Defense of the Faith": 56/3 *Perspectives on Science and Christian Faith: Journal of the American Scientific Affiliation* (September, 2004), 189-203, and reprinted in Montgomery, *Christ As Centre and Circumference (op. cit.),* Part. 2, chap. 2; also, Montgomery, *Computers, Cultural Change, and the Christ* (trilingual ed. [English, French, German]; Wayne, NJ: Christian Research Institute, 1969).
[22] Cf. Michael Behe's powerful use of the black box analogy in his refutation of classical Darwinism and support of Intelligent Design: *Darwin's Black Box: The Biochemical Challenge to Evolution* (2d ed.; New York: Free Press, 2006).

posed to operate with sharp probabilities and utilities although the judgments and discernments are only partially ordered. The advantage of this theory is that it is dead realistic ... The purpose of the theory is to enlarge the body of beliefs and to detect inconsistencies in it, whereupon the judgments need revision ...

If we imagine a futuristic robot making use of a subjectivistic theory it is obvious that all it can do at any given moment is to use the judgments that it has made up to that moment. I can see no reason to suppose that a person could do any better without divine guidance.[23] This is a sufficient reason for calling my theory subjectivistic rather than credibilistic. But I regard it as mentally healthy to think of subjective probabilities as estimates of credibilities although I am not sure that credibilities exist. It's like half-believing in God. One might say that a belief in credibilities constitutes a religion, whereas subjective probabilities emerge more directly from ordinary experience.[24]

Good is certainly correct that we cannot fathom the inner working of this black box. But it is surely possible to move from subjective probabilities to credibilities – from half-believing in God to a firm faith in him – from ordinary experience (the ordinary experience of the Apostolic company who experienced the "many infallible proofs" of Jesus' divinity[25]) to the one religion that is solidly grounded in empirical fact. Good recognizes the distinction between analytical assertions that are true by definition and synthetic assertions that depend on factual investigation of evidential probabilities.[26] It is precisely such probability that should move the serious seeker to credible faith in Jesus Christ.

## Where to Go from Here?

Good's "subjectivist states his judgments whereas the objectivist sweeps them under the carpet by calling assumptions *knowledge,* and he basks in

---

[23] Cf. Plato, *Phaedo,* 85d (cf. Montgomery, *The Shape of the Past* [reprint ed.; Eugene, OR: Wipf & Stock, 2009], p. 295), and Ludwig Wittgenstein (cf. Montgomery, *Tractatus Logico-Theologicus, op. cit.,* pp. 7-9). Unlike the vast majority of representatives of the philosophical tradition, Plato and Wittgenstein had the humility to recognize their limitations and to see the need for transcendent revelation.

[24] *Ibid.,* p. 153.

[25] Acts 1:3.

[26] Good, *Probability and the Weighing of Evidence (op. cit.),* pp. 19 ff, 34-35.

the glorious objectivity of science."²⁷ Good regards the "objective probablist" as a dogmatist who thinks that his conclusions are absolute and are supported by the "assured results of modern science." What is needed is a bit of humility: the recognition that no factual evidence ever reaches 100% certainty, but that it may nonetheless be more than sufficient for practical certainty and reasonable action in this world.

The case for Christian truth is of this very nature – though, sadly, Good never apparently applied his sound probabilistic method to investigating the evidence in its behalf.

And if solid evidence does exist, when should we act upon it? Good deals with this in principle 25 of his "Twenty-Seven Principles of Rationality": "The time to make a decision is largely determined by urgency and by the current rate of acquisition of information, evolving or otherwise. For example, consider chess timed by a clock."²⁸

Thus the exhortation of Holy Scripture: "Now is the accepted time; behold, now is the day of salvation."²⁹

---

[27] *Good Thinking (op. cit.)*, p. 16.
[28] *Ibid.* p. 18.
[29] 2 Corinthians 6:2.

## 12. Miracle Evidence: How Philosophers Go Wrong

In a recent perambulation in an English second-hand bookstore, I obtained a copy of *An Introduction to Philosophical Analysis* (4th ed., 1997) by John Hospers, emeritus professor of philosophy at the University of Southern California. The UK publisher is Routledge; the original American editions were issued by Prentice-Hall/Simon & Schuster. The cover informs us by an over-stamp: "Over 150,000 copies sold." The book provides a basic introduction to the gamut of philosophical fields – from metaphysics to ethics, including scientific method and mind-body dualism. You can well imagine my glee in purchasing the book for a mere five pounds sterling.

I soon discovered, however, that I had not received a great bargain, considering the author's treatment of philosophy of religion. The short section, pp. 212-16, on "the argument from miracles" (as attesting religious truth) is so typical of the cavalier dismissal of miracles in university and college-level religion and philosophy courses that it deserves our examination here. We shall take up the author's major arguments *seriatim*.

> 1) *"We could never know that the event could not be subsumed under some laws."*

This is, of course, quite true; as another philosopher once said, "Anything is possible but squeezing toothpaste back into the tube." But the fact that there *might* be a yet undiscovered law to explain the "miracle" – thus preventing us from so designating it – hardly tells us whether that approach would be the most reasonable course of action. Example: how likely is it that a new physical law might be discovered that would provide a satisfactory explanation of Jesus' resurrection from the dead after the systematic work of a Roman crucifixion team and three days in the grave?[1] In science, law, and ordinary life, one needs to make decisions by probabilistically examining the facts, not reaching conclusions on the basis of cosmic possibilities.

> 2) *"No testimony,"* wrote Hume, *"is sufficient to establish a miracle unless the testimony be of such a kind that its falsehood would be more miraculous than the fact which it endeavors to establish."*

---

[1] Cf. W. D. Edwards, W. J. Gabel, F. E. Hosmer, "On the Physical Death of Jesus Christ," 255 *Journal of the American Medical Association* [JAMA], 1455-63 (1986).

David Hume, to be sure: the standard counter to placing a value on miracle evidence. But Hospers ought surely to realize that the Humean argument depended squarely on an 18th-century, absolutist view of natural law, impossible today in an Einsteinian, relativistic universe. Hume believed that our existing knowledge of the universe was sufficient to establish the cosmic unlikelihood of a miracle vs. the likelihood of lying, deception, or incredible naïveté on the part of the witnesses to it. In point of fact, one cannot second-guess the universe as to what is likely or unlikely to happen; philosophers (just like the rest of us) must get off their deductivistic *derrières* and examine the empirical evidence for each miracle claim without prejudice for or against. That is the only way to avoid the gross circularity built into the Humean argument: miracles (obviously) will never occur if there is, as Hume asserted, "uniform experience" against the miraculous; but to assume such uniform testimony in the face of genuine miracle claims just begs the question![2] And why – by the by – did not Hospers later revise his material in light of non-Christian philosopher John Earman's decimation of the Humean argument: *Hume's Abject Failure: The Argument Against Miracles?*[3]

> 3) "Most alleged miracles were reported by people in times long past, so we can no longer check their claims – people who were not well trained in reporting what they saw without adding anything to the observed facts."

Here the reader receives a good dose of historical chauvinism: people of "the long past" were naïve simpletons who could not distinguish between fact and fable. In reality, moderns are much more prone than the ancients to swallow gross falsities (Marxisms, totalitarianisms, conspiracy theories, flying saucer myths, etc., etc.) than were the ancients. And are we really to suppose that the ancients couldn't tell the difference between dead people and live ones? (If so, they must have been burying the wrong bodies.)[4] The early Christian witnesses to Jesus' miracles and the resurrection insist that "we were not following "cunningly devised fables [Gk., *mythoi*] when we made known to you the power and coming of our Lord Jesus Christ, *but*

---

[2] See the discussion of this issue in Montgomery, *The Shape of the Past* (rev. ed.; Eugene, OR: Wipf & Stock, 2008), pp. 288-93. 296-98.

[3] New York: Oxford University Press, 2000. See also, Montgomery, "Science, Theology, and the Miraculous," in his *Faith Founded on Fact* (Nashville, TN: Thomas Nelson, 1978), pp. 43-73.

[4] See Thomas Sherlock, *The Tryal of the Witnesses of the Resurrection of Jesus* (1729), reprinted in Montgomery (ed.), *Jurisprudence: A Book of Readings* (rev. ed.; Strasbourg, France: International Scholarly Publishers, 1980).

*were eyewitnesses of His majesty"* (2 Peter 1:16). And these reports were in circulation when hostile witnesses of the life of Christ were still alive; had the early Christians fabricated their accounts, can we imagine that those who had been instrumental in the death of Christ would not have had the means, motive, and opportunity to refute their false claims or exaggerations?[5]

> 4) *"Each religion has its own stock of miracles to bolster its claim to authenticity."*

Here our author gratuitously blends the miracle claims without regard to particular religion or particular claim. But – to coin a phrase – "though all miracles are equal, some are more equal than others." Most world religions are *experiential* in focus: they assert their value based not on miracles but on personal experience (Buddhism, Hinduism, New Age, Mormonism and other contemporary cults and sects). And when miracles are claimed, the degree of evidence offered differs immensely. Thus Mohammed's miraculous night journey on a heavenly steed occurred so rapidly that no one observed it.[6] Contrast this with Jesus' resurrection from the dead – observed by over five hundred witnesses, most of whom were still alive in 56 A.D. (1 Corinthians 15). Each miracle claim must be evaluated in terms of the testimony for it or against it. Generalisations of the kind expressed by Hospers are of no value in such investigations.

> 5) *Suppose, however, that there was some super miracle that we could all observe and could not explain away ... If all killers were were thenceforth executed by thunderbolts in accordance with the [universal, heavenly] announcement, this would ... be mightily impressive ... It would certainly be evidence for the existence of 'a powerful being out there' – perhaps not a being who was omnipotent, or infinitely wise, or the cause of the universe, or a 'necessary being' – but at least something for whose existence we had thus far had no direct evidence."*

---

[5] Montgomery, *History, Law and Christianity* (3rd ed.; Irvine, CA: 1517. Legacy Project/New Reformation Press, 2014).

[6] Shaykh Muhammad and Mitwalli Al-Sha'rawi, *The Miracles of the Qur'an*, trans. M. Alserougii (n.p.: Dar-Al-Taqwa, n.d.), pp, 189-91. Such miracle claims qualify as what the analytical philosophers term "meaningless" or "nonsensical" assertions, since there is no evidence to count for or against them. See, in general, Montgomery, *Tractatus Logico-Theologicus* (5$^{th}$ ed.; Bonn, Germany: Verlag für Kultur und Wissenschaft, 2012); the *Tractatus* is available in the U.S. from Wipf & Stock, Eugene, OR.

Here our philosopher states the conditions that would impress him and lead (perhaps) to his acceptance of a miracle claim as genuine. This reminds one of Dives, the rich man in the parable of Lazarus and the rich man. The latter, owing to his self-centred, egotistical life, arrives in hell and asks Abraham to send back the beggar Lazarus, now in heaven, to warn his brothers so that they will not end up in the same eternal condition. Response: "Abraham saith unto him, They have Moses and the prophets; let them hear them. And he said, Nay, father Abraham: but if one went unto them from the dead, they will repent. And he said unto him, If they hear not Moses and the prophets [i.e., the existing biblical revelation], neither will they be persuaded, though one rose from the dead" (Luke 16). The point here being, first, that a little humility might be in order as to the provision of miracle evidence (perhaps the Lord is in the best position to determine the kind of miracle he prefers to offer to a sinful and fallen race); and, secondly, unbelievers will always find some way to discount the evidence for a miracle, no matter how good it in fact is.

If Jesus indeed conquered death – the most fundamental of human problems (it can really ruin your day – along with all your plans, hopes, dreams, and relationships), you will never have a better reason to worship. And it is certainly more reasonable to take the explanation of the miracle from the one who performed it than to speculate on its cause when one has not been capable of performing such a miracle oneself. Jesus explained His miraculous life and resurrection on the ground that He was God incarnate ("I and the Father are one"; "he who has seen Me has seen the Father"; etc.), and therefore omnipotent, infinitely wise, the cause of the universe, and a necessary being.

> 6) "Even a very extraordinary event, one contrary to known laws of nature, will not impress people as a candidate for the miraculous nearly as much as will occurrences with a 'personal touch' – that appear to be the work of a will, a personality of some kind ... [Something] might well be counted as miraculous, not merely because of the event itself, because of the prior warning from the clouds: it would be a manifestation of a will, backed up by power, both of which are universally considered to be distinctive features of a deity."

Most interesting – not because of Hospers' repeated use of an outmoded notion of the "laws of nature," but because of his concession that a miracle would be the most persuasive if (1) predicted beforehand and (2) a clear manifestation of "will" and "power." The prophetic material in the Old

Testament and fulfilled in detail in the life and ministry of Jesus Christ offers a staggeringly persuasive "prior warning from the clouds."[7] And Jesus' miracles are part and parcel of a life displaying will and power ("I came down from heaven, not to do mine own will, but the will of him that sent me" –John 6:38; "no one ever spoke as this man does" –John 7:46; "you shall see the Son of man sitting on the right hand of power, and coming in the clouds of heaven" – Matthew 26:64).

> 7) *"Even raising someone from the dead might not be found particularly impressive – physicians have revived people after thier [sic] heartbeat and brainwaves have stopped; it would more likely be thought of as a medical triumph than a miracle."*

Oddly enough, this is not how Lazarus apparently thought of it – or how his skeptical family evaluated the situation prior to Jesus's raising him from the dead ("Lord, by this time he stinketh: for he hath been dead four days" – John 11:39). And if one cannot comprehend the significance of Christ's own resurrection ("because I live, ye shall live also" – John 14:19), it is passing difficult to know what kind of divine act could possibly impress.

---

[7] See Montgomery, "Prophecy, Eschatology and Apologetics," in his *Christ Our Advocate* (Bonn, Germany: Verlag für Kultur und Wissenschaft, 255-65. This material may also be found in David W. Baker (ed.), *Looking Into the Future* (Grand Rapids, MI: Baker, 2001).

# 13. The Heritage of the Reformation – and Why It Should Be Defended[1]

*Abstract:* After a brief discussion of the positive values of the Reformation, as lauded in past and present centennials, we deal with the most trenchant contemporary negative critique: that of Brad S. Gregory in his book, *The Unintended Reformation: How a Religious Revolution Secularized Society*. We argue that modern secularism, rather than being an "unintended product" of the Reformation, arose from ideologies directly in opposition to Reformation beliefs.

Five hundred years have passed since Luther's posting of the Ninety-Five Theses, and another Reformation centennial is upon us. Studies of the four preceding centennials (1617, 1717, 1817, and 1917) make interesting reading.[2] There is no doubt that perspectives have undergone change. Thus, it has been noted that the 1817 and 1917 centennials, in line with modern nationalistic sentiments, emphasized the effects of the Reformation on the rise of the national state to an extent absent in earlier centennial celebrations, when the Holy Roman Empire was still in existence.[3]

But one thing is sure: every centennial has rung the changes on the positive value of the Reformation. Here is a short list of the contributions to civilization regularly attributed to Luther's break with Roman Church:

- By its insistence on locating the source of salvation as within God's grace alone, the Reformation freed religious believers from the burden of self-salvation and redirected human effort to serving others – becoming, to use Luther's felicitous phrase, "a little Christ to one's neighbour[4]
- By strengthening the power of secular rulers over against ecclesiastical authority, the Reformation contributed to the rise of the

---

[1] Keynote Address at 1517 Legacy & ChristHoldFast's "Here We Stand: a Reformation Conference," San Diego, CA, 19 October 2017.
[2] See, for example, Hartmut Lehmann, *Luthergedächtnis 1817 bis 2017* ("Refo 500," Bd. 8; Göttingen: Vandenhoeck & Ruprecht, 2012).
[3] The Empire was officially abolished by Napoleon I. My professor of German history at the University of California at Berkeley applied T. S. Eliot's line from *The Hollow Men*: the Holy Roman Empire ended "not with a bang but a whimper."
[4] See George Forell, *Faith Active in Love* (reprint ed.; Eugene, OR: Wipf & Stock, 2000).

modern state and, ultimately, to the expansion of religious liberty by way of the separation of church and state – thus preserving religious belief from state control
- By its stress on the priesthood of all believers, the Reformation promoted the equality of every person before God and contributed to the equality of all citizens before the law
- By its insistence on the individual's right to read and interpret the Scriptures, the Reformation moved society in the direction of universal public education and the responsibility of the individual to make personal religious decisions, rather than merely relying on ecclesiastical authority[5]
- By its conviction that God reveals himself both in Scripture and in the natural world, the Reformation provided a key motivation for 17th- and 18th-century advances and discoveries in the natural sciences[6]
- The Reformation's emphasis on individual decision-making may well have contributed to the remarkable economic and social gains in Protestant lands, particularly in northern Europe and north America, during subsequent centuries[7]

To be sure, the Reformation was certainly not considered a positive influence by everyone. Roman Catholics were hardly enthusiastic and, until the present centennial, have stayed well away from such celebrations. Revealing is the treatment of Luther by the 19th-century Catholic historian Ignaz von Döllinger – whose understanding of Luther moved from the psychobiographical (cf. Erik Erickson's *Young Man Luther*) to a guarded recognition, following Döllinger's excommunction for refusing to accept papal infallibility after Vatican I, of the Roman church's responsibility for the break:

> In his 1871 lectures on church reunion, Döllinger offered the most mature statement of his new perspective, stressing the fundamental crisis among the German Church and people, which would have drawn them away from Rome even without the "Titan of the world of mind." In elaborating on the

---

[5] See John Warwick Montgomery, "Luther, Libraries, and Learning," in his *In Defense of Martin Luther* (new ed.; Milwaukee, WI: Northwestern Publishing House, 2017), pp. 115-39.

[6] See Montgomery, "Cross, Constellation, and Crucible," *ibid.*, pp. 87-114; also, Montgomery, *Cross and Crucible* (2 vols.; "International Archives of the History of Ideas," 55; The Hague: Nijhoff, 1973).

[7] Cf. the Weber/Tawney thesis ("religion and the rise of capitalism").

Curia's heavy responsibility for the Reformation schism, Döllinger emphasized the decades of papal silence in the face of manifest abuses and doctrinal confusion, and a refusal to confront the question of reform because of the threat to papal power and profits. No longer is the Reformation understood as the product of Luther's diseased and violent mind. Rather Luther is seen as the catalyst of reform in a Church which had been unable to bring about the changes it desperately needed.[8]

As for Enlightenment rationalists and contemporary secularists, they have seen little of value in the Reformation aside from its rejection of church authority and its opening of the door to varieties of both belief and unbelief.

> As the seventeenth century yielded to the eighteenth ... a fundamental reassessment of the Reformation inheritance became inescapable as a result of major shifts in European intellectual life. Cartesian philosophy, Newtonian science, and the political theories of Thomas Hobbes and John Locke amounted to a radical questioning of all tradition and implied a relativizing of the European religious experience. What had appeared to be transcendent and self-evident truth was increasingly understood as circumstantial and cultural variation.[9]

One of the most sophisticated current onslaughts *contra* Luther's split with the church of his day is a recently published work by a distinguished University of Notre Dame historian. We quote at length the author's argument:

> On the eve of the Reformation, Latin Christianity comprised for good or ill the far from homogeneous yet institutionalized worldview within which the overwhelming majority of Europeans lived and made sense of their lives. Diversely, early twenty-first-century Westerners live in and think with and even feel through the historical results of its variegated rejections and appropriations in such knotted ways that it is difficult even to see, much less to analyze, them. In getting from the early sixteenth to the early twenty-

---

[8] A. G. Dickens and John M. Tonkin, *The Reformation in Historical Thought* (Oxford: Basil Blackwell, 1985, pp. 182-83. In the *Encyclopedia of the Reformation* (4 vols.; New York: Oxford University Press, 1996), the article on "Reformation Studies" (III, 398-410) correctly describes Dickens' work as "the most comprehensive study available of the historiography of the Reformation over nearly five centuries."
[9] Ibid., pp. 402-403 (John Tonkin). Cf. Harold Mah, *Enlightenment Phantasies: Cultural Identity in France and Germany 1750-1914* (Ithaca, NY: Cornell University Press, 2003).

first century, this study develops the claim from my first book that "incompatible, deeply held, concretely expressed religious convictions paved a path to a secular society." ...

[T]he exclusion in the secularized academy of any religious claims or metaphysical assumptions besides naturalism has eliminated any possibility of justifying the belief that members of the species *Homo sapiens* are persons, or that rights are real. There are certainly no grounds for thinking that rights are *natural*, rooted in nature as many Enlightenment theorists claimed ... Rights and dignity can be real only if human beings are more than biological matter. The modern secular discourse on human rights depends on retaining in some fashion – but without acknowledging – the belief that every human being is created in the image and likeness of God, a notion that could be rooted in nature so long as nature was regarded as creation, whether overtly recognized as such or not. But if nature is not creation, then there are no creatures, and human beings are just one more species that happened randomly to evolve, no more "endowed by their creator with certain unalienable rights" than is any other bit of matter-energy. Then there simply are no rights, just as there are no persons, and no theorizing can conjure them into existence. The intellectual foundations of modernity are failing because its governing metaphysical assumptions in combination with the findings of the natural sciences offer no warrant for believing its most basic moral, political, and legal claims.[10]

Professor Gregory's argument is redolent of philosopher Charles Taylor's *A Secular Age*,[11] based on Taylor's 1998 Gifford Lectures sketching Western history of ideas from the Reformation to our era of radical pluralism. Gregory holds that (1) modern secularism cannot sustain its laudable beliefs in the areas of civil liberties and human rights – simply because "inalienable rights" require an inalienable, metaphysical foundation, and (2) that foundation was made impossible by the Reformation's destruction of the medieval synthesis and the consequent loss of what had been a virtually universal reliance on a single, established religious authority and Christian worldview.

Now, we would surely not dispute Gregory's first claim. Indeed, we have argued precisely the same point in our numerous apologetics publications.[12] The case bears repeating here:

---

[10] Brad S. Gregory, *The Unintended Reformation: How a Religious Revolution Secularized Society* (Cambridge, MA: Belknap Press, 2012), pp. 2, 380-81.
[11] Cambridge, MA: Harvard University Press, 2007.
[12] E.g., *Faith Founded on Fact*; *Christianity for the Toughminded*; *History, Law and Christianity*; *The Law Above the Law*; *Human Rights and Human Dignity*; *Tractatus Logico-Theologicus*; *Christ Our Advocate*.

The importance of religious argument in behalf of human rights lies especially in the principle enunciated by Ludwig Wittgenstein in his *Tractatus Logico-Philosophicus* that "ethics is transcendental." Metaphorically expanding on this theme in his posthumously published "Lecture on Ethics," Wittgenstein says: "[W]e cannot write a scientific book, the subject matter of which could be intrinsically sublime and above all other subject matters. I can only describe my feeling by the metaphor, that, if a man could write a book on Ethics which really was a book on Ethics, this book would, with an explosion, destroy all the other books in the world." In other words, to arrive at inalienable rights one would have to move beyond the limited, finite perspective of human opinion and go "outside the world" to a "transcendental" realm of values. Only there could "intrinsically sublime" standards be found. Wittgenstein's insight seems entirely in accord with common sense. Water does not rise above its own level; why should we think that absolute legal norms could arise from relativistic human situations? Archimedes said that if he were given a lever long enough and a fulcrum outside the world he could move it – but the *sine qua non* is that the fulcrum be located outside the limited world of human experience.

On this basis, religious traditions have asserted that their revelations (Bible, Qur'an) constitute that transcendent source of absolute ethical principles and human rights ... Christians affirm not only that the Old and New Testaments constitute the transcendent basis of an absolute ethic (the Ten Commandments, the Sermon on the Mount) but also that a personal relationship with Jesus Christ is the only way to transform human nature so that the human being will indeed consider the rights of others as deserving of equal recognition with her own rights.

But religious declarations certainly cannot be accepted on the basis of the claims themselves. After all, the religions of the world present views of the world which are mutually incompatible, so they cannot all be true. Thus the student must pose the key epistemological question: Is there any way to test these incompatible revelational claims to see if any one of them might be veracious? Were the latter to be the case, a solution to the problem of justifying human rights would indeed be possible.[13]

But what of Gregory's second point – that the modern loss of meaningful transcendence is ultimately the product of the Reformation?

The fallacy here is that of *post hoc, ergo propter hoc*. No doubt, the modern secular belief system arose from Enlightenment ideologies in the 18th century; but was "the Age of Reason" the *logical consequence* of Reformation

---

[13] John Warwick Montgomery, "The Need for Philosophical Sophistication in Human Rights Teaching," in his *Christ As Centre and Circumference* (Bonn, Germany: Verlag für Kultur und Wissenschaft, 2012), pp.206-207.

beliefs? Gregory is careful to say that the modern dilemma was but an "unintended" product of the Reformation; but was it a *necessitarian product of the Reformation at all*?

Suppose the worldview of the Enlightenment did not follow from the Reformation, but was in fact in diametric contrast to it and arose from other ideological roots. Were that so, the Reformation could not legitimately be blamed for the modern inability to establish a satisfactory value system for society. This is what we shall argue here.

What are the characteristics of modern secularism? Gregory properly describes them: "there are such things as persons and they have such things as rights." The modern secularist holds in principle to the values of "self-discipline, self-denial, self-sacrifice, ethical responsibility for others, duty to one's community, commitment to one's spouse and children." But modern secular liberalism attempts to ground these rights and responsibilities in individual autonomy: "it does not prescribe what citizens should believe, how they should live, or what they should care about."

Was this the Reformation position? The answer lies in Luther's celebrated "Here I Stand" declaration before the Holy Roman Emperor Charles V at the Diet of Worms:

> Unless I am convinced by the testimonies of the Holy Scriptures or evident reason (for I believe in neither the Pope nor councils alone, since it has been established that they have often erred and contradicted themselves), I am bound by the Scriptures that I have adduced, and my conscience has been taken captive by the Word of God; and I am neither able nor willing to recant, since it is neither safe nor right to act against conscience.[14]

Note well: the authority appealed to here is *not* conscience: it is "Holy Scripture," "the word of God." Luther is not calling for anarchy based on personal conviction. He is calling on the authorities to substitute one authority for another – or, better, to return Christendom to its original authority, not an ecclesiastical institution but Holy Scripture, the written word of God.

Every major Reformer – whether Lutheran, Calvinist, or Anglican – took precisely that position. One can rarely find autonomous, conscience-driven theologies in the Reformation era, and then only at the periphery of the so-called Anabaptist, radical Reformation. One must move to the 18th-century Enlightenment (Thomas Paine *et al.*) for such notions.

---

[14] WA 7, 836-38. See Montgomery, *Crisis in Lutheran Theology* (2 vols. in 1; new ed.; Irvine, CA: NRP Books/1517.The Legacy Project, 2017), *passim.*

So how does one make the Reformers the "inadvertent" source of modern autonomy? Presumably, because their authority (Scripture) was thought to present a single, clear message that needed to be personally read and accepted as revelatory. This is the heart of Gregory's claim that the Reformation was the unintended source of modern secular pluralism:

> What did the Bible say? *That* was the question, and there had never been anything remotely resembling a consensual answer despite centuries of Protestant claims about scripture's perspicuity. The institutionalization of individual religious freedom, pioneered in the United States, was the definitive beginning of the end of the magisterial Reformation. It revealed what the Reformation as such produced absent the power of political authorities standing behind hermeneutic authorities: the aggregate of whatever individuals happen to prefer. This fit perfectly with the ideology of American individualism that so struck Tocqueville and other nineteenth-century European visitors to the United States. But it did not fit at all with knowledge-making ... The fissiparous particularity of Protestant truth-claims, theology, and experiential knowledge was an insuperable problem. So knowledge had to be secularized and religious truth-claims excluded from nascent academic disciplines just as religious convictions had to be privatized, indeed regarded as subjective beliefs and individual opinions no matter their content or the religious tradition in question ...
>
> [T]he Reformation is the most important distant historical source for contemporary Western hyperpluralism with respect to truth claims about meaning, morality, values, priorities, and purpose. Despite the hopes and dreams of Reformation protagonists, the result of their distinctive appeal to scripture alone was not a set of clear mandates for reforming human life according to "the Gospel," but an undesired, open-ended range of rival truth claims about answers to the Life Questions. Because what was at stake was so important, and because Christianity informed all of human life, exegetical disagreements were translated into doctrinal disagreements that were in turn expressed in socio-moral division and political contestation. Against the intention of anti-Roman reformers but as a result of their actions, the church became the churches.[15]

But was the theology of the medieval church supposed to be accepted *per se*, just because it was there – with no reflection or personal decision? Granted, baptismal regeneration may suggest such, but surely the defining theologians of the Middle Ages, such as Thomas Aquinas, insisted on the

---

[15] Gregory, *op. cit.*, pp. 355, 369.

presence of free will in conversion,[16] and medieval missionary work – one thinks of Ramón Lull's activities among Muslims – was predicated on convincing the non-Christian to accept the superiority and veracity of Christian belief.[17]

Should the Reformers, faced with the Roman Church's gross doctrinal errors touching the very way of salvation, have stayed in communion with that body simply because of its long historical existence–or because it was universally accepted in the West at the time? *Consensus gentium* does not guarantee truth (after all, medieval man universally believed that the sun went around the earth), and even in the 16th century there were two, not just one, churches – the Eastern Orthodox as well as the Roman Catholic, and that split had occurred as long ago as 1054.[18] Religious decision-making was not a Reformation innovation.

Moreover, the medieval church displayed – and the Roman Church today manifests – remarkable variety and pluralism of activities and ideas within it. Consider, on the contemporary scene, the spread from traditionalist, sacerdotalist members of the Curia to American charismatic Catholics to wild theological liberals (Hans Küng, *et al.*).[19]

Among Protestants, there was no jettisoning of authority; there was simply an attempt to return to the *fons* – the source – of proper religious authority. True, the right of private interpretation led ultimately to a variety of ecclesiastical confessions, but the only way to have prevented that would have been to deny any right of personal decision-making in the religious realm, which would surely have contradicted Jesus' teachings (Mt 23:37; Luke 13:34; John 7:17) – as well as militating against personal freedom of choice in society at large.

And the problem is not, *pace* Gregory, the Reformation's formal principle of *Sola Scriptura* and its corollary, that Scripture is in fact perspicuous.

---

[16] Cf. John Warwick Montgomery, "The Holy Spirit and the Defense of the Faith," "The Freewill Issue in Theological Perspective," "Some Remarks on Punishment and Freewill in Legal Theory & Classical Christian Theology," *Christ As Centre and Circumference (op. cit.)*, pp. 138-46, 270-85.

[17] See Montgomery, "Computer Origins and the Defense of the Faith," *ibid.*, pp. 78 ff.

[18] The fallacy of the Petrine theory defense of Roman claims may be seen in Montgomery, *The Shape of the Past* (rev. ed.; Eugene, OR: Wipf & Stock, 2008), pp. 351-57.

[19] See John Warwick Montgomery, "The Approach of New Shape Roman Catholicism to Scriptural Inerrancy: A Case Study," in his *God's Inerrant Word* (Minneapolis: Bethany, 1974), pp. 263-81; and Robert Campbell, O.P.'s companion volumes, *Spectrum of Protestant Beliefs* (Milwaukee: Bruce, 1968) and *Spectrum of Catholic Attitudes* (Milwaukee: Bruce, 1969). The present writer was a contributor to the first of these collections, which show the same spread of doctrinal views in the contemporary Roman Church as among Protestants.

As Luther pointed out, in refuting Erasmus, the difficulty does not lie with a lack of clarity on the part of Scripture but with the interpreter who will not listen to and accept the biblical message:

> The notion that in Scripture some things are recondite and all is not plain was spread by the godless Sophists (whom now you echo, Erasmus) ... I certainly grant that many passages in the Scriptures are obscure and hard to elucidate, but that is due, not to the exalted nature of their subject, but to our own linguistic and grammatical ignorance ... Who will maintain that the town fountain does not stand in the light because the people down some alley cannot see it, while everyone in the square can see it?[20]

If Scripture were really not a clear revelation, isn't it strange that all major branches of Christendom – Eastern Orthodox, Roman Catholic, and Protestant – agree on the Ecumenical Creeds (the Apostles', the Nicene, and the Athanasian) as setting forth fundamental Christian beliefs?

The explanation for the modern secular dilemma is not the Reformation's supposed advocacy of autonomy but the Enlightenment's rejection of biblical authority, followed and reinforced by biblical criticism in the 19th and 20th centuries.

Thomas Paine advocated the substitution of the "Book of Nature" for the "Book of Scripture." Sadly, though God is indeed the author of nature, nature is not in propositional form and is open to much wider diversity of interpretations than is Holy Scripture (witness contemporary cosmological theories!). And when Darwin offered an (empirically unjustified but culturally comforting) alternative of natural selection and natural "Progress," and German higher critics of Scripture provided an (empirically unjustified but presumably scientific) humanization of the biblical materials, it was easy enough to jettison God's authoritative value system for self-centred, contemporary standards.

Is there a solution? Very definitely. But it does not consist of (1) dumping the Reformation and somehow returning to the Medieval Synthesis,[21] or (2) doing little more than once again commemorating the Reformation as an heroic historical movement.

What is required is, first, focusing on what the Reformation centrally teaches: salvation by grace through faith (the material principle of all true theology) as set forth in the Holy Scriptures alone (the formal principle of

---

[20] *De servo arbitrio*, WA, 18, 606.
[21] Gregory, to his credit, realizes that that is impossible.

all veridical theology); and, secondly – no less importantly – preaching and defending these truths *for personal decision*.[22]

We perhaps made some in the audience uncomfortable with our earlier remark about the Anabaptist wing of the Reformation. Let me now balance the scale. Throughout Baptist history, the stress has been on personal decision for Christ. Baptists have always been fearful that church membership can and often does become little more than a cultural tradition, devoid of personal commitment. This is a legitimate and genuine concern, as illustrated by the "dead orthodoxy" in so many churches – and as classically critiqued by Søren Kierkegaard in his *Attack Upon "Christendom"* (represented, sadly, by the Danish State Lutheranism of his day).

This is not to denigrate infant baptism in the least. But, as Luther taught, the grace of God is not irresistible; the saving grace imparted in baptism can be lost (1 Cor. 9:27; 2 Tim. 4:10). The rite of Confirmation is supposed to make sure that those joining the church still hold to their baptismal faith. It is sad to see how many pastors allow Confirmation to become a routine, assembly-line rite of passage rather than an opportunity to confront the confirmand with the need to experience Christ personally.

Today, with the staggering pressures toward secularism arising from all quarters in our modern society, the need for the church to seek "decisions for Christ" is more important than ever. The Baptists and the Methodists became major denominations in America because they went forth into exceedingly difficult frontier conditions seeking lost souls. The evangelical revivals of the 18th and 19th centuries placed an indelible stamp on the American character – whilst many Lutherans and Anglicans were satisfied to stay on the East Coast, conducting liturgical services.[23] I had a Baptist grandmother, who introduced me to the Bible and to a religion that could not be limited to church attendance or to formal church membership.[24]

In my Lutheran circles, I am saddened by a theological current that ridicules so-called "decision theology." When teaching at the Concordia Seminary, then in Springfield, Illinois, I wandered into the student lounge and

---

[22] See John Warwick Montgomery and Gene Edward Veith (eds.), *Where Christ Is Present: A Theology for All Seasons on the 500th Anniversary of the Reformation* (Irvine, CA: NRP Books/1517.The Legacy Project, 2015).

[23] See John Warwick Montgomery, *The Shaping of America* (Minneapolis: Bethany, 1976), *passim*.

[24] John Warwick Montgomery, *Fighting the Good Fight: A Life in Defense of the Faith* (Bonn, Germany: Verlag für Kultur und Wissenschaft; Eugene, OR: Wipf & Stock, 2016).

heard students criticizing Billy Graham and his "Hour of Decision" on television. In point of fact, they were actually criticizing St Paul, who, in answer to the Philippian jailor's question, "What must I do to be saved?," gave the following straightforward answer: "Believe on the Lord Jesus and you will be saved" (Acts 16:31). The same Apostle who declared that "by grace you have been saved through faith, and that not of yourselves, lest anyone should boast" (Eph. 2:8-9) insisted on personal decision for salvation. How often Lutherans forget that in classical Lutheran theology saving faith cannot be limited to *notitia* (formal, doctrinal knowledge) or even to *assensus* (public connection with the church), but must reach the level of *fiducia* (personal trust in Jesus Christ).

"Synergism" and "works-righteousness" occur only if *after making a decision for Christ* one attributes the decision to oneself and not to the Holy Spirit – who alone saves. (In fact, this is as rare as the drowning victim's praising himself for having grabbed the life preserver thrown to him by the lifeguard.)

Ironically, preachers of every denomination expect their flock to make decisions on the basis of their sermons and counseling; surely this should suggest that there is nothing wrong with endeavouring to bring the uncommitted to a meaningful decision to centre one's life on Christ.

Listen to Luther: "Each of us is at risk in how we believe, and we must all see to it that we believe rightly. Just as nobody else can go to heaven or hell for me, so nobody else can believe or disbelieve for me.[25]

If we expect a Reformation centennial to be more than a cultural or ecclesiastical exercise, we need to present the content of the Reformation gospel for personal decision. What is the matter with evangelistic services? with door-to-door evangelism? Just because the Jehovah's Witness cult does it, should we avoid it? (The fact that Muslims brush their teeth does not suggest that Christians should pull theirs out.)

And, finally, we need to realize that a proclamation of the Reformation message without any defense will make little impact in our pluralistic world. In the modern societies of the West, the widest diversity of religious and philosophical options exists. We must therefore offer concrete, historical evidence that "God was in Christ, reconciling the world unto himself" (2 Corinthians 5:19). We must provide solid evidence of the historical and factual accuracy of the biblical documents. Otherwise, why would anyone choose the Reformation answer in preference to all the other *Weltanschauungen* available in the contemporary marketplace of ideas?

---

[25] WA 11, 264 ("Temporal Authority").

What would such a Reformation apologetic entail? The following is the key argument in outline:

1) The NT materials can be shown to be reliable historical documents (cf. Montgomery, *History, Law and Christianity*)
2) The writers can be shown to be reliable eyewitnesses (cf. Bauckham, *Jesus and the Eyewitnesses*)
3) The eyewitnesses inform us that Jesus himself claimed to be the Divine Savior
4) Jesus' claims are validated by fulfilled OT prophecies concerning him and by the miracles he performed, especially his resurrection from the dead
5) Jesus considered the OT inerrant revelation and promised his Apostles a special gift of the H.S. to recall what he had taught them (John 14:26); apostolic writings thus have the same inerrant, revelational character (including Paul's writings, since he was accepted as a genuine Apostle by the original apostolic company – see II Peter 3:15-16).
6) Conclusion: Jesus is indeed God incarnate, come to earth to die for our sins and offer us the way to eternal life; and all of Holy Scripture is God's reliable and inerrant revelation of the divine will for a fallen race.

Without a transcendental, God-breathed charter of rights, as provided in Holy Scripture, and absent the opportunity to counteract fallen man's selfcentredness through personal salvation by way of God's free grace via the Cross of Christ, there is simply no hope for the human race, individually or societally. The Reformation message and the evidence supporting its truth therefore become, not an option but the sole answer to our ideological, personal, and societal dilemmas.

We conclude with Luther's plea – more relevant now, if possible, than when it was first penned – and with a wonderful French Reformation hymn:

> Lord, keep us steadfast in Thy Word;
> Curb those who fain by craft and sword
> Would wrest the Kingdom from Thy Son
> And set at naught all He hath done.
>
> Lord Jesus Christ, Thy pow'r make known,
> For Thou art Lord of lords alone;

Defend Thy Christendom that we
May evermore sing praise to Thee.

O Comforter of priceless worth,
Send peace and unity on earth.
Support us in our final strife
And lead us out of death to life.[26]

\* \* \* \* \*

Demeure par ta grâce
Avec nous, Dieu Sauveur!
Quand l'ennemi menace,
Protège-nous, Seigneur!

Conserve ta Parole,
Parmi nous ici-bas;
Qu'elle soit la boussole
Qui dirige nos pas.

Eternelle lumière,
Dont la vive splendeur
Nous guide et nous éclaire,
Garde-nous de l'erreur[27]

---

[26] *Erhalt uns, Herr, bei deinem* Wort; trans. Catherine Winkworth. Luther's original text contained the line: "Restrain the murderous Pope and Turk" – the equivalents in the Reformation era to the secular humanism of our day that would "wrest the Kingdom from God's Son."

[27] Words: Jean-Frédéric Monnier (d. 1813); melody, Melchior Vulpius 1609 (*Christus, der ist mein Leben*).

# 14. The Apologetic Thrust of Lutheran Theology

Can the truth of Christianity be "proven" to an unbeliever? Ought the Christian try to "demonstrate" the veracity of the gospel to the non-Christian? Should one attempt to "establish evidentially" the Bible's claim to be the very word of God? Here are two representative twentieth-century Lutheran judgments on these questions:

> The certainty of Christian faith is not dependent upon the demonstrable character of divine revelation. The idea that scientific studies and investigations should provide a solid foundation for faith and give it certainty is contrary to the nature of both science and faith. If this were indeed possible, it would mean that science, within the empirical reality, which is the object of its study, could discover something of that revelation of which faith speaks. The discoveries of science would in that case verify faith. But this would obviously be to ask something of science which it cannot give without ceasing to be scientific. Whether it be a question of a scientific investigation of nature or history, such a study cannot penetrate to that which is decisive for faith – the revelation of God.[1]

> Christian theology is the ability to exhibit, or preach, the Gospel, but not to prove it true by human arguments of reason or philosophy. As the Christian theologian proclaims the truth, he wins souls for Christ, but not as he endeavors to prove true the mysteries of faith by principles of human reason. This also is the meaning of the axiom: "The best apology of the Christian religion is its proclamation." Let the Gospel be made known, and it will of itself prove its divine character. Christian apologetics has therefore only one function: it is to show the unreasonableness of unbelief. Never can it demonstrate the truth with "enticing words of man's wisdom."[2]

Only the presence of biblical citations in the second quotation and the absence of them in the first might suggest a difference in apologetic viewpoint on the part of these two theologians. The first statement derives from Gustav Aulén, the renowned spokesman for Lundensian theology, who categorically set himself against "biblicism" (the verbal inspiration

---

[1] Gustav Aulén, *The Faith of the Christian Church*, trans. Wahlstrom and Arden (Philadelphia: Fortress, 1948), 107; cf. 95-96.
[2] J. Theodore Mueller, *Christian Dogmatics*, vol. 1 (St. Louis: Concordia 1950), 109.

and infallible authority of Holy Scripture)[3] and depreciated the substitutionary ("Latin," "Anselmian") doctrine of Christ's Atonement.[4] The second affirmation expresses the viewpoint of J. Theodore Mueller, the great Missouri Synod dogmatician, who throughout his long career stood fast for the inerrancy of Scripture and the Christology of the historic church, and vigorously opposed Lundensian theology as a Lutheran variant of reformed neo-orthodoxy.

Yet the apologetic stance of these two Lutheran thinkers is virtually indistinguishable! Both claim that Christian revelation stands beyond proof and beyond demonstration – and that any attempt to offer an apologetic to establish its validity is to misunderstand the nature of the Christian gospel. As I have pointed out in other writings, very much the same antipathy to positive apologetic argument is displayed throughout contemporary Protestantism; it has been equally characteristic of the old modernism, of the Barthian "crisis theology" that reacted against modernism, of Bultmannian existentialism, and of the orthodox Calvinism and pietistic fundamentalism which have fought the errors of liberalism, neo-orthodoxy, and Bultmannianism.

The question we wish to pose in this essay is the difficult but exceedingly important one concerning the proper relation between Lutheran faith and the apologetic task: *Ought* the confessional Lutheran to feel the same antipathy toward the positive defense of the faith as is experienced by liberal Lutherans and non-Lutherans alike? Or does Lutheran theology demand an apologetic for the word as aggressive as its proclamation of the word? Should orthodox Lutheranism share the anti-apologetic bed with contemporary theology, or have we inadvertently picked up the wrong room key altogether?

## An Existential Luther with Aristotelian Followers

We are told that, as those who go by Luther's name, we should be the last to approach Christianity apologetically. Jaroslav Pelikan, in his influential little monograph, *From Luther to Kierkegaard,* maintains that the young Luther had little interest in "natural theology" – in the knowledge of God or of divine truth which can be attained by the sinner in his unregenerate state – and that even as an old man when he did deal with the question, he

---

[3] Aulén, *The Faith of the Christian Church,* 81-85.
[4] Aulén, *Christus Victor* (New York: Macmillan, 1969), *passim.* For a critique see J. W. Montgomery, ed., *Chytraeus on Sacrifice* (St. Louis: Concordia, 1962), 139ff.

orientated it "around the concept of dread."[5] In other words, Luther's fundamental approach was not objective, cognitive, factual, but rather existential: he approached truth-questions, as Søren Kierkegaard would later, in terms of dynamic, personal experience. We are told that Kierkegaard's aphorism that "truth is subjectivity" strikes closer to Luther's worldview than any kind of objective arguments for Christianity's validity. Was Kierkegaard not expressing the spirit of Luther's position when he said that to question or defend the truth of Christ is like a husband seriously asking himself whether he could love another woman – even to ask such a question labels his love as unreal?

Pelikan's sketch of the history of theological ideas between Luther and Kierkegaard presents essentially an arid territory of orthodox Lutheran dogmaticians who, while rejecting Aristotelian adulterations of the content of Christian theology, unwittingly incorporate Aristotelian philosophical methodology into their labors, thereby eventually corrupting Luther's existential insights and paving the way for the victory of rationalism. The stress on proofs for God's existence in such later orthodox dogmaticians as David Hollaz is clear evidence that Luther's disinterest in "natural theology" did not long remain among his followers.

One of the chief sources of Pelikan's interpretation, as evidenced by his own bibliographical notes, was the brief section on natural theology at the outset of Werner Elert's *Morphologie des Luthertums*. There Elert – who himself relies heavily on Ernst Troeltsch's *Vernunft und Offenbarung bei Joh. Gerhard und Melanchthon* (1891) – claims that Philipp Melanchthon inconsistently maintained in his *Apology to the Augsburg Confession* that "God can be known in no other way than through the Word," yet he "already accepted the essential elements of the later 'natural theology'" and "demonstrates the natural proofs of the existence of God."[6] From this point things went from bad to worse, both in Melanchthon himself and in the orthodox theologians of the next century and a half: Chemnitz, Gerhard, Calov, Hollaz, Baier. (Only Flacius deserves real praise, for he unqualifiedly condemned sinful man's *ratio*.) Tragically, dogmaticians such as these set forth positive apologetic arguments for biblical truth, and the Lutheran astronomer-mathematician Johann Kepler actually endeavored to harmonize scientific discoveries with the word of God! "How far away from Luther we now are!" cries Elert, and concludes:

---

[5] Jaroslav Pelikan, *From Luther to Kierkegaard* (St. Louis: Concordia, 1950), 23.
[6] Werner Elert, *The Structure of Lutheranism*, vol. 1, trans. Walter A. Hansen (St. Louis: Concordia, 1962), 51. The English translation is preceded by revealing commendatory introductions by Pelikan and ALC theologian Robert C. Schultz.

The development of "natural theology" is the march of history from Luther's primal experience (*Urerlebnis*) up to the Enlightenment. It ended with the ominous error that Christian faith in God and "natural knowledge of God" are essentially identical. For the naive apologists, for many a dogmatician, even for many a politician who wanted to "preserve religion for the people," this was a comfort and a satisfaction. For the church Philistine, as Tholuck addressed him, it was reason for no longer knowing of an anguished conscience. But then came Ludwig Feuerbach. Then came Karl Marx and Nietzsche. They showed that the knowledge of "natural" man arrives at a totally different result. And when it came to the great test of the revelation of God's goodness, faithfulness, and mercy on land, at sea, and in the air – which Zöckler and many others taught – the result was decidedly negative. Was it surprising that the generation of the war and the collapse declared the Christian belief in God to be a delusion because it had been refuted by the terrors and the fate that they had experienced?[7]

The Bultmannian and post-Bultmannian Lutherans carry this line of argument even farther. Does Bultmann tear away all objective grounding for faith by declaring that the ostensively historical descriptions of our Lord's miraculous acts are really the mythological garb in which the primitive church clothed its existential experience of "authentic self-understanding"? Fine! In this "one sees in unmistakable outlines the shadow of Luther,"[8] for Bultmann is removing the objective, intellectual props by which modern man may attempt to "justify himself," even as Luther removed the props of moral works-righteousness from sixteenth-century man. Bultmann thus continues Luther's task of stripping away all the externals from faith – leaving it as it really is, a naked leap, which can never be aided, much less established, by objective evidence or factual demonstration. This viewpoint has been expressed with particular forcefulness by such post-Bultmannian advocates of the new hermeneutic as Ernst Käsemann:

> Neither miracle nor the canon nor the Jesus of history is able to give security to our faith. For our faith there can be no objectivity in this sense. That is the finding which New Testament scholarship has made plain in its own fashion. But this finding is only the obverse of that acknowledgment which Luther's exposition of the third article of the Creed expresses.[9]

---

[7] Elert, *The Structure of Lutheranism*, 53, 57-58.
[8] Robert Scharlemann, "Shadow on the Tomb," *Dialog* 1 (Spring, 1962), 22-29.
[9] Ernst Käsemann, *Exegetisch Versuche und Besinnungen*, vol. 1, 2d ed. (Göttingen, 1960), 236.

In sum, Luther's central conviction that a man is justified by grace through faith and his concomitant refusal to confuse law with gospel supposedly eliminated for him, if not objective grounds for faith, at least all uses of objective evidences in "defending" the faith. Luther's immediate followers, however, allegedly returned like the dog to its Aristotelian vomit in endeavoring to establish the truth of faith and to convince others of its veracity by objective argument. Such argumentation is foreign to true Lutheran belief, we are told, and must be excised as a cancer.

## Luther and the Classical Dogmaticians Revisited

Energy, existential or otherwise, need not be expended here in refuting the contention that Luther had no objective grounding for his faith. Merely his affirmation at Worms – "I am bound by the Scriptures that I have adduced, and my conscience has been taken captive by the word of God" – should be enough to show that for Luther truth was hardly "subjectivity." For those interested in a detailed analysis of this issue, a previous essay of mine should prove useful.[10] Our task here is the more specialized one of determining to what extent Luther's theology allows for and encourages the *apologetic use* of Christianity's factual character in setting the faith before an unbelieving world. Granted that for Luther God's word was objectively true; does it follow that its truth can be established and defended in the marketplace of ideas, or is the sinful character of the human situation an absolute barrier to such an operation? This is the question before us – and we shall now take it up (not forgetting, however, the sobering consideration that the strongest opponents of a Lutheran apologetic are those who base their anti-apologetic stance on the conviction that Christianity is, after all, non-objective!).

Even the reading of Pelikan leaves us a bit shaky as to the dichotomy between an allegedly existential Luther and his Aristotelian-apologetic followers. In Luther, admits Pelikan, "we do have at least one passage in which he expounds what virtually amounts to an argument [for God's existence] from the analogy of being. The detailed commentary on Genesis, our chief source for the old Luther, deals with natural theology several

---

[10] J. W. Montgomery, "Luther's Hermeneutic vs. the New Hermeneutic," in *In Defense of Martin Luther* (Milwaukee: Northwestern Publishing House, 1970), 40-85. For other publications of this essay in English, and for published versions in German and French, see the "Acknowledgments" in the same volume.

times."[11] But this apologetic emphasis is attributed to "the old Luther" – not to the Reformer in his theological prime.

We could answer with E. M. Plass that Luther's Genesis commentary comprises the "longest and, in many respects, the maturest of his lectures."[12] However, this approach is unnecessary, for, as Luther scholars such as Philip S. Watson have shown, the Reformer's concern with natural theology was by no means limited to his later years. As early as 1525, Luther is expressly teaching in *The Bondage of the Will* that "the knowledge of predestination and of God's prescience has been left in the world [after the fall] no less certainly than the notion of the Godhead itself."[13] In his Galatians commentary (1531) – considered by many to be the greatest of all Luther's writings – he condemns all attempts by the sinner to justify himself on the basis of the natural knowledge of God, while at the same time stoutly defending the existence of such natural knowledge and encouraging the Christian to dispute intelligently with unbelievers on the basis of it:

> When you are to dispute with Jews, Turks, Papists, Heretics, etc., concerning the power, wisdom, and majesty of God, employ all your intelligence and industry to that end, and be as profound and as subtle a disputer as you can.[14]

> Such arguments [arguments for divine truth based on human and earthly analogy] are good when they are grounded upon the ordinance of God. But when they are taken from men's corrupt affections, they are naught.[15]

Though all efforts at self-salvation through natural theology must be unqualifiedly condemned, Luther sees the natural knowledge of God and of his law inscribed on every man's heart as the point of contact – the common ground – which makes the evangelistic task possible.

> If the natural law were not written and given in the heart by God one would have to preach long before the conscience were smitten. One would have to preach to an ass, horse, ox, or cow for a hundred thousand years before they accepted the law, although they have ears, eyes and heart as a man. They too can hear it, but it does not enter their heart. Why? What is wrong? Their

---

[11] Pelikan, *From Luther to Kierkegaard*, 22. The Genesis commentary references are to be found in WA 42:291-92, and 374.
[12] E. M. Plass, ed., *What Luther Says*, vol. 3 (St. Louis: Concordia, 1959), 1618.
[13] WA 18:618.
[14] Luther's comment on Galatians 1:3.
[15] Comment on Galatians 3:15. Cf. Luther's *Tischreden* assertion that he found Cicero's ideological argument for God's existence very moving.

soul is not so formed and fashioned that such a thing might enter it. But a man, when the law is set before him, soon says: Yes, it is so, he cannot deny it. He could not be so quickly convinced, were it not written in his heart before.[16]

P. S. Watson summarizes the case in the best traditions of dry Oxbridge humor:

> He [Luther] had, after all, read his New Testament; and the first two chapters of the Epistle to the Romans, along with other passages dear to the natural theologians, could not escape his notice. He had, furthermore, too much reverence for the sacred text to ignore such passages, or to dismiss them as unimportant.[17]

*However*, retorts the anti-apologetic Lutheran, does this really penetrate to the heart of Luther s position? Granted that he held to natural knowledge of God; he nonetheless refuses to allow such knowledge a place in salvation. As specialists on Luther's view of "reason" have pointed out (one thinks especially of B. A. Gerrish[18] and Robert H. Fischer[19]), Luther indeed encourages rational operations in the secular realm (the earthly kingdom) but categorically rejects reason as a normative rule in the realm of salvation (the spiritual kingdom). Reason must never be allowed to govern or restrict God's word; where this occurs, reason becomes Frau Hulda and Madam Jezebel – the devil's whore.

> The Kingdom of Reason embraces such human activities as caring for a family, building a home, serving as a magistrate, and (as Rörer's MS. adds) looking after cows. All that can be demanded of me by God in such a sphere of activity is that I should "do my best". The important thing not to overlook is that this Kingdom has its boundaries; the error of the sophists is that they carry the saying "to do one's best" *(facere quod in se est)* over into the *regnum spirituale,* in which a man is able to do nothing but sin. In outward affairs or in the affairs of the body man is master: "He is hardly", as Luther drily remarks, "the cow's servant." But in spiritual affairs he *is* a servant or slave, "sold under sin". "For the Kingdom of Human Reason must be separated as far as possible from the Spiritual Kingdom."[20]

---

[16] WA 16:447.
[17] P. S. Watson, *Let God Be God!* (London: Epworth, 1947), 84. See also Paul Althaus, *Die Theologie Martin Luthers,* 2d ed. (Gütersloh, 1963), ch. 3.
[18] B. A. Gerrish, *Grace and Reason* (Oxford: Clarendon Press, 1962).
[19] R. H. Fischer, "A Reasonable Luther," in *Reformation Studies: Essays in Honor of Roland H. Bainton,* ed. F. H. Littell (Richmond, VA: John Knox, 1962), 30-45.
[20] Gerrish, *Grace and Reason,* 72-73.

And what possible good can an apologetic do when, in Luther's thinking, natural knowledge of God offers no substitute whatever for the Word of God in Jesus Christ? Knowledge of the *Deus absconditus* can only impart terror; the *Deus revelatus* – God in Christ – offers the sole avenue to peace and salvation, and he is accessible, not to reason and demonstration, but to the eyes of faith. Thus even Christ's miracles did not convince those who would not accept his word: "When miracles are performed, they are appreciated only by the pious."[21] One must come in faith to the lowly Christ of the manger and there, paradoxically, one will meet the divine Savior. Luther's theology calls for proclamation of this truth, not for an impossible defense of it which invariably appeals to the "natural man" desiring to justify himself.[22]

Here we arrive at the core of the matter. Luther very definitely distinguished two kingdoms, the earthly and the spiritual, and in fact considered this distinction to be one of the most valuable aspects of his theology.[23] But does this distinction dichotomize the world into a secular realm where reason and proof operate, and a spiritual realm where evidence has no place? This is precisely the impression given by virtually all modern interpreters of Luther. Especially revealing is Robert Fischer's declaration that for Luther "such insights [reason, experience, common sense] operate in what would later be called the phenomenal realm; they do not penetrate the noumenal."[24] The use of the terms "noumenal" and "phenomenal" (borrowed from the Kantian critical philosophy, which is itself dependent upon a Platonic separation of the realm of "ideas" or "ideals" from the phenomenal world of sense experience) is most significant. Luther is painlessly being absorbed into the idealistic-dualistic frame of reference characteristic of virtually all contemporary Protestant thought. Why can neoorthodox and other varieties of current theology confidently hold to their "theological insights" while simultaneously accepting the most destructive judgments of biblical critics regarding alleged factual errors in the biblical material and the supposed historical unreliability of the scriptural accounts of our Lord's life? Simply because the (noumenal) truth of

---

[21] WA 25:240 (a comment on Isa 37:30).
[22] So Regin Prenter interprets Luther in *Spiritus Creator*, 2d ed. (Copenhagen, 1946), especially chaps. 2 and 3. *Ratio* and *lex* are presented as "belonging together;" faith is "in contrast to all *sensus*" (i.e., to all "experience which relies on that which can be observed in the visible world"); God's revelation in flesh as the Christ "is placed in absolute opposition to our human *sensus* and *ratio*; "theological epistemology" consists of the *transformatio sensus* by the Creator Spirit.
[23] WA 38:102 ("Defense against Duke George," 1533).
[24] Fischer, "A Reasonable Luther," 39.

theological statements, we are told, is in no way dependent on the phenomenal, secular issues connected with biblical history. After all, the Bible conveys *religious,* not scientific or historical truth! "The Bible is not a textbook of science," etc.

Is Luther to be assimilated to the Platonic-Kantian perspective? The answer will depend squarely on what kind of *connection* Luther saw between the two kingdoms. If he in fact kept them in water-tight compartments, then a positive apologetic originating in the secular realm could not in principle justify truths lying in the spiritual sphere. The mere fact of Luther's belief in a natural theology, in the sense previously shown, strongly suggests some kind of connecting link between the kingdoms in his thinking; but what precisely is the nature of the link?

Troeltsch (whom we have already met in passing as one of the sources of Elert's and Pelikan's anti-apologetic view of Luther) is best known in Reformation studies for his negative views of Luther's social ethic.[25] He claims that Luther's theology produced social quietism because Luther never connected the theological insights operative in his spiritual kingdom with the activities of the earthly kingdom. This allegation has been decisively refuted by George Forell, who shows that, in the first place, Luther's two kingdoms are connected as to origin, for "these two separate realms are ultimately both God's realms"; and, even more important, they are linked in practice by the individual Christian believer, who is a citizen of both simultaneously ("Luther explains that a point of contact between the secular realm and the spiritual realm exists in the person of the individual Christian").[26] A parallel vindication of Luther is needed epistemologically.

As the individual Christian unites the two kingdoms in his person, thereby bridging the sociological gap between them, so *the Incarnate Christ himself* links the two realms epistemologically. The incarnational center of Luther's theology eliminates entirely the possibility of making him an advocate of "two-fold truth" – a kind of sixteenth-century Averroës. In the sharpest possible opposition to Platonic dualism – and to the related modern dichotomies of Kantianism and of Lessing's ditch between historical fact and absolute truth – Luther declares that Jesus Christ, in his own person, offers immediate access to God. One begins with the earthly and finds

---

[25] See Ernst Troeltsch, *The Social Teaching of the Christian Churches,* vol. 2, trans. Olive Wyon (Chicago: University of Chicago Press, 1981), 461-575. Cf. K. Penzel, "Ernst Troeltsch on Luther," in *Interpreters of Luther: Essays in Honor of Wilhelm Pauck,* ed. Jaroslav Pelikan (Philadelphia: Fortress, 1968), 275-303.

[26] G. W. Forell, *Faith Active In Love* (Minneapolis: Augsburg, 1959), 121, 149.

the heavenly. Luther's words should be carefully pondered in the final version of his Galatians commentary:

> Paul is in the habit of linking together Jesus Christ and God the Father so frequently: he wants to teach us the Christian religion, which does not begin at the very top, as all other religions do, but at the very bottom. Paul commands us to ascend on the ladder of Jacob, at the top of which God Himself is resting, and the feet of which touch the earth next to the head of Jacob (Gen. 28:12f.). Therefore if you would think or treat of your salvation, you must stop speculating about the majesty of God; you must forget all thought of good works, tradition, philosophy, and even the divine Law. Hasten to the stable and the lap of the mother and apprehend this infant Son of the Virgin. Look at Him being born, nursed, and growing up, walking among men, teaching, dying, returning from the dead, and being exalted above all the heavens, in possession of power over all. In this way you can cause the sun to dispel the clouds and can avoid all fear and all errors too. And this view of God will keep you on the right path.[27]

Luther insists that the search for God begin at the connecting link between earth and heaven, which exists at the point of the incarnation. There we find a genuine human being ("nursed and growing up," "dying") but also very God of very God ("returning from the dead and being exalted above all the heavens"). "Philosophy," which starts elsewhere, must be forgotten; absolute truth is available only here. Why does Luther concentrate relatively little on traditional proofs for God's existence (even though he considered such argumentation valid)? Because for him it did not constitute the proper point of departure:

> If you begin your study of God by trying to determine how He rules the world, how He burned Sodom and Gomorrah with infernal fire, whether He has elected this person or that, and thus begin with the works of the High Majesty, then you will presently break your neck and be hurled from heaven, suffering a fall like Lucifer's. For such procedure amounts to beginning on top and building the roof before you have laid the foundation. Therefore, letting God do whatever He is doing, you must begin at the bottom and say: I do not want to know God until I have first known this Man; for so read the passages of Scripture: "I am Way, the Truth, and the Life"; again: "No man cometh unto the Father but by Me" (John 14:6). And there are more passages to the same effect.[28]

---

[27] WA 40/1:79ff. (published 1535 and 1538).
[28] WA 36:61 ff. (sermon of 6 Jan. 1532, on Micah 5:1).

Luther is not anti-apologetic; he is, rather, exceedingly careful in his starting-point. The *point de depart* must be Christ; in methodology one must "begin at the bottom" with the incarnation; and no reasoning (or anything else, for that matter!) can be legitimately regarded as ground for works-righteousness or self-justification.

Admittedly, Luther did not build a formal apologetic from this incarnational starting-point. His task was not to defend the soundness of the biblical history or of its picture of Christ. In the sixteenth century, no reputable theologians of any school of thought questioned the veracity of the scriptural text. The cold winds of rationalistic biblical criticism had not yet begun to blow. (To be sure, Renaissance humanists such as Lorenzo Valla would later be regarded as precursors of such criticism, but they constituted no negative apologetic threat to biblical authority in Luther's time.) Luther often said that he did his best work when angry; that is, he recognized that his theological activities were determined in large part by the contemporary pressures upon him. These pressures came not from unbelievers doubting the authority of the word but from churchmen who misinterpreted it. Thus Luther's battles were necessarily hermeneutic rather than apologetic in character.

Moreover, since he was especially confronted by the traditional Romanist on the right and the fanatic *Schwärmer* on the left, both of whom appealed to extra-biblical miracles in their midst, Luther preferred to fight on the common ground of the word, emphasizing the truth – which must never be forgotten apologetically in our contingent world! – that those who *want* to discount the clear evidence of God's miraculous dealings can always find some way (improbable though it may be) of doing so.

But the fundamental themes of Luther's theology were most definitely hospitable to a positive apologetic and bore fruit apologetically when, not so many years later, the very authority of the word came under fire. We have already stressed the central role the incarnation played in Luther's thought – eliminating theological schizophrenia and offering a bridge from ordinary human experience to the divine truth of God's revelation. Related themes of great apologetic consequence in his theology include (1) his psychosomatic *holism* (Luther's refusal, in debate with Zwingli and others, to separate Christ's spirit from his body; he thereby avoided the trap of "spiritualist" theology which is in the last analysis unverifiable and indefensible – as was the claim of Reformed modernists in the last century that Christ rose from the dead "spiritually" but not necessarily in body);[29]

---

[29] See J. W. Montgomery, "Inspiration and Inerrancy: A New Departure," in *Crisis in Lutheran Theology*, vol. 1, 2d ed. (Minneapolis: Bethany, 1973), 15-44.

(2) Luther's constant epistemological insistence on the *objectivity* of Christian truth (his repeated assertions that to find the true meaning of the gospel one must always go from "the outward to the inward" and that the gospel lies entirely *extra nos* not only precluded subjectivism and auto-salvation, but also provided the foundation for the teaching of the orthodox Lutheran dogmaticians that *notitia* – objective fact – must always ground *fiducia* – personal, subjective commitment – and that Christian heart conviction can be justified by external evidence);[30] (3) Luther's *sacramental teaching* (his firm maintenance of the *finitum est capax infiniti* principle places him most definitely outside the Platonist camp and opens the way to the widest variety of apologetic operations, since every fact in the world – "even the most insignificant leaf of a tree," to use Luther's own expression – becomes a potential avenue to Christ);[31] and, (4) finally, his *inductive methodology* (Luther's requirement that one discover what Scripture is actually saying and not force it into alien categories – such as Zwingli's metaphysical speculations about the nature of "bodies" – made possible the defense of the faith in a world about to recognize the necessity of open, inductive, scientific procedure in the discovery of truth. Those who followed Luther's hermeneutic, as opposed to the deductive model of Ramist Calvinism, were thus – as in the case of Tycho Brahe and Kepler – at the forefront of both scientific advance and the apologetic reconciliation of Scripture and scientific discovery).[32]

Though not himself an apologist in the strict sense, Luther provided, through such theological insights, the basic orientation necessary for the apologetic emphases of the classical Lutheran dogmaticians. Elert finds it especially galling to admit that in regard to the efforts of the dogmaticians and Lutheran scientists such as Kepler to harmonize Science and Scripture, "Luther had led the way with related interpretations of Genesis."[33] But is it not far more reasonable to see a positive relationship between the apologetic activity of the great Lutheran theologians following Luther and the work of Luther himself, rather than to claim that somehow all of these theologians – who were evidently trying to be faithful to the great Reformer

---

[30] See J. W. Montgomery, "The Theologian's Craft," in *Suicide of Christian Theology* (Minneapolis: Bethany, 1970), 267-313; this essay has been reprinted in Montgomery, *Christ As Centre and Circumference* (Bonn, Germany: Verlag für Kultur und Wissenschaft, 2012), pp. 40-77.
[31] See J. W. Montgomery, "Cross, Constellation, and Crucible," in *In Defense of Martin Luther*, 87-94.
[32] Montgomery, "Cross, Constellation, and Crucible," 94-113.
[33] Elert, *The Structure of Lutheranism*, 57.

– somehow managed to pervert his theology by latching on to peripheral aberrations in his thought?

Even Elert and Pelikan have to admit that hardly a great name in Lutheran dogmatics from Luther's time to the eighteenth century disregarded "natural theology" and the objective defense of Christian truth. The following concise apologetic bio-bibliography should offer sufficiently intimidating evidence in this regard; the citations, taken together, constitute a veritable catalog of apologetic argumentation by the sixteenth- and seventeenth-century Lutheran fathers:

Chemnitz (1522-1586): *Loci Theologici* (Frankfurt & Wittenberg, 1653), Pt. 1, pp. 19ff. ("De notitia Dei"); *Examen Concilii Tridentini*, ed. Preuss (Leipzig, 1915), pp. 6ff. ("De Sacra Scriptura").

Heerbrand (1521-1600): *Compendium theologiae* (Leipzig, 1585), pp. 33ff.

A. Hunnius (1550-1603): *Tractatus de sacrosancta maiestate, autoritate, fide ac certitudine Sacrae Scripturae* (Frankfurt, 1591), passim.

Hafenreffer (1561-1619): *Loci theologici*, 3d ed., (Tübingen, 1603), pp. 30ff.

Gerhard (1582-1637): *Loci Theologici*, vol. 1, ed. Frank (Leipzig, 1885), pp. 266ff. (on the question of God's existence), pp. 25ff. (on the authority, canonicity, and reliability of the biblical books).[34]

J. V. Andreae (1586-1654): *Sol veritatis sive religionis christianae certitudo*, in his *Rei christianae & literariae subsidia* (Tübingen, 1642), pp. 1-120. (The *Sol veritatis* is an abridgement of Hugo Grotius' *De veritate religionis christianae*, "commonly held to be the pioneer work in modern apologetics."[35])

---

[34] An examination of these sections of Gerhard's *Loci* will reveal how wide of the mark is Robert Scharlemann's attempt, in his book, *Thomas Aquinas and John Gerhard* (New Haven: Yale University Press, 1964) to relate Gerhard to Kant's critical philosophy, modern German existentialism, and Bultmannian theology by finding in him a dualistic separation between an alleged finite realm of formal, conceptual, objective knowledge and the realm of faith where only the "dialectical word" and "acoustic knowledge" hold sway (see especially pp. 28-37).

[35] J. H. Crehan, "Apologetics," in *A Catholic Dictionary of Theology*, vol. 1 (London, 1962), 117. On Andreae and his interest in Grotius' apologetic, see J. W. Montgomery, *Cross and Crucible: Johann Valentin Andreae (1586-1654), Phoenix of the Theologians*, vol. 1 ("International Archives of the History of Ideas," 55; The Hague: Nijhoff, 1971), 42, 90-91.

Calov (1612-1686): *Systema locorum theologicorum* (Wittenberg, 1655-1677), *loci* on God (e.g., Pt. 2, pp. 61-86) and Holy Scripture.

Quenstedt (1617-1688): *Theologia didactico-polemica* (Wittenberg, 1685), pp. 97-102 ("An per alia κριτηρια persuaderi possit Sac. Scripturae autoritas?"), 250 ff. ("De Deo, ejusque naturali notitia").

Baier (1647-1695): *Compendium theologiae positivae,* ed. Walther, vol. 1 (St. Louis, 1879), pp. 121-31 (catalog of arguments leading to *fides humana,* with references to apologetic arguments in still other dogmaticians of classical Lutheran orthodoxy – not included here for want of space – e.g., Huelsemann and Dannhauer).

Hollaz (1648-1713): *Examen theologicum acroamaticum* (Stockholm & Leipzig, 1750), pp. 106ff. (the external evidences of the divine origin of Holy Writ), 188ff. (the natural knowledge of God).[36]

It will be noted that these citations range across the entire period of Lutheran orthodoxy, beginning with the generation of Luther's and Melanchthon's own students. Moreover, the list could be readily extended by the addition of the names of exegetes such as Chytraeus (of whom Elert says sarcastically that he finds "in every chapter of the First Book of Moses the proof for one or more *loci* of dogmatics"[37]) and authors of works defending the Bible against charges of contradiction and error (e.g., Andreas Althamer, whose *Conciliationes locorum Scripturae* of 1527 went through at least sixteen editions).

But did these Lutheran apologists not inevitably weaken the biblical picture of man's total depravity, deemphasize the scriptural teaching concerning the Holy Spirit's work in salvation, and introduce a subtle synergism into the preaching of the gospel of divine grace? Not at all. They recognized (though Elert seemed to have difficulty in doing so) that the Flacian alternative to the view that man retained his thinking and reasoning process after the fall is nothing less than heresy; for if original sin meant the loss of the very image of God in man (including the loss of his rational faculty), man would have ceased to be man, no subsequent revelation could even in principle have been communicated to man, and Christ

---

[36] Cf. J. Pelikan, "Natural Theology in David Hollaz," *Concordia Theological Monthly* 15 (1947), 253-63. See also, at the close of the era of classical Lutheran orthodoxy, H. G. Masius, *A Defense of the Lutheran Faith on the Eve of Modern Times,* trans. and ed. John Warwick Montgomery (Milwaukee: Northwestern Publishing House, 2016).

[37] Elert, *The Structure of Lutheranism,* 57.

could not even have become man without becoming an irrational sinner! In retaining Luther's view of the incarnation as the center of theology, the orthodox dogmaticians rightly opposed any Flacian attempt to dehumanize man by a concept of the fall that would lead to a loss of man's ability to distinguish truth from falsehood in secular matters or (which is the same thing) to distinguish true from false claims that God was in fact incarnate in the secular sphere.

Nor did this apologetic approach produce a "de-pneumatized" theology. The dogmaticians rightly maintained that the *fides humana* or "historical faith" could not in itself save. *Notitia* is possessed by the devils also, who tremble but are not saved because of it. There must be the personal commitment – the commitment of the whole person – to Christ for salvation, and that is brought about solely by the Spirit's work. At the same time, however, the orthodox theologians correctly refused to say (as the modern neoorthodox do) that this personal commitment through the work of the Holy Spirit somehow "produces" the *notitia* or offers the only evidence of its reality. Hardly! The facts of God's existence and of his incarnate revelation in Jesus Christ stand as objectively true and evidentially compelling wholly apart from belief in them; faith in no sense creates their facticity. They stand over and against man, judging him by their sheer veracity and compelling force – and unless he volitionally refuses to believe, and goes against all sound reasoning in so doing, they will move him to a Spirit-produced conversion and living relationship with Jesus Christ.

"Synergism"? Hardly, for everything is done by God, not by man. The evidential facts are God's work, and the sinner's personal acceptance of them and of the Person on whom they center is entirely the product of the Holy Spirit. To argue that the Lutheran dogmaticians fell into synergism because they defended the faith and expected a rational response from the sinner would require our condemning their *preaching* as well (and, indeed, all Christian preaching), on the ground that it presupposes a responsible decision on the sinner's part. But the same Paul who asserted unqualifiedly that men are saved by grace alone (Eph 2:8, 9) told the Philippian jailer to "believe on the Lord Jesus Christ" (Acts 16:31), defended God's truth in philosophical terms on the Areopagus (Acts 17) and cited historical evidence for Christ's resurrection in conjunction with his very statement of the nature of the gospel (1 Cor 15). All appeals to the sinner, whether in evangelistic preaching, or in evidential argument, must assume the existence of rational faculties to permit communication at all; synergism exists only when, following conversion, the justified man is led to believe that in any way *whatever* (rational, moral, volitional) he contributed to his own salvation. Lutheran theology particularly – in comparison with other theological traditions – keeps the knife-edge of this mystery sharp, thereby making possible a most aggressive apologetic combined with a most salutary theocentrism.

## Agony in Search of the Ecstasy: the Contemporary Mission Field

And yet, our anti-apologetic Lutheran offers his final counter: Surely the "defense" of Christianity violates the most fundamental aspect of Lutheran theology, the law-gospel principle! When arguments are offered for the truth of the word, sinners are led, even when the apologist does not intend it, to rely upon themselves (the misuse of the law) rather than, in realization that *lex semper accusat*, to come to God solely on the ground of his free grace (the gospel).

Let me suggest, however, that the situation is the *exact reverse* of this: the neglect of apologetics is the surest way to *confuse* law and gospel, particularly in our day.

If we go back to the beginning of this essay, we find a strange phenomenon: the orthodox Mueller and the Lundensian Aulén occupying the same anti-apologetic bed. Both argue that "proof" is incapable of being marshaled to justify their positions. One bases his beliefs on an inerrant Scripture, the other upon an erring Scripture and undefined elements in the church's heritage of faith. Note that, under these conditions, an individual standing outside these two commitments has no way of "testing the spirits" to see which view, if either, is worthy of his commitment. "Begin with inerrant Scripture!" cries Mueller. "Begin with my understanding of 'the faith of the Christian Church'!" cries Aulén. In the absence of an apology that will make sense to the uncommitted, it is impossible, even in principle, to decide between these views. But if this is where the religious question is left, then the non-Christian will make an *arbitrary* decision – which will be dependent on *himself alone* (not on evidence outside himself) – and his commitment (even if to the true position) will be man-centered and therefore *legalistic*. The neglect of an apologetic for Christian truth thus inevitably confuses law with gospel by turning gospel into arbitrary, self-centered law. Only a genuine apologetic based on external, objective fact as presented in general and special revelation preserves religious decision from arbitrariness, keeps the gospel truly *gospel*, and (to use Watson's felicitous phrase) "lets God be God."

Moreover, let us note well that the options before the unbeliever today are by no means limited to a Mueller and to an Aulén. Ours is an age of religious cacophony, as was the Roman Empire of Christ's time. From agnosticism to Hegelianism, from devil-worship to scientific rationalism, from theosophical cults to philosophies of process: virtually any worldview conceivable is offered to modern man in the pluralistic marketplace of ideas.[38] Our age is indeed in ideological and societal agony, grasping at anything and everything that can conceivably offer the ecstasy of a cosmic relationship or of a comprehensive *Weltanschauung*. Will Lutherans, having perhaps the strongest theological and apologetic resources in Christendom, continue to hide behind our traditions and our ecclesiastical structures, fearing the world of intellectual unbelief, or will we yield to the Holy Spirit – the Spirit of truth – who can overcome our inertia and bring us into the agoras of our time, there to establish by "many infallible proofs" the true character and message of the Unknown God?

---

[38] I have developed this point, over against the Reformed presuppositionalists Gordon Clark and Cornelius Van Til, in my essays "Gordon Clark's Historical Philosophy," in J. W. Montgomery, *Where Is History Going?* (Minneapolis: Bethany, 1972) and "Once Upon an A Priori," in J. W. Montgomery, *Faith Founded on Fact: Essays in Evidential Apologetics* (Nashville: Thomas Nelson, 1978).

# 15. Christian Apologetics in the Light of the Lutheran Confessions

"What indeed has Athens to do with Jerusalem?" queried the church father Tertullian,[1] expecting a negative as the only possible answer. In the same vein one might ask, "What indeed .has apologetics to do with the Lutheran Confessions?" A confession is, after all, a public declaration of belief, not an argument. The very title given in 1580 to the official collection of Lutheran confessional writings was *Concordia: Book of Concord* – suggesting the peace and unity of common belief, not the disputatious refutation of other viewpoints.

And even if the controversial nature of material in the *Concordia* is recognized, must one not also admit that the controversies leading up to it occurred strictly within Christendom – between the Lutherans, on the one hand, and the Roman Catholics, the Sacramentarians, etc., on the other – not between Christians and unbelievers?[2] Aside from a few passing references to the "Turks," the Lutheran Confessions seem largely unaware of the existence, beyond the confines of internal Christian doctrinal discussion, of a world of unbelief to which apologetic argument ought to be addressed. Could one not apply to the Confessions with even greater force the tongue-in-cheek remark made concerning Thomas Aquinas, that when he wrote his *Summa contra gentiles* (his apologetic against the pagans) he had never met a pagan? In short, is not the *Book of Concord* simply a compendium of Christian belief-statements, written for an audience of believers, and is not its range of controversy limited to the correction of false doctrine within the narrow sphere of Christian profession? If so, the apologetic significance of the *Concordia* would seem, *ipso facto*, to be minimal at best.

There is another side to the matter, however. It is widely agreed that even the Ecumenical Creeds of the Patristic age, which are incorporated into the *Book of Concord* and form its first section, arose in a context of disputation and set forth orthodox doctrine in specific contradistinction to such heresies as Arianism and non-Christian belief-systems as Gnosticism.[3]

---

[1] Tertullian, *De praescriptione haereticorum*, VII.
[2] Cf. Johann Georg Walch, *Introductio in Libros Ecclesiae Lutheranae Symbolicos, observationibus historicis et theologicis illustrata* (lenae [Jena]: sumtu viduae Meyer, 1732).
[3] See, inter alia, the writings of J. N. D. Kelly (*Early Christian Creeds; Early Christian Doctrines: The Athanasian Creed*).

Could not one go so far as to say that a true confession is always at the same time an apologia?

The very title of one of the chief Lutheran confessional writings, the *Apology of the Augsburg Confession*, displays a concern that goes well beyond the mere proclamation of a theological position. Professor Allbeck does not exaggerate when he declares:

> Looking back from our time to the sixteenth century, we see the Apology as an outstanding example of the theological writing of the Reformation age. Those who would sample the literary style and the patterns of thinking of that day would do well to read the Apology. ... The purpose of the Apology to defend the Confession, and with it the gospel doctrine, against a specific opponent was accompanied by a vigorous mood. For the Apology is a piece of polemical writing.[4]

Indeed, the tone of the Reformation Lutheran Confessions in general, with their constant stress on refuting "antitheses" as well as setting forth "theses," reveals a veritable preoccupation with the defense of sound teaching over against falsehood. Leonhard Hutter's great work, *Concordia concors: de origine et progressu Formulae Concordiae*, appropriately begins with a book-length "Praefatio Apologetica," refuting views such as those of the Calvinist Hospinian.[5]

And if such considerations are regarded merely as further proof that the Lutherans, even when engaged in controversy, never went beyond intra-Christian disputation, it must not be forgotten that in those days doctrinal dispute was taken so seriously that particularly offensive views, even though maintained by professing Christians, were refuted as non-Christian. At Marburg Luther did not shrink from declaring that the sacramentarian views of Zwingli manifested another Christ from his own, and the Confessions retain this same perspective.[6] The *Book of Concord*, holding that justification by grace through faith is the "article by which the church stands or falls," classes Roman Catholic doctrinal works-righteousness as nothing short of Antichristic. When the Lutheran Confessions engage in apologetic controversy, they speak not primarily to minor internal differences within Christendom but more especially to fundamental issues dividing the true church from varieties of pseudo-Christian religiosity. The

---

[4] W. D. Allbeck, *Studies in the Lutheran Confessions* (Philadelphia: Muhlenberg Press, 1952), pp. 142-43.

[5] Leonhard Hutter, *Concordia concors: de origine et progressu Formulae Concordiae* (Witebergae [Wittenberg]: Clement Berger, 1614).

[6] See Hermann Sasse, *This Is My Body* (Minneapolis: Augsburg, 1959), pp. 148-55.

# Christian Apologetics in the Light of the Lutheran Confessions

Lutheran Confessions do not tilt against windmills; they endeavor to storm the bastions of serious religious aberration.

And is this not what one would expect, after all? In my essay, "Lutheran Theology and the Defense of Biblical Faith," I have shown that both Luther himself and the Lutheran theologians of the Age of Orthodoxy maintained vigorous apologetic principles.[7] It would be strange indeed if the Lutheran Confessions – which historically link Luther and the Orthodox theologians together and whose authors include students of Luther and Melanchthon (such as David Chytraeus) and Orthodox fathers in their own right (e.g., Martin Chemnitz) – were not to display the apologetic perspective and concerns of those who preceded and followed them in the same theological tradition.[8]

But deduction from "historical necessity" is a notoriously unreliable way to answer factual questions. We must turn from general speculation to the Lutheran Confessions themselves to see what degree of apologetic insight they manifest.

## How Apologetic Are the Lutheran Confessions?

The task of the Christian apologist may be said to embrace three major activities: (1) clarification (he defends the faith by disabusing the unbeliever of misconceptions concerning its nature), (2) refutation (he defends the faith by showing the fallacies and unworthiness of opposing positions), and (3) positive argumentation (he defends the faith by offering positive reasons to accept the Christian world-view in preference to other philosophical or religious options).[9] To what extent, if any, does the *Book of Concord* engage in apologetic activity along these lines?

Undeniably present throughout the Lutheran Confessions are arguments of a clarifying and refutory nature in defense of biblical religion.

---

[7] Published in Swedish in *Ditt Ord ar Sanning: En Handbok om Bibeln, tillagnad David Hedegaard*, ed. Seth Erlandsson ("Biblicums Skriftserie," 2; Uppsala: Stiftelsen Biblicum, 1971), pp. 234-58. Available in English in the *Lutheran Synod Quarterly*, XI, 1 (Special Issue; Fall, 1970), and in John Warwick Montgomery, *Faith Founded on Fact* (New York and Nashville: Thomas Nelson, 1978).

[8] Cf. Montgomery, *Chytraeus on Sacrifice* (St. Louis, Mo.: Concordia, 1962); Montgomery, *Cross and Crucible* ("Archives Internationales d'Histoire des Idees," 55; The Hague: Martinus Nijhoff [now New York: Springer], 1973), 2 vols.; and Montgomery, "Chemnitz on the Council of Trent," in *Soli Deo Gloria: Essays in Reformed Theology; Festschrift for John H. Gerstner*, ed. R. C. Sproul (Nutley, N.J.: Presbyterian and Reformed Publishing Co., 1976), pp. 73-94.

[9] See Montgomery, *Christianity for the Toughminded* (Minneapolis: Bethany, 1973) and *Myth, Allegory and Gospel* (Minneapolis: Bethany, 1974).

Among innumerable examples of attempts to defend the orthodox position by clarifying its true nature is the following:

> We herewith condemn without any qualification the Capernaitic eating of the body of Christ as though one rent Christ's flesh with one's teeth and digested it like other food. The Sacramentarians deliberately insist on crediting us with this doctrine, against the witness of their own consciences over our many protests, in order to make our teaching obnoxious to their hearers. On the contrary, in accord with the simple words of Christ's testament, we hold and believe in a true, though supernatural, eating of Christ's body and drinking of his blood, which we cannot comprehend with our human sense or reason.[10]

Negative, refutory arguments are even more frequent. We have already noted the standard inclusion of "antitheses" throughout the *Concordia*. In the Preface written both for the *Formula of Concord* and for the whole *Book of Concord*, Jakob Andreae and Martin Chemnitz spend considerable time expressly justifying such material. "Condemnations," they declare, "cannot by any means be avoided," for (as Andreae noted in a marginal revision to the printed draft) "the responsibility devolves upon the theologians and ministers duly to remind even those who err ingenuously and ignorantly of the danger to their souls and to warn them against it, lest one blind person let himself be misled by another." Typical of the refutory argumentation of the Confessions is the *Formula of Concord's* direct citation of Luther (WA, XXVI, pp. 321-22):

> If Zwingli's *alloeosis* stands, then Christ will have to be two persons, one a divine and the other a human person, since Zwingli applies all the texts concerning the passion only to the human nature and completely excludes them from the divine nature. But if the works are divided and separated, the person will also have to be separated, since all the doing and suffering are not ascribed to the natures but to the person. It is the person who does and suffers everything, the one thing according to this nature and the other thing according to the other nature, all of which scholars know right well.

---

[10] F. C. Ep. VII, 42 (486.42). Throughout this essay, citations to the *Concordia* follow the standard system employed by Schlink in his *Theologie der lutherischen Bekenntnisschriften*. For convenience we have also added in parentheses page and paragraph references to the Tappert edition of the *Book of Concord* (Philadelphia: Muhlenberg Press, 1959), and unless otherwise indicated, English translations of Confessional sources have been quoted from that edition.

Therefore we regard our Lord Christ as God and man in one person, neither confounding the natures nor dividing the person.[11]

To be sure, those who question the apologetic character of the Lutheran Confessions will not be especially disturbed by the presence of clarifying or refutory arguments in these documents – even when such arguments appear there with great frequency (as they do). The real issue will be said to lie with the third type of apologetic reasoning as set forth above, viz., the presence or absence of *positive proofs*, consciously designed to convince an unbelieving opponent through the marshalling of facts and evidence in behalf of orthodox religious truth. Proofs of this kind are held by many to be not only absent but in fact utterly foreign to the teaching of the Confessions. "Proving the faith," we are told, contradicts confessional Lutheranism in the following respects: (1) it gives reason a place in man's salvation and therefore constitutes a return of the dog to the vomit of works-righteousness; (2) it elevates "historical knowledge" *(fides historica)* to the level of saving faith and ignores the monergistic work of the Holy Spirit in salvation; (3) it disregards the total depravity produced by the fall and the noetic effects of original sin; and (4) it is oblivious of the fact that Scripture does not make sense to the unbeliever through argumentation but solely through illumination of the Spirit and the influence of justification by grace through faith.

If this is indeed the viewpoint of the Confessions, a positive Lutheran apologetic would admittedly be excluded on principle: at best the confessional Lutheran could only defend his position by attempting to remove misconceptions concerning it or by endeavoring to point out fallacies in his opponents' reasoning. (Indeed, as I have maintained elsewhere,[12] the problem for the witnessing Christian would be far more acute, for the just-stated understanding of total depravity as precluding meaningful positive argument to the sinner would *also* make any clarifications or refutations correspondingly ineffective when presented to him!) But we shall quickly see that the Confessions do not at all require us to avoid positive apologetic argument. Let us analyze confessionally each of the four points raised.

---

[11] F.C. S.D. VIII, 43 (599.43).
[12] See my essays, "Clark's Philosophy of History," in *The Philosophy of Gordon H. Clark: A Festschrift*, ed. Ronald H. Nash (Nutley, N.J.: Presbyterian and Reformed Publishing Co., 1968), pp. 353-90, 505-11; and "Once Upon an A Priori," in *Jerusalem and Athens: Critical Discussions on the Theology and Apologetics of Cornelius Van Til*, ed. E. R. Geehan (Nutley, N.J.: Presbyterian and Reformed Publishing Co., 1971), pp. 380-92, 482-83. (These essays have been reprinted, respectively, in Montgomery, *Where Is History Going?* and *Faith Founded on Fact*.)

(1) *The problem of reason.* Every Lutheran is familiar with Luther's explanation of the Third Article of the Apostles' Creed in his *Small Catechism:* "I believe that by my own reason or strength I cannot believe in Jesus Christ, my Lord, or come to him."[13] Does this mean that a rational defense of the faith – any positive apologetic for Christian truth – turns out to be superfluous at best and highly dangerous at worst? Edmund Schlink comments:

> The opinion that man can arrive at a true knowledge of divine matters on the basis of human thought and emotion is again and again traced in the most diverse doctrines of the opponents, refuted, and finally made ridiculous. All this is only *"multa fingere,"* to "invent many things in one's own brain," which leads only to such opinions as are "totally unfounded in Scripture and touch neither above nor below" (Ap. XII, 178). Reason cannot even come to a knowledge of original sin, but this "must be believed because of the revelation in the Scriptures" (S.A. III, i, 3).[14]

Indeed, the Confessions seem to exclude reason from even a preparatory role in the evangelistic task: "There is no power or ability, no cleverness or reason, with which we can prepare ourselves for righteousness and life or seek after it."[15]

But a closer look at the Confessional passages just cited will show that they do not condemn reason (in the sense of the rational process) as such: they condemn a particular *misuse* of man's rational faculty. What this misuse is will become plainer from other references in the *Concordia*.

The *Apology* roundly criticizes those "scholastics, Pharisees, philosophers, and Mohammedans" who "reason" that justification can be attained through the law. Such "reasoning" is just another name for "human wisdom," and is the exact opposite of "the foolishness of the Gospel": "We know how repulsive this teaching is to the judgment of reason and law and that the teaching of the law about love is more plausible; for this is human wisdom."[16] What is being condemned here is a non-Christian value system which passes itself off as "rational" but which in reality is one hundred and eighty degrees removed from true wisdom. As would later occur in the eighteenth century "Age of Reason" (the misnamed "Enlightenment"), the idea of rationality was being elevated to the status of a philosophy of life, and an anti-Scriptural philosophy at that. The Lutheran Confessions are

---

[13] S.C. II, 6(345.6).
[14] Edmund Schlink, *Theology of the Lutheran Confessions*, trans. P. F. Koehneke and H. J. A. Bouman (Philadelphia: Muhlenberg Press, 1961), pp. 3-4.
[15] F.C. S.D. II, 43 (529.43).
[16] Ap. IV, 229-30 (139.229-30).

simply declaring that they will tolerate no such competition with God's saving message.

What did the scholastics' pseudo-rational value system entail? In a word, works-righteousness. When the Confessions set the Gospel over against "reason," they are employing the word "reason" as a synonym for works-righteousness. "Blind reason," says Luther in the *Smalcald Articles*, "seeks consolation in its own works."[17] Throughout the long article on Justification in the *Apology* the same emphasis is to be found: "The scholastics have followed the philosophers. Thus they teach only the righteousness of reason – that is, civil works – and maintain that without the Holy Spirit reason can love God above all things."[18] "It is false that by its own strength reason can love God. ... Reason cannot free us from our sins or merit for us the forgiveness of sins."[19] "Being blind to the uncleanness of the heart, reason thinks that it pleases God if it does good."[20] Here, reason is not being rejected *per se*; it is being rejected only when it evinces the irrational pretention to self-salvation.

Since man is incapable of saving himself, his only hope lies in a revelation from God. God's thoughts are higher than man's thoughts (Is. 55:9), so God's Word will necessarily contain truths that go beyond man's comprehension. The *Book of Concord*, while never suggesting that Christian revelation contradicts good reasoning, emphasizes that when Scripture does transcend man's rational categories it must be accepted anyway. Thus human reason needs to bow to God's transcendent truth in such areas as the depth and extent of original sin,[21] predestination,[22] our Lord's descent into hell,[23] and his real presence in the Holy Eucharist.[24]

In technical theological parlance, the *Concordia* rejects not the *ministerial*, but the *magisterial* use of reason. "We take our intellect captive in obedience to Christ," declare the authors of the *Formula*.[25] As long as reason is brought into genuine captivity to Christ, and is not allowed to usurp a self-justifying role in the salvatory operation, the Confessions in no way exclude its apologetic use. Indeed, major confessional authors such as David Chytraeus were so emphatic in marshalling proofs for biblical revelation

---

[17] S.A. III, iii, 18 (306.18).
[18] Ap. IV, 9 (108.9).
[19] Ap. IV, 27-31 (111.27-31).
[20] Ap. IV, 288 (151.288).
[21] F.C. Ep. I, 9 (467.9); F.C. S.D. I, 8 (510.8); F.C. S.D. II, 60 (519.60).
[22] F.C. Ep. XI, 9, 16 (495.9; 497.16); F.C. S.D. XI, 26, 91 (620.26; 631.91).
[23] F.C. Ep. IX, 4 (492.4); F.C. S.D. IX, 3 (610.3).
[24] F.C. S.D. VII, 102-106 (587.102-588.106).
[25] F.C. Ep. VII, 42 (486.42); F.C. S.D. VIII, 96 (609.96).

that they have made orthodox Lutherans of our own day a bit uncomfortable.[26]

(2) *The problem of "historical knowledge."* Nonetheless, it is argued that the depreciation of *fides historica* by the Lutheran Confessions renders apologetic argument of little or no consequence. If the Holy Spirit and not factual knowledge does the saving, what possible good can apologetics serve?

One must note first of all that the *Concordia* does not reject historical knowledge as such, any more than it rejects reason as such. In virtually every instance where the *Book of Concord* speaks negatively of the *fides historica*, it carefully qualifies the condemnation (generally by the words "merely" or "only"), as in the following typical examples from the *Apology*: "Our opponents imagine that faith is *only* historical knowledge"; "The faith of which the apostles speak is not *idle* knowledge, but a thing that receives the Holy Spirit and justifies us"; "As we have often said, faith is not *merely* knowledge but rather a desire to accept and grasp what is offered in the promise of Christ"; "We are not talking about *idle* knowledge, such as even the demons have"; "Faith is not *merely* knowledge in the intellect but also trust in the will"; "The scholastics ... interpret faith as *merely* a knowledge of history or of dogmas, not as the power that grasps the promise of grace and righteousness, quickening the heart amid the terrors of sin and death."[27]

What is here being taught becomes particularly plain in the Latin text of the *Augsburg Confession*, where we read: "The term 'faith' does not signify *merely* knowledge of the history (such as is in the ungodly and the devil), but it signifies faith which believes not only the history but also the effect of the history."[28] The Roman Catholic opposition had restricted the meaning of "faith" to factual, historical knowledge of saving truth so as to be able to argue that works were also essential to salvation; therefore the Confessional writers had to point out that the proper biblical understanding of faith, as set forth by Saint Paul, embraced "not only the history but also the effect of the history."[29] This did not mean, however, that the Confessions were denigrating historical knowledge! The Lutheran fathers

---

[26] Robert D. Preus, *The Theology of Post-Reformation Lutheranism* (2 vols.; St. Louis, Mo.: Concordia, 1970-1972), I, pp. 100-103; II, p. 35.
[27] Ap. IV, 48, 99, 227, 249, 304, 383, (113.48; 121.99; 139.227; 142.249; 154.304; 165.383).
[28] A.C. XX, 23 (44.23).
[29] See Carpzov's discussion of this point: Johann Benedict Carpzov, *Isagoge in Libros Ecclesiarum Lutheranarum Symbolicos*, ed. Johann Olearius and Johann Benedict Carpzov, Jr. (3rd ed.; Lipsiae [Leipzig]: David Fleischer, 1699), pp. 206-207, 224, 286.

were anything but *Schwaermer* or modern existential mystics. They believed thoroughly that the assent *(assensus)* and trust *(fiducia)* elements of faith had to be grounded in objective knowledge *(notitia)*.[30]

Such kndwledge could go only so far: it could not justify or save; only the Holy Spirit imparting faith to the heart could do that. But since the Spirit works through the Word, and since the Word sets forth accurate historical knowledge of Christ's life and saving work, the Confessions hardly preclude the apologetic use of such evidence. Historical knowledge, like reason, can be misused by sinful man; but it – again like reason – can be brought into obedience to Christ and employed ministerially to persuade men to accept the historical Christ as Lord of their personal history.

(3) *The problem of original sin.* But what value can apologetic arguments have – even if based upon sound logic and historical fact – when the sinner is incapable of appreciating them and is actively engaged in twisting them to justify himself? Schlink understands the Confessions to paint such a picture; his discussion is worth quoting *in extenso*:

> God is hidden from the empirical observation of human reality. He is completely hidden behind the *simul* of creatureliness and corruption. Neither God the Creator nor God the exacting Lawgiver, neither God's love nor God's wrath can be recognized in this fallen world. ...
>
> At first glance this seems to be contradicted when it is occasionally said of "man's reason or natural intellect" in a subordinate clause, "... although man's reason or natural intellect still has a dim spark of the knowledge that there is a God, as well as of the teaching of the law (Rom. 1:19 ff.)" (S.D. II, 9; cf. V, 22). A similar thought is hidden in the expressions concerning the loss of the *"notitia Dei certior"* of paradise (Ap. II, 17), where already the German text, however, passes over the problem of the comparative. How do the Confessions arrive at equating this "spark" of the knowledge of God with ignorance of God?
>
> This question occupied the Confessions surprisingly little. They give no direct answer. The problem involved in the natural knowledge of God is treated in the Confessions as so unimportant and insignificant that apparently no need of harmonizing the opposing formulations was felt. Only indirectly can we seek to attain clarity in the matter. ...
>
> By analogy, then, we may say of the natural knowledge of God in general:
> a) Man has a "dim spark of the *knowledge that there is a God*" (S.D. 11,9).
> b) This knowledge, however, is only "a dim spark," an indefinite and general knowing.

---

[30] Cf. John Warwick Montgomery, *The Suicide of Christian Theology* (Minneapolis: Bethany, 1970), pp. 289 ff.

c) As soon as man tries to take this vague knowing seriously and to put it into practice concretely by calling God by name and devising a ritual for him, he only falls more deeply into sin with his natural obedience to the law and does not come to God but to idols. ...

Thus natural man knows that there is a God but not who God is, and so he does not know God the Creator. He knows in part what is demanded but not who demands it, and therefore he does not recognize God's wrath. He knows neither God nor his own reality; the innate internal uncleanness of human nature is not seen by him, and "this cannot be adjudged except from the Word of God" (Ap. II, 13; cf. 34). "This hereditary sin is so deep a corruption of nature that reason cannot understand it. It must be believed because of the revelation in the Scriptures" (S.A. III, i, 3; cf. also Ep. I, 9; S.D. I, 8). Original sin is "ultimately the worst damage ..., that we shall not only endure God's eternal wrath and death but that we do not even realize what we are suffering" (S.D. I, 62). Thereby our creatureliness too is hidden from the natural knowledge.[31]

Schlink's catena of passages from the *Book of Concord* showing the effect of man's fall upon his natural knowledge of God is a fair and accurate one, but the general interpretation he places upon these passages is too extreme. The Confessions deal with this issue to make clear beyond all doubt that no natural knowledge on the part of fallen man is capable of bringing him to salvation. Natural knowledge has precisely the same limitations as reason or historical knowledge: not one of them or all of them in combination can form a ladder reaching to heaven. The *Smalcald Articles* declare it to be "nothing but error and stupidity" to hold "that after the fall of Adam the natural powers of man have remained whole and uncorrupted, and that man by nature possesses a right understanding and a good will, as the philosophers teach."[32] Salvation is a gift, and is brought home to the heart only by the sovereign work of God the Holy Spirit.

But it by no means follows that in the *Concordia* "God is hidden from the empirical observation of human reality." As Schlink admits (grudgingly), the authors of the Confessions allow the natural man knowledge that there is a God; and their overwhelming emphasis on the reality of the incarnation – the personal union of the divine and human natures – makes them the strongest possible supporters of the biblical affirmation that God submitted to the "empirical observation of human reality" by becoming true Man in Jesus Christ.

---

[31] Schlink, *op. cit.* (in note 14 above), pp. 48-52.
[32] S.A. III, i, 3-4 (302.3-4).

Thus there is nothing in the Confessions which would in principle militate against the use of apologetic arguments for God's existence from nature, or for the deity of our Lord and Savior Jesus Christ from empirical observation of His resurrection appearances, or for the inspiration of Scripture from fulfilled prophecy and other external proofs – as long as such arguments do not purport to substitute for the Spirit's converting work in the heart. As already noted, the orthodox Lutheran theologians of the post-Reformation time – including the authors of the confessional documents – feel comfortable with apologetic arguments of this kind; indeed they seem driven to use them because of their great concern to employ every legitimate means to bring men to the Savior and to His revealed truth (cf. I Cor. 9:22; I Pet. 3:15).

(4) *The problem of spiritual illumination.* Yet does not the *Book of Concord* teach that the very scriptural revelation God gives to a fallen race remains a closed book until the sinner's eyes have been opened – not by argument, but by God's Spirit who teaches him to read it from the vantage point of justification by grace through faith? Again let us hear Schlink:

> Without the knowledge of the Gospel the Bible remains unintelligible and useless. Only from the Gospel do all individual statements of Scripture receive their proper place and meaning. Erasmus, Zwingli, the peasants, and the Enthusiasts had also waged their battle with Bible quotations, as did also the Roman adversaries. By means of Scripture texts employed "in either a philosophical or a Jewish manner" it is possible to abolish the certainty of faith and to exclude Christ as mediator (Ap. IV, 376). Only in the light of the Gospel can we determine which words of Scripture are commands and promises, which words serve to terrify or to comfort, which words are valid for us as God's commandments, and which commandments of the Old Testament have been abolished by Christ. Only by faith in the Gospel can Scripture be interpreted correctly, that is, by receiving the benefits secured for us by the crucified Christ.[33]

What we have said repeatedly earlier in this paper applies here with equal force: the Confessions will not allow a man to save himself by any work, rational, cognitive – or even biblical! The sinner cannot pull himself up to heaven by the bootstraps of his own ability to interpret the Scriptures. God alone can give fallen man the illumination necessary to comprehend the Bible in a salvatory way.

---

[33] Schlink, *op. cit*, p. 7.

However, the *Book of Concord* never suggests – as Schlink does – the modern Neo-Orthodox teaching that the Bible possesses no inherent clarity, but somehow waits for the Spirit's work on the heart to acquire the meaning God intended for it. After discussing a number of biblical passages and their relationship to justification by grace through faith, the *Apology* bluntly says: "No sane man can judge otherwise."[34] Then Melanchthon goes on to quote Romans 10:10 and states: "Here we think that our opponents will grant that the mere act of confessing does not save, but that it saves only because of faith in the heart."[35] Later the same confessional writing utters the following imprecation: "May God destroy these wicked sophists who so sinfully twist the Word of God to suit their vain dreams!"[36]

Such passages from the *Concordia* show beyond question that the confessional authors believed that Scripture is inherently perspicuous – that it speaks clearly and ought to say exactly the same thing to their opponents as it did to them. If it did not, the reason was simply that the opposition twisted it by sinful sophistry. Indeed, it should be obvious that had the confessional writers not been convinced that the Bible could speak clearly and persuasively to their opponents, they would not have gone to the trouble of continually presenting and arguing from Scriptural texts!

And since their opponents were particularly of the Roman Catholic camp and therefore did not believe in justification by grace through faith, the confessional authors could not have cited Scripture against them and at the same time have held the Bible to be a closed book to those who had not already accepted the Scriptural teaching on justification. They believed that the Bible itself was capable of convincing their opponents as to the proper view of justification, and they quoted it to that end.

Likewise with the Sacramentarians. In arguing for Christ's real presence in the Holy Eucharist, the *Formula of Concord* stresses that the words of Scripture are clear and plain and that the only reasonable course for any Bible reader to take is to accept Jesus' own understanding and interpretation of Scripture:

> There is, of course, no more faithful or trustworthy interpreter of the words of Jesus Christ than the Lord Christ himself, who best understands his words and heart and intention and is best qualified from the standpoint of wisdom and intelligence to explain them. In the institution of his last will and testament and of his abiding covenant and union, he uses no flowery language but the most appropriate, simple, indubitable, and clear words, just as he

---

[34] Ap. IV, 375 (164.375).
[35] Ap. IV, 383-84 (166.383-84).
[36] Ap. XII, 123 (200.123).

does in all the articles of faith and in the institution of other covenant-signs and signs of grace or sacraments, such as circumcision, the many kinds of sacrifice in the Old Testament, and holy Baptism. And so that no misunderstanding could creep in, he explained things more clearly by adding the words, "given for you, shed for you."[37]

In sum, though only the Holy Spirit can apply Biblical texts in a salvatory way to human hearts, believers can and should employ Scripture to convince unbelievers of the nature and truth of God's message. Good interpretation can be distinguished from bad interpretation in such a way as to lead opponents to discover the meaning of the Biblical texts. Both an apologetic for Scripture and an apologetic through Scripture must be seen as compatible with the *Book of Concord*.

## Fundamental Apologetic Axioms in the Lutheran Confessions and Their Contemporary Application

Admittedly, we have done no more than to show that the *Concordia* opens the door to apologetic operations. Can we go beyond this point (which, *nota bene*, should not be minimized, considering the number of anti-apologetic Lutherans who have tried to eliminate all apologetics on the basis of supposed confessional teaching!), and find positive apologetic substance in the *Book of Concord*? To be sure, we should not expect to discover any general programmatic against unbelief in confessional documents composed before the rise of modern secularism in the eighteenth century.[38] But we can derive from the *Concordia* a fundamental apologetic axiom-set which will serve as a kind of template outlining the characteristics which a truly confessional apologetic would need to display. Wittgenstein observed that though the propositions of logic do not describe the world they do serve as a "scaffolding" to show the shape of the world;[39] the Lutheran Confessions, *mutatis mutandis*, do not provide an apologetic for an age of unbelief, but they can display the shape such an apologetic ought to have

---

[37] F.C. S.D. VII, 50 (578.50). See also Gottfried Olearius, *Isagoge Anticalvinistica secundum Formulae Concordiae* (Lipsiae [Leipzig]: Johann Wittigau, 1662), pp. 91-114; and Sebastian Schmidt, *Articulorum Formulae Concordiae repetitio* (Argentorati [Strasbourg]: Josias Staedel, 1696), pp. 348-74.

[38] Cf. Montgomery, *The Shaping of America* (Minneapolis: Bethany, 1976).

[39] "Die logischen Satze beschreiben das Gerust der Welt, oder vielmehr, sie stellen es dar. Sie 'handeln' von nichts" (Ludwig Wittgenstein, *Tractatus Logico-Philosophicus*, 6.124; cf. 3.42 and 4.023).

to be Scripturally meaningful and doctrinally sound. We shall list the fundamental apologetic axioms derivable from the *Book of Concord*, and then, on the basis of them, say a few words as to the apologetic challenge facing confessional Lutheranism today.

(i) *Fallen man retains the ability to reason deductively – to employ logic.* Note how, throughout the Confessions, when bad reasoning is condemned, proper logic is offered as a substitute and opponents are expected to respond to its force:

> If the old witch, Dame Reason, the grandmother of the *alloeosis*, would say that the deity surely cannot suffer and die, then you must answer and say: That is true, but since the divinity and humanity are one person in Christ, the Scriptures ascribe to the deity, because of this personal union, all that happens to the humanity, and vice versa. And this is likewise within the bounds of truth, for you must say that the person (pointing to Christ) suffers, dies. But this person is truly God, and therefore it is correct to say: the Son of God suffers. Although, so to speak, the one part (namely, the deity) does not suffer, nevertheless the person who is true God suffers in the other part (namely, in the humanity). For the Son of God truly is crucified for us – that is, this person who is God, for that is what he is – this person, I say, is crucified according to the humanity.[40]

(ii) *Fallen man also retains the ability to reason inductively – to draw correct factual inferences from empirical data.* The Augsburg Confession quotes approvingly from the pseudo-Augustinian *Hypognosticon*: "We concede that all men have a free will which enables them to make judgments according to reason,"[41] and the *Apology* comments: "Human nature still has reason and judgment about the things that the senses can grasp."[42] The Confessions evidently regard the inferential functioning of man's mind, in regard both to logic and to facts, as an aspect of the human essence. Man did not lose this essence when he fell, for had he done so he would have ceased to be human. The *Concordia* guards itself carefully from the Flacian error – the gross doctrinal mistake of Matthew Flacius, who in attempting definitively to answer the semi-Pelagians and synergists, toppled into the opposite error of holding that Adam's fall resulted in a different essence in man.[43]

---

[40] F.C. S.D. VIII, 41-42 (599.41-42). The *Formula of Concord* is here quoting Luther (WA, XXVI, 321-22).
[41] A.C. XVIII, 4 (39.4); we follow the Latin text here.
[42] Ap. XVIII, 4 (225.4).
[43] Cf. Henry W. Reimann, "Matthias Flacius Illyricus," *Concordia Theological Monthly*, XXXV (February, 1964), pp. 69-93.

(iii) *A common ground of logic and fact unites believer and unbeliever, so that the believer can persuasively employ the unbeliever's own reasoning against him.* Note how the *Apology* engages in just such an argumentative process in the following passage:

> Where is the "divinely instituted order that we should take refuge in the help of the saints"? ... Perhaps they derive this "order" from the usage at royal courts, where friends must be used as intercessors. But if a king has appointed a certain intercessor, he does not want appeals to be addressed to him through others. Since Christ has been appointed as our intercessor and high priest, why seek others?[44]

(iv) *The common ground of logic and fact uniting believer and unbeliever permits the effective use of analogy-reasoning to convince the unbeliever.* In the same section of the *Apology* from which the preceding illustration is taken, Melanchthon offers this persuasive analogy-argument for the biblical doctrine of propitiation, as against the invocation of saints:

> If one pays a debt for one's friend, the debtor is freed by the merit of another as though it were his own. Thus the merits of Christ are bestowed on us so that when we believe in him we are accounted righteous by our trust in Christ's merits as though we had merits of our own.[45]

(v) As demonstrated in detail in the previous section of this paper, the Confessions hold that *fallen man is capable of acquiring natural knowledge of God's existence, historical knowledge ("fides historica") of Biblical events, and understanding as to the meaning of the perspicuous Scriptural text.*

(vi) However, the Confessions are even more concerned to emphasize, as we have seen, that *none of the above capacities of the unregenerate man* (or any other abilities he may possess, for that matter) *are such as to permit him to mend his broken God-relationship: the Holy Spirit and the Holy Spirit alone, converts men to Christ.* "To be born anew, to receive inwardly a new heart, mind, and spirit, is solely the work of the Holy Spirit."[46]

Now what kind of apologetic approach ought today's confessional Lutheran to build on this axiomatic foundation? Let us be very clear, first of all, as to what approach he must *not* take. He must not fall into the trap of *presuppositionalism* or *apriorism* so attractive to orthodox Calvinists of the

---

[44] Ap. XXI, 24 (232.24).
[45] Ap. XXI, 19 (231.19).
[46] F.C. S.D. II,'26 (526.26).

Dutch school (Van Til, Dooyeweerd,' et al.). Even the ostensibly milder, revisionist presuppositionalism advocated in Reymond's provocative little work, *The Justification of Knowledge*, cannot be accepted by a confessional Lutheran. Reymond correctly sees that Van Til's epistemology destroys the divinely created common ground between believer and unbeliever: "The solution to all of Van Til's difficulties is to affirm, as Scripture teaches, that both God and man share the same concept of truth and the same theory of language."[47] But Reymond still rejects any positive apologetic to the unbeliever on the theory that the universe of facts and possible interpretations is so vast that the unbeliever can consistently interpret all evidence in line with his sinful presuppositions.

The *Book of Concord* much more wisely perceived that the unbeliever, living in the same universe with the Christian and using the same inferential faculties of mind, should respond to reasoning that proceeds by analogy from ordinary decisionmaking in secular affairs to the meaning and significance of biblical evidence. If the unbeliever refuses to do so, he acts irrationally by analogy with his ordinary experience and displays his *real* reason for rejecting the truth; not intellectual dissatisfaction but willful egocentricity.

Here, on the basis of the apologetic axioms of the *Concordia*, the contemporary Lutheran apologist begins to discover his battle plan. What will be its characteristics?

The Lutheran apologist will not be afraid to "become all things to all men that by all means some may be saved": convinced of the common ground of logic and fact between believer and unbeliever, he will argue by analogy that bad reasoning leads to religious heresy just as it produces catastrophe in the secular realm, and that the same good reasoning as is essential to survival in ordinary life, if applied to religious issues, will vindicate the Holy Scriptures and their Christ.

The contemporary confessional apologist will not be afraid of developing effective modern arguments for God's existence (such as is afforded by the application of the classical contingency proof to the Second Law of Thermodynamics, or such as Peter Berger creates on a sociological base in his *Rumor of Angels*); but – in line with the fundamental stress of Lutheran theology on the incarnation, the Gospel, and the Cross – he will especially

---

[47] Robert L. Reymond, *The Justification of Knowledge: An Introductory Study in Christian Apologetic Methodology* (Nutley, N.J.: Presbyterian and Reformed Publishing Co., 1976), p. 105. Dr. Robert H. Countess provides an excellent review of this work in *Christianity Today*, November 18, 1977, pp. 34-35. 48.

endeavor to provide a case for the deity of our Lord and Savior Jesus Christ beginning from, but not limited to, the *fides historica*.[48]

Rather than giving today's religious seeker the impression that the Missouri Synod's uncompromising stand on the inerrancy of the Bible is an aprioristic asylum of invincible ignorance, the Lutheran apologist will offer the best evidence in support of our Lord's own assertion that Scripture cannot be broken.

Finally, the confessional apologist will see himself not as a Holy-Spirit-substitute but as a John the Baptist in the wilderness of a secular age, preparing the way of the Lord, making the paths intellectually straight which lead to the Lamb of God – to the only One who can take away the sins of the world.

Admittedly, such an apologetic is not provided, full-blown, in the *Book of Concord*. Apologetics speaks to the fallen man, and the *Zeitgeist* constantly changes. There is no absolute apologetic; the apologetic task faces each generation of Christians anew. But we of the Lutheran Church-Missouri Synod have taken a giant step forward to meet that challenge. A Lutheran Council in the U.S.A. news release of December 1, 1977, quotes the report of a five-year official LCUSA theological study observing that "the LCA and ALC have not felt it necessary to adopt doctrinal statements in addition to the confessional articles. The LCMS, on the other hand, has reserved for itself the right to restate its positions on doctrinal matters throughout its history."

The Missouri Synod has rightly seen that modern secularism requires new confessional responses; she has not been intimidated into accepting modern heresies such as result from the application of historical-critical hermeneutics just because the 16$^{th}$ century Confessions antedated them. Surely, then, in the realm of apologetics – a domain far less static than dogmatics – we can no longer employ our theology as the fundamentalists do their sociological blue laws, to wall the church off from the real challenges of the age. Only the Word of God remains forever; nothing else is changeless. Now that our battle for the Bible has been won, let us with apologetic vigor show modern secular man that the Holy Scriptures still have the last Word.

---

[48] See Montgomery, *Sensible Christianity* cassette series (3 vols.; Santa Ana, Ca.: Vision House/One Way Library, 1976); now available from the Canadian Institute for Law, Theology and Public Policy (http://www.ciltpp.com).

# 16. The Kloha Catastrophe

## I. Beyond the "Plastic Text": the Plot Thickens

*Abstract:* A new approach to textual criticism is being advocated by a New Testament professor at the Concordia Seminary, St Louis, one of the two theological centers for the training of pastors in the Lutheran Church-Missouri Synod. It is the conviction of the present essayist that this approach amounts to the destruction of the denomination's commitment to scriptural inerrancy; returns biblical scholarship to the subjectivism of the higher criticism; and, if pursued, could cause that conservative church body to face again the theological difficulties that came close to destroying the LC-MS in the Seminex controversy of the 1970s.

Readers may well recall my critique of Jeffrey Kloha's "plastic text" essay.[1] I have learned (unofficially) that church authorities have met with Dr Kloha, that he admitted to no doctrinal problems, and that the church authorities were comfortable with this. A major debate between Dr Kloha and this author ensued on 15 October 2016; this writer's presentation and rebuttal to Dr Kloha are included in the present chapter.

The seriousness of the issues involved for the historic doctrine of the inerrancy of the Holy Scriptures requires additional examination of Dr Kloha's biblical orientation. This will focus on his contribution to the Festschrift for his mentor, Professor J. Keith Elliott,[2] with additional comments on Kloha's "plastic text" essay and a reaction to his paper entitled "The Authority of the Scriptures," delivered at the 2010 Concordia Seminary St. Louis symposium ("The Scriptures: Formative or Formality").[3]

---

[1] John Warwick Montgomery,"The Problem of a 'Plastic Text': The Kloha Essay on 'Text and Authority,'" 24/4 *Modern Reformation* (July/August, 2015). This material has also been published in *Christian News*, and appears as an Appendix to the present paper. Kloha's essay may be found at http://thebarebulb.files.wordpress.com/2013/12/text-and-authority.pdf

[2] *Texts and Traditions: Esssays in Honour of J. Keith Elliott,* ed. Peter Doble and Jeffrey Kloha (Leiden: Brill, 2014). Another contributor to this volume is James W. Voelz, Kloha's New Testament Department head at Concordia Seminary, St. Louis, who has found no problems with Kloha's methodology or theology.

[3] https://gudribassakums.files.wordpress.com/2012/07/jeffrey-kloha-scriptures-symp2010.pdf

## The Magnificat *(traitement pas du tout magnifique)*

Kloha's Festschrift contribution carries the title: "Elizabeth's Magnificat (Luke 1:46)."[4] The author argues that it is more appropriate to attribute the Magnificat to Elizabeth than to Mary.

To be sure, whether Mary or Elizabeth spoke those words poses no doctrinal issue whatsoever. But the way in which Kloha arrives at his attribution is fraught with the most serious consequences for the authority and factual inerrancy of the text – and, by implication – for all other biblical material.

Kloha, as textual critic, first sets forth the manuscript evidence for the two readings of Luke 1:46. "Turning to the continuous-text manuscript tradition of Luke," he properly notes, the Marian reading "is consistently attested in all Greek MSS at Luke 1:46" (p. 205). This, to be sure, is why "no editions of the Greek New Testament produced in the last half-century" accept any reading other than the Marian one (p. 200). The only readings of any consequence attributing the Magnificat to Elizabeth are non-Vulgate Latin readings, Irenaeus (a divided authority, however, since in one place he explicitly attributes the song to Mary), Origen (indecisive, as with Irenaeus), and a little-known, hardly impressive late 3d-, early 4th-century Latin preacher, one Nicetas of Remesiana. The fact that these authorities are earlier than the authoritative Greek texts (Codex Sinaiticus and Codex Vaticanus, early to mid 4th century) is hardly a strong argument for the Elizabeth attribution, since they are non-Greek versions/translations and contradict the Greek texts.[5] Kloha admits this.

So why does he favour the Elizabeth reading – against the powerful weight of textual authority? Answer: because he accepts the philosophy of textual criticism exposued by his mentor, Professor J. Keith Elliott. In the Introduction to the Festschrift, we are told that "Keith's career has seen him refocus his work from searching for an 'original text' to what may be reasonably be said of the history to which texts point." Kloha revealingly quotes Elliott at the beginning of his article in the following terms: the textual critic, according to Elliott, "feels able to select freely from among the available fund of variants and choose the one that best fits the internal criteria" (p. 200).

In accord with this methodology, Kloha selects Elizabeth over Mary. Example of the reasoning employed: "Were the Magnificat placed on the

---

[4] *Texts and Traditions*, pp. 200-219.
[5] See, for example, the Nestle/Aland *Novum Testamentum Graece* (Stuttgart: Württ. Bibelanstalt) at Luke 1:46.

lips of Mary, it would be the only time she verbalizes praise to the Lord. Such a verbalization would not be consistent with her characterization elsewhere in Luke" (p. 217).

What is going on here? Luke's Gospel is being treated as a constructed literary work, such that the critic/interpreter can "select freely" among possible readings and accept those readings that fit best his or her understanding of the literary style and organization of the text. This is, of course, the very opposite of an understanding of the biblical text as an historical account of events, determined simply by taking the best manuscript readings as representing the authorial text.[6]

An analogy or two may make this clear. I deliver a lecture in which I organize my material in the order of A, B, and C. A news article on my lecture appears, in which the writer, out of great respect for me and a knowledge of my other writings, says that I presented my material in the order of B, A, and C – on the ground that this makes more literary sense and is more consistent with my usual style. That reporter has prostituted his journalistic calling: he has not reported what actually occurred, but rather doctored it to fit what he thinks would *better* have occurred.

Or consider the battle of Waterloo. The standard French accounts of the battle agree that one factor in Napoleon's defeat was General Ney's error in thinking that a movement of casualties from Wellington's centre was the beginning of a retreat. Suppose an early Romanian translation of a non-primary, no longer existent French account attributed the error to General Grouchy. Would any competent historian choose that account – on the ground that Grouchy provided a better source of the Napoleonic defeat because his "characterization" is more appropriate to an effective narrative? Of course not: the issue is *what occurred historically*, not what narrative would be most effective from a literary standpoint.

---

[6] The same approach – regarding the biblical text as a literary construction – can be found in Kloha's department chairman's essay in the same volume. James W. Voelz writes, in his paper, "The Characteristics of the Greek of St. Mark's Gospel": " It may be that the latter portion of the Gospel, containing as it does more well-known scenes or periscopes (e.g., Jesus' trial before the procurator [15:1-15], as opposed to the healing of the multitudes who come from many regions [3:7-12]), was more popular, more frequently related, and, ultimately more "worked over" by those who handed such material on. (If this is, in fact, the case, then it is not surprising that portions of chapter 6 display characteristics of chapters 8-16. The death of John the Baptist and the feeding of the 5000 could well have attained the status of periscopes from the Passion Narrative.) Characteristics of such periscopes would, then, tend to be accommodated to a more common and Attic-influenced Greek" (*Tests and Traditions*, p. 152).

But suppose one were to argue that to presuppose historicity in the case of biblical materials is gratuitous and that one should instead view them primarily as literary creations? After all, are they not "religious" in nature? The answer to this is that the New Testament authors themselves claim, again and again, that they are setting forth history.[7] "That which we have seen and heard," they write," declare we unto you" (I John 1:3). "We have not followed cunningly devised fables, when we made known unto you the power and coming of our Lord Jesus Christ, but were eyewitnesses of his majesty" (II Peter 1:16).

In Luke's case, the argument is even stronger. The very chapter containing the Magnificat begins with the author's prologue, in which he insists on the solid historicity of what he is going to narrate: "Forasmuch as many have taken in hand to set forth in order a declaration of those things which are most surely believed among us, even as they delivered them unto us, which from the beginning were eyewitnesses, and ministers of the word; it seemed good to me also, having had perfect understanding of all things from the very first, to write unto thee in order, most excellent Theophilus, that thou mightest know the certainty of those things, wherein thou hast been instructed" (Luke 1:1-4). This claim to precise historicity has been compared not only to classical historians such as Tacitus but also with the aims of Von Ranke and German historical schools of the 19th-century to represent the past *"wie es eigentlich gewesen."*[8]

Kloha's approach to the biblical text alters it from an historical account into a constructed literary narrative, and as such denatures it. It imposes literary categories on the text, changing the author's intention to provide an accurate record of the events of Jesus' life and ministry.

But, apart from the bad scholarship involved in such a transformation of the biblical materials, Kloha's operation moves away from classic textual criticism to the very error at the heart of the so-called "higher criticism," namely, allowing subjective judgments as to style, vocabulary, "characterization," etc., to determine the ultimate meaning of the biblical text.

It is precisely this move from objective to subjective that lay at the heart of the Seminex view of how one is to handle the Sacred Writings. A typical example from that era is Norman C. Habel's essay, "The Form and Meaning of the Fall Narrative," in which the author contended that "it is

---

[7] Cf. Richard Bauckham, *Jesus and the Eyewitnesses: The Gospels As Eyewitness Testimony* (Grand Rapids, MI: Eerdmans, 2008).

[8] Cf. John Warwick Montgomery, *The Shape of the Past: A Christian Response to Secular Philosophies of History* (2d ed.; Eugene, OR: Wipf & Stock, 2008).

legitimate to consider this narrative a literary form which may be described as a 'symbolical religious history,' but that we should not confuse the truth that the writer is stating with this particular mode of saying it, a mode which is especially appropriate for the world in which he lived, and a mode which has at least partial analogies in the epic literature of his day."[9]

It should also be noted that as soon as the biblical text is regarded not as historical narrative but as the product of literary construction, the very notion of "inerrancy" disappears. There is no such thing as "inerrant" literature (what Fagan or Winnie the Pooh does or does not do cannot be evaluated in terms of "truth" or "error"). Perhaps this is why the literary approach is so attractive in mainline theological circles: if we don't have to regard the Scriptures as fact-orientated, we avoid the messy problem of their factual reliability and no longer have to worry about apparent errors and contradictions in the biblical books. (We also, to be sure, lose a factual revelation that can deal objectively with the reality of our sinful condition through God's real work in history.)

Two generations ago, the biblical scholar J. Barton Payne, in a classic essay, argued that a bad hermeneutic – a bad approach to the interpretation of Scripture – can destroy a meaningful doctrine of biblical inerrancy.[10] The Seminex professors achieved this through the use of higher criticism as a hermeneutic tool. Kloha and company are doing this by way of a philosophy of lower or textual criticism that dehistoricizes the biblical text, reducing it essentially to a literary phenomenon.

Of more than routine interest is the diametric contrast between Kloha's handling of biblical texts as literature and Luther's insistence on treating them as *de facto* history. In conflict with Erasmus on the issue of freewill and with Zwingli on the real presence of Christ in the Sacrament, Luther continually insisted that literary metaphor was the devil's tool and that one must understand the Scriptures in their plain, literal sense. Thus, against Erasmus:

> Let this be our conviction: that no "implication" or "figure" may be allowed to exist in any passage of Scripture unless such be required by some obvious feature of the words and the absurdity of their plain sense, as offending

---

[9] An essay presented to the Missouri Synod's Conference of College Presidents and Seminary Faculties on 2 December 1963. For other (agonizing) examples of such reduction of biblical material to literary forms, see Montgomery, *Crisis in Lutheran Theology* (2d ed., 2 vols. In 1; Grand Rapids, MI: Baker Book House, 1973), I, 81-123.

[10] J. Barton Payne, "Hermeneutics as a Cloak for the Denial of Scripture," 3/4 *Bulletin of the Evangelical Theological Society* 93-100 (Fall, 1960).

against an article of faith. Everywhere we should stick to just the simple, natural meaning of the words, as yielded by the rules of grammar and the habits of speech that God has created among men; for if anyone may devise "implications" and "figures" in Scripture at his own pleasure, what will all Scripture be but a reed shaken with the wind, and a sort of chameleon? ["Plastic," perhaps – ed.] There would then be no article of faith about which anything could be settled and proved for certain, without your being able to raise objections by means of some "figure." All "figures" should rather be avoided, as being the quickest poison, when Scripture itself does not absolutely require them.[11]

## Plasticity, Inerrancy, and Seminex (*déjà vu – all over again*)

If the textual critic may "select freely from among the available fund of variants and choose the one that best fits the internal criteria" (Kloha. quoting with approval Professor Elliott), then it becomes evident why he regards the biblical text as "plastic." Because the New Testament books were regarded as divine revelation, there are vast numbers of manuscript copies and, consequently, thousands of variant readings (almost all of them of no significance or value), but thousands nonetheless. If the critic is allowed to choose freely among them, including the doubtful ones – as we have seen Kloha do in his treatment of the Magnificat passage in Luke – basing serious textual arguments thereon, the scriptural text does indeed become plastic.[12]

Note that once this approach is taken, the real decision as to which text to accept is made on "internal criteria," i.e., the reading is chosen which best accords with the subjective judgment of the critic as to "characterization," vocabulary, stylistic shifts, alterations in logic, etc. In other words, just as with the higher criticism, where the objective text becomes a pretext for subjective authorial judgments, so here the choice of variant readings (and thus the text itself) becomes a matter of the subjective opinion

---

[11] Luther, *De servo arbitrio,* WA 18, 700-701. Cf. Montgomery, *In Defense of Martin Luther* (Milwaukee: Northwestern Publishing House, 1970), pp. 40-85.

[12] To be sure, in the exceedingly rare case where two solid readings were evenly balanced, one would be forced to appeal to "internal" criteria in choosing between the two – but, even then, these would need to be the internal considerations best supporting the historicity of the narrative, not those offering the greatest literary effectiveness in the eyes of the textual critic. That Kloha's "internal" approach is not limited to such rare cases is painfully evident from his handling of the authorship of the Magnificat in Luke 1:46.

of the critic as to which variant can produce the literary result most attractive to the critic. With thousands of variants, there is indeed nothing but plasticity.

And inerrancy? We have already noted that the concept is meaningful only if a text is regarded as setting forth factual/historical data. Kloha's textual philosophy, being literary and not historical, therefore eschews any meaningful issues of the reliability of the biblical material: it is a literary construction. We may speak of its "effectiveness," but certainly not of its truth.

This creates quite a problem for one who is a Lutheran in a conservative denominational tradition and who, moreover, teaches at a prestigious theological seminary of his church body. Kloha can hardly avoid speaking to the inerrancy issue. Here is how he does so in his "Authority of the Scriptures" essay:

> If you want to rip Romans 15 and 16 out of my Bible, I can live with that. If you want Hebrews, James, Revelation torn out too, I can live with that. If you force me to look only at p46 or the bizarre majuscule manuscript W or one of thousands of Byzantine minuscules and use them as my New Testament – I can live with that. Give me only Codex Boernarianus, one of the most poorly copied, misspelled, error filled copies of Paul's letters, and I can live with that. I could live with or without any of those, because even these poorly copied, corrupted by people, edited, to use Luther's words, preach Christ. And if they preach Christ, they are of the Spirit, for preaching Christ is the Spirit's work. And if they preach Christ, they are apostolic, for the apostle can speak nothing other than what he has been sent to speak. So apostles, no matter who they are, even one who has been aborted yet lived like Paul, who once persecuted the church, preach the death and resurrection of Jesus Christ. I can live without a perfect Bible. I cannot live without God raising Jesus from the dead.
>
> On the other hand, force me read only the Gospel of Thomas, I cannot live with that. Or the Koran, or the Book of Mormon. Not because the are not "inerrant" or "perfect," or even "human," but because there is no Gospel: There is no new life in Christ.

Observe what is going on here. Kloha says that inerrancy is not the ground for his believing that the Bible – or any other book – is revelatory. Right: the mere fact that a book is inerrant doesn't make it God's Word (think of Euclid's *Geometry* – no errors there). But the *presence* of errors will certainly destroy a book's claim to being a divine revelation, since God does not err.

Thus Kloha must face the issue of biblical errors. These do not in principle or in fact bother him; he has no trouble living with poor manuscripts and textual and content errors – for his revelational criterion is the presence of the gospel. As long as the Bible "preaches Christ," fine.

This, of course, is the old Gospel Reductionism of Seminex and of the liberal Lutherans in general. Arthur Carl Piepkorn: "Where the stress is on a religious purpose, his [the human biblical author's] concern with the precise and literal accuracy of concomitant historical or scientific detail may recede into the background."[13] Joseph Sittler, Lutheran Church in America (now ELCA) theologian, beloved of the Seminex people: "All verbal forms, all means of communication through speech, prove too weak for this massive bestowal [of Gospel] ... We must ask after the Word of God in the same way faith asks after Jesus Christ. That is to say, that the Word of God *becomes* Word of God for us ... To assert the inerrancy of the text of scripture is to elevate to a normative position an arbitrary theological construction."[14]

The contrast with Luther's view of Holy Writ could hardly be more pronounced. Luther maintained that the entire canonical Scripture was authoritative, inerrant, and perspicuous. He refused to dismiss as trivial even the most minute assertions in the Bible – for they were the product of the Holy Spirit's inspiration. He refused to accept any contradiction in the Bible, even if he himself could not resolve the problem. And he insisted that the text be accepted on its own ground, literally and factually. For him, the Scripture was 180 degrees removed from "plasticity." Here are just a few of the many passages from Luther that could be quoted as to his biblical convictions:

> I have learned to ascribe the honor of infallibility only to those books that are accepted as canonical. I am profoundly convinced that none of those writers has erred.[15]

> He who carefully reads and studies the Scriptures will consider nothing so trifling that it does not at least contribute to the improvement of his life and morals, since the Holy Spirit wanted to have it committed to writing.[16]

---

[13] Arthur Carl Piepkorn, "What Does 'Inerrancy' Mean?," 36 *Concordia Theological Monthly* 577-93 (September, 1965).

[14] Joseph Sittler, *The Doctrine of the Word* (Philadelphia: Muhlenberg Press, 1948), pp. 62-63, 68 (Sittler's italics).

[15] Luther, "Defense Against the Ill-tempered Judgment of Eck," WA, 2, 618.

[16] Luther, WA, 42, 474 (on Gen. 12:11-13); cf. WA, 15, 1481: "The Scriptures have never erred."

> We see with what great diligence Moses, or rather the Holy Spirit, describes even the most insignificant acts and sufferings of the patriarchs.[17]

I end on a personal note. One of my theological seminary professors (the late T. A. Kantonen) once remarked that he always had wanted to become famous. Then it occurred to him that to become famous in theology or biblical study would require that he present something genuinely new. However, he came to realize that since the Bible had been around for a very long time, was clear (*not* plastic) and the church's doctrine had been derived from it, innovation on his part would inevitably entail heresy. Thus, said he, I gave up my quest for fame.

Contemporary theology goes for fame at the expense of biblical fidelity. Students go from orthodox theological seminaries to liberal graduate schools in America and Europe, write "original" – or ostensibly original – dissertations,[18] and ape their professors. All too often the result is, tragically, corruption of the faith once delivered to the saints and corruption of the institutions created to preserve and promote it.

Brethren, these things ought not to be.

# Appendix

## The Problem of a "Plastic Text": the Kloha Essay on "Text and Authority"

The "Text and Authority" paper by Concordia Seminary, St Louis, Associate Professor and Provost Jeffrey Kloha has been published on the internet,[19] so I am not violating Matthew 18 in critiquing it. Fascinatingly, it was delivered at the Lutherische Theologische Hochschule in Oberursel, where, in the old days, I had a wonderful relationship with the late Prof. Dr Wilhelm Oesch – who, by the by, would have been appalled by the reasoning and theological consequences of Kloha's essay. When most German theologians could not see the catastrophic effect of modern critical biblical scholarship on the dogmatics of the church – and were frightened silly of evaluating it for lack of linguistic skills – Dr Oesch was well aware that the

---

[17] Luther, WA, 44, 91-92 (on Gen.32: 21-24). See Montgomery (ed.). *God's Inerrant Word: An International Symposium on the Trustworthiness of Scripture* (Minneapolis: Bethany, 1974), pp. 63-94.

[18] There is, to be sure, the process by which at least some doctoral dissertations come into existence: the candidate "digs up material from one graveyard, rearranges it, and buries it in another."

[19] http://thebarebulb.files.wordpress.com/2013/12/text-and-authority.pdf

issue was not linguistic but that of bowing at the shrine of secularist New Testament scholarship without a sufficient understanding of the underlying assumptions prevalent in the field – and that such naïveté was a recipe for theological disaster.

Since Bart Ehrman, textual critic and former evangelical, has been issuing his broadsides at the notion of biblical inerrancy, two kinds of response have appeared on the American theological scene. On the one hand, it has been correctly noted that Ehrman does not give the benefit of the doubt to the best textual readings of the New Testament (as one would do, following Aristotle, in treating Homer's writings or other ancient texts), and that he suffers from an egregious anti-supernatural bias. The other approach operates, in effect, with the tag "if you can't beat 'em, join 'em": one can approach the textual criticism of the New Testament much as Ehrman does and still hold to historic Christian faith. The latter seems to be the tack taken by Kloha, who claims that, owing to the progress of contemporary textual studies, one need not – and should not – hold that biblical inspiration occurs as single divine events producing an inerrant, once-for-all original text to be recovered as fully as possible through lower, textual criticism. Rather, says Kloha, just as it took the church some time to arrive at its view of the canon of Scripture, so inspiration itself is a continuing process and the decisions as to what indeed constitutes inspired Scripture must be made by the Church as it is led by the Spirit in the course of advances in textual understanding.

Kloha admits that his approach is diametrically opposite to that of the Lutheran fathers – both those of the Age of Orthodoxy (Quenstedt) and those who formulated the theology of the Lutheran Church-Missouri Synod (Pieper). The present author readily admits that those patriarchs could have been grossly mistaken (*errare humanum est*). But, if they were, what are the implications of the Kloha recension?

1) The mainline biblical scholarship of the 19th and 20th centuries in liberal theological circles eliminated an authoritative text through the application of the so-called "higher criticism" – subjective determinations of the "real origins" of the text and the relegation of the best text resulting from lower or textual criticism to a product of later editing and revision in light of the sociological and theological *Sitz im Leben*.

Kloha achieves much the same result by his approach to lower, textual criticism: the Nestle-Aland text, for example, is not to be viewed as a means of arriving as closely as possible to original, inerrant autographs, but as the current state of a "plastic" process which must never be reduced to the status of a propositionally inerrant revelation. To quote Kloha: "We now have a plastic text of the New Testament. It is *plastikos*: moldable, shapeable, changeable ... The transmission history of the New Testament text has ... forced us to reckon with the 'death of the text.'"

In light of his departure from the Lutheran fathers' approach to the nature of biblical inspiration, how does Kloha see himself as a Lutheran – particularly as a conservative Missouri Synod Lutheran? The answer lies in his promotion of an analogy between the divine/human natures of the incarnate Christ and the divine/human character of Holy Scripture. He criticizes liberal Lutheranism (the ELCA) for overstressing the human side of Scripture – but he is similarly convinced that the classical Lutheran theology, as reflected in the Lutheran Church-Missouri Synod, has committed the equal but opposite error of overemphasizing the divine side of the biblical texts.

The severe theological difficulty of Kloha's reconstruction is, to be sure, not just the mistake of pushing an Incarnation-to-Bible analogy much too far (we surely know that the Scripture does *not* in fact have two natures!), but particularly in his disregard of the fundamental Lutheran teaching of the *communicatio idiomatum*: the truth that in the God-man the divine nature is communicated to the human nature whilst the divine nature is never humanised or the human nature divinitised.[20] Calvinism's discomfort with this formulation has produced immense problems in Reformed circles, as Herman Sasse (strangely, one of Kloha's most cited authors) has emphasized. If one wishes to analogise from living Word to written Word, therefore, one must *never* allow the human side of Scripture (including the work of the lower/textual critic) to overwhelm the divinely inspired character of it. Scripture is first and foremost God's divine, inerrant revelation to a fallen race; textual activity must operate *ministerially*, not *magisterially*, in relation to that fundamental perspective.

2) In Kloha's view, final theological authority cannot reside in a Bible produced by single acts of divine inspiration. Rather, that authority must lie in the Church herself as she continually reevaluates the results of the labours of textual scholarship. The text, like the canonicity question, is never finally closed, but remains an open and continuing task for the Church. Writes Kloha: "Who then decides? As always, the gathered baptized, those who hear the voice of the shepherd and follow where he leads

---

[20] See in particular Johann Gerhard, *Loci theologici*, ed. Fr. Frank, I (2d ed.; Leipzig: J. C. Hinrich, 1885), pp. 527-91 (Locus IV, chaps 10-13: "De communicatione idiomatum").

... The church decides, but the church has been and continues to be led by the Spirit into all truth as it hears ever again the Word."²¹

Such a viewpoint would work perfectly in a Roman Catholic context, where an "organic" view of revelation prevails, and where the Magisterium is essential for determining the true meaning and theological application of Scripture in the life of the Christian community; this is the Church as the "continuing incarnation of Christ in time."²²

Needless to say, on such a view it becomes impossible to employ the Scriptures as the final authority by which the Church is judged – since it is the Church that in reality creates the Scriptures by its handling of them. Indeed, the Preface to the Formula of Concord, declaring that the Scriptures are the authority by which "all teachers and writings must be judged," can no longer have any significant meaning.

And one cannot avoid this catastrophic result by arguing dialectically, as do Roman Catholics and Anglicans, that the Scriptures judge the Church whilst the Church is judging the Scriptures, for this leaves the Christian community in a logical and practical impasse: which judgment ultimately prevails? Do we really want to return to the notion that the Spirit somehow manages to keep the Church on track in spite of there being no objective, propositional revelation by which the Church's activity can be evaluated? Had this view been maintained by Luther, how could his Reformation ever have occurred?²³

3) Practically, what would the Kloha approach mean in the day-to-day life of the parish? A pastor would never be able to say with assurance, "Thus says the Lord" – since all of the sacred texts suffer from plasticity. And the individual believer would be unable to have confidence in the text as a declaration of God's will or as a source of life-giving teaching – since its meaning is subject to the latest decisions of textual scholars (such as Kloha). As

---

21 Remarkably, though Kloha's specialty is the New Testament text, he does not seem to realise that "the leading into all truth" (John 16:13) like the bringing "all things to your remembrance, whatsoever I have said unto you" (John 14:26) were special gifts of the Spirit bestowed by Jesus on the original apostolic band, and thus the guarantee that their recounting of divine truth would be infallibly reliable – not a general promise to the church that it would function as the vehicle of revelatory truth. Pre-eminent New Testament scholar Oscar Cullmann referred to this as the "gift of total recall."

22 See Montgomery, "The Approach of New Shape Roman Catholicism to Scriptural Inerrancy," in his *God's Inerrant Word* (Minneapolis: Bethany, 1974), pp. 263-81.

23 Cf. Montgomery, *In Defense of Martin Luther* (Milwaukee: Northwestern Publishing House, 1970; reprint edition in press for the 500th anniversary of the Protestant Reformation, 2017).

for the Lutheran Church-Missouri Synod, it really should not attempt to make theological decisions or pronouncements on issues such as women pastors, for as with one of Kloha's major exegetical illustrations, the plastic text of I Corinthians 12-14 may well not at all be prohibiting women to exercise authority in the church but rather may simply be giving advice on the conduct of husband-wife relations.

To say, as Kloha does, that these staggering difficulties can be resolved by making Christ and his gospel central to our hermeneutic is piously moving but of no assistance whatever. It smacks of the "gospel reductionism" of the Seminex movement; but, far more important, if the biblical text is indeed "plastic: moldable, shapeable, changeable," *so is the Christ of Scripture and so is His gospel of free grace.*

We have nothing against odd theological views; indeed, we have successfully championed religious liberty before the European Court of Human Rights on several occasions. America is a free country, and if one wishes to believe in the Great Pumpkin, that is an available option. But historic Lutheranism is not Roman Catholicism, and the two theologies are mutually incompatible – especially when it comes to the locus of theological authority. A plastic Bible cannot support the theology of the Book of Concord. If we think it can, we make precisely the same mistake the Seminex professors made when they believed that the higher criticism was compatible with Lutheran orthodoxy.[24] Now it's a question of a new philosophy of lower criticism, but in Kloha's case that's a distinction without a difference.

## Addendum to the Appendix: A Word or Two About Textual Criticism

Against the criticisms just presented, one might argue that textual criticism need not be evaluated, much less critiqued theologically, since it must precede all theological discussion. After all, only when one has arrived at a reliable sacred text can one begin to determine proper Christian doctrine and correct Lutheran teaching.

From a logical and scientific standpoint, this is of course correct. One must have a Bible before one can do biblical theology. In that sense, textual

---

[24] Montgomery, *Crisis in Lutheran Theology* (2 vols., 2d rev. ed.; Minneapolis: Bethany, 1973). It seems quite remarkable that Pastor Martin R. Noland can write that "I can't find anything theologically wrong or defective in his [Kloha's] essay." Noland is clearly overwhelmed by the fact that, as he puts it, "Dr. Kloha is the only non-retired academically-qualified text-critic we have in the LCMS right now."

criticism is a heuristic discipline; it functions analogously to formal logic and scientific method – which precede content investigations of the world and need no justification. However, the issue cuts deeper than this, owing to the existence of at least two *philosophies of textual criticism*. The classic philosophy, maintained through the history of the discipline and represented by such scholars as Sir Frederic Kenyon and F. F. Bruce (and the perspective that Kloha is at pains to replace) views the task of textual or lower criticism as our attempt to arrive as closely as possible at the original, autograph text through an examination of the textual material actually available to us.[25]

The "plastic" philosophy espoused by Kloha, however, directs us to the ephemeral character of 1$^{st}$ century writing and publication, and argues that since one cannot always with certainty declare one variant reading better than another, we have a fluid, continually modifiable text, and that just as the early church, unable to decide on the canonicity of certain books, held them in suspension, so the church today, by the work of the Spirit, must embrace and live with the plasticity of the biblical text.

Note the overwhelming problems with such a philosophy of textual criticism.

1) The nature of letter writing and book production in the ancient world is irrelevant to the question of the revelatory character of the biblical text. Just as the Old Testament prophets were often unaware of the ultimate value of their utterances (II Peter 1:21), so the fact that an apostle or associate of an apostle directed his letter to a single congregation has no significance as to the general revelatory significance or inerrancy of that writing for the whole church. If, as Oscar Cullmann and others have maintained, Jesus in fact bestowed the gift of the "total recall" of his ministry and teachings upon the apostolic company – and no serious textual critic, including Kloha, would deny the textual value of John 14:26) – then apostolic writings constitute valid Scripture *regardless* of the immediate intent of the apostle when writing or transmitting what he wrote. Note also that in the New Testament itself, Peter classes Paul's

---

[25] "The province of Textual Criticism is the ascertainment of the true form of a literary work, as originally composed and written down by its author ... The function of textual criticism, then, is to recover the true form of an author's text from the various divergent copies that may be in existence ... The task of textual criticism, then, in relation to the New Testament, is to try to extract the actual words written by the apostles and evangelists" (Sir Frederick G. Kenyon, *Handbook to the Textual Criticism of the New Testament* [2d ed.; Grand Rapids, MI: Eerdmans, 1953], pp. 1, 2, 6).

writings with "the other Scriptures [*ta graphe*]," i.e., with Old Testament revelation (II Peter 3:15-16).

2) The fact that in some cases a variant reading in a given passage cannot be definitively regarded as better than another does not offer any ground for the "plasticity" theory. It simply underscores the nature of a fallen world: our best efforts sometimes do not result in success. The proper approach in such instances is to suspend judgment until better information becomes available, not to declare both variants as somehow equally revelatory, or to believe that Holy Spirit, through the visible Church, will somehow reveal which variant we should follow. Note also that the early church, by continually refining its investigation of apostolic origins, *did* finally come to definite decisions on the canonical content of the New Testament, and those decisions were confirmed during the Reformation period when it was recognized by Protestants that one could not accept the books of the New Testament on the ground that the Church said so. It follows that canonicity today cannot be regarded as something "plastic."

3) One must always remember that instances of indeterminate New Testament textual variants are minuscule – a minute fraction of the entire New Testament text falls into this category – and that none of those variants are determinative for the establishment of theological doctrine.[26]

---

[26] "[Hort, *Introduction to the New Testament in the Original Greek* (1882), p. 2] says: 'The proportion of words virtually accepted on all hands as raised above doubt is very great, not less, on a rough computation, that seven-eighths of the whole. The remaining eighth, therefore, formed in great part by changes of order and other comparative trivialities, constitutes the whole area of criticism ... This area may be very greatly reduced. Recognising to the full the duty of abstinence from peremptory decision in cases where the evidence leaves the judgment in suspense between two of more readings, we find that, setting aside differences of orthography, the words in our opinion still subject to doubt only make up about one-sixtieth of the whole New Testament. In this second estimate the proportion of comparatively trivial variations is beyond measure larger than in the former; so that the amount of what can in any sense be called substantial variation is but a small fraction of the whole residuary variation, and can hardly form more than a thousandth part of the entire test.' It is further to be remembered that, although some doubt attaches to the record of certain incidents and sayings of great interest and value, yet no doctrine of Christianity rests solely upon a disputed text. The Christian student can approach the subject without misgiving, and may follow whithersoever honest inquiry seems to lead him, without thought of doctrinal consequences. His researches should unquestionably be conducted in a reverent spirit, but he may avail himself, without hesitation or mistrust, of all the resources of secular science" (Kenyon, *op. cit.*, pp. 6-7).

"The great mass of the New Testament ... has been transmitted to us with no, or

That being the case, there is no reason whatever, in the face of advances in textual criticism or theory, to move to a "plastic Bible." We are so close to the original autographs (unavailable not just for the New Testament but for all ancient, and most modern writings) that pastors and laymen can "read, mark, and inwardly digest" with confidence the biblical material as inerrant divine revelation. It is *still* the case that *Verbum Dei manet in aeternum*.

As is so often true, the difference between orthodoxy and heresy does not depend on factual or scientific data per se: it depends on the philosophical stance and methodology of the theological investigator. When engaged in or evaluating the work of the textual critic, it would therefore not be amiss to keep in mind the Montgomery clan motto: *Gardez bien*.

## II. Textual and Literary Judgments on the Biblical Text – What Happens to the Lutheran Commitment to Scriptural Inerrancy?[1]

### Part I: Initial Presentation

Our subject is textual (or lower) criticism and its impact on the formal principle (Holy Scripture) of Lutheran – and all biblical – theology. We are especially concerned with the views of Dr Jeffrey Kloha of the Concordia Seminary, St. Louis.

Some preliminaries. First, I have never met Dr Kloha and therefore what I have written and published elsewhere on this topic – and what I

---

next to no, variation; and even in the most corrupt form in which it has ever appeared, to use the oft-quoted words of Richard Bentley, 'the real text of the sacred writers is competently exact; ... nor is one article of faith or moral precept either perverted or lost ... choose as awkwardly as you will, choose the worst by design, out of the whole lump of readings.' ... The autographic text of the New Testament is distinctly within the reach of criticism in so immensely the greater part of the volume, that we cannot despair of restoring to ourselves and the Church of God, His Book, word for word, as He gave it by inspiration to men" (B. B. Warfield, *An Introduction to the Textual Criticism of the New Testament* [1896], pp. 14-15).
The above estimates of textual accuracy should be followed – rather than those given by Norman Geisler in the *Baker Encyclopedia of Christian Apologetics* and elsewhere, allegedly based on Bruce Metzger's *Chapters in the History of New Testament Textual Criticism*, since Metzger there does not in fact present the estimate attributed to him by Geisler.

[1] This essay was presented, in debate with Dr Kloha, at Concordia University Chicago on 15 October 2016.

shall be presenting today – must not be considered any kind of personal vendetta. I am much impressed by Dr Kloha's linguistic knowledge and the laborious analyses of textual minutiae in his doctoral thesis. *Our problem is with the philosophy of textual criticism he espouses and its implications for the doctrine of scriptural inerrancy.*

Secondly, Dr Kloha has repeatedly said that I "do not understand him"[2] and that, because my scholarly specialties are not in the area of textual criticism, I have no business critiquing him. I have pointed out that, with a classics major at Cornell University, a master's degree in New Testament, years of teaching Greek at graduate level, three earned doctorates, and two published translations of previously untranslated Latin works of the 17th century, I am entirely capable of raising issues as to his position; and, far more important, that these issues do not relate to the technicalities of textual criticism but to the *underlying philosophy of textual criticism espoused*. It has been common for atheists such as Richard Dawkins to argue that only someone with his/the unbeliever's scientific specialty (in Dawkins' case, evolutionary biology) has a right to criticize the secular position. This is, of course, errant nonsense, since the problems arise, not from the science *per se* but from the *philosophy of science* being presented. A generation ago, Dr Gordon Clark, a distinguished philosophy professor, wrote a little book on textual criticism. In it, he defended his authorship against the charge that he himself was not a textual critic:

---

[2] In this I am by no means alone. Dr Kloha said the same thing of Dr Alvin Schmidt after Dr Schmidt published a critique of Kloha's position in the 9/1 *Lutheran Clarion* (Sept. 2016): http://lutheranclarion.org/images/NewsletterSep2016.pdf Do Dr Kloha's crtics not understand him – or do they understand him all too well?

For those who think that I don't know anything about textual criticism and have misrepresented Kloha, here is the evaluation of Dr Paul D. Wegner, director of the PhD/ThM Program at Gateway Seminary, Ontario, CA, and author of the standard text, *A Student's Guide to Textual Criticism of the Bible* (Downers Grove, IL: IVP Academic, 2006): "You are very correct in your critique of Kloha's thorough-going eclecticism view. At the end of the day you have no objective criteria to evaluate the text. At least with manuscripts you have something that actually exists and not just your assumptions about which reading is favored by internal evidence ... Because there is so little evidence on how an author can say things and if they can ever say something new or unique causes a serious problem for the thorough-going eclecticism view. You have hit the nail on the head for the problem; is the text a revelatory construction or merely a literary one? If it is revelatory, then we must start with original or as close to original sources as possible" (personal communication, 20 August 2016).

> Although the present writer is not a textual critic, he will be bold enough to make some small claim to acquaintance with logic ... If someone argues, "All insects are quadrupeds, and all quadrupeds are edible, therefore all edibles are insects, "the writer can with some degree of assurance declare the syllogism invalid, even though he may not know whether or not a bumble bee is an insect ... Similarly, if a textual critic asserts that manuscript B has the correct reading for Luke 5:33, and that therefore B has the correct reading for Jude 22, we must suggest a course in logic for the critic, even though we might think that B was discovered in 1624 and represents the Byzantine text.[3]

Thirdly, this is not a call for an *auto da fé*. It up to Dr Kloha's academic and theological superiors to deal with the consequences of his views. I am sure that he is Christian believer who wishes to identify himself with the Lutheran Church-Missouri Synod. The question is: *How realistic is it that someone with his biblical orientation teach future pastors of that church body?*

## Philosophies of Textual Criticism

Let us begin with the most esoteric aspect of the issue – textual criticism *per se*. Here are two standard dictionary definitions of the field: "the study of a literary work that aims to establish the original text"; "the technique of restoring texts as nearly as possible to their original form."

The field is by no means limited to theological materials – classical studies and Shakespearean scholarship are equally concerned to arrive at the best representations of what authors originally wrote.

The problem is that we do not have – in the case of all ancient and most modern literature – the "autographs" of the authors (their original, handwritten texts). It is therefore necessary to compare copies, together with quotations of the work from other writers, so as to arrive as closely as possible to the authorial originals.

In the case of the Bible, this task is made particularly difficult by the sheer number of copies, as well as numerous citations in sermons, in liturgies, and in the writings of early churchmen. The books now in our New Testament were (rightly) considered of such eternal consequence that they were copied, recopied, and quoted again and again from apostolic times to the invention of printing from movable type in the West (the 15th century). So how should the textual critic proceed?

---

[3] Gordon H. Clark, *Logical Criticisms of Textual Criticism* (Jefferson, MD: Trinity Foundation, n.d.), pp.10-11.

There are several theories of textual criticism in the biblical field. These differ particularly in the value they place on *internal, literary criteria* for determining the choice of a reading. We shall focus on the theory espoused by Dr Kloha, following his doctoral mentor J. Keith Elliott, one of the chief advocates of the approach termed *thoroughgoing eclectism*.[4] Here is Professor Elliott's statement of that philosophy – in contrast with the classic approaches:

> The majority of textual critics grudgingly apply principles of intrinsic probability to text-critical problems only when their preferred external evidence is unhelpful or ambiguous. Thoroughgoing eclecticism, by contrast, operates the other way round, that is to say the initial questions asked when variants need to be resolved are: Which reading is in accord with our author's style or language or theology? and Why and how did the alternative readings occur?[5]

A follower of Professor Elliott, Charles Landon, in his *A Text-Critical Study of the Epistle of Jude* (one of the very few attempts to apply thoroughgoing eclecticism to an entire New Testament book), says in his definition of the eclectic method that the methodology relies "mainly on internal evidence

---

[4] We do not commit ourselves to a particular theory; our object here is, rather, to show the great dangers for the doctrine of scriptural inerrancy attendant on the theory espoused by Dr Kloha, following J. Keith Elliott. A far less subjective approach is that of the "single text model" – the model generally chosen being Codex Sinaiticus: "[A]ncient editors would have had access to much earlier and better manuscripts than modern editors and therefore would have probably been in a better position to make text-critical decisions" (Stanley E. Porter and Andrew W. Pitts, *Fundamentals of New Testament Textual Criticism* [Grand Rapids, MI: Eerdmans, 2015], p. 95). The latest efforts to arrive at the *Ausgangstext*/source text of the NT on a more solid, objective foundation is the Coherence-Based Genealogical Method (CBGM). Tommy Wasserman's paper on the subject (57/2 *Novum Testamentum* 206-218 [2015]) and his lecture at the 2014 annual meeting of the Society for Biblical Literature (San Diego, CA) apply the method, *inter alia*, to NT material (I John, Jude) for which we have an apparatus by way of the Editio Critica Maior project at the University of Münster; the result is a substantial critique of Bart Ehrman's claim to "orthodox corruption" of NT texts (textual changes due to Christological controversies) – cf. below, our note 16.

[5] J. K. Elliott, *New Testament Textual Criticism: The Application of Thoroughgoing Principles* ("Supplements to *Novum Testamentum*" 137; Leiden: Brill, 2010), pp. 41-42. See also Elliott, "Thoroughgoing Eclecticism in New Testament Textual Criticism," in: Bart D. Ehrman and Michael W. Holmes, *The Text of the New Testament in Contemporary Research* (2d ed.; Leiden: Brill, 2014), pp. 745-79.

to choose the best reading whenever the MSS divide, [and] places minimal reliance on external evidence."[6]

In practice, this means that, though the thoroughgoing eclectic uses external text evidence (how could he avoid doing so?), the factors that most influence his conclusions are the internal, literary character and context of the work for which he is trying to establish the best reading of a given passage. Thus the following factors loom large in the eclectic's decision-making:

> A variant's conformity to the author's style ... vocabulary [and use of rhetoric]
> A variant's conformity to the author's theology or ideology[7]

Thoroughgoing eclectics have tried to deflect the charge of literary subjectivism that such a philosophy inevitably entails, but without great success. Here is a recent evaluation of that methodology:

> While thoroughgoing eclectics insist on the objectivity of their criteria, issues of style, language, use, theology, and other internal considerations are rarely as formally based as they propose or as clear-cut as they need to be. A wholesale diminishing of external evidence ends up placing the entirety of the decision upon the shoulders of the critic, without due consideration of the objective controls provided by external considerations. This represents the primary reason why most NT textual critics have rejected thoroughgoing eclecticism.[8]

---

[6] Charles Landon, *A Text-Critical Study of the Epistle of Jude* (Sheffield, England: Sheffield Academic Press, 1996), p. 25.

[7] *Ibid.*, p. 26. Landon approves these criteria – to be found in E. J. Epp and G. D. Fee, *Studies in the Theory and Method of New Testament Textual Criticism* (Grand Rapids, MI: Eerdmans, 1993), pp. 163-64. The square brackets are Landon's – who wishes the "rhetorical" style of the author (in his case, Jude's) to be taken into account when evaluating the choice of variant readings to be accepted.

[8] Porter and Pitts, *op. cit.*, pp. 93-94. Not so incidentally, a milder position, "reasoned eclecticism," falls under the same axe: "The same criticisms are applicable to reasoned eclecticism as are lodged above against thoroughgoing eclecticism. There are not clear criteria regarding the balance between external and internal criteria" (*ibid.*, p. 95). Fascinatingly, Elliott himself provides a commendatory recommendation of the Porter and Pitts book.

To prevent misunderstanding, we are not saying that internal criteria must *never* be employed by the textual critic. As in the "construction" (interpretation/exegesis) of legal documents, internal factors can be taken into account in the limiting case where the text as arrived at objectively makes no sense. This so-called "golden rule" in the construction of legal documents states that "the grammatical and ordinary sense of the words may be modified, so as to avoid ... absurdity and inconsistency *but no farther* (*Grey v Pearson* [1857], 6 HL Cas 61, Parke B; our italics).

The same point is made in a review of Elliott's book, *Textual Criticism: The Application of Thoroughgoing Principles* (2010):

> The claim that thoroughgoing eclecticism is "by no means subjective" (19) – indicating that decisions are not made on a whim but on the basis of clearly established criteria – overlooks the fact that the very selection of any criteria is a subjective enterprise.[9]

Another critic of thoroughgoing eclecticism writes:

> What Elliott fails to address, however, is the assumptions upon which a preference for internal criteria depend; for example, in his attention to the variant in Mark 1:4 ... Elliott accepts "the probability of Markan consistency"; indeed, his entire argument depends in part on the assumption that the author is – or would be – consistent in his usage.[10]

The use of stylistic considerations for the determination of text authorship and origins has quite rightly been rejected in other academic fields. Thus, in computer investigations of texts:

> A collection of newspaper articles and an autobiographical account all by the same author may differ considerably in their measurable style. Clearly, then, stylistic analyses are fallible and cannot provide positive identification of a text's authorship or literary heritage.[11]

Parallels with the "higher criticism" should be evident: (1) reliance on subjective, internal, literary considerations in evaluating texts, and (2) the non-acceptance of such approaches outside the narrow confines of a (generally liberal) theological community. It is especially noteworthy that thoroughgoing eclecticism has never been accepted or employed in the textual criticism of Shakespeare; there, one relies objectively on a best text

---

Cf. Montgomery, *Law and Gospel* [2d ed.; Edmonton, Alberta: Canadian Institute for Law, Theology and Public Policy, 1994], chap. 12, pp. 23-26).

[9] Juan Hernandez, Jr. (Bethel University): http://www.academia.edu/6858603/Textual_Criticism_on_the_Basis_of_Thoroughgoing_Principles [accessed 15 September 2016].

[10] Kim Haines-Eitzen (Cornell University), Review of *Rethinking New Testament Textual Criticism*, ed. David Alan Black, *TC: A Journal of Biblical Textual Criticism*, 2003.

[11] Daniel I. Greenstein, *A Historian's Guide to Computing* (New York: Oxford University Press, 1994).

(e.g. the First Folio). As one writer has put it: "*All* modern Shakespeare critics are historical/documentary critics."[12]

There is also a serious logical problem inherent in the philosophy of thoroughgoing eclecticism. If, in the final analysis, one determines a reading by what best fits the internal content of the work as a whole, *how did one discover the proper readings constituting that work as a whole?* One needs to have a solid text in order to judge what variant reading best fits it – so one can hardly claim that literary "fit" is the fundamental factor for deciding which given variant is to be chosen. This is of course why the standard critical editions of the Greek New Testament (Nestle/Aland *et al.*) have generally used Codex Sinaiticus, Codex Vaticanus, the Corpus Paulinum, and the earliest major papyri as their starting points.[13]

## Dr Kloha's Approach to the Biblical Texts

We have noted that Dr Kloha regards himself as a thoroughgoing eclectic. In the conclusion to his doctoral dissertation, he writes: "The goal of this

---

[12] Cf. Peter Alexander (ed.), *Studies in Shakespeare: British Academy Lectures* (London: Oxford University Press, 1964), pp. 128-30. There, bibliographer Ronald B. McKerrow notes Dr Samuel Johnson's reliance on the First Folio and his evaluation of Edward Capell's editorial approach to the Shakespeare texts as "gabble." Capell had "the idea that if an editor likes a reading, that reading is (a) good, and (b) attributable to Shakespeare." This uncomfortably reminds us of how Dr Kloha handles the sacred text (*infra*).

[13] See above, our note 4. Michael W. Holmes concedes that "the effort to identify the earliest text form to which we have access will always have a certain logical and diachronic priority, inasmuch as it provides a point of reference from which to assess and evaluate later changes and developments in the transmission of the text. As Epp has observed, 'we need a baseline'" (M. W. Holmes, "From 'Initial Text' to 'Original Text'," in Ehrman and Holmes, *op. cit.* [in our note 4 *supra*], p. 643). In his discussion of Codex Sinaiticus, David C. Parker notes that "Myshrall's analysis of approximately three thousand corrections in the Gospels revealed that the vast majority of them are minor – orthographical or just changing word breaks across a line. Only a tiny number are textually significant" (D. C. Parker, "The Majuscule Manuscripts of the New Testament," in Ehrman and Holmes, *op. cit.*, p. 58). And Barbara Aland, after noting the careful transmission of the earliest major papyri ($\mathfrak{P}^{45}$, $\mathfrak{P}^{46}$, etc.), states: "If we do not see radical changes in the transmission of a text later on, it follows that we should not see them earlier on either, before the initial text. And thus we should be able to trust the initial text as being fairly close to the original text" (B. Aland, "New Testament Textual Research, Its Methods and Its Goals," in: Stanley E. Porter and Mark J. Boda, *Translating the New Testament: Text, Translation, Theology* [Grand Rapids, MI: Eerdmans, 2009], p. 24).

study has been realized: To apply the principles of thoroughgoing eclecticism to the readings of the Greek manuscripts of I Corinthians, in order to determine how and, where possible, why the manuscripts were altered in the earliest period of transmission, that is, up to the fourth century."[14]

But what does this mean in practice? The fact that thoroughgoing eclecticism privileges subjective, internal, literary criteria for the choice of biblical texts does not *per se* mean that Dr Kloha falls into this methodological pit. We must therefore examine how Dr Kloha does in fact make his textual decisions.

Kloha's doctoral dissertation provides innumerable illustrations of the consequences of his acceptance of thoroughgoing eclecticism. Here are but two instances that point up very clearly the incompatibility of his approach with the classic doctrine of biblical inerrancy – that the Bible speaks the truth in everything it teaches or touches.

In his treatment of I Cor. 7:33-34, Dr Kloha rejects the "archetypal" reading reflected in our modern translations (based on the foundational MSS $\mathfrak{P}^{15}$ B P) on the grounds that "the influence of the parallelism of the context, the difficulty of several syntactical features, and the development of terminology and practice in the early church led to several simultaneous alterations that cannot be attributed to accidental corruption."[15]

At the end of his thesis, Kloha speaks of "the contexts of individual witnesses." He asserts that these contexts "can be known only in the case of a handful of witnesses (for example F G), and even there only imperfectly. Nevertheless, the theological, ethical, and even linguistic developments that were taking place during the first few centuries of the transmission of the *Corpus Paulinum* must be understood. For example, only after a highly-developed Trinitarian theology took hold could the addition of 8:6 have been made."[16] It should be observed that if this view is accepted, no pastor should preach I Corinthians 8:6 as if it were the Word of God.

---

[14] Kloha, "A Textual Commentary on Paul's First Epistle to the Corinthians" (unpublished Ph.D. dissertation, University of Leeds, 2006). Vol. 2, p. 714 [hereafter cited as "Kloha thesis"]. Only the first two volumes are text; the remaining volumes consist of lists of MSS readings, bibliography, and the reproduction of a previously published article. The thesis demonstrates impressive labour; what it lacks is awareness of the theological implications of the philosophy of textual criticism it slavishly follows.

[15] Kloha thesis, I, 186-87.

[16] Kloha thesis, II, 717. It is clear that Kloha agrees here with Bart Ehrman: "As Ehrman has argued, at least some passages of the NT manuscripts have been altered in light of the christological controversies with which the scribes, presumably,

In the Festschrift for his mentor Elliott, Dr Kloha identifies the author of the *Magnificat* as Elizabeth and not Mary.[17] To be sure, whether Mary or Elizabeth spoke those words poses no doctrinal issue whatsoever. But the way in which Kloha arrives at his attribution is fraught with the most serious consequences for the authority and factual inerrancy of the text – and, by implication – for all other biblical material.

Klohe first sets forth the manuscript evidence for the two readings of Luke 1:46. "Turning to the continuous-text manuscript tradition of Luke," he properly notes, the Marian reading "is consistently attested in all Greek MSS at Luke 1:46" (p. 205). This, to be sure, is why "no editions of the Greek New Testament produced in the last half-century" accept any reading other than the Marian one (p. 200). The only readings of any consequence attributing the *Magnificat* to Elizabeth are non-Vulgate Latin readings, Irenaeus (a divided authority, however, since in one place he explicitly attributes the song to Mary), Origen (indecisive, as with Irenaeus), and a little-known, hardly impressive late 3d-, early 4th-century Latin preacher, one Nicetas of Remesiana. The fact that these authorities are earlier than the authoritative Greek texts (Codex Sinaiticus and Codex Vaticanus, early to mid 4$^{th}$ century) is hardly a strong argument for the Elizabeth attribution, since they are non-Greek versions/translations and contradict the Greek texts.[18] Kloha admits this.

So why does Dr Kloha favour the Elizabeth reading – against the powerful weight of textual authority? Answer: because he accepts the philosophy of textual criticism espoused by J. Keith Elliott. In the Introduction to the Elliott Festschrift, we are told that "Keith's career has seen him refocus his work from searching for an 'original text' to what may be reasonably be said of the history to which texts point." Kloha revealingly quotes Elliott

---

would have been familiar" (*ibid.* I, 26). Ehrman's (and Kloha's) hypothesis of "orthodox corruption" has been shown by Tommy Wasserman to be unnecessary in several instances (cf. above, our note 4). My appreciation to Wasserman for an email that helped to make my argument more precise on this point.

[17] Kloha, "Elizabeth's *Magnificat* (Luke 1:46)," *Texts and Traditions: Esssays in Honour of J. Keith Elliott,* ed. Peter Doble and Jeffrey Kloha (Leiden: Brill, 2014), pp. 200-219. Another contributor to this volume is James W. Voelz, Kloha's New Testament Department head at Concordia Seminary, St. Louis, who (naturally!) has found no problems with Kloha's methodology or theology.

[18] See, for example, the Nestle/Aland *Novum Testamentum Graece* (28$^{th}$ ed.; Stuttgart: Württ. Bibelanstalt) at Luke 1:46. Throughout his doctoral dissertation on the text of I Corinthians, Kloha shows particular bias for early, non-Vulgate Latin readings – in spite of the tremendous problem that it is impossible to identify the original Greek text they were attempting to translate. See below, our Appendix A, for two simple illustrations of the irrationality of Dr Kloha's approach.

at the beginning of his article in the following terms: the textual critic, according to Elliott, "feels able to select freely from among the available fund of variants and choose the one that best fits the internal criteria" (p. 200).[19]

If such an approach is accepted, the result is what might well be termed a "designer New Testament": variants are chosen according to the literary criteria of the textual critic, the idea being to arrive at a text which has the literary quality (similarity of vocabulary, style, structure, etc.) with which the critic is comfortable. This is, of course, to deny the *historical* claims of the New Testament books (e.g., Luke 1:1-4, which precedes the *Magnificat* passage in the same chapter!). Note well: *any* New Testament text would be subject to the same treatment. Dr Kloha's students, as future pastors and teachers, could hardly miss the lesson: if Kloha can do it, so can I.

The central problem with thoroughgoing eclecticism and Dr Kloha's employment of it lies in the unrestrained discretion given to the textual critic. Here one observes a significant parallel with the evils of uncontrolled judicial discretion.[20] A proper jurisprudential philosophy will limit judicial discretion to those rare cases where the law is unclear. A proper biblical theology will limit textual discretion to those rare cases where external evidence *per se* cannot provide a solution based on the weighing of MS authority.

Even recognizing the unfortunate results of Dr Kloha's textual philosophy in practice, can we not say that, considering the overwhelming similarity of textual readings and therefore the virtual identity of modern translations based on commonly accepted Greek texts of the New Testament (almost never the product of thoroughgoing eclecticism), no harm is really done?

Sadly, much harm is done. This is due to the fact that Dr Kloha draws a logical but deadly conclusion from the fundamental principle of thoroughgoing eclecticism that *all* variant readings are in theory deserving of consideration. Since the number of existing texts, good, bad, and indifferent, is legion – and since there is always the possibility of uncovering previously undiscovered ones – the text of the New Testament is indeed never settled ("plastic," to use language that he has ceased to use for political reasons). This means that the biblical text is always in a state of flux. Dr Kloha declares: "We now have a text of the New Testament that makes no

---

[19] More detail on this issue can be found in the first section of the present chapter.
[20] "Judicial power is never exercised for the purpose of giving effect to the will of the judge, always for the purpose of giving effect to the will of the legislature; or, in other words, to the will of the law" (John Marshall, C. J., *Osborn v. Bank of the United States*, 22 U. S. 738 (1824).

claim to being fixed and stable, for it is subject to continuous improvement and change."[21]

That being the case, how can it be authoritative for the pastor or the layman? When can one say with confidence, "Thus says the Lord?" Dr Kloha sees the historical church as the solution: it is the church that ultimately decides on the text to be accepted at any point in time. And since the church is the body of Christ, led by the Holy Spirit, we need not be troubled by an ever-changing Bible.

In Kloha's view, the attempt to get back to the original autographs of Scripture is a chimerical task. One cannot even be sure that the *Corpus Paulinum* gives us the *ipsissima verba* of the Apostle. Indeed, final theological authority cannot reside in a Bible produced by single acts of divine inspiration. Rather, that authority must lie in the church herself as she continually reevaluates the results of the labours of textual scholarship. The text, like the canonicity question, is never finally closed, but remains an open and continuing task for the church. Writes Kloha:

> How, then is it decided which *reading* is apostolic and has been received as such by the church? The church has been and continues to be led by the Spirit into all truth as it hears ever again the Word. And the church has always taken the greatest care to ensure that what it teaches and preaches is indeed apostolic. That work continues today, in light of new evidence and historical study ... [T]o speak of a single act of inspiration ... leaves us vunerable ... God works in history. The Spirit created the church.[22]

---

[21] Kloha, "Theological and Hermenuetic Reflections on the Ongoing Revisions of the *Novum Testamentum Graece*," in: Achim Behrens and Jorg Christian Salzmann (eds.), *Listening to the Word of God: Exegetical Aprpoaches* (Göttingen: Edition Ruprecht, 2016), p. 180. (This is the revision of Kloha's "Plastic Text" essay delivered at the Lutherische Theologische Hochschule, Oberursel, Germany, in November, 2013.)

[22] *Ibid.*, pp. 198, 200. The proof-texts Kloha cites in support of his view have, literally, nothing whatever to do with the issue (I Cor. 1:21, Acts 2:38-41). In his original "Plastic Text" paper, he wrote: "Who then decides? As always, the gathered baptized, those who hear the voice of the shepherd and follow where he leads ... The church decides, but the church has been and continues to be led by the Spirit into all truth as it hears ever again the Word." Remarkably, though Kloha's specialty is the New Testament text, he does not seem to realise that the *"leading into all truth" (John 16:13) like the bringing "all things to your remembrance, whatsoever I have said unto you" (John 14:26) were special gifts of the Spirit bestowed by Jesus on the original apostolic band, and thus the guarantee that their recounting of divine truth would be infallibly reliable - not a general promise to the church that it would function as the vehicle of revelatory truth.* Preeminent New Testament scholar Oscar Cullmann referred to this as the "gift of total recall." See below, our note 32 and Appendices C and D.

This, of course, is exactly the Roman Catholic solution to textual problems and biblical authority.

It is *not*, however, the Lutheran answer. Had it been, Luther's Reformation would never have occurred. He could hardly have said at Worms, "My conscience is captive to the word of God" and set biblical teaching against that of the Roman church of his day. One cannot have it both ways: if the Scripture is created by the church, it can hardly be used to criticize the church's errors.

Moreover, of course, such a solution is pure *Schwärmerei*: the Holy Spirit, instead of working through the objective Word to "reprove the world of sin, and of righteousness, and of judgment" (John 16:8), becomes a *deus ex machina* to justify the subjective literary judgments of the textual critic as to the proper content of the biblical text. In a very real sense, when "the church led by the Spirit" justifies the text, it is really justifying the literary perspective of the textual critic(s). Unless the text is justified by Christ's promise to the apostolic band, i.e., by its apostolic character, there will be no adequate case for its revelatory and inerrant nature. Without this, the Christian falls into the sectarian category of proclaiming as God's word what cannot be shown to be such (as with the *Bhagavad gita, Qur'an, Book of Mormon, Science and Health*, etc.).

And what happens to the Lutheran commitment to the *inerrancy* of Holy Writ? Inerrancy refers to issues of *truth:* whether the Bible is factually correct in all its assertions. When the content of Scripture is treated as a literary production – texts being chosen that presumably fit better the literary context – inerrancy becomes impossible in principle. A literary production can be effective and moving, but it cannot be "true" or "false." (Think, for example, of *Winnie the Pooh*.)

To be sure, one can redefine "inerrancy" – to mean, say, "effective and moving" – doing in every instance "what God wants it to do." This is precisely how the Seminex professors handled the matter. They never outrightly denied the inerrancy of the Bible; they merely downplayed it at best and redefined it at worst (example: Arthur Carl Piepkorn).[23]

Hear Dr Kloha on the inerrancy issue, and ask yourself: How does this differ from simply jettisoning the doctrine and going with Seminex "gospel reductionism" (the Bible is true in the sense that it presents the gospel):

---

[23] See A. C. Piepkorn, "What Does 'Inerrancy' Mean?" 36 *Concordia Theological Monthly* 577-93 (September, 1965). Cf. for numerous other illustrations: Montgomery, *Crisis in Lutheran Theology* (2d ed., 2 vols. in 1; Grand Rapids, MI: Baker Book House, 1973), I, 81-123 (especially pp. 96-97, 116-17).

If you want to rip Romans 15 and 16 out of my Bible, I can live with that. If you want Hebrews, James, Revelation torn out too, I can live with that. If you force me to look only at p46 or the bizarre majuscule manuscript W or one of thousands of Byzantine minuscules and use them as my New Testament – I can live with that. Give me only Codex Boernarianus, one of the most poorly copied, misspelled, error filled copies of Paul's letters, and I can live with that. I could live with or without any of those, because even these poorly copied, corrupted by people, edited, to use Luther's words, preach Christ. And if they preach Christ, they are of the Spirit, for preaching Christ is the Spirit's work. And if they preach Christ, they are apostolic, for the apostle can speak nothing other than what he has been sent to speak. So apostles, no matter who they are, even one who has been aborted yet lived like Paul, who once persecuted the church, preach the death and resurrection of Jesus Christ. I can live without a perfect Bible. I cannot live without God raising Jesus from the dead.

On the other hand, force me read only the Gospel of Thomas, I cannot live with that. Or the Koran, or the Book of Mormon. Not because the are not "inerrant" or "perfect," or even "human," but because there is no Gospel: There is no new life in Christ.[24]

Finally, it has been argued that, since Dr Kloha has not denied any Lutheran doctrine, there is no issue to be faced anyway. Such a conclusion is comfortable politically, but represents staggering naiveté.[25]

We mentioned Seminex in passing. The Seminex professors accepted as legitimate the higher criticism. Higher critics receive from the lower/textual critics the best biblical texts, and then endeavor to go "higher" (or deeper) by subjecting the biblical material to internal, stylis-

---

[24] Kloha, "The Authority of the Scriptures," Concordia Seminary St. Louis 2010 Symposium ("The Scriptures: Formative or Formality?"). The logical slippage in the above argument should not be overlooked (cf. above, the Gordon Clark quotation at out note 3). Says Kloha: "*if they [texts] preach Christ, they are apostolic, for the apostle can speak nothing other than what he has been sent to speak. So apostles, no matter who they are ...*" BUT preaching Christ does not make the preacher an Apostle ("apostolic") – or everyone who has ever preached the gospel would be an Apostle! In reality, solely *being an Apostle* makes one's utterances per se apostolic.

Not so incidentally, *pace* Dr Kloha, the reason for textual critic Bart Ehrman's defection from biblical Christianity was *not* his prior commitment to a traditional, evangelical understanding of the inerrancy of given-once-for-all biblical texts; it was his acceptance of a rationalistic, anti-miraculous, secular worldview which made any kind of transcendent revelation impossible (*finitum non capax infiniti* vs. the biblical – and Lutheran – *infinitum capax finiti*).

[25] See Appendix B to this essay.

tic, literary analysis. On finding what they believe to be errors, inconsistencies, vocabulary and stylistic differences, etc., they arrive at the conclusion that there must have been earlier sources, earlier authors, and earlier editors of the material. The fact that such earlier documents are nowhere to be found does not bother the higher critic – for his approach, like that of thoroughgoing eclecticism, focuses not on the objective, but on subjective, literary, stylistic judgment. In both cases, one might say – perhaps unkindly, but realistically – an objective God who objectively reveals is replaced by the Critic whose subjective determinations provide whatever "revelation" there is.

Is it really important whether biblical revelation is destabilized by higher criticism or by an unfortunate philosophy of lower criticism? The result is the same. Unless one gives the Holy Spirit a function Scripture does not, or unless one accepts the Roman Catholic belief that the church visible is the justifier of Scripture, these views must be rejected. One simply cannot be permitted to hold such views as a confessional Lutheran.

*A Cautionary Tale in Conclusion*

In the preceding analysis, we have assiduously avoided *ad hominem* argumentation. But, in conclusion, it cannot be omitted – owing to the lesson it carries.

On the recommendation of his department head, Dr James Voelz, Jeffery Kloha proceeded to the University of Leeds (England) to obtain the Ph.D. under Professor J. Keith Elliott.[26] The English Ph.D. is not like the American degree of the same nomenclature: it requires neither a year or more of advanced course work in the field nor any comprehensive, written, qualifying examinations; the entire responsibility of the candidate is to produce an original thesis that will satisfy his doctoral mentor, advisor(s), and sometimes external examiners chosen by the doctoral mentor. In his doctoral thesis, Kloha lavishly praises Elliott for his guidance and his personal kindnesses.[27] In point of fact, Professor Elliott, during his career, has been a vicious critic of scholars who do not agree with him. Here are but two painful examples:

---

[26] Note: not a theological doctorate from a theological faculty.
[27] "Prof. J. K. Elliott has provided his meticulous guidance throughout. It has been an honor to work under his direction. I only hope that I can begin to emulate his model of outstanding scholarship and warm collegiality" (Kloha thesis, I, 1).

A review by Professor Elliott in the *Journal of Theological Studies* was so offensive that the editors subsequently published the following notice in its New Series (2013):

> **Editorial Apology.** In April 2010 *JTS* published a review of Professor Chris Keith's book *The Pericope Adulterae, the Gospel of John, and the Literacy of Jesus* (New Testament Tools, Studies, and Documents 38; Leiden: E. J. Brill, 2009). Pp. xvi+350. Hardback Euro121.00/$166.00. ISBN 978 90 04 17394 1. The editors wish to apologize unreservedly for the publication of this review, and for the unprofessional and personal criticisms of the book and its author which it contained. The editors have also invited Professor Keith to respond in the article which follows to the academic criticisms of his book which were made in the review and a new review of the book has been commissioned."

Professor Elliott's review of the late Dr Harold Greenlee's *The Text of the New Testament: From Manuscript to Modern Edition* (2008) in the *Review of Biblical Literature* was so objectionable that one commentator used the adjective "vituperative" to describe it.[28] It is noteworthy that Professor Elliott has been especially disturbed by evangelicals (in his view, fundamentalists) such as Dr Greenlee.

Plainly, Professor Elliott does not suffer gladly those whom he considers fools, and deviation from the thoroughgoing eclectic textual theory for which he has become the major spokesman would be difficult to tolerate. Success in obtaining the English doctorate requires the wholehearted support of one's major professor. I am myself acquainted with sad cases of students' ruffling the feathers of their doctoral advisors at English and commonwealth universities and never receiving their degree.[29]

Is it too much to suppose that, with so much at stake academically, Jeffery Kloha moved inexorably into the orbit of his mentor's textual theory – even though there is no possible way to make it compatible with the classic Lutheran view of Scripture (or any understanding of the Bible as inerrant revelation, for that matter)?

---

[28] http://evangelicaltextualcriticism.blogspot.com/2009/02/greenlee-review-keith-elliott-responds.html [accessed 15 September 2016].

[29] Since I possess two earned European doctorates (as well an an American one), this evaluation can hardly be dismissed as "sour grapes." See my article, "On Taking a European Theological Doctorate," in Montgomery, *The Suicide of Christian Theology* (Minneapolis: Bethnay, 1970), pp. 174-80.

If so, it would hardly be a unique phenomenon. American seminary graduates – especially those from theological faculties of in-grown denominations where the student has spent virtually his entire academic life in the institutions of that church body – arrive in Europe and are blown-out-of-the-water by a professorial atmosphere where, all too often, you either become a disciple of your major professor or return home with no doctorate and nothing to show for all the time and money expended. Example: Daniel Fuller (son of the famed radio evangelist Charles Fuller) whose doctrine of biblical inerrancy disappeared as he studied for the theological doctorate under the aegis of Karl Barth at the University of Basel.[30]

Those American theology students who do proudly return to the U.S. with European doctorates often receive teaching positions at conservative theological seminaries, colleges, and bible schools. The institutional administrators are so impressed with the newly-crowned doctors that their beliefs are seldom questioned – as long as they use the proper creedal and denominational lingo (without being asked to define their terms, of course). For a while, the professors continue to use the old language of biblical "infallibility" or "inerrancy," but eventually that goes by the board – and the institutions move to a "moderate" or "quasi-liberal" theological stance (Princeton Seminary, Fuller Theological Seminary, and a host of others).

"Professor" is, etymologically, "one who professes" something. A seminary professor, above all, should be presenting, stressing, and reinforcing his students' confidence in Holy Scripture – not offering new and original viewpoints that do exactly the opposite. Our entire culture pressures the church and its clergy to give up confidence in God's inerrant Word. Sadly, our Lutheran seminaries offer little or no meaningful answers and little, if any, serious apologetics for the truth of the faith once delivered to the saints. This is scandalous, and declining church membership is often but a reflection of inadequate seminary instruction.

One of the major themes of J. R. R. Tolkien's novels *The Hobbit* and *The Lord of the Rings* is the ease with which we come to believe that, if evil is decisively conquered on one occasion, we shall have nothing to fear in the future. But, in fact, Middle Earth – and *our* earth – is never free of the dangers of the old Dragon's return. Only Christ's coming will end the struggle.

In the Lutheran Church-Missouri Synod, many have believed that, with the purification of the church (and especially the St Louis seminary) from

---

[30] As told me by Daniel Fuller in persona conversation. Daniel Fuller became subsequently one of the main influences in the Fuller Theological Seminary's jettisoning of its doctrinal commitment to biblical inerrancy.

the Seminex contamination, the church body became immune to scriptural and doctrinal problems. "Now, all we need to worry about are the church growth movement and increased administrative centralism." Nonsense.

If I were C. S. Lewis's demonic Uncle Screwtape, I would not bother with liberal denominations: they aren't saving people anyway. I would focus my efforts on destroying the few church bodies that still hold to the entire truth of God's Word (Scripture and Gospel). They are the ones to corrupt – and the best place to start is the faculties of theology, and the best place in the seminaries to do devilish work is the exegetical department. Why? Because a corrupt view of Scripture will – as the night follows the day – inevitably result in the corruption of systematic and practical theology – and thus impact what will be preached from the pulpit by the seminary graduates. And I would always push any viewpoint that stresses subjective decision-making, since, at all costs, the demonic strategy is to downplay the fundamental truth that God's Word is always *extra nos*.

For Uncle Screwtape to succeed, all it takes is naïve seminary and church administrators: seminary presidents, deans, and department heads who value "scholarship" or "academic reputation" above doctrine; church presidents who want peace and any price, and value, above doctrinal truth, good ecumenical relations with sister denominations or with wider ecclesiastical life.

"The secret of freedom is courage" (Thucydides). But in church and seminary bureaucracies today, courage is the virtue encountered the least. Why do theological seminaries and churches go liberal – as virtually all have done? Answer: the pusillanimous attitude that refuses courageously to root out whatever is incompatible with the formal or material principles of any truly confessional theology.

Our concluding recommendations: (1) Refuse to tolerate textual philosophies that employ internal (stylistic) criteria as the preferred standard for the choice of readings – just as we have refused to tolerate higher critical theories that employ internal (stylistic) criteria to determine the origin and authorship of the biblical books.[31] (2) Insist upon a serious commitment to biblical inerrancy – which necessarily means that scriptural material purporting to present historical facts (e.g., Luke's Gospel) be treated as objective history and not transformed into literary productions where the content depends upon stylistic considerations as theorized by

---

[31] Cf. Kurt E. Marquart, "The Incompatibility between Historical-Critical Theology and the Lutheran Confessions," in: *Studies in Lutheran Hermeneutics*, ed. John Reumann (Philadelphia: Fortress Press, 1979), pp. 313-33.

critics or interpreters. (3) Continue to oppose all varieties of gospel reductionism – all positions that maintain, in one fashion or another, that biblical revelation consists of nothing more than expressions of the gospel and that whatever else is there can be treated as the product of human fallibility. (4) Maintain and present to a dying world the objective, factual, evidential work of God as exemplified by a totally trustworthy Bible and a historical Christ whose human life and divine ministry are precisely as described in the biblical records.[32]

---

[32] For a summary of the serious difficulties in Dr Kloha's approach, see Appendix C (*infra*).
N.B. I had suspected that a good part of Dr Kloha's problem was a tacit commitment to a presuppositionalist stance, comparable to that present in much Calvinist/Reformed epistemology (Cornelius Van Til, *et al.*). This is confirmed in Kloha's recent essay, "Manuscripts and Misquoting, Inspiration and Apologetics," presented at the Lutheran Concerns Association Annual Conference, 19 January 2015: "In the end, we either trust the promises of Christ, or we do not ... 'But when the Comforter comes, whom I will send to you from the Father, the Spirit of truth who proceeds from the Father, he will testify to me' (John 15:26) ... We cannot *make* the Scriptures authoritative, we cannot prove them to be authoritative; any foundation or method which depends on our interpretation or reconstruction is, by definition, self-referential, self-serving, and ultimately uncertain. Only one based on Christ and his promises, which we know through his Word, is certain" (p. 16). Three comments: (1) If the text is not factually certain, how do we "know Christ and his promises through his Word"? The gospel will be uncertain if the text of Scripture is uncertain. (2) As we have pointed out earlier, John 15:26 and the other passages in John dealing with Jesus' gift of truth and recall through the Spirit are directed specifically to the apostolic company, *not* to the church across the centuries – unless we commit ourselves to some kind of "apostolic succession" as does Roman Catholic theology (see *supra*, our note 22; also our Appendix D, *infra*). (3) The presentation of factual evidence for the correctness of a viewpoint is *not* "self-referential" or "self-serving." Without such evidence for biblical truth, the unbeliever in a secular age is left without an effective witness. Dr Kloha's presuppositionalism may be a comfort to those already Lutheran; it is a hopeless fideism in a pluralistic world of unbelief crying out for Christians who will "be ready always to give an answer [Gk *apologia*] to everyone that asks you a reason for the hope that is in you" (I Peter 3:15). (See my numerous apologetics publications in this area, and especially "Christian Apologetics in the Light of the Lutheran Confessions," in: Montgomery, *Christ As Centre and Circumference* [Bonn, Germany: Verlag für Kultur und Wissenschaft, 2012], pp. 147-63; and reprinted as a chapter in the present volume.)

## Coda

Debates tend to harden the positions of the debaters. This is unfortunate. I believe that Dr Kloha wants to be a truly Lutheran professor of theology, faithful to its beliefs and to those of the historic church.

May I therefore suggest that

- he rethink the eclectic position and move in the direction of a more objective textual philosophy, such as that of the Coherence Based Genaalogical Method;
- he realize that the authority of the NT rests with its *apostolic character*, objectively guaranteed by Jesus' promise to the apostles that the Holy Spirit would cause them to remember accurately exactly what he had told them (and their subsequent approval of Paul as a genuine apostle);
- he accept the necessary consequence of this promise, that a divinely guaranteed inspiration establishes the truth of the NT writings, not just in a narrow theological sense ("gospel reductionism") but in everything they present as historical fact;
- he agree that these writings, *not created but confirmed by the church*, can and should function as the standard "by which all teachers and writings must be judged" (Formula of Concord, Epitome);
- he undertake a serious study of apologetics – to see how this factually true biblical revelation can be successfully proclaimed and defended in a world where the number of Lutheran church members continues to diminish but where the growing number of unbelievers must be presented with a religion of truth, not just a religion of personal faith;
- he clearly and explicitly convey these essentials to his students and future pastors, as well as to the scholarly, ecclesiastical, and general public – and that he publish in the same media as have publicized his earlier views his re-orientation of perspective in these several areas of critical doctrinal concern.[33]

---

[33] Dr Kloha might also consider joining the Evangelical Theological Society, the doctrinal basis of which states: "The Bible alone, and the Bible in its entirety, is the Word of God written and is therefore inerrant in the autographs."

# Appendix A: Why We Should Not Employ Kloha's Textual Approach: Two Hypotheticals

*The Reagan Hypothetical*

Suppose 200 years have passed since the death of President Reagan. Textual scholars are concerned to arrive at the proper reading of one of his speeches. No autograph original of the speech has survived.

The majority of textual critics rely on several MSS of the speech that are dated some 100 years after Reagan's time. These are in the English language.

Now Critic K points to another MS of a portion of the speech that can be dated some 50 years after the speech was delivered. It is in Spanish and fragmentary. This text uses an expression that, when translated back into English, Reagan used during the *Iran-Contra* hearings ("I have no recollection of that"). The widely accepted, English MSS of the speech say, instead, "How could I remember a thing like that?"

Critic K argues for the reading in the Spanish MS – on the grounds that (1) stylistically, it's more "Reaganesque" – it fits better from a contextual standpoint than does the reading in the English MSS, and (2) it is earlier than the MSS relied on by the majority of textual scholars.

What do we say to this? Surely, we should reject Critic K's argument. Why?

(1) No writer or speaker has to be consistent in style, vocabulary, structure, etc., and people do not in fact operate that way. The task of the critic is to determine what Reagan actually said – as a historical fact – not what the critic thinks would provide a better or more consistent literary version of the speech.

(2) *Earlier* is not necessarily *better* – particularly when a translation (version) is involved. Reagan never delivered speeches in Spanish, and there is always the possibility of mistranslation in trying to construct the original from a translation..

Note the close parallel with the determination of whether or not to accept the "Elizabeth" rather than the "Mary" reading of the *Magnificat*. Codices Siniaticus and Vaticanus ("Mary") are admittedly later (4$^{th}$ century) than the 2d-3d century Latin readings ("Elizabeth") relied upon by Kloha. However, those questionable earlier readings are not in the common Greek (*koiné*) – the *lingua franca* of the Apostles' time – and no one maintains that any NT book was originally written in Latin. As for literary style, do we really want a biblical text that reflects what the critic thinks the Apostles *should* have written – as opposed to a text based on the most widely accepted Greek MSS and therefore presumably a better record of *what historically – in fact – occurred?*

## The Vinific Hypothetical

Let us suppose that a 2d century non-Vulgate Latin version of the wedding of Cana pericope in John 2 is discovered in the ruins of an Egyptian monastery. This MS has the words for "wine" (*vinum*) and "water" (*aqua*) reversed throughout, so that Jesus changes wine into water. This reading also occurs once in Irenaeus and once in Origen, and is employed in an anti-drunkenness sermon of the 4th century ascetic A. Teetotalus.

Dr C. R. I. ("Carry") Nation, is a prominent textual critic of the thoroughgoing eclectic persuasion. From Dr Nation's literary standpoint, the acceptance of the Latin reading – doubtless derived from a now lost, early Greek text of the Gospel – would far better fit the New Testament concern to reduce inebriation (e.g., "Be not drunk with wine, wherein is excess; but be filled with the Spirit" – Eph. 5:18). And it is much earlier than the baseline Greek MSS Codex Sinaiticus and Codex Vaticanus (early to mid 4th century).

As a result of his internal analysis, Dr Nation opts for the Latin reading as best fitting the literary context and theology of the Gospel – even though there is almost uniform agreement among the best texts against it.

Dr Nation has followed the underlying principle of thoroughgoing eclecticism: he has allowed internal, literary considerations to trump objective, external MS evidence.

In spite of his being highly praised by the Baptist and independent fundamentalist churches, which have always been uncomfortable with the historical fact that Jesus turned water into fermented wine, *Dr Nation should be locked up for his own good and for the good of the church.*

## Appendix B: Consequences of Kloha's Viewpoint

"Some folks who have followed this controversy may wonder how I could state about Dr. Kloha's revised essay in Behrens and Salzmann ... that "I find nothing in it that is false doctrine" ("Noland Replies to Christian News," *Christian News* 54 #19 (May 9, 2016): 3, col. 1) and at the same time disagree with some aspects of that essay or see such aspects as 'problems.' That is because I agree with the LC-MS about what constitutes a 'doctrine.' In LC-MS Constitution Article II, we define our 'doctrine' as that which agrees with the Scripture and the Lutheran Confessions. In the Brief Statement (1932), Article 44, the LC-MS also stated what is *not* doctrine: 'Those questions in the domain of Christian doctrine may be termed open questions which Scripture answers either not at all or not clearly.' Neither Scriptures nor the Lutheran Confessions answer the questions raised by textual variants, therefore we have no formal or official 'doctrine' in the Lutheran church with regard to the matter of textual criticism. This is affirmed by the 'Statement of Scriptural and Confessional Principles' (1973, under 'The Infallibility of Scripture') which states 'We recognize that there are apparent contradictions or discrepancies and problems which arise because of uncertainty over the original text.' BUT – even though we don't have an official doctrine in the field of textual criticism, it therefore does not follow that every philosophical assumption, method, criteria, or statement made in that field is *congruent with our doctrine of Scripture*. My concern in the present article is the lack of such congruence, and I share that concern with Dr. Montgomery. For more on the LC-MS approach to open questions and theological problems, see Francis Pieper, *Christian Dogmatics*, vol. 1 (St Louis: CPH, 1950), 93-102; and C. F. W. Walther, 'On Syncretism,' 'The False Arguments for the Modern Theory of Open Questions,' and 'Theses on the Modern Theory of Open Questions,' in *Church Fellowship*, Walther's Works (St. Louis: CPH, 2015), 81-143." – Martin Noland, "Why Dr. John Warwick Montgomery Is Right," 9/1 *Lutheran Clarion* (Sept. 2016), p. 4. n. 3: http://lutheranclarion.org/images/NewsletterSep2016.pdf

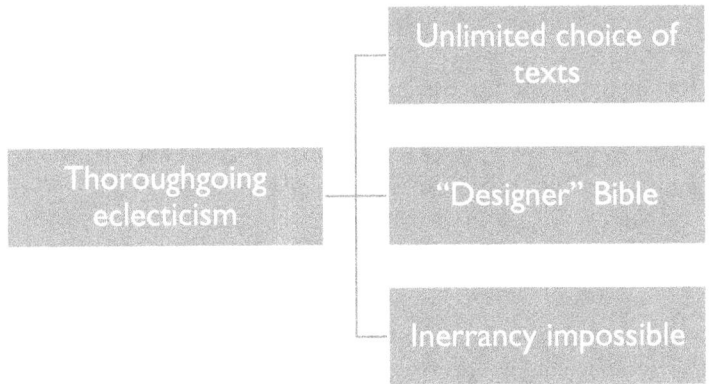

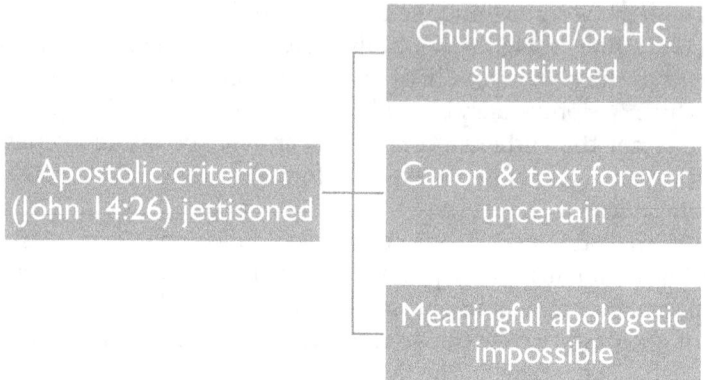

## Appendix C: Kloha vs. Classic Theology

| The Classic Position | Kloha's Position |
|---|---|
| 1. NT texts chosen with minimal reliance on internal, literary considerations | 1. NT texts chosen primarily on the basis of internal, literary considerations (thoroughgoing eclecticism) |
| 2. Inspiration of NT documents based on their *apostolicity* (written by apostles or in apostolic circles) | 2. Authorship of NT documents unimportant revelationally, since "if a text preaches Christ, it *is* apostolic" |
| 3. Inspiration of NT documents a once-for-all act, limited to the apostolic company, including St Paul (accepted as a genuine apostle by the original apostles); *Scripture critiques the church* | 3. Inspiration is a continuous process in the history of the church, guided by the Holy Spirit; the church guarantees that the text is indeed revelatory[34] |

---

[34] Kloha relies on John 13-17 to argue that Jesus' promise to "lead into all truth" was a promise made to the whole church through the centuries – and thus that the church, by way of the Spirit, can presumably create the canon and validate on a continuing basis the scriptural texts to be accepted as revelatory. However, those utterances of our Lord were *specific to the apostolic company*, as 14:26 makes crystal clear (bringing "all things *to your remembrance*, whatsoever I have said to you"). The personal references are exclusively to apostles (Peter, 13:36; Thomas, 14:5;

| | |
|---|---|
| 4. Original autographs of NT writings inerrant; best texts approximate the autographs | 4. "We now have a text of the New Testament that makes no claim to being fixed and stable, for it is subject to continuous improvement and change" |
| 5. The Scriptures are correct in all their assertions, not just when they present the gospel (vs. gospel reductionism) | 5. Textual errors are unimportant as long as "Christ is preached" |
| 6. The Scriptures are defensible as divine revelation to an unbelieving world | 6. "Proving" Christian revelation is "self-referential" and "self-serving" (Kloha a *fideist*) |

## Appendix D. Epistemological Fallacies in Asserting Biblical Inerrancy

*A. The Common Varieties*
1) Confusing inerrancy with canonicity
2) "Secular" vs. "spiritual" biblical content
3) Gospel reductionism
4) "Hermeneutics as a cloak for the denial of biblical inerrancy" (Barton Payne)
5) Ecclesiology as a cloak for the denial of biblical inerrancy
6) Pneumatology as a cloak for the denial of biblical inerrancy

*B. The Core Problem*

Is it true that "as long as one asserts biblical inerrancy, it makes no difference what constitutes one's *epistemological authority* for that belief"? Is there a valid parallel with the notion that salvation comes from a simple relationship with Christ, such that one need have no epistemological or apologetic understanding to enter into the salvatory relationship?

Note the confusion: Of course, to be saved there is no need to work through philosophical issues that do not trouble the believer; but if one does not, for example, hold to the factuality of Jesus' life, miraculous acts, preaching, etc., one cannot be "saved by Christ" – since one isn't believing

---

Philip 14:8; Judas 14:22); see also 15:27 ("you have been with me *from the beginning*"); 17:12 (Judas Iscariot the only one lost). Not until 17:20 does Jesus shift attention to the whole church.

in the only Christ who factually saves. The saved thief on the cross knew little theology, but he accepted the facticity of Jesus' declaration that they would be together in Paradise; not to have accepted that would have precluded his salvation.

Likewise, if one's basis for holding to "inerrancy" is of such a nature that it (1) redefines inerrancy to embrace de facto errors in the biblical text, or (2) grounds inerrancy in an authority that is fallible or subjectively indefensible, the consequence is an "inerrancy" devoid of meaningfulness. Such an "inerrancy" will be incapable of sustaining Christian faith in a secular world and will so weaken Christian proclamation that the believer will be unable to declare "Thus saith the Lord" in any persuasive fashion.

A few examples of how *not* to ground biblical inerrancy:

- I believe that the Bible is inerrant because, as an Irishman, I was visited by a leprechaun who informed me of its nature.
- I believe that the Bible is inerrant because of a vision I experienced and an angelic word confirming biblical authority.
- I believe that the Bible is inerrant because the Book of Mormon assumes its inerrant authority.
- I believe that the Bible is inerrant because the Roman Church maintains in the Canons and Decrees of the Council of Trent that it is such.
- **I believe that the Bible is inerrant because the Holy Spirit guides the church across the centuries toward solid textual authority; de facto errors in the text or higher critical analyses do not therefore upset my belief in biblical inerrancy. [Kloha]**
- I believe that the Bible is inerrant because that belief warms my heart.

## C. The Proper Basis for Inerrancy

*The historical Christ's position on the nature and value of Holy Scripture.*
See below, the 6-point argument at the end of the Rebuttal.

## Part II: Montgomery's Rebuttal to Kloha

*Positive*

- Dr Kloha cites an impressive list of Lutheran fathers dear to the heart of conservative Lutherans: Chemnitz, Sasse, Pieper, the Preuses. (It is noteworthy, however, that he offers these citations even when they are not in fact on point with the disputed issues to be treated in this debate.)

- His presentation today is very different in tone from that of his prior publications. (Is it possible that Dr Kloha takes his audience's worldview into account, presenting material incompatible with biblical inerrancy to audiences not holding to inerrancy, and the reverse in contexts such as the present one? Is he perhaps *disingenuous?*)

## Negative

- More interesting is *what he has left out* than what he has presented:
+ He glosses over the essence/the distinguishing feature of thoroughgoing eclecticism: its privileging of internal criteria over objective external evidence in determining the choice among variants. Note the citations corresponding to **notes 5-10** in my initial presentation.

Here I should perhaps clarify my criticism of the use of internal factors in choosing text readings. I made clear in **footnote 8** that I was not opposing *all* use of internal considerations – only those offering unrestrained discretion to the critic according to his literary views. Here are several additional items from Epp's list of internal criteria (cf. my presentation, **note 7**):

- ✓ A variant's status as the shorter or shortest reading
- ✓ A variant's status as the harder ot hardest reading
- ✓ A variant's fitness to account for the origin, development, or presence of all other readings
- ✓ A variant's conformity to Koiné (rather than Attic) Greek
- ✓ A variant's conformity to Semitic forms of expression

There is, in principle, nothing the matter with employing these more objective internal-criteria rules – which differ markedly from choosing readings on the basis of a supposed consistency of the author's vocabulary and style, or conformity with what the critic supposes to be the author's theology or ideology.

Worth noting also are the potential conflicts in the choice of the internal criteria to be employed in any given instance. For example, non-Semitic-style readings would presumably be the "harder" readings. Do we, then, disregard the "Semitic" rule and choose a "harder," non-Semitic reading? A hierarchy of criteria has to be employed, but such a hierarchy is invariably *implicit*; it will perforce be chosen and applied *ad hoc* by way of the subjective judgments of the critic. This problem becomes especially acute when we recall that, for the thoroughgoing eclectic, *internal considerations always trump external MS evidence.*

The dangers are particularly great in the two areas we cited in our initial presentation: "A variant's conformity to the author's style, vocabulary, and rhetoric" and "A variant's conformity to the author's theology or ideology." But these are *the very criteria Kloha employs to argue for Elizabeth and not Mary as author of the* Magnificat.³⁵

+ Kloha agrees with Michael Holmes, advocate of "reasoned eclecticism" (cf. our initial presentation, **note 8**) that "hopes for some sort of genealogical or documentary method that will somehow bring clarity out of confusion are illusory" (Kloha's paper, pp. 15-16). This perhaps explains why the Editio Critica Maior and the Coherence Based Genealogical Method receive only cursory reference in two footnotes of the Kloha essay (notes 6 and 63). In point of fact, this revolutionary method, which will eventually be used throughout the Nestle/Aland *Novum Testamentum Graece* and which has already provided the text of the Catholic Epistles in the 28th edition, offers a significant advance in text critical methodology. As Klaus Wachtel of the University of Münster's Institute for NT Research has said in his essay on "The Coherence Method and History": "Pre-genealogical coherence ... is independent of any subjective element. It is based solely on the degree of agreement between witnesses" (*TC: A Journal of Biblical Textual Criticism* [2015]: http://rosetta.reltech.org/TC/v20/TC-2015-

---

35  Martin R. Noland has suggested in a personal communication the following helpful rules for a proper handling of the external and internal criteria in choosing one variant reading over another:
– (AGE) if a word or phrase comes from the oldest extant Greek MS, and there are no variants from that century in Greek, it should be considered the original text.
– (GEOGRAPHICAL ORIGIN) if there are two or more variants for a word or phrase that come from the oldest extant Greek MSS, then the independence of the MSS witnesses indicated by differing provenance or geographical origins (if known) should determine which is the original text.
– (GENEALOGY) if there are two or more variants for a word or phrase that come from the oldest extant Greek MSS, and such MSS have the same provenance or geographical origins, then the genealogy of the variants – determined by text types or the Coherence-Based Genealogical Method – should determine which is the original text.
– (MORE OBJECTIVE INTERNAL CRITERIA) if there are two or more variants for a word or phrase that come from the oldest extant Greek MSS, and geographical origins and genealogy are identical, then "the more objective" internal criteria may be used in order to decide which text is the most probable, with the alternates indicated in study bibles and Greek texts with apparatus – but subjective internal criteria, such as the author's alleged style, language, theological views, etc. should never be used to make these judgments.

CBGM-history.pdf). This is not to say that the Coherence Based Genealogical Method or the Editio Critica Maior rejects the use of internal criteria; but these are employed in a better, less subjective, relation to the external, MS evidence.

+ In his presentation, Dr Kloha criticizes Bart Ehrman's argument that there has been "orthodox corruption" of early NT texts (p. 21). However, Kloha does not bother to mention that, in his doctoral dissertation, he himself approvingly cites Ehrman's argument in behalf of that very orthodox corruption! (See my initial presentation, **notes 4 and 16**.) Did Luther validate "orthodox corruption" theory by rejecting I John 5:7? Certainly not, for that verse is properly to be rejected owing to its appearance only in eight late MSS (none of them earlier than A.D. 1215, and four of them providing the reading as no more than a marginal note qualifying as a scribal commentary).

+ Dr Kloha offers no repudiation of any of his previously published material – the source of the current concern with his views. Specifically, he apparently still has no problem with

1) his assertion that "we now have a text of the NT that makes no claim to being fixed and stable, for it is subject to continuous improvement and change"; *and*
2) his effort to substitute a continuous inspiration by way of the Holy Spirit's work in the history of the church, rather than centering, as do the Lutheran fathers, on the "single act of inspiration" through Apostolic authorship (which, he says, "leaves us vulnerable").

+ Only 2 ½ pages at very end of his 24-page paper touch on the **inerrancy** aspect of the topic, and he gives us *no definition of what he means by the term.* Does he believe that the biblical texts are *factually correct in all they say*? That, for example, the Apostle Peter is the author of II Peter and is speaking of his eyewitness presence on the Mount of Transfiguration (1: 1, 16-18)? How about the authorship of other NT materials, where the text explicitly names the author (e.g., I and II Timothy – or Kloha's favorite, I Corinthians)? Was Quirinius in fact governor of Syria and was there really a census at the time of our Savior's birth (Luke 2:1-2)?

- It is noteworthy also that Dr Kloha rejects the *higher criticism* without apparent awareness that his philosophy of *lower criticism* moves in precisely the same direction. The higher critic uses internal, stylistic considerations to discover allegedly earlier, "source" texts; Kloha (as his *Magnificat* analysis clearly shows) privileges internal, stylistic considerations to arrive at the proper choice of variants, and thus the true nature of the biblical text. He – mercifully – does not hypothesize earlier sources for the text, but he determines *the nature of the text itself* by employing subjective, internal, literary analysis. In both instances, the result is a "designer" Bible, the historicity of which is lost in literary "fit."

- Finally, let's look at *what he does emphasize* – at the very end of his paper (his page 24). Here we find material taken directly from the essay he delivered at last year's Lutheran Concerns Association's Annual Conference [2015] and is obviously so important to Dr Kloha that it warranted repeating on this occasion. Dr Kloha dismisses apologetic attempts to justify biblical inerrancy or, presumably, Christian truth-claims in general. I have treated this in **note 32** of my paper, and I read from there. It also appears on the screen for your convenience.

Now, if I found myself trying to reconcile Dr Kloha's textual approach with biblical inerrancy, I, too, would doubtless have no choice but to jettison all objective apologetic argument and dive into the bottomless pit of presuppositionalism and fideism. Fortunately, if one doesn't go with Kloha's textual philosophy, such a perilous route need not be taken.

In conclusion, then, let us examine Kloha's assertion that all attempts to demonstrate the factual truth of biblical revelation are "self-referential" and "self-serving." In reality, these expressions are properly applicable, not to those who have a solid understanding of biblical inerrancy and present historical evidences for the Christ of Scripture to unbelievers, *but to the very fideism Dr Kloha substitutes for any kind of evidential foundation*. Offering evidence for Christ and a solid NT text shifts the ground from the believer to the Word, and is therefore 180° away from the "self-serving" or the "self-referential."

It is only when one privileges dogmatic certainty over evidences that provide overwhelming historical probability, refusing to offer the latter to today's unbeliever, that the unbeliever will quite rightly see our evangelistic efforts as "self-referential and self-serving." Why? because then there is no reason to think that the basis for believing is anything other than the believer's personal faith, not an objective ground for accepting biblical texts as God's revelation.

Far from being "self-referential" and "self-serving," the defender of biblical truth *refers the unbeliever to Christ by way of reliable scriptural evidence*. His work, like that of John the Baptist, is to point *away from himself to the historical Christ* who died on the Cross and whose truth is attested by solid witnesses and solid historical documentation. Cf. the crucifixion panel of the Grünewald altarpiece at the Unterlinden museum in Colmar, Alsace, France.

*Apologetic Finale*

If one refuses to support biblical claims by evidence, one reduces Christian faith to the level of other world's religions and the cults. Two quick examples: one Islamic, one Mormonic (not moronic).

Some years ago, I debated Imam Shabir Ali at the Inns of Court School of Law in London. When pressed as to why he believed that the Gospel writers had perverted the original picture of Jesus, he answered: because the Qur'anic portrait of Jesus presents Jesus as a prophet, not as a "Son of God" and certainly not as divine. But, I queried, why accept the Qur'an on the subject – seven centuries after the time of Jesus and not written by eyewitnesses to the life of Jesus? Ali's answer: because the Qur'an is Allah's final revelation. Ali would not (and could not) offer evidence in behalf of the revelation in which he believed (in a 100% presuppositional, fideistic manner). Do we, as Christian believers and inheritors of Luther's replacement of inner, subjective conscience with the objective, perspicuous Word of God (as at Worms), want to present the biblical gospel as unfounded and unjustifiable to a fallen world, desperate for genuine divine truth?

About the same time as the Ali debate, two Mormon missionaries arrived at our flat in Strasbourg, France. I asked them why they believed in the Book of Mormon. Answer: because of the "burning in the bosom," i.e., the inner conviction of its truth. Sadly, they could not support the Book of Mormon by historical or archeological evidence, and appealing to Joseph Smith accomplished little (he never demonstrated deity by rising again from the dead). Do we want our evangelism to have no objective foundation and appear to the unbeliever as nothing more than another subjective claim to religious truth?

In broadest outline, here is the *Christ-referential and Christ-serving* apologetic we advocate:

1) The NT materials can be shown to be reliable historical documents (cf. Montgomery, *History, Law and Christianity*)
2) The writers can be shown to be reliable eyewitnesses (cf. Bauckham, *Jesus and the Eyewitnesses*)
3) The eyewitnesses inform us that Jesus himself claimed to be the Divine Savior
4) Jesus' claims are validated by fulfilled OT prophecies concerning him and by the miracles he performed, especially his resurrection from the dead
5) Jesus considered the OT inerrant revelation and promised his Apostles a special gift of the H.S. to recall what he had taught them; apostolic writings thus have the same inerrant, revelational character (including Paul's writings, since he was accepted as a genuine Apostle by the original apostolic company – see II Peter 3:15-16).
6) Conclusion: Jesus is indeed God incarnate, come to earth to die for our sins and offer us the way to eternal life; and all of Holy Scripture is God's reliable and inerrant revelation of the divine will for a fallen race.

# 17. Christian Concern UK: Evangelicals contra Irreligion in an Increasingly Secular Britain[1]

*Abstract:* Christian Concern and its litigation arm have in recent years been the most vocal spokesmen for conservative evangelicalism in Britain's political and legal arenas. Founded by former practicing barrister Andrea Williams within the Lawyers' Christian Fellowship (Horace Rumpole's 'Lawyers As Christians'), it has actively promoted the evangelical agenda and taken legal cases as far as the European Court of Human Rights in Strasbourg. Among its concerns are: fighting abortion, euthanasia, assisted suicide, and same-sex relations; and defending Christian practices in the public square such as personal evangelism, the employment of Christian symbolism, and the distribution of Christian literature. This paper will briefly evaluate Christian Concern's biblically-orientated program, degree of success, and future prospects.

## I. Introduction: Christian Concern UK

This evangelical Christian organization originated as a network within the Public Policy Unit of the Lawyers' Christian Fellowship in the United Kingdom. Owing to concerns on the part of some of the leadership of LCF that the Unit's growing activism could jeopardise charitable status, the head of the Policy Unit, Andrea Minichiello Williams, separated it from LCF in 2008, whilst maintaining amicable relations with the Fellowship. The litigation arm of Christian Concern UK is the Christian Legal Centre, most of whose cases are handled by barrister Paul Diamond.

The official website of Christian Concern UK states the aims of the organization in the following terms: 'At Christian Concern we have a passion to see the United Kingdom return to the Christian faith. Our nation has been shaped and defined by this faith for hundreds of years. Yet in the last few decades, the nation has largely turned her back on Jesus and embraced alternative ideas such as secular liberal humanism, moral relativism and

---

[1] Invitational presentation at the God, Religion and Politics Conference, Institute for Interdisciplinary Biblical Studies, University of Sheffield (U.K.), 8-9 April 2015.

sexual licence. The fruit of this can be seen in widespread family breakdown, immorality and social disintegration'[2]

The Christian Legal Centre, in its own words, serves to 'defend Christians in the public sphere and to protect the freedom of Christians to live their lives in accordance with their Christian beliefs'[3]

Among the major 'concerns' addressed by the organization and listed as such in their materials are: Abortion, Same-sex marriage and parenting, End-of-life, Employment, Religious freedom and Freedom of speech, Islam, International persecution, and Social concerns.

In consequence, the organization has campaigned, *inter alia*,

1) against abortion rights
2) against gay marriage and gay parenting
3) against euthanasia and assisted suicide legislation
4) against Islamic expansion and mosque-building
5) against persecution of Christians internationally
6) against films offensive to Christian believers such as Scorsese's *Last Temptation of Christ*
7) in favour of street evangelism and evangelism in public places
8) in favour of the Christian demonstration of their faith by the wearing of crosses and other Christian symbols at work

The Christian Legal Centre has handled cases such as the following:[4]

1) Defense of street preachers and preaching in town centres (e.g., Mike Overd of Somerset, arrested for allegedly violating the Public Order Act in the Taunton town centre)
2) Defense of Christians distributing Christian literature to or attempting to evangelise Muslims in a public-employment context (e.g., Victoria Wasteney, senior occupational therapist, suspended by NHS)
3) Defense of Christians expressing religious viewpoints in a job context (e.g., nurse Sarah Mbuyi, dismissed by a London children's nursery for saying that marriage should be only between one man and one woman)
4) Defense of Christians refusing to work on Sunday (e.g., the Celestine Mba case)
5) Defense of Christians refusing to provide sex counseling to homosexual partners (e.g., the Gary McFarlane case)

---

[2] http://www.christianconcern.com/about [retrieved 14 March 2015]
[3] http://www.christianconcern.com/christian-legal-centre [retrieved 14 March 2015]
[4] For details of a number of these cases, see http://www.christianconcern.com/cases [retrieved 14 March 2015].

6) Defense of Christians refusing to officiate at same-sex partnership ceremonies (e.g., the Ladele case, where Ms Ladele, a registrar of births, deaths and marriages, was fired because of her conscientious objection to doing such)
7) Defense of Christians refusing to place children into the care of homosexuals (e.g., Sheffield magistrate Andrew McClintock, forced to resign)
8) Defense of guest-house owners applying their "married couples only" policy to refuse a room to same-sex partners (e.g., Peter and Hazel Mary Bull case)
9) Defense of cross-wearing in public employment (e.g., the Shirley Chaplin case, in which the NHS Trust refused to allow any such display unless it was doctrinally "mandatory" in the wearer's religion; and the Eweida case, in which a British Air stewardess was told not to wear a cross on pain of discharge)

As noted, the major influence behind Christian Concern UK and its litigation arm is barrister Andrea Minichiello Williams. Andrea is an attractive, dynamic wife and mother of Italian background. Her dynamism and strong emotional stands betray her Italian heritage. Some years ago, when her husband's professional activity required their presence in the United States for a year, she returned to England deeply impressed by the activism in American evangelical life. She remarked on one occasion that she really preferred that religious lifestyle to the non-confrontational, passive, essentially relational and ingrown style of English church life. Although never a full-time barrister or litigator, she saw the law as a means of asserting the values of traditional Christianity in an increasingly secular UK. Andrea's theology is that of conservative evangelicalism: belief in the entire correctness of biblical teachings and the essentiality of personal commitment to Christ for personal salvation. In line with the late Jerry Falwell's American 'Moral Majority,' she endeavours to impact the society with what she sees as Christian values.

## II. Theological examination

Since Christian Concern UK operates as an activist theological organization, it is only proper to ask whether its concerns and approach are theologically sound by its own standards. Here, some serious problems arise.

First, in terms of the concerns it addresses, one confronts a mixed bag. Many of the organisation's concerns are genuinely biblical and of great importance, particularly those relating to medical ethics. Holy Scripture is patently prolife: it affirms the existence of the person from the moment of conception;⁵ it therefore opposes as a logical consequence abortion and genetic manipulation (stem cell cloning, etc.).⁶ The Bible places such a high value on human life that every instance of suicide in the Scriptures is treated negatively.⁷ Moreover, the Bible condemns in unqualified terms homosexual practices (Romans 1) and understands marriage monogamously and as the union of one man with one woman.⁸ Finally, since the biblical position is that the preaching of the gospel is the *sine qua non* for personal and societal salvation, Christian Concern UK stands for freedom of evangelism and freedom of Christian expression.⁹ In Christian Concern UK's furtherance of these goals, it is surely acting in accord with its fundamental principles.

At the same time, a number of the emphases of the organization can hardly be justified as biblically mandated. Thus, efforts to reduce the activity and influence of other religions and the censorship of films obnoxious to Christian faith, even in a country (England, Scotland) where a state church exists, can very well be seen as an attempt to stifle religious freedom in general. The irony of this lies in the fact that Christian Concern UK rightly strives to increase freedom of expression for Christians (public evangelism in particular), but does not seem to realise that religious freedom must be accorded to all non-socially-deleterious religious viewpoints in order to make possible genuine, freely chosen commitments to Christianity. The choice afforded by a single religion can hardly be defined as a choice at all!

Moreover, support for sabbatarian positions is very hard to justify scripturally in light of the New Testament abolition of the requirements of Jewish ceremonial law (circumcision, feast days, dietary laws). Christian

---

[5] See John Warwick Montgomery, *Slaughter of the Innocents* (Westchester, IL: Crossway, 1981).

[6] See John Warwick Montgomery, 'The Embryo Cloning Danger in European Context,' in his *Christ Our Advocate* (Bonn, Germany: Verlag für Kultur und Wissenschaft, 2002), 197-218.

[7] See John Warwick Montgomery, 'Whose Life Anyway? A Re-examination of Suicide and Assisted Suicide,' *ibid.*, 169-95.

[8] Cf. Christopher Wolfe (ed.), *Same-Sex Matters: The Challenge of Homosexuality* (Dallas, TX: Spence Publishing, 2000).

[9] See John Warwick Montgomery, 'The Freewill Issue in Theological Perspective' and 'Some Remarks on Punishment and Freewill in Legal Theory & Classical Christian Theology,' in his *Christ As Centre and Circumference* (Bonn, Germany: Verlag für Kultur und Wissenschaft, 2012), pp. 270-85; and Angus J. L. Menuge (ed.), *Legitimizing Human Rights: Secular and Religious Perspectives* (Farnham, Surrey, England: Ashgate, 2013), *passim*.

Concern UK's uncritical support of such smacks more of American fundamentalism and Calvinist legalism than of biblical teaching.

More serious are the indirect effects of the organisation's activism in a secular British society. There are three prominent approaches in Christendom as to how the Christian should react in a secular context: stay as far away as possible from secular government and secular society (what might be termed the monastic/Mennonite/Amish approach); dominate the secular society (the Constantinian approach, also characteristic of Calvinistic reconstructionisms); and the viewpoint which 'distinguishes law from gospel' (the Lutheran view, held also by many Anglicans).[10]

The monastic viewpoint can hardly be justified biblically, since Christians are supposed to be 'lights in the world' – raising the moral level of society to accord with biblical standards. The Constantinian/Calvinist solution – what Luther termed a *theologia gloriae* (a triumphalist 'theology of glory') – in endeavouring to force biblical morality on a recalcitrant society makes genuine evangelism exceedingly difficult, since after ramming biblical morality down the throats of unbelievers it becomes very difficult to present the gospel to the secularist as a matter of free choice.

The Lutheran approach, termed a *theologia crucis* (a 'theology of the cross') has as its fundamental principle that *evangelism should almost always trump ethical amelioration* – the biblical ground for this being Jesus' 'Great Commission' declared to the church at the close of his earthly ministry (Matthew 28): 'to preach the gospel to every creature,' not 'to raise the moral level of society.' This approach can be described in a serious of propositions;

1) One mustn't try to force the institutionalisation of Christian values (in the U.S., this would in any event run up against the First Amendment separation of church and state)
2) One mustn't try to force biblical ethics on the non-Christian through Christian political blocs
3) One mustn't legislate non-revelational mores in the name of revelation, or to legislate even genuinely scriptural moral teachings when they lack demonstrable social necessity
4) However, the Christian has a responsibility to raise the moral standards of our culture: to achieve this, believers need to impact the climate of

---

[10] Cf. John Warwick Montgomery, 'Should We Legislate Morality?' in *Christians in the Public Square: Law, Gospel & Public Policy; Essays by C. E. B. Cranfield, David Kilgour, M.P. [and] John Warwick Montgomery* (Edmonton, Alberta, Canada: Canadian Institute for Law, Theology and Public Policy, 1996), 69-79.

opinion by convincing the non-Christian public of the legitimacy of biblical moral standards so that they also vote in accord with scriptural standards; to achieve this, *persuasive common-ground arguments* must be employed

5) The fundamental principle: *Evangelism trumps moral improvement*
6) The sole exception: right-to-life (abortion, euthanasia, etc.) The justification of this exception lies in the fact that the right to life is fundamental for the operation of any and all other rights; once one is dead, other rights are irrelevant; thus it would have been monstrous for Christian during the Third Reich to refuse to oppose the death camps on the ground that by doing so evangelism to death-camp guards would have been imperiled.[11]

Our misgivings about some of the goals of Christian Concern UK lie in the (perhaps unwitting) Calvinism of the organisation's approach and style: they seem little concerned with the negative effect on evangelism inevitably produced by the confusion of truly biblical with traditional moral positions and, even more important, with the negative effects of forcing Christian values on a secular society by social pressures and litigation. Where right-to-life is concerned, the latter may well be justifiable; in other areas, that is surely not the case and can be seriously counter-productive for the Christian cause.

## III. Sociological/Pragmatic Evaluation

American evangelicalism, whose theology and practice have so deeply influenced Christian Concern UK through the experiences of its founder, is heavily impregnated with Puritan-Calvinist values. During the 17th and 18th centuries, Puritan Calvinism was the dominant influence in the American colonies, and it deeply impacted 18th- and 19th-century evangelical 'awakenings,' even when the revivalism regarded itself as Methodist or even Arminian.[12] Baptist Jerry Falwell's 20th-century 'Moral Majority' would have been right at home in Calvin's Geneva or in Cromwell's Commonwealth. Christian Concern UK reflects this tradition – with not a small dose of the revivalistic passion characteristic of the American evangelistic movement.

To be sure, Christian Concern UK is reacting to a tectonic shift toward secularism in the UK, including its legal professions.

---

[11] This discussion is further developed in John Warwick Montgmery, *The Shaping of America* (Minneapolis: Bethany, 1976), 152 ff.
[12] *Ibid.,* 37-46, 123-33.

When I read for the English bar, the most influential figures on the English legal scene were serious, practicing Christians: Lord Chancellor Hailsham, whose first autobiography, *The Door Wherein I Went*, contains an important legal apologetic for Christian faith[13]; Lord Diplock, who worshipped regularly at the barristers' Temple Church; and Lord Denning, president of the Lawyers' Christian Fellowship. Now the atmosphere has radically changed: the English judge who denied the appeal of Christian relationships counselor Gary McFarlane, fired for refusing to provide sex counseling to a homosexual couple, stated that religious justifications were 'irrational.'[14]

A very recent YouGov survey shows the extent of the problem.

> Religious figures have the least influence on the lives of young Britons – and more say religion is a force for evil than a force for good
> 
> In the 2011 Census, 59% of the population described themselves as Christian and only a quarter reported having no religion. But a new poll of young people ... by YouGov finds that the place of religion in the lives of young Britons is smaller than ever.
> 
> YouGov asked 18-24 year olds which figures have influence on their lives, and religious leaders came out on bottom: only 12% feel influenced by them, which is far less than even politicians (38%), brands (32%) and celebrities (21%).
> 
> The reputation of religion amongst young people is actually more negative than neutral: 41% agree that 'religion is more often the cause of evil in the world' and only 14% say it is a cause for good.
> 
> When asked if they believe in God, only 25% say they do. 19% believe in some non-Godlike 'spiritual greater power' and a further 38% believe in no God or spiritual power whatsoever.[15]

All of which may account, at least in part, for Christian Concern UK's lack of much success in litigation (it is impossible to gauge its success in influencing public opinion, but one is not encouraged by the organisation's limited focus on convincing those already within the Christian community –

---

[13] Reprinted in Vol. 4 (1984-1985) of *The Simon Greenleaf Law Review*, under my editorship.

[14] See Montgomery, 'Religious "Irrationality" and Civil Liberties,' *Amicus Curiae: Journal of the Society for Advanced Legal Studies* [U.K.], Summer, 2010.

[15] https://yougov.co.uk/news/2013/06/24/british-youth-reject-religion/ [retrieved 14 March 2015] Full poll results are available at http://cdn.yougov.com/cumulus_uploads/document/jgdvn3vm4b/YG-Archive-Pol-Sun-results-190613-youth-survey.pdf

a kind of 'preaching to the converted'). The *Wikipedia* article on the Christian Legal Centre accurately states: 'Since its inception, the CLC has provided legal support in a number of high-profile cases in the UK. Most of them have been unsuccessful.'[16] One of the factors in this lack of success appears to be the litigation style of their chief advocate, barrister Paul Diamond. Diamond cannot be faulted for lack of courage, but his aggressiveness and lack of sensitivity have certainly not helped in cases he has argued. At the concluding session of the Inner Temple/Middle Temple conference on 'Magna Carta, Religion, and the Rule of Law' (7 June 2014), Diamond was roundly criticiaed for his advocacy by academics and judges on the programme. His argumentative style suggests that of convert from Judaism and founder of the American Centre for Law and Justice, Jay Sekulow (who, however, has had much greater success – perhaps understandably – in the American courtroom and before the U.S. Supreme Court).[17]

On balance, Christian Concern UK is filling a definite need. As former French president Nicolas Sarkozy said in a visit to the Pope a number of years ago, Christians should be more, not less, vocal in a democratic society. This is particularly true when the values of that society are changing in a direction that sidelines Christian belief and the high principles of the faith that have been a glory of western civilization. At the same time, it is essential for Christians, such as those in Christian Concern UK, to distinguish law from gospel; truly biblical teaching from mere conservative traditionalism; and the important cultural differences between America and Europe.

---

[16] http://en.wikipedia.org/wiki/Christian_Legal_Centre [retrieved 14 March 2015]. This article lists additional cases in which the Centre has been involved. For Christian Concern's own efforts to show a success rate worthy of attracting contributors, see its Christian Legal Centre publication, *Case Summaries 2006-2015.*

[17] On Sekulow, a protégé of Pat Robertson, see, *inter alia,* the *American Bar Association Journal,* June, 1998, 30-32,

# 18. A Non-Politically-Correct Remedy to Muslim Terrorist Immigration[1]

*Abstract:* It is commonly assumed that little can be done legally to stem the tide of Muslim terrorist immigration. This paper argues that (1) immigration is controlled in international public law by the principle of national sovereignty; (2) refugee treaty ratification is likewise a question of national sovereignty; (3) the exclusion by national law of socially obnoxious political parties has been upheld by the European Court of Human Rights; (4) individuals dangerous to the state are regularly prohibited from entering western nations; (5) a religious position can, by its fundamental beliefs and history, fall into the category of the socially deleterious; (6) Islamic extremism constitute such a category; and (7) strict immigration standards can therefore be established, without violating recognized religious freedoms, to require those of Islamic belief wishing to immigrate or to enter the frontiers of a western state to disavow fundamental Quranic and Shari'a teaching as a condition of acceptance. In making this argument, the paper offers analogies with other religious and quasi-religious positions having socially questionable beliefs and practices (anthropophagy, Aztec human sacrifice, Mormon polygamy) and deals with the basic question, in the case of Islam, whether the atrocities committed historically and contemporaneously in its name are aberrational or inherent to the fundamental belief structure of that religion.

## Introduction

When attending the cinema in France, a notice often appears on the screen in the case of a film not already vetted by the national cinema authority. It reads (our translation): "Before seeing this film, the viewers are invited to verify for what audience the film is appropriate." Perhaps such a notice should accompany this paper, since it will be exceedingly offensive to politically-correct readers. Our plea is to reserve judgment and pay close attention to the reasoning. It is just possible that the logic of the paper can

---

[1] Invitational presentation at the IVR World Congress on the Philosophy of Law and Social Philosophy, Washington, D.C., July 27-31, 2015; and at the 67th Annual Meeting of the Evangelical Theological Society, Atlanta, GA, November 17-19, 2015.

displace perspectives based on rhetoric and lead to a more realistic approach to one of the most serious cultural problems in contemporary western society.

## Two Hypotheticals

In accord with jurisprudential practice, we begin with two hypothetical situations relating to the acceptance of non-citizens into a country either as tourists, temporary visitors, or immigrants.

> 1) The Immigration Authorities of a western nation are confronted with the application of M. Saveur Bonappetit, a native of Fiji. He is the chief priest of a native Fijian religion, Cosmic Anthropophagy, and wishes to lead many of his followers to the west. This religion, in accord with ancient custom and practice, believes in eating one's neighbor on ritual occasions, thereby absorbing a greater portion of the World Soul, of which each individual represents a segment.[2] M. Bonappetit is widely read, and frequently cities Michel de Montaigne's essay on cannibalism, in which Montaigne praises cannibal society and asserts: "Every one gives the title of barbarism to everything that is not in use in his own country."[3]
> 
> 2) The same Immigration Authorities must also deal with the application of Judas Iscariote Zabotec. This gentleman, a Mexican citizen, is the archpriest of a religious revival of ancient Mesoamerican Aztec belief, Aztecs Redivivi, and hopes to be the first of many co-believers to immigrate to western countries in need of a new spirituality. For Zabotec and his followers, as with their ancestors, the gods once sacrificed themselves, so we must likewise engage in ritual human sacrifice. On-going sacrifice sustains the Universe; everything is *tonacayotl*: "spiritual fleshhood" on earth.[4] He points with particular pride to the 10 to 80,000 sacrifices at the re-consecration of the Great Pyramid of Tenochtitian in 1487.[5]

What are the Immigration Authorities to do? Should their policy be to exclude (1) just these two individuals; (2) all applicants from Fiji and from

---

[2] Cf. Peggy Reeves Sanday, *Divine Hunter: Cannibalism As a Cultural System* (Cambridge: Cambridge University Press, 1986)

[3] Michel de Montaigne, "Of Cannibals," *Essays* [1575], trans. Charles Cotton, ed. W. C. Hazlitt (1877), chap. 30, p. 167.

[4] Cf. Miguel León-Portilla, *Aztec Thought and Culture: A Study of the Ancient Náhuatl Mind*, trans. J. E. Davis ("Civilization of the American Indian," 67; Norman: University of Oklahoma Press, 1963), p. 111.

[5] Ross Hassig, "El sacrificio y las guerras floridas," 11 *Arqueología mexicana*, 47 (2003).

Mexico; (3) all members of the two religious sects; (4) those applicants not willing to give up their particular beliefs or to cease practicing those beliefs whilst present in the western country they wish to visit or where they want to settle?

## Determinative Legal Principles

International Public Law provides certain relevant bedrock principles.

First, since at least the beginnings of the Nation-State in the 18th century,[6] the right to enter the territory of a State has been solely within the prerogative of that State. National sovereignty is the determinant of immigration policy. One of the early modern classics in the field states the legal position thusly:

> The jurisdiction of a state over aliens within its territory is very extensive. The absolute right of exclusion of all foreigners would hardly be maintained by any civilized state, *though it could be deduced from the doctrine of sovereignty* ... The right of expulsion is, however, generally maintained ... The right to conditional admission is generally allowed, *as seen in laws in regard to immigration. The foreign state may impose such restrictions upon settlement as it sees fit.*[7]

A recent illustration of this principle was the February, 2014, Swiss referendum "Against Mass Immigration," which will reduce immigration into Switzerland through a quota system.

To be sure, a State may limit its sovereignty in immigration by ratifying bilateral or multilateral treaties. The most common such limitation is the refugee treaty, committing a State to accept legitimate refugee requests from those persecuted or potentially subject to inhuman treatment in their own countries. Refugee treaty ratification, however, is still a matter of national discretion.[8]

---

[6] Emmanuel Aubin, *Droit des Etrangers* (2d ed.; Paris: Gualino, 2011), p. 24.
[7] George Grafton Wilson and George Fox Tucker, *International Law* (New York: Silver, Burdett, 1901), pp. 131-32; *italics ours*. Note that dual citizenship for Americans is possible only if the second country is deemed not be hostile to American interests. Non-citizens such as the notorious fraudster Charles Ponzi (1882-1949) have been deported from the U.S. as undesirable aliens. The U.S. and the U.K. regularly refuse tourist visas to those identified with extremist organisations or movements.
[8] See especially Katharina Röhl, *New Issues in Refugee Research: Working Paper No. 111* (Geneva, Switzerland: Evaluation and Policy Analysis Unit, United Nations High

In American law, it is noteworthy that national sovereignty is taken with particular seriousness where immigration matters are concerned. Though labeled by some critics as racist,

> It is a central premise of modern American immigration law that immigrants, by virtue of their non-citizenship, are properly subject to an extra-constitutional regulatory authority that is inherent in national sovereignty and buffered against judicial review. The Supreme Court first posited this constitutionally exceptional authority, which is commonly known as the "plenary power doctrine," in the 1889 Chinese Exclusion Case. There, the Court reconstructed the federal immigration power from a form of commercial regulation rooted in Congress's commerce power, to an instrument of national self-defense.[9]

Secondly, even where human rights treaties (such as the European Convention of Human Rights) have been ratified, freedom of religious practice is not absolute. Thus the second paragraph of Article 9 of the ECHR, for example, qualifies religious rights by allowing for "such limitations as are prescribed by law and are necessary in a democratic society in the interests of public safety, for the protection of public order, health or morals, or for the protection of the rights and freedoms of others."[10]

Thirdly, a State may exclude political parties or sectarian groupings when their principles are such that, were they to gain control of the State or become the majority influence within it, the freedoms of the rest of society would be imperiled. The leading authority in this regard is the 2003 Strasbourg case of *Refah Partisi (Welfare Party) v Turkey*, where the ECHR upheld the Turkish ban of a political party on the ground that its Islamic

---

Commissioner for Refugees, 2005). In 2013, I was privileged to attend a multi-session continuing legal education course on Les Droits des Etrangers presented under the auspices of the Paris bar.

[9] Matthew J. Lindsay, "Immigration, Sovereignty, and the Constitution of Foreignness," 45/3 *Connecticut L.R.* (February 2013); University of Baltimore School of Law Legal Studies Research Paper No. 2013-08; Abstract. That American law has operated along the same lines since the early years of the Republic can be seen from the section "Of Aliens and Natives" in James Kent's *Commentaries on American Law*, ed. O. W. Holmes, Jr. (12th ed., 4 vols.; Boston: Little, Brown, 1873), II, 50-51.

[10] The language here closely parallels that of the United Nations Civil and Political Covenant, Art. 18, para. 3. See John Warwick Montgomery, "Restrictions on Religious Freedom: When and How Justified?," in *Legitimizing Human Rights: Secular and Religious Perspectives*, ed. Angus J. L. Menuge (Farnham, Surrey, England: Ashgate, 2013), pp. 143-56.

agenda was incompatible with fundamental democratic principles.[11] This is by no means the only example of such legally valid exclusions.[12]

Finally, even granting the legitimacy of general bans such as the above, a State must treat immigration applications individually and with appropriate due process/natural justice. The State must not engage in mass exclusions; *refoulement* must be carried out only on an individual basis. Thus, in the leading ECHR case of *Hirsi Jamaa and Others v Italy*, the Grand Chamber judged that the Italian government violated the human rights of some two hundred Somali and Eritrean nationals by "collective expulsion" – returning them to Libya *en masse* without "a fair and effective procedure to screen asylum seekers."[13]

## Solving the Hypotheticals

If we were to apply the just-described principles of international public law to our two immigration hypotheticals, what will be the result?

It is clear that, in both cases, the results would be the same. The western Immigration Authorities are faced with the adherents of two religious belief systems who, if allowed to enter the country, would engage in activities not merely obnoxious but exceedingly deleterious to the body politic (cannibalism, human sacrifice). Thus, refusing them entrance does not violate the principle of religious non-discrimination; their beliefs trigger the Article 9, para. 2 qualification in the ECHR and in parallel international human rights treaties.

At the same time, to refuse immigration automatically to all the citizens of the countries involved would hardly be justified, since those citizens would not necessarily be adherents of the belief-systems of the two applicants in the hypotheticals.

Moreover, mass exclusion of all adherents of those religions would appear to violate the principle of *non-refoulement* – that forcing the applicant to return to his or her own country can only be carried out legitimately through the particular examination of individual applications.

The only justification for a general exclusion of all adherents of those faith positions would be, as in the case of outlawing an extremist political party, successfully demonstrating that the antisocial conduct (here, can-

---

[11] *Refah Partisi (Welfare Party) v. Turkey*, 2003-II Eur. Ct. H.R. 267, 271.
[12] Gur Bligh, "Defending Democracy: A New Understanding of the Party-Banning Phenomenon," 46 *Vanderbilt J. Transnational L.* 1321-79 (2013).
[13] *Hirsi Jamaa and Others v Italy*, Application No. 27765/09 (23 February 2012).

nibalism, human sacrifice) is so inherently a part of the given religious position that it would necessarily be practiced by its adherents should they be allowed to enter the country. In theory, adherents could conceivably pledge to give up those beliefs – or at least not to carry out practices dictated by those beliefs – whilst in the western state.

## The Threat of Muslim Extremism and Its Ideological Source

Now, in light of our discussion to this point, let us turn to the problem of extremist Muslim immigration per se.

The 21$^{st}$-century world has been subjected to unparalleled acts of barbarism by terrorists. One thinks especially of the 9/11 destruction of the Twin Towers in New York, the killing of *Charlie Hebdo* journalists in Paris on 7 January 2015, and the 13 November 2015 slaughters in Paris But the list goes far beyond these archetypical events and has been chronicled in detail elsewhere.[14]

The common ground of these terrorist acts is the perpetrators' attribution to Muslim faith of the acts they or their "martyrs" have carried out. Thus, Muhammed Atta and the other hijackers who flew two aircraft into the Twin Towers were connected directly or indirectly with Osama ben Laden's Muslim crusade against the west. The *Charlie Hebdo* attackers cried "Allah akbar" before opening fire on the defenseless journalists; subsequently, Al-Qaida in Yemen has claimed responsibility for those Paris murders. The Islamic Nation/ISIS has taken credit for the November, 2015 killings of 129+ innocent civilians in Paris.

Though one cannot discount the political dimension of these atrocities (intense resentment over the decline of Islamic influence in modern times, as compared with great political and cultural success in its first century of existence and during the middle ages),[15] it is plain that a powerful religious factor is present. Indeed, when Muslim terrorists term their organization "The Islamic State/Daech" (Coulibaly claimed this connection for the Paris atrocities of 7 January 2015), they make clear that they wish to be regarded as having religio-political aims. The religious factor is plainly integral to such claims, and no degree of reductionism can eliminate it. Every single

---

[14] See especially Ibn Warraq, *Pourquoi je ne suis pas musulman* (Lausanne, Switzerland: Editions L'Age d'Homme, 1999), and cf. also Jean Robin, *Le livre noir de l'Islam* (Paris: Editions Tatamis, 2013), and Raymond Ibrahim, *Crucified Again: Exposing Islam's New War on Christians* (Washington, D.C.: Regnery, 2013).

[15] This is discussed in detail in the publications of Bernard Lewis, for example, *What Went Wrong?: Western Impact and Middle Eastern Response* (new ed.; London: Weidenfeld & Nicolson, 2002).

instance of serious terrorism in our time has been connected, directly or indirectly, with the Muslim religion. No terrorist acts whatever have been the product of Christian (or, for that matter, Buddhist or Hindu) religious believers. Lumping Christian fundamentalists into the same category as Muslim fundamentalists ignores this fact; no Christian fundamentalists, however extreme, have engaged in suicide attacks against adherents of other faiths or have attempted in some fashion to establish Christianity through the killing of others.

The key question here is whether Muslim terrorist extremism is an aberration, unjustified by the Muslim faith, or whether it in fact follows from the core beliefs of that faith. The former explanation is generally assumed. I recall Tony Blair, when prime minister, commenting at Lincoln's Inn (where we are both barrister members) that he had perused the Qur'an on a weekend and found it an innocuous and attractive read.[16] However, the sacred writings and the religious history of Islam simply belie such anodyne interpretations.

We shall take just a few definitive examples from the Qur'an and from the most sacred traditions of Islam (the Shari'a).

The Qur'an calls upon the faithful to war against the infidel. Sura 4: "Let those fight on the path of God ... Whoever fighteth on God's path, whether he be slain or conquer, we will in the end give him a great reward ... They who believe, fight on the path of God ... Fight therefore against the fiends of Satan ... The might of the infidels haply will God restrain, for God is the stronger in prowess, and the stronger to punish." Sura 9: "Contend against the infidels and the hypocrites, and be harsh with them: Hell shall be their dwelling place!"

Writes German specialist on Islam Prof. Dr Christine Schirrmacher:

> Extremists who apply the early Muslim community's struggle against "infidels" to present-day conflicts can hardly be accused of misinterpreting the Koran, for people who resist the spread of Islam can scarcely be considered as "innocent victims," particularly in Israel, where there is not a family without someone serving in the armed forces. From the extremists' perspective it is easy to see how even those not involved in the war can be considered enemies of Islam. According to this view, it is legitimate to take the life

---

[16] More contemporaneously, following the Charlie Hebdo atrocity, film director Francis Ford Coppola was interviewed in Paris by *Le Figaro*; said he: "*Charlie Hebdo* would have done better in its issue following the attack to have published the Qur'an, so that everyone would read it. They would have seen that there's nothing bad in it" (29 January, 2015).

of Islam's enemies, who resist its spread, as Israel does by its very existence, as this ultimately counts as defending Islam.[17]

From the perspective of the Muslim extremist, there is no way that the Quranic teaching on Jihad can today be restricted (as contemporary defenders of Islam have tried to argue) solely to defensive warfare on Islamic territory. Western nations, by their support of Israel, by their lax willingness to allow published satires of the Prophet and his teachings, and by their belief in an open society are in fact engaged in an all-out war against the fundamental religious teachings of Islam; their citizens therefore deserve to become the objects of Jihad and have only themselves to blame for the carnage that can ensue.

One of the foremost Islamic scholars of our day has written in his impressive treatment of the Shari'a:

> The goal of jihad is to subdue the Abode of War to the dominion of the Abode of Islam ... The Christians, Jews and Magians were to be fought with the view of either converting them to Islam or subjecting them to Islamic rule while allowing them to maintain their religious beliefs. If the latter, then they were under the obligation to pay the poll-tax (*jizya*). However, pagans enjoyed no such options, having been obliged to convert to Islam or fight to the death.[18]

The application of this rule to non-Muslims in countries maintaining Shari'a law has had crushing social and human rights consequences.[19]

We cannot here go into the sad historical record of Islamic warfare and conversions by the sword. That has been done elsewhere and the data are readily available.[20] But the message is clear: when Muslim terrorists in our

---

[17] Christine Schirrmacher, *Islam and Society: Sharia law – Jihad – Women in Islam* ("WEA Global Issues," 4; Bonn, Germany: Verlag für Kultur und Wissenschaft, 2008), p. 113. See also Christine Schirrmacher, *Islamismus: Wenn Religion zur Politik wird* (Holzgerlingen, Germany: SCM Hänssler, 2010).

[18] Wael B. Hallaq, *Shari'a: Theory, Practice, Transformations* (Cambridge: Cambridge University Press, 2009), p. 327.

[19] See Bat Ye'or, *Islam and Dhimmitude: Where Civilizations Collide,* trans. M. Kochan and D. Littman (Madison, NJ: Fairleigh Dickinson University Press, 2002); and Robert Spencer (ed.), *The Myth of Islamic Tolerance: How Islamic Law Treats Non-Muslims* (Amherst, NY: Prometheus Books, 2005). Cf. also Spencer's *The Politically Incorrect Guide to Islam (and the Crusades)* (Washington, DC: Regnery, 2005).

[20] See standard encyclopedia treatments of "Jihad," "Dhimmi," and "Conversion" such as to be found in Dominique and Janine Sourdel, *Dictionnaire historique de l'Islam* (Paris: Presses Universitaires de France, 1996). Cf. also Geoffrey Robertson, *An*

time plan and carry out their appalling activities, they have solid historical precedent for spreading their faith and eliminating opposition in that manner.

## An Immigration Remedy and Its Legal Legitimacy

Now to the concrete issue. What can be done – without transgressing international public law and human rights standards – to stem the tide of extremist Muslim infiltration into the democratic, western world?

We suggest an individual examination of applicants who wish to enter western countries, based upon questions to be asked of all such applicants:

1) Do you consider yourself a Muslim by background or by personal belief?
2) If the answer to the previous question is Yes, are you willing to affirm under oath that, if allowed to enter State X, you will, during your permitted time within the borders of that State, *either*
   a) renounce belief in Jihad in any form whatsoever, as well as renouncing the use of force, violence, military or terrorist action; *or*
   b) whilst not renouncing such beliefs, personally agree to not engaging in any such practices or aiding or abetting others in that regard, including direct or indirect financial support or aid; and covenanting to inform the appropriate police authorities should you discover or learn of any such activities?
3) Are you now or have you ever been a member of a Muslim religio-political organization? If so, list the organization(s), address(es), and years of contact with it or them. List the mosques you have attended in the last 10 years, with addresses and dates of contact.
4) I understand that by signing this declaration under oath I give the Immigration Authorities of State X the unqualified right to investigate my background so as to determine whether I have been a member of any organization, religious or otherwise, that advocates Jihad or any form of violence against the State or private organisations, churches, or other social groups; and I agree that if it can be demonstrated that I have committed perjury in making this application to visit or to immigrate to State X, I shall be subject to appropriate criminal penalties and/or immediate expulsion from the country.

---

*Inconvenient Genocide: Who Now Remembers the Armenians?* (London: Biteback Publishing, 2014); and John Warwick Montgomery, "'Ararat,' the Armenians, and Missionary Doctor Clarence Ussher," 3/3 *Global J. Classical Theology* (June, 2003) [access: http://www.globaljournalct.com/a-note-from-our-editor/ararat-the-armenians-and-missionary-doctor-clarence-ussher/].

Several points need to be raised in conjunction with this proposal.

First, even if one grants that the proposal fits the public law and human rights criteria discussed earlier, *is it at all realistic?*

Are not Muslims so committed religiously that they would never agree to such interrogation? At a recent Paris legal conference in the week of the Charlie Hebdo atrocity, one distinguish speaker naively stated that the problem was simply the lack of successful integration of the young terrorists into French society[21]; he was sublimely unaware that the force of Muslim conviction made such integration impossible for them.[22]

This, however, is hardly true of all Muslims. The Latter Day Saints may offer an illustration as to the practicality of the approach we are suggesting. Polygamy has been an inherent Mormon belief since the origins of that cult in 19th-century America. Even Mormon believers today acknowledge the fact that cult's founder, Joseph Smith, was an active polygamist, having 30 to 40 wives. But in order for Utah to obtain statehood, the Mormon Church (whose headquarters and major influence were in the Utah territory) officially banned the practice of polygamy in 1890. Though polygamy still raises its head among the Mormons, it is officially condemned by that sectarian body. Here we have an instance of a religion voluntarily agreeing to forego a practice doctrinally and historically accepted by them in order that they could function legally within American society. It is certainly conceivable that individual Muslims, even though they might not be willing to go back on Quranic or Shari'a beliefs, would be willing to agree not to practice such tenets as a condition of being allowed into western nations.[23]

But what about Muhammed's teaching that the end justifies the means – that lying is allowable when one is fighting for the true faith?[24] Would

---

[21] Le Club des Juristes and l'Institut Montaigne: "Les Assises du Droit et de la Compétitivité," 9 January 2015, closing session.

[22] "Extremists think of their faith before nationality," *Connexion* [Paris], February, 2015.

[23] This analogy may have particular force owing to the religious similarities between Mormonism and Islam; see religious sociologist Alvin J. Schmidt's work, *The American Muhammad: Joseph Smith, Founder of Mormonism* (Saint Louis, MO: Concordia, 2013).

[24] "The Prophet said, 'War is deception'" – *Riyad as-Salihin*, Bk. 11 (The Book of Jihad), citing two of the most authoritative hadith collections, Al-Bukhaari and Muslim b. al-Hajjaj. The Qur'an, Sura 16 contains the interesting verse: "Whoso, after he hath believed in God denieth him, if he were forced to it and if his heart remain steadfast in the faith, shall be guiltless"; the passage is certainly capable of justifying subjective "belief with a steadfast heart" whilst denying the faith publicly as a result of persecution or social pressure – or because such denial would be the only path to immigration for achieving holy jihad??

not the terrorist simply prevaricate when faced with the interrogation we are suggesting? This is of course possible. Indeed, an immigration judge in England told me on one occasion that 95% of the refugee applicants who came before him lied about their true motives (economic and social) for entering the U.K. However, it will be noted that the above proposal includes depth investigation of the background of the applicant and draconian penalties for lying applicants. The proposal would not eliminate all terrorist immigration, but it would certainly reduce its scope.

And what about the fact that a good deal of radical Muslim extremism is homegrown (example: Djokhar Tsarnaïev, the author of the Boston marathon bombings in April, 2013)? Our proposal is not capable of eliminating extremists who are already ensconced in western countries; that is a matter for the police and investigative authorities of those countries, Interpol, etc. But the application of the interrogation questionnaire given above could certainly be expanded to provide a legal check on the ideological stance of those of Muslim belief already in western countries. Doubtless, such examinations would be instantly opposed by civil libertarians, but, in principle, they would not be a violation of international law or of human rights standards.

Finally, would not our proposal create a chilling effect on legitimate tourism and immigration from Muslim areas of the world or among foreigners of Islamic background and belief? Admittedly, this might indeed be the case in practice, though quantification is impossible. One can certainly imagine some Muslims simply not wanting to be so questioned or put in a position where the potential conflict between their cherished beliefs on the one hand and western democratic and cultural values on the other would be placed under a bright administrative searchlight. However, this result, even if the case, might not be entirely negative for the western nations employing the methodology we are suggesting. The late, unlamented Libyan Muslim dictator al-Gaddafi once remarked that Jihad was not really necessary for the ultimate triumph of Islam; the high Muslim birthrate, as contrasted with that of the non-Muslim west, would eventually guarantee victory for Islam.[25] The west, therefore, might not in fact suffer great loss if there were secondary effects following the legal reduction – or even the stamping out – of Muslim terrorist immigration.

---

[25] "We have 50 million Muslims in Europe. There are signs that Allah will grant Islam victory in Europe – without swords, without guns, without conquest – will turn it into a Muslim continent within a few decades" (speech, 10 April 2006).

# 19. Religious Fraud: Its Etiology and Prevention

*Abstract:* Sadly, fraud occurs in the religious context. The present essay endeavours to understand how and why this happens in churches and Christian organisations, and provides guidance to reduce ecclesiastical fraud with its consequential harm to the body of Christ and to the effectiveness of gospel proclamation.

One of my hats is that of an international Certified Fraud Examiner (CFE). Certification followed the successful passing of four examinations – Fraud Prevention & Deterrence; Investigation; Law; and Financial Transactions & Fraud Schemes.[1] I was introduced to the area by one of my student attendees at our annual International Academy of Apologetics, Evangelism and Human Rights in Strasbourg, France.[2] He (an American lawyer) said that he had gained apologetics insights from the CFE programme relative to the Gospel writers' testimonies to Jesus' life, miracles, and resurrection – in that there was no way that modern sophisticated fraud analysis could impugn what they had written. I found that indeed to be the case, and it reinforced evidential conclusions I had reached on the basis of my own legal studies. (More on this later.) But once I myself had entered into CFE fraud training, additional theological applications of fraud analysis soon displayed themselves.

Fraud is rampant in modern life. Not only are there the frequent repetition of the Ponzi schemes – causing immense misery to untold numbers of victims (the Madoff catastrophe, to cite but the best-known recent illustration) – but on a far smaller, yet no less harmful scale the activities of those engaged in identity theft, credit card and bank account pilferage, and e-mail ("Nigerian") scams. The problem is truly international: the French anti-fraud watchdog (the DGCCRF) has recently reported that no less than 47% of French second-hand car dealers engage in fraudulent activity.[3]

But surely the religious sphere is exempt from such? Not at all! We mention here but two egregious contemporary examples:

---

[1] www.acfe.com
[2] www.apologeticsacademy.eu
[3] *Connexion,* June, 2016.

*Jim Bakker*: In 2008, the televangelist and founder of the highly successful PTL ("Praise the Lord") Ministries, was indicted on federal charges of mail and wire fraud and of conspiring to defraud. The PTL operation involved a 2,200-acre resort (Heritage USA), where time-shares were knowingly sold beyond the capacities of the resort. Bakker received a 45-year sentence, subsequently reduced to eight years, and was released from prison in 1994. He is currently engaged in new "ministries."

*Cal Switzer*: As pastor of the Victory Christian Centre in Edmonton, Canada, he owned 98% of the church's common shares, and was thus the proprietor of his own church! In 2008, he entered into a real-estate deal with a questionable developer and condo flipper who had a long history of failed real-estate dealings. When the bubble finally burst in 2013 – a $14-million financial scandal – the pastor blamed it on the developer and "Satan." Switzer then (with his co-pastor wife) re-branded as pastor of "Studio Church," which in 2015 also suffered judicial eviction.

That such horror stories are not unique is evident from the fact that the total amount of money "leaking out" of churches and Christian philanthropic activities owing to fraud averages some $27-billion annually – "about 6 percent of the global total of $410-billion given to Christian charities," according to Bert Hickman, research associate with Gordon-Conwell Theological Seminary's Center for the Study of Global Philanthropy.[4]

## History and Etiology

Religious fraud is not, however, a recent phenomenon.

Consider the classic New Testament example, from the earliest days of the Christian church:

> Neither was there any among them that lacked: for as many as were possessors of lands or houses sold them, and brought the prices of the things that were sold, and laid them down at the apostles' feet: and distribution was made unto every man according as he had need ...
> But a certain man named Ananias, with Sapphira his wife, sold a possession, and kept back part of the price, his wife also being privy to it, and brought a certain part, and laid it at the apostles' feet. But Peter said, Ananias, why hath Satan filled thine heart to lie to the Holy Ghost, and to keep back part of the price of the land. Whiles it remained, was it not thine own? and after it was sold, was it not in thine own power? why hast thou conceived this thing in thine heart? thou hast not lied unto men, but unto God. And Ananias hearing these words fell down, and gave up the ghost: and great

---

[4] EP service, *Christian News,* May 18, 2009.

fear came on all them that heard these things. And the young men arose, wound him up, and carried him out, and buried him.

And it was about the space of three hours after, when his wife, not knowing what was done, came in. And Peter answered unto her, Tell me whether ye sold the land for so much? And she said, Yea, for so much. Then Peter said unto her, How is it that ye have agreed together to tempt the Spirit of the Lord? behold, the feet of them which have buried thy husband are at the door, and shall carry thee out. Then fell she down straightway at his feet, and yielded up the ghost: and the young men came in, and found her dead, and, carrying her forth, buried her by her husband.

And great fear came upon all the church, and upon as many as heard these things.[5]

Was this actual or attempted fraud in the legal sense?[6] Absolutely, whether one thinks in terms of the Anglo-American common law of fraud or the European civil law understanding of the crime:

*Common Law Fraud, Requiring Five Elements:*

(1) a false statement of a material fact, (2) knowledge on the part of the defendant that the statement is untrue, (3) intent on the part of the defendant to deceive the alleged victim, (4) justifiable reliance by the alleged victim on the statement, and (5) injury to the alleged victim as a result.

*Code Pénal, Art. 313-1 (Escroquerie):*

Fraudulent obtaining is the act of deceiving a natural or legal person by the use of a false name or a fictitious capacity, by the abuse of a genuine capacity, or by means of unlawful manoeuvres, thereby to lead such a person, to his prejudice or to the prejudice of a third party, to transfer funds, valuables or any property, to provide a service or to consent to an act incurring or discharging an obligation.

Fraudulent activity has been present throughout the history of the church. Medieval examples include the fabrication of the so-called "Donation of Constantine" in the papal chancery in the year 850.[7] This document purported to give to the papacy temporal authority over secular princes, and

---

[5] Acts 4:34-5, 5:1-11 (AV).
[6] The concept of fraud, in popular parlance, often signifies mere deception or chicanery; see, for example, Tighe Hopkins, *The Romance of Fraud* (London: Chapman and Hall, 1914).

was a key element in assertions of the temporal authority of the papacy throughout the Middle Ages, especially during the Investiture Controversy. The Donation was revealed as a forgery by Renaissance scholar Lorenzo Valla. A detailed study has been made of medieval forgeries in England.[8]

Forged relics have been endemic in Roman Catholic church history, particularly when cathedrals and churches and princes vied to collect those having the greatest sanctity and therefore the greatest appeal to pilgrims and donors. The valuable relic collection of Luther's prince, Frederick the Wise, was perhaps the greatest personal obstacle to his eventual conversion to the Reformation (and Pauline) doctrine of salvation by grace alone through faith.

The following incident is anything but unique:

> In Sicily, near Palermo, in a shrine in a cave on Pellegrino mountain, the bones of Saint Rosilia are venerated.
>
> When a teenager, Rosalia lived as a hermit until dying of natural causes in 1166. Her bones lay undisturbed for centuries, until a plague struck Palermo in 1624. Residents began having visions of "the Little Saint," and a hunter, looking for any kind of cure, went to her cave, dug up her bones, and paraded them through the streets. The plague ceased. Her cave became a place of worship; she became the patron saint of Palermo and Sicilians subsequently prayed to the bones.
>
> However, in 1825, British geologist and theologian William Buckland, on his honeymoon, made an examination of the relics, finding them "non-human" – apparently the bones of a goat. He also concluded that dark spots on another church's floor being presented as "drops of martyr's blood" were, in fact, drops of bat urine. However, the church, rather than fixing the mistake and getting rid of the goat remnants, has the same bones on display today.[9]

---

[7] "The three books of the Pseudo-Isidorian Decretals contain in book i. sixty letters of Roman bishops from St Clement to the beginning of the fourth century, all of which are spurious. Book ii. contains other famous documents, such as the forged Donation of Constantine" (Reginald L. Poole, *Lectures on the History of the Papal Chancery* [Cambridge: Cambridge University Press, 1915], p. 26). See also E. H. Davenport, *The False Decretals* (Oxford: B. H. Blackwell, 1916), and, in general, Antoine Gavin, *Le Passe-Par-Tout de l'Eglise Romaine, ou l'histoire des trumperies ... en Espagne* (London: J. Stephens, 1726), and G. D. Emerline, *Frauds of Papal Ecclesiastics* (New York, 1835).

[8] Alfred Hiatt, *The Making of Medieval Forgeries: False Documents in Fifteenth-Century England* (London: British Library, 2004).

[9] For the detailed account, see Elizabeth Oke Gordon, *The Life and Correspondence of William Buckland* (London: J. Murray, 1894), pp. 95-96.

So why has there been a history of fraud in the church? The answer, of course, is original sin – stemming from our first parents. They tried to deceive God by hiding in the Garden of Eden after they had violated his will, and humanity, even after receiving the grace of Christ, is still subject to the Adamic temptation. As the Lutheran Reformers properly recognized, even the believer is *simul justus et peccator*. A perfect church requires the return of its perfect Saviour.

## Fraud Prevention: Some General Principles Applicable to the Church and Christian Organisations

Let us now apply some of the basic principles of sophisticated, contemporary fraud analysis to the religious sphere.

We focus on Donald Cressey's classic "Fraud Triangle"[10]:

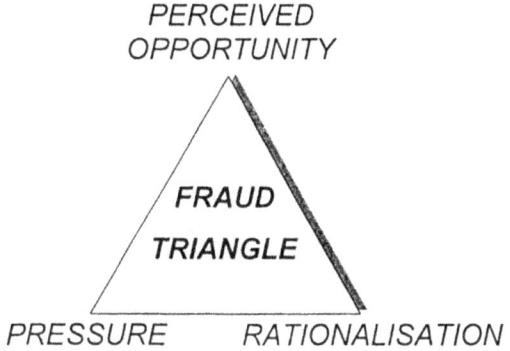

The Fraud Triangle identifies the three key factors in identifying the likelihood of fraud in an organization: *opportunity* (the absence of sufficient controls), *pressure* (personal or social on the potential fraudster), and *rationalization* (the capacity of the individual to justify to himself or herself the committing of an illegal/immoral act).

We mentioned above the non-applicability of the Triangle to the apostolic reporting of Jesus' miraculous life in the New Testament records. (1) The *opportunity* did not exist, owing to the presence of hostile witnesses to our Lord's life and ministry – hostile witnesses still alive at the time the Gospel records were circulated (they had crucified Jesus, so they would

---

[10] *ACFE Fraud Examiners Manual 2008* (UK version).

certainly have had means and motive to identify and condemn false testimony to his acts or teachings, had such existed). (2) Any social or personal *pressure* on the New Testament witnesses would have produced the opposite effect, since the Jewish context was hostile to the unique messianic claims that had been set forth by Jesus and that the New Testament writers asserted. (3) The apostolic witnesses and New Testament authors would hardly have been able to *rationalize* the proclamation of a false picture of Jesus, since they were followers of a Jesus who unqualifiedly condemned lying and deception (John 8:44).

Observe, however, the applicability of the Fraud Triangle to potential or actual fraud in the church and in Christian organisations today. The Triangle offers a fine preliminary checklist of red flags to fraud. In your church or charitable organization, ask:

1) Are our financial controls rigorous – so as to reduce the *opportunity* of fraud? Specifically: Have we segregated duties (collection of monies and payment of bills, recording of receipts, auditing of accounts)? Do we vary the vacation times of those handling the different financial aspects of our operation? Do we authorise frequent and independent audits? Such controls are particularly important for churches, since they are exempted from the requirement that nonprofits must file informational tax returns with the IRS.

2) Do we make an effort to understand the lives of our staff and the financial *pressures* they face – so as to be able to recognise the potential risks a staff member may pose within the organization? Specifically: Have we done financial checks on our employees or those seeking to work with us? Any history of gambling or previous criminal or civil actions involving financial mismanagement? Significant credit card debts? Sudden acquisition of property (e.g., an expensive car) beyond apparent income level?

3) How high is the moral level of our employees and staff members? The higher the ethical level, the less likely their ability to rationalize fraudulent activities hurtful to the organisation. Personal conduct in the marital area is often a barometer to one's ethical level in general: any mistreatment of the spouse or cheating on the spouse? And do we provide adequate salaries for our employees and sufficient public praise for their efforts – thereby reducing the chances of their being able to justify stealing or misappropriations on the ground of ill treatment or favoritism?

## Fraud Prevention: Some Specific Principles Applicable to the Church and Christian Organisations

The Evangelical Council for Financial Accountability[11] sets forth "Seven Standards of Responsible Stewardship." Even though these standards relate more to large charitable organizations that to the local church, they deserve our attention.

*Standard 1 – Doctrinal Issues*

Every organization shall subscribe to a written statement of faith clearly affirming a commitment to the evangelical Christian faith or shall otherwise demonstrate such commitment, and shall operate in accordance with biblical truths and practices.

*Standard 2 – Governance*

Every organization shall be governed by a responsible board of not less than five individuals, a majority of whom shall be independent, who shall meet at least semiannually to establish policy and review its accomplishments.

*Standard 3 – Financial Oversight*

Every organization shall prepare complete and accurate financial statements. The board or a committee consisting of a majority of independent members shall approve the engagement of an independent certified public accountant, review the annual financial statements, and maintain appropriate communication with the independent certified public accountant. The board shall be apprised of any material weaknesses in internal control or other significant risks.

*Standard 4 – Use of Resources and Compliance with Laws*

Every organization shall exercise the appropriate management and controls necessary to provide reasonable assurance that all of the organization's operations are carried out and resources are used in a responsible

---

[11] www.ecfa.org

manner and in conformity with applicable laws and regulations, such conformity taking into account biblical mandates.

## Standard 5 – Transparency

Every organization shall provide a copy of its current financial statements upon written request and shall provide other disclosures as the law may require. The financial statements required to comply with Standard 3 must be disclosed under this standard.

An organization must provide a report, upon written request, including financial information on any specific project for which it has sought or is seeking gifts.

## Standard 6 – Compensation-Setting and Related-Party Transactions

Every organization shall set compensation of its top leader and address related-party transactions in a manner that demonstrates integrity and propriety in conformity with ECFA's Policy for Excellence in Compensation-Setting and Related-Party Transactions.

## Standard 7 – Stewardship of Charitable Gifts

### 7.1 Truthfulness in Communications

In securing charitable gifts, all representations of fact, descriptions of the financial condition of the organization, or narratives about events must be current, complete, and accurate. References to past activities or events must be appropriately dated. There must be no material omissions or exaggerations of fact, use of misleading photographs, or any other communication which would tend to create a false impression or misunderstanding.

### 7.2 Giver Expectations and Intent

Statements made about the use of gifts by an organization in its charitable gift appeals must be honored. A giver's intent relates both to what was communicated in the appeal and to any instructions accompanying the gift, if accepted by the organization. Appeals for charitable gifts must not create unrealistic expectations of what a gift will actually accomplish.

### 7.3 Charitable Gift Communication

Every organization shall provide givers appropriate and timely gift acknowledgments.

### 7.4 Acting in the Best Interest of Givers

When dealing with persons regarding commitments on major gifts, an organization's representatives must seek to guide and advise givers to adequately consider their broad interests.

An organization must make every effort to avoid knowingly accepting a gift from, or entering into a contract with, a giver that would place a hardship on the giver or place the giver's future well-being in jeopardy.

### 7.5 Percentage Compensation for Securing Charitable Gifts

An organization may not base compensation of outside stewardship resource consultants or its own staff directly or indirectly on a percentage of charitable contributions raised.

\* \* \*

A religious organization has particular, built-in vulnerabilities to fraud. We shall now consider, in conclusion, their nature and what can be done to reduce the dangers stemming from their inevitable presence.

First, *the nature of the leadership.* Even in hierarchical church bodies, such as the Roman Catholic Church or Anglican bodies (where a bishop supervises the local clergy or charity in his diocese) or in Presbyterian/Reformed denominations (where the presbytery is the final ruling authority), the pastor or priest is a towering authority figure. In independent churches (Baptist, local evangelical, charismatic), there is generally no authority above the pastor himself (or herself). Abuse of authority is therefore a perennial danger.

The solution is therefore clear: the pastor must *not* own an interest (particularly not a controlling interest) in the church's property – directly or indirectly – and he must not be the final word on the organization's temporal, financial matters. A church council must oversee and provide adequate, independent financial auditing. One simply asks for trouble, for example, when the pastor can appoint a church secretary of his choosing (in some cases his own wife), the secretary then handling the church collections, recording the monies received, paying the bills, and writing the cheques. Such an unsupervised arrangement is an invitation to skimming, collusion (monies paid to relatives or friends for services to the organization), illicit expense reimbursements, etc., etc.

Horror stories illustrating these problems could be multiplied but they would be only the tip of the iceberg. Most discoveries of such defalcations result in little more than a quiet firing of the culprit and no recovery of losses – since the church is too embarrassed to reveal what has occurred and too fearful of bad publicity that would presumably harm the church's reputation and its gospel proclamation.

Secondly, *the character of certain religious orientations*. The vast majority of serious religious frauds in recent years have occurred within the so-called charismatic sphere. One should therefore be especially careful in financial dealings involving charismatic leaders, tele- and radio-evangelists, and their ilk. Why is there a special problem here? The difficulty is not because those folk hold to the continuing, miraculous work of God the Holy Spirit. (Any believer has witnessed such in his or her own life repeatedly.) The problem is that the charismatic – like too many an evangelical – is at root a *subjectivist*, one who stresses feelings rather than objective truth. The consequence is that when "it feels good" the charismatic has little difficulty in viewing the action as morally (and theologically) permissible. This is the key to comprehending the sex-scandals of charismatic leadership – and their proclivity to engage in out-and-out fraud or the naïve acceptance of fraudulent schemes proposed by others.

Finally, *our strength may also be our weakness*. Christian believers are committed to help the poor and the outcast and are at the forefront (beyond even the lawyers) in believing everyone innocent until proven guilty. Fine! But often the result is a *naïveté* bordering on childishness. We tend to believe every cry for financial help from those who cross our path, and if a financial scheme is promoted by a persuasive, clean-cut, politically conservative salesman, we readily fall into the trap. Churches and Christian charities are especially vulnerable to what is known technically as "affinity fraud" when they accept without proper evidence of legitimacy proposals or actions by fellow believers (or those who claim to be such). We neglect proper financial controls and independent advice. We ignore the sage adage that "If a project or profit-making scheme is too good to be true, that's probably because it is." A more serious view of original sin and the nature of a fallen world could serve the evangelical church as serious fraud insurance. And it might even strengthen our theology.[12]

---

[12] Relevant articles in the ACFE's *Fraud* magazine: "Pilfering in the Pews" (January/February 1999); "Stealing from the Collection Plate" (November/December 2005); "Fraud in Houses of Worship" (January/February 2012); "Affinity Is Only Skin Deep" (March/April 2013); "Fleecing the Shepherds" (March/April 2014); "God's Money Is Now My Money" (July/August 2015).

# 20. Doctrinal Fidelity in the Light of Comparative Professional Negligence

*Abstract:* In most professional fields, such a medicine, law, and real estate brokerage, practitioners are held to a high standard in what they present as fact to their lay clients. Intentional or negligent misrepresentation is grounds for discipline, including removal of the professional license to practice. This paper surveys such requirements and then examines various homiletic and public statements by influential clerics to determine their compatibility with professional standards presumably applicable in church contexts.

## Introduction

We might paraphrase George Orwell: "all the professions are equal, but some are less equal than others." In law and real estate brokerage, there are almost universal requirements of continuing education, with a strong ethics component. Examples: the Paris bar, which requires 20 hours annually of continuing legal education, or the California Department of Real Estate, which mandates 45 hours of continuing education in the field every four years to maintain one's broker's or salesperson's license. No such requirement appears to exist for clergy of any denomination.

The result is interesting. It was once suggested to me that the personal library of the average clergyperson contained serious theological titles obtained whilst in seminary, and little more than popular, sermonic and counseling materials thereafter. Moreover, other professions are very serious about disciplining professionals who violate professional standards, in particular those who misrepresent facts to their clients or to the general public. The theory is that the professional, owing to his specialized education and training, owes a higher – a fiduciary – duty to the lay person not to mislead or to provide false or unfounded representations that, if relied upon, could produce harm to the victim. The physician who advises exercise to cure cancer will be struck off.

In this paper, we shall be taking examples from the practice of real estate brokerage – and we shall follow that by examining some egregious examples of what can and does occur in the ecclesiastical realm.[1]

## Ethics in Real Estate Brokerage

One of the most important cases in the field is that of *Easton v Strassburger* [152 Cal. App. 3d 96 (1984)]. We quote from the California Court of Appeals judgment, upholding liability against the real estate broker (the defendant property vendors – the Strassburgers – had filed for bankruptcy and were therefore no longer in the picture).[2]

> The property which is the subject of this appeal is a one-acre parcel of land located in the City of Diablo. The property is improved with a 3,000-square-foot home, a swimming pool, and a large guest house. Respondent purchased the property for $170,000 from the Strassburgers in May of 1976 and escrow closed in July of that year. Appellant was the listing broker in the transaction.
>
> Shortly after respondent purchased the property, there was massive earth movement on the parcel. Subsequent slides destroyed a portion of the driveway in 1977 or 1978. Expert testimony indicated that the slides occurred because a portion of the property was fill that had not been properly engineered and compacted. The slides caused the foundation of the house to settle which in turn caused cracks in the walls and warped doorways. After the 1976 slide, damage to the property was so severe that although experts appraised the value of the property at $170,000 in an undamaged condition, the value of the damaged property was estimated to be as low as $20,000. Estimates of the cost to repair the damage caused by the slides and avoid recurrence ranged as high as $213,000.

The real estate agents conducted inspections of the property prior to the sale to one Leticia Easton. Red flags indicated potential soil problems, but they made no effort to obtain soil stability tests or mention a possible problem to the purchaser. There had in fact been major slides during the Strassburgers' ownership of the property, but these were not revealed to

---

[1] The author is a licensed California real estate broker, as well as a member of the California, Washington State, Virginia and District of Columbia bars, the U.S. Supreme Court bar, a barrister (England and Wales), and an *avocat, barreau de Paris*. He is also a pastor emeritus of the Lutheran Church-Missouri Synod, and holds a doctorate in theology from the University of Strasbourg, France.

[2] We are appalled at the surname of the property sellers, and can only hope that their family roots were not in French Alsace.

Easton or to the real estate agents. After closing, soil shifts severely damaged the property, and Easton filed suit against the Strassburgers and the real estate agents. A jury found all the defendants liable for negligence and apportioned the damage, such that the real estate agents were required to pay a percentage of the total.

The real estate brokers appealed, supported by an amicus brief from the National Association of Realtors, contending

> that a broker is only obliged to disclose known facts and has no duty to disclose facts which "should" be known to him "through reasonable diligence." In effect, appellant maintains that a broker has no legal duty to carry out a reasonable investigation of property he undertakes to sell in order to discover defects for the benefit of the buyer.

The appellate court was not impressed by this argument.

> If a broker were required to disclose only known defects, but not also those that are reasonably discoverable, he would be shielded by his ignorance of that which he holds himself out to know. The rule thus narrowly construed would have results inimical to the policy upon which it is based. Such a construction would not only reward the unskilled broker for his own incompetence, but might provide the unscrupulous broker the unilateral ability to protect himself at the expense of the inexperienced and unwary who rely upon him. In any case, if given legal force, the theory that a seller's broker cannot be held accountable for what he does not know but could discover without great difficulty would inevitably produce a disincentive for a seller's broker to make a diligent inspection. Such a disincentive would be most unfortunate, since in residential sales transactions the seller's broker is most frequently the best situated to obtain and provide the most reliable information on the property and is ordinarily counted on to do so.

This holding has been essentially incorporated into California law by subsequent statute and is grounded in the fiduciary duty real estate brokers and salespersons owe to the general public. Specifically, the real estate agent, by virtue of his or her licensure, training and knowledge not possessed by the general public, must be held legally to a high standard. If the agent does not perform as one with that education and training should reasonably perform, he or she shall be legally liable in negligence.

Should the agent undertake to serve in a capacity that necessarily involves the possession and exercise of a special skill, such as that of a lawyer, stockbroker, or real estate broker, he or she is required to exercise the skill ordinarily possessed by competent persons who pursue that particular calling. In the case of *Timmsen v. Forest (1970) 6 C.A. 3d 860*, a broker can be held liable to the seller for procuring and recommending a financially unsound offer. In *Timmsen,* the court held that a broker could be liable for misadvising a seller about the effect of a subordination provision in the seller's contract.

The courts have consistently equated the duty owed by an agent-to-principal with the duty owed by a trustee-to-beneficiary. This rule of agency is specifically mentioned in the California Real Estate Law, and its violation is cause for revocation or suspension of a real estate license (Section 10176 (d) of the California Business and Professions Code).

Fine. But what has all this to do with theology or preaching in the church?

## Professional Negligence in the Ecclesiastical Sphere

One does not have to look very far to see the results in church circles of the disregard of such basic professional principles as we have been describing.

Clergy hold themselves out, on the basis of three- to four-years of theological seminary training, as expositors of Christian faith. Laity and the general public are therefore supposed to be able to rely on their preaching and teaching as representing classic Christianity. Clergy thus have a fiduciary responsibility to those less well informed theologically to present the true teachings of Christian faith. Are they doing so?

Answer: Not with any consistency. We offer just a few examples, from different theological traditions.

*The Baptists: Harry Emerson Fosdick.* Fosdick, in the early 20th century, was the spokesman in the United States for theological liberalism. One of his books, *The Modern Use of the Bible,* maintained that Holy Scripture was by no means inerrant, but in scientific and historical matters erred continually.[3] One of Fosdick's most famous sermons was titled "The Peril of Worshiping Jesus."[4] Since the Ecumenical Creeds of all Christian churches (Eastern Orthodox, Roman Catholic, and Protestant) affirm Trinitarian belief and the Deity of Christ, and since the Protestant Reformation maintained as central the formal principle of total biblical reliability, one can only conclude that Fosdick violated egregiously his fiduciary responsibility as a Christian

---

[3] As a young Christian, I preached the gospel to an individual at a Presbyterian summer conference. Later, she wrote me, rejecting what I had presented after reading Fosdick's book. See my autobiography, *Fighting the Good Fight: A Life in Defense of the Faith* (Bonn, Germany: Verlag für Kultur und Wissenschaft, 2016).

[4] See 5/3 *Church Monthly* 43-48 (January, 1931).

clergyman in that he mislead laity and the non-churched concerning the true nature of Christian faith. He was never disciplined. Even the conservative Lutheran Church-Missouri Synod includes one of his hymns in their most recent official hymnbook.[5]

*The Episcopalians: Bishop James Pike.*
Pike, a lawyer, became an Episcopal priest, a theological seminary professor, and ultimately a bishop. During his career he moved from a relatively conservative neo-orthodox theology to extreme liberalism and ultimately spiritualism. He was particularly known for his public declarations that he could "sing the Creed but not say it," and that he had "jettisoned the Trinity, the Virgin Birth and the Incarnation." When I debated him at McMaster University in Canada, he was on his way to Israel with his current mistress to write "the definitive biography of Jesus." Apparently, the Lord did not want a definitive biography, and Pike died of exposure in the Palestinian desert.[6]

In spite of laudatory, hagiographical biographies by journalists of Pike's liberal persuasion, it is painfully obvious that what he preached and taught was 180° removed from classic, creedal Christianity. Pike, as an ordained clergyman and bishop, had a fiduciary responsibility to provide accurate information on the Christian faith to those with less training and knowledge of it than he possessed. Instead, he misled the public, committing negligent misrepresentation of the nature of Christian belief.

*The Lutherans: Professor Kloha and Dual Representation.*
Another aspect of professional misconduct in the real estate field consists of acting as agent for both the seller and the buyer without revealing the dual agency. Dual representation is not illegal *per se* but it becomes such when both principals in the transaction are unaware of the agent's dual role.

The reason for this ethical and legal requirement goes back to our Lord's caution against "serving two masters" (Matthew 6:24). Fiduciary duty to the one may well result in a violation of fiduciary duty to the other. For example: what is the broker to do if the buyer states that he or she is willing to pay more than the seller has offered? What if the seller has told the broker that he or she would accept less than the asking price? Whatever choice the broker makes – to reveal or not to reveal information to

---

[5] The hymn is entitled "God of Grace and God of Glory."
[6] See Montgomery, "Agent 666: Bishop Pike and His Treasure Hunt," in *The Suicide of Christian Theology* (Minneapolis: Bethany, 1970), pp. 47-61.

the other party – one of the principals will be hindered from achieving his or her objectives. And withholding information may ensure that the broker's duty of disclosure is breached as well. The agent who tries to act as agent for both parties is highly prone to committing fiduciary breaches.

If this occurs – and very definitely if the agent does not reveal the dual nature of his or her representation – the professional consequences are dire. They include: (1) the right of either principal to cancel the transaction whether or not either principal incurred damages; (2) the right of either principal to hold the licensee responsible for damages actually incurred; (3) the right of either principal to refuse to compensate the licensee; (4) the possible suspension or revocation of the licensee's real estate license.

Recently, I debated Professor Jeffrey Kloha of the Concordia Seminary, St. Louis, on theories of textual criticism and their impact on the doctrine of scriptural inerrancy.[7] One of the major issues in the debate was Dr Kloha's paper, presented in a European Festschrift, that argues for Elizabethan, not Marian, authorship of the Magnificat (Luke 1). In the debate, when asked about this, Kloha said that when he taught a lay class on the subject in church, he never mentioned the issue. I criticized this as dissembling and dishonest.

Shortly after the debate, one of Professor Kloha's seminary colleagues defended him in a blog in the following terms: "Kloha is not disingenuous or contradictory. He simply does not need to detail every step of his work to those in his field in the same way that he does for the person who does not work in that field."[8]

I replied:

> *Pace* Herrmann, this is not a matter of Kloha's simplifying for Lutherans the views he has espoused in a more technical manner in European scholarly Festschriften. There, before audiences of non-confessional academics, Kloha presents views incompatible with biblical stability and reliability – and then avoids saying the same thing to the Christian laity in his own church body. Egregious example: he argues, on the basis of poor MS sources and thoroughgoing eclecticism's principle of choosing variant readings according to subjective, literary fit, that Elizabeth and not Mary spoke the Magnificat. Then, teaching in church on the very same Lucan passage, he never even refers to the question – giving his audience the obvious message that he goes along with the Marian reading as do all the standard translations based on

---

[7] See, elsewhere in this volume, the chapter titled, "The Kloha Catastrophe."
[8] Reprinted in *Christian News*, 7 November 2016.

solid Greek texts. This is simply dishonest. If that is the kind of scholarship and churchmanship practiced at the Concordia Seminary, St Louis, I tremble for the future of the LCMS.[9]

As an ordained clergyman of the Lutheran Church-Missouri Synod and an associate professor at its major theological seminary, Kloha presents himself as having specialized knowledge in his field well beyond that of laity or the general public. In the capacity of teacher or preacher, therefore, he has a fiduciary responsibility not to present misleading information – and certainly not to engage in a dual agency. Here, he has advocated a critical viewpoint in a scholarly context where that would be acceptable and, by implication, the opposite viewpoint to laity in an ecclesiastical framework where he knew well that a denial of Marian authorship of the Magnificat would not only be disturbing but surely raise immediate issues as to the compatibility of his text critical views and the denomination's commitment to a reliable Scripture. He took as his "master" in one context the non-confessional scholarly community and in the other his denomination's fidelity to a solid biblical text. But Kloha appears to be in no danger whatever of being disciplined, much less of losing his license to practice.

## Conclusion

The Real Estate profession maintains its rigorous standards out of concern for the general public. Owing to the seriousness of real estate purchases (probably the most expensive outlays of money in the average person's lifetime) and the real estate broker's or salesperson's superior training and knowledge, the lay client should be able to accept the real estate professional's factual assertions as representing objective truth. If the broker or salesperson presents an unfounded opinion as fact, or a reasonable person would construe the broker's statement of opinion as an assertion of fact, and the layman acts to his or her detriment in reliance on the statement, the professional is liable in either intentional or negligent misrepresentation.

Example: broker suggested that the buyer purchase an eleven-unit apartment house. To induce the plaintiff to purchase, the broker made representations that the apartment would be worth $140,000 if the rents were raised. The increased rents would produce a net spendable $500 per month. At the close of escrow, every unit was occupied, and the new owner sent rent increase notices to each tenant. Within two months, 65% of the

---

[9] *Christian News,* 14 November 2016.

apartments were vacant, and no new tenants could be secured at the higher rent. The eventual result was a loss of the property, together with $42,000 less rental income to the buyer instead of the profit the broker had represented. In the subsequent lawsuit, the plaintiff-buyer was successful in obtaining a verdict against the real estate agency.[10]

In California, as in virtually all other common law jurisdictions, the standard of care owed by the real estate broker to a prospective purchaser is the degree of care a reasonably prudent real estate licensee would exercise, and is measured by the degree of knowledge through education, experience, and examination required to obtain a real estate license under state law [C.C. § 2079.2].

What application does this have in the ecclesiastical realm? One might argue that with the number of untrained clergy, especially in charismatic ministries (one is often "ordained" simply on the individual's testimony that he or she has been "called by the Spirit"), laity should have no reasonable expectation of fiduciary responsibility on the cleric's part. But virtually all denominations maintain theological seminaries, Bible schools, and training for their clergy. Even in Baptistic and "free church" contexts, where authority is not centralized but is maintained by the local church, those local churches are members of associations that maintain licensing standards of some kind. Furthermore, even in the most extreme cases – the self-styled, uneducated clergyperson – the mere title of "Reverend" suggests a theological authority (and responsibility) beyond that of the layman or member of the general public.

This being the case, is it too much to expect that pastors and theologians operate with at least the minimum standards of secular professionals? There is a theme in Scripture that one should at least expect the believer to maintain the minimal ethics of unbelievers (cf. Jesus' parables of the unjust steward and the unjust judge –Luke 16 and 18). Moreover, the theological professional is informing others about heavenly mansions and how to get there (John 14:2). He or she is making asseverations about eternity – presumably of an importance surpassing even that of the purchase of a homestead here on earth. The preacher or theologian is making what appear to be factual declarations about (1) God's truth as revealed in God's own biblical revelation to mankind, and (2) salvation – how to enter into a relationship with God that will result in heaven and avoid hell.

Under these circumstances, shouldn't the professional standard parallel the importance of the subject matter? If so, may we suggest that the

---

[10] Cf., in general, Stuart Hershman and Joyce G. Mazero, *Financial Performance Representations* (Chicago: American Bar Association, 2009).

laxity in Christian denominations and theological seminaries – even those of conservative and evangelical reputation – is appalling. The real estate profession has long progressed beyond leaving the layman to the mercies of *caveat emptor* – "let the buyer beware." How sad that the church, in general, has not.

# Part Three:

## Short Essays on Critical Topics

## 21. Lesser-of-Evils

A key ethical issue particularly plagues evangelical believers. Evangelicals (like Roman Catholics engaged in moral casuistry and the quest for "sainthood") desperately want to fulfil John Wesley's desire for moral perfection. But how is this possible in a fallen world where ethical ambiguities can leave one with no choice that is inherently good? Take the standard torture example: suppose that only by physically torturing a terrorist can we find out where he has planted a bomb that, if and when it goes off, will kill one hundred school children. Most rational people would – as a lesser-of-evils – torture the terrorist, but such an act is, nonetheless, morally reprehensible.

Or take war. Here is a telling passage from Scott Turow's second-world-war novel, *Ordinary Heroes*; the narrator is a soldier who took part in the D-Day landings:

> "It was the devil's hell, all right. Sitting in church, having the preacher tell me where the sinners was gonna find their ugly selves, and thinking so hard about it, that was what I'd seen. The banging, the screaming, the pain. Even the smells of the bombs and the artillery rounds. That's a saying, sir, you know, war is hell, but it's a truth. The souls screaming and sinking down. And the skies falling. When I get to thinking about it, sometimes I wonder if I'm not dead after all."

One of the most widely accepted ethical solutions for evangelicals is what Norman Geisler has denominated "graded absolutism." In essence, this view says that biblical commands vary in importance and if one chooses to violate a "lower" command in order to follow a "higher" command, one is not sinning at all. Thus, in Corrie ten Boom's "hiding place" dilemma, if one lies to protect Jews, one does not commit sin and one's sanctification remains intact. Of course, the problem with such a viewpoint is simply the flat biblical assertion that "whosoever shall keep the whole law, and yet offend in one point, he is guilty of all" (James 2:10).

Far more satisfactory (and biblical) is the Reformation position that sees such ethical "hells" as negating a doctrine of perfectionism. When one sins, one sins; and the only proper recourse is to go back to the Cross of Christ for forgiveness and restoration. One chooses the "lesser-of-evils" – but a "lesser" evil does not become a good by virtue of the fact that its pragmatically negative consequences are less than the opposing choice. Of course, it is better to lie than to sacrifice the lives of fellow human beings, but lying is *still* wrong; indeed, Jesus classifies lying as devilish (John 8:44).

Geisler makes three points in arguing against the Reformation ethic, which he terms "ideal absolutism" or "conflicting absolutism" or "the lesser-of-evils view" (*Options in Contemporary Christian Ethics* [Baker, 1981], pp. 81-101). Here they are, with our commentary: (1) The Reformation view "holds the individual guilty for doing his best in an unavoidably bad situation." But this is precisely God's judgment against every generation of mankind since Adam fell: "When you shall have done all those things which are commanded you, say, We are unprofitable servants" (Luke 17:10).

(2) "There is always at least one right thing to do – 1 Corinthians 10:13." But the temptation referred to in this passage, and which we need never give in to, is that of *irresponsibility*: not bothering to go through the agonizing process of choosing the lesser-of-evils. (3) Reformation ethics "would render the sinlessness of Christ either impossible or meaningless." But to be true man, Christ neither had to have every particular human experience (he never experienced old age, for example) nor had to experience every particular human temptation (he was never in the military and he was apparently never presented with the "hiding place" situation). To be "touched with the feeling of our infirmities" and "tempted in all points like as we are, yet without sin" (Hebrews 4:15) requires *qualitative*, not quantitative, identification with fallen mankind. God was incarnate "in the fullness of time" (Galatians 4:4): doubtless one aspect of God's choice of time and place was to ensure that during his sojourn on earth he would not have to choose even a lesser evil; and his omniscience (except as to the hour of the Second Coming) whilst in the earthly state gave him the knowledge totally to avoid ethically compromising choices.

In contrast to so-called "situation ethics," which is totally lacking in ethical absolutes (save for "love," which, being undefined, loses absolute quality in any case), Reformation ethics takes biblical principle so seriously that it recognises genuine moral conflicts in a fallen world. The difficulty is not with the principles (of course both lying and betraying one's fellow man are contrary to scriptural principles!) but with the depravity of the world which we have made – in Adam as our representative and in the selfishness that penetrates our every decision and action. (Cf. Joseph Fletcher and John Warwick Montgomery, *Situation Ethics - True or False: A Dialogue* [2d ed.; Calgary, Alberta: Canadian Institute for Law, Theology and Public Policy, 1999], *passim*, but especially pp. 64-66.)

So, whether in the case of war or torture or the "hiding place," we need to give up our chimerical belief in realisable holiness in this life. With Luther, there are occasions where we must "sin bravely" – "but believe and rejoice in Christ even more bravely, for he is victorious over sin, death and the world" (*WA*, 2, 371). When we must act in such ambiguous situations, let us not dissemble but courageously pray, "O Lord, forgive me for my participation in this sinful and fallen world. Without thy death for me, I would be lost forever. Raise me up by thy sacrifice and take me into thy presence in spite of what I have had to do. When I am called out of this world may I spend eternity in that land where sin is no more and which thou hast prepared for those who know that they cannot save themselves." (See Montgomery, *Human Rights and Human Dignity* [2d ed.; Calgary, Alberta: Canadian Institute for Law, Theology and Public Policy, 1995], notes 347 and 376.)

In conclusion, a word from another character in Turow's *Ordinary Heroes*; in this instance, a battlefield general who eventually becomes a theologian:

"We're lost. Utterly lost. Because we need God, Dubin. Every man out here needs God ... Do you know why we need God, why we must have him? ...

"Well, I'll tell you, Dubin. Why we need God. Why I need God. To forgive us," he said then, and with the words his anger almost instantly subsided to sadness ... "Because when this is over, this war, that's what we'll need, all of us who have done what war requires and, worse, what war permits, that's what we'll need, in order to be able to live the rest of our lives."

## 22. Reflections on John 7:53-8:11

Once in a while your author gets into a sermonic mood (he is, after all, a Lutheran clergyman). Here's a take on John 7:53-8:11 which may be new to you.

But first, a preliminary word for readers schooled in textual criticism.

Writes Bruce Metzger (*A Textual Commentary on the Greek New Testament* [2d ed.; Stuttgart: Deutsche Bibelgesellschaft, 1994], pp. 187-89): "The evidence for the non-Johannine origin of the pericope of the adulteress is overwhelming ... At the same time the account has all the earmarks of historical veracity. It is obviously a piece of oral tradition which circulated in certain parts of the Western church and which was subsequently incorporated into various manuscripts at various places." In other words, though we do not know exactly where the story should be placed within Jesus' earthly ministry, it surely represents an event that really occurred during his ministry.

The essence of the event lies in Jesus' assertion to the religious leaders and their followers about to stone the woman: "He who is without sin among you, let him cast a stone at her." Response? "And they who heard it, being convicted by their own conscience, went out one by one, beginning at the eldest, even unto the last."

Even the scribes and the Pharisees, with their holier-than-thou legalism, had to admit that they themselves were sinners – and that therefore they were in no position to condemn the woman to a horrible death.

The late Professor Norman Cohn, in his classic *The Pursuit of the Millennium: Revolutionary Millenarians and Mystical Anarchists of the Middle Ages* (1957), observed that violent revolutionary movements such as the 16th century Anabaptist commune in Muenster became even more dangerous and destructive when led by someone "who believed that he had attained a perfection so absolute that he was incapable of sin."

Today, in our world of rampant and increasing secularism, many have lost all understanding of sin. And when that happens, there is no reason not to commit atrocities and human rights violations in dealing with those one disagrees with or whom one despises as inferior.

Doesn't this go far to explain why the secular régimes of the 20th century (Hitler's Germany, Stalin's U.S.S.R., Pol Pot, Idi Amin, Mugabe) have had no problem killing and maiming whoever opposes them – or even those they imagine to be a threat to them?

Our modern secular era has been the most destructive of human life in all the centuries of recorded history. When one loses consciousness of one's personal and societal sin, that result is inevitable. A good reason, one would suppose, to oppose secularism tooth and nail–and, on the positive side, to do everything possible to maintain a God-fearing national identity and an evangelism committed to preaching the eternal gospel of sin and grace worldwide.

## 23. Secularism and Stupidity in the Fast Lane

Secularism has been around for a long time; though (*pace* Francis Schaeffer) it did not become dominant during the Renaissance, it certainly became mainline ideology in the western world beginning with the 18$^{th}$ century (misdesignated) Enlightenment. As for stupidity, that has been around even longer – ever since our first parents in the Garden of Eden believed the lies of the serpent.

But, unless my imagination is running wild, during the last few decades the incremental rates of both stupidity and secularity have been rising at an unprecedented rate.[1] Here are just a few examples:

1) The wide acceptance of evolutionary arguments à la Dawkins that, given enough time, one can explain developmental change without resorting to intelligent design. The problem here is that time contains no causal element. A birdhouse can sit for an infinite period of time and will still be a birdhouse; it will not change into a castle.[2]
2) In the Union of South Africa, public holidays of ecclesiastical significance such as Ascension Day have been scrapped in favour of humanistic festivals ("Women's Day," "Worker's Day," "Youth Day," etc.).
3) When I read for the English bar, the most influential figures on the English legal scene were serious, practicing Christians: Lord Chancellor Hailsham, whose first autobiography, *The Door Wherein I Went*, contains an important legal apologetic for Christian faith[3]; Lord Diplock, who worshipped regularly at the barristers' Temple Church; and Lord Denning, president of the Lawyers' Christian Fellowship. Now the atmosphere has radically changed: an English judge recently denied the appeal of a Christian relationships counselor who was fired for refusing to provide sex counseling to a homosexual couple, stating that religious justifications were "irrational"[4]; and two civil servants have been told not to

---

[1] P. T. Barnum remarked that "there's a fool born every minute." To be sure, the birthrate was lower during his time than it is in ours ...
[2] Cf. Montgomery, *Global Journal of Classical Theology*, Vol. 6, No. 1 (May, 2007): http://www.globaljournalct.com/the-irrationality-of-richard-dawkins/
[3] Reprinted in Vol. 4 (1984-1985) of *The Simon Greenleaf Law Review*, under my editorship.
[4] See Montgomery, "Religious 'Irrationality' and Civil Liberties," *Amicus Curiae: Journal of the Society for Advanced Legal Studies* [U.K.], Summer, 2010.

wear crosses to work – the English courts agreeing and the government taking the same position before the European Court of Human Rights.

4) In the 2012 French presidential race, Sarkozy, the experienced president, lost to Hollande, a man with zero experience in running a government and even less experience in foreign affairs. This occurred against the background of the desperate need for financial austerity as promoted by Sarkozy – whilst the *département* headed by Hollande had the biggest financial deficit in the entire country. The more committed to Christianity one was, the more he or she voted for Sarkozy, whilst Hollande was heavily favoured in the national election by those with no religion – and by the Muslims. Here are the statistics of the percentage of each religious category voting for Sarkozy, as reported by *Le Figaro* (8 May 2012):

| | |
|---|---|
| Regularly practicing Roman Catholics | 73% |
| Protestants | 61% |
| Occasionally practicing Roman Catholics | 58% |
| Non-practicing Roman Catholics | 51% |
| No religion | 34% |
| Muslims | 7% |

Hollande received 52% of the total national vote, becoming the first divorced French president with an unmarried "partner."

5) Meanwhile, evangelicals are engaged in systematic dumbing down – charismatic emotionalism, pabulum theologies, and mega-church populism (focused on the overhead projector rather than the cross) substituting for the serious theologies of the Reformation past. Even the graduates of respected theological seminaries have trouble understanding the writings of professionals in their field.[5]

So what can be done? Perhaps nothing; history moves in cycles and we may be experiencing another Dark Age. But a classical education, with a strong dose of formal logic, would certainly help – as would serious study of the writings of the great theologians of the past: Augustine, Luther, Calvin, B. B. Warfield, C. F. W. Walther, Herman Sasse. At very minimum, they might teach us how to think.[6]

---

[5] The reader will forgive a personal example. One anonymous net review of the author's book, *Suicide of Christian Theology* reads as follows: "I found the writing so complicated that I had difficulty following the intricately woven arguments. I actually had to take some of his sentences and rewrite them in simpler terms before I understood what he meant ... PS. I am no dummy either. I have a 3.96 GPA at Trinity Evangelical Divinity School." Other reviewers – who had nothing but praise for the book – did not seem to have this problem.

[6] It was Sasse who said that the modern Christian has lost the ability to "think theologically."

## 24. "Intolerant Religion" As Threat To "Tolerant-Liberal Democracy"?

The title of the present article makes reference to a recent book – *Intolerant Religion in a Tolerant-Liberal Democracy* (Hart, 2015). Though the book contains little legal analysis, its author – Yossi Nehushtan – is a senior lecturer at the Keele University School of Law and co-director of its MA programme in human rights, globalization and justice. Thus, an analysis of the book's arguments would appear to fall without difficulty within the scope of religio-jurisprudential discussion.

Nehushtan is convinced that a strong correlation exists between religion and intolerance and he endeavours to show that religious commitment poses a genuine threat to contemporary "tolerant-liberal" democracy. In light of such events as the appalling terrorist attacks in Paris on 13 November 2015 by Muslim commandos of Daesh, this claim might seem self-evidently correct. It is the purpose of the present article to show how superficial Nehushtan's argument is in fact.

The two fundamental errors that suffice to destroy the author's thesis are (1) the disparity between his definition of intolerance and the actions of the religious, and (2) his apparent inability to distinguish among the diversity of religious belief systems. We shall take up each in turn.

Nehushtan defines *tolerance* as follows: "Tolerance exists when the tolerant person makes an adverse judgement of a certain type about another, the adverse judgement provides the tolerant person with reasons to harm the other, but the tolerant person restrains himself and avoids harming the other – for whatever reason" (p. 25). Note that this definition (properly) distinguishes between holding adverse judgments of another's position and *harming that person* because of the difference in viewpoints. Thus, merely holding that another is wrong in his beliefs should not constitute intolerance; harming him because of the difference would be required for genuine intolerance to exist.

All good and well. But then our author offers sociological survey after sociological survey to show that religionists are intolerant – based on their "intolerant" beliefs that other positions than their own are false. To make his case, the only proper route would be to show that, *by way of their obnoxious treatment of unbelievers,* the religionists *as a class* demonstrate intolerance.

To be sure, such actions can be shown in certain instances – the Muslim terrorists being an obvious example. But to generalize from such cases would require ignoring the differences in religious beliefs and religious communities historically, geographically, and ideologically. Tarring every religious believer with the same brush is hardly good logic or good scholarship.

Both the Qur'an and the Shari'a provide strong reasons to maltreat unbelievers. The Qur'an calls upon the faithful to war against the infidel. Sura 4: "Let those fight on the path of God ... Whoever fighteth on God's path, whether he be slain or conquer, we will in the end give him a great reward ... They who believe, fight on the path of God ... Fight therefore against the fiends of Satan ... The might of the infidels haply will God restrain, for God is the stronger in prowess, and the stronger to punish." Sura 9: "Contend against the infidels and the hypocrites, and be harsh with them: Hell shall be their dwelling place!"

Writes German specialist on Islam, Prof. Dr Christine Schirrmacher: "Extremists who apply the early Muslim community's struggle against 'infidels' to present-day conflicts can hardly be accused of misinterpreting the Koran, for people who resist the spread of Islam can scarcely be considered as 'innocent victims,' particularly in Israel, where there is not a family without someone serving in the armed forces. From the extremists' perspective it is easy to see how even those not involved in the war can be considered enemies of Islam. According to this view, it is legitimate to take the life of Islam's enemies, who resist its spread, as Israel does by its very existence, as this ultimately counts as defending Islam" (Christine Schirrmacher, *Islam and Society: Sharia law – Jihad – Women in Islam* ["WEA Global Issues," 4; Bonn, Germany: Verlag für Kultur und Wissenschaft, 2008], p. 113).

From the perspective of the Muslim extremist, there is no way that the Quranic teaching on Jihad can today be restricted (as contemporary defenders of Islam have tried to argue) solely to defensive warfare on Islamic territory. Western nations, by their support of Israel, by their lax willingness to allow published satires of the Prophet and his teachings, and by their belief in an open society are in fact engaged in an all-out war against the fundamental religious teachings of Islam; their citizens therefore deserve to become the objects of Jihad and have only themselves to blame for the carnage that can ensue.

We cannot here go into the sad historical record of Islamic warfare and conversions by the sword. But the message is clear: when Muslim terrorists in our time plan and carry out their appalling activities, they have solid historical precedent for spreading their faith and eliminating opposition in that manner.

The contrast with the teachings of Jesus could hardly be greater. His Sermon on the Mount insists on "turning the other cheek" rather than reacting violently against the opponent. At the same time, Jesus declares that he is "the Way, the Truth, and the Life"; no one comes to the Father by any route than Himself (John 16:4; cf. Acts 4:12). Here, then, we have an exclusive belief system, but one that must by its very nature tolerate the existence of other convictions.

Nehushtan does, occasionally, recognize differences among religionists – though without modifying his blanket negative evaluation of religious belief in general. Thus, he sees the special problem of fundamentalism in Israel (pp. 84-86). However, whilst having to report survey results showing that "intrinsic [evangelical] faith is associated with a rejection of prejudice against anti-homosexual sentiment, even though homosexual behavior was still regarded as a moral problem," he makes the astounding claim that "evangelicals are less tolerant than other religious Americans" (p. 86). It is noteworthy that the author gives no concrete evidence that American evangelicals as a class have caused harm to homosexuals – which, by his own definition of intolerance, would have to be shown to demonstrate the evangelicals' intolerant character.

And the author naively accepts the politically-correct view that the more liberal one is religiously, the less likely he or she is to be intolerant. Many years ago, I did a study of the library catalogue titles in two theological faculty libraries – a renowned "conservative" and a celebrated "liberal" institution. The conservative faculty had both liberal and conservative books in roughly equal numbers; the liberal faculty had virtually no conservative titles (Montgomery, "Bibliographical Bigotry," *Christianity Today*, 19 August 1966).

Throughout his book, Nehushtan presents generalisations that simply cannot be pasted onto all religionists. Examples: "Religion aspires to gain formal control over its believers, other religious believers, and heretics alike ... Religion identifies morality and law with the divine, hence generally it rises above human criticism and reform" (p. 93). Apparently, the author has never heard of such law reforms as the abolition of slavery and the slave trade – brought about specifically by the efforts of evangelical Christian believers (cf. Montgomery, "Slavery, Human Dignity and Human Rights," in his *Christ As Centre and Circumference* [Verlag für Kultur und Wissenschaft, 2012; and, in general, Alvin J. Schmidt, *How Christianity Changed the World* [Zondervan, 2004]). And it is more than ironic that the most extensive violations of human rights in human history have been the product of atheistic governments and their leaders (the holocaust under the pagan Third Reich and the gulags under the atheistic-materialistic Soviets).

It should go without saying that genuinely intolerant religion needs to be opposed legally. The European Court of Human Rights was entirely correct in its judgment upholding the refusal of the Turkish government to register an extremist religio-political party on the ground that, if that party gained control of the state, it would eliminate the civil liberties to which Turkey had committed itself by ratifying the European Convention of Human Rights (*Refah Partisi v Turkey*, Applications nos. 41340/98, 41342/98, 41343/98 and 41344/98); judgment of 13 February 2003). But to regard intolerance as a defining mark of religion in general goes beyond all rational limits.

Nehushtan concludes his book with "A Note about Religion, the Academic World and the Real World" – in which he bewails the fact that intellectuals have not been sufficiently moved by the "troubling theoretical and empirical links" between religion and intolerance "when we decide political and legal disputes about religion in a tolerant-liberal democracy."

Perhaps there is good reason, after all, for the intellectuals not accepting Nehushtan's call to arms.

# 25. The New Age of Christian Martyrdom

Among the so-called "new atheists" it is common to rail against Christianity for its persecution of dissidents – the Crusades, the Spanish Inquisition, the 17th-century witchcraft trials. To be sure, there are definitive refutations of these critiques (see, as but a single illustration, my treatment of the witchcraft trials in my book, *The Law Above the Law*); and the positive contributions of Christianity to civilization across the centuries far outweigh the historic church's – in fact fairly rare – deviations from Christ's standards (consult Alvin J. Schmidt's survey, *How Christianity Changed the World*).

But any attempts to condemn Christianity for persecuting others pale to insignificance in the face of the miseries being faced by Christian believers at the present moment. And this is coming to be recognized not just by Christian believers and human rights organizations of Christian persuasion (e.g., the World Evangelical Alliance's International Institute for Religious Freedom, of which I am Honorary Chairman of the Academic Board), but even by the secular world. Example: the 11-20 October 2010 issue of the distinguished French weekly news magazine *Le Nouvel Observateur*, whose full-page column by Jacques Julliard is devoted to "La chasse aux chrétiens" (Open Season on Christians).

This article makes so many important points that I am going to present its essence in translation and paraphrase. – And in what follows, please note my careful use of quotation marks. I want to avoid at all costs the charge of plagiarism, properly directed to civil rights advocate and liberal pastor Martin Luther King, whose academic career involved the continual, unacknowledged use of other people's material: see the *Martin Luther King Papers*, ed. Clayborne Carson (6 vols.; Berkeley: University of California Press, 1992-2007, I, 49-50, II, 7-8).

The subtitle of Julliard's article reads: "Christianity has become, by far, the most persecuted religion. But the West plays ostrich." These two points are then supported in spades.

1. The extent of the persecution and its major source. "It's really nothing: nothing but Christians and Christian communities being eaten alive. Where? Just about everywhere Christians are in the minority: in India, Bangladesh, China, Vietnam, Indonesia, North Korea. But especially in Muslim lands – and not just in Saudi Arabia where Christian worship is punished by the death penalty, but also in Egypt, Turkey, and Algeria. In today's world, Christianity is by far the world's most persecuted religion."

"However, it is in the Near East – the very birthplace of Christianity – where the situation is the gravest. In Turkey, the most ancient Christian communities, antedating Islam, are on the verge of disappearing entirely. In Coptic Egypt and in Maronite Lebanon they are closing in upon themselves or immigrating to the West. A miniature religious genocide is taking place."

Why the current Muslim persecutions of Christians? "During many centuries, Christians were able to live in peace with the followers of Islam, even when the latter became the majority. Why the change in the last fifty years? The reason lies in the Islamic revival in the Near East – a revival of an aggressive and fundamentalist sort – which considers the Near East as belonging exclusively to the Muslims. Example: at Naj Hammadi, sixty kilometers from Luxor, Egypt, on the 6th of January this year, the Muslim Brotherhood attacked a car carrying Coptic Christians who were returning home from a Christmas mass (result: 7 dead)."

"Ironically, the democratization of former colonial regimes has reinforced Muslim intolerance and exclusivity. Even under Saddam Hussein Christians were less persecuted in Iraq than they are today. The fact is that the Near Eastern despots were very often beneficiaries of traditional pluralism. Now in almost all of those countries, Islam has become the state religion and anti-Western jihad has focused on Christians as representing the evil West."

2. Current indifference in Christian countries. "Meanwhile, the West plays ostrich. With but few exceptions, when faced with this issue the Western human rights professionals run for cover. A new kind of cultural Yalta seems to be coming about: in the East, a monopoly created by a single religion – Islam – which displays more and more intolerance; in the West, pluralism, tolerance, and secularism. And this Yalta is, like the previous one, the source of cold war (to put it mildly). *It is therefore mandatory that we, without any second thoughts or namby-pamby complacency, defend the right of existence of Eastern Christians.*"

I have italicized the final sentence of Julliard's article – which deserves to be generalized to embrace persecuted Christians everywhere.

# 26. "Ararat," the Armenians, and Missionary Doctor Clarence Ussher

The film to which we point our readers is not easy to find, though it was released late in 2002 and has an international cast, including Christopher Plummer (remember him as Captain Von Trapp in *The Sound of Music*?) and distinguished French actor (better known as singer and composer of popular French *chansons*) Charles Aznavour. The film is titled "Ararat" and was produced in Canada (in English, with some subtitled French and Armenian). It is now showing in Paris, where I recently saw it, as well as in select movie houses in major cities in other countries.

"Ah," you, say, "Ararat. Of course Montgomery could not resist, having carried on extensive Ark research on the said mountain in the 1970s and even climbed to the peak of that formidable mountain." (See my *Quest for Noah's Ark*, which Bethany Fellowship Publishers has allowed to go out of print, presumably to make way for the evangelical romantic novels they now publish.) But No! The film "Ararat" does not in the least deal with the search for the Ark, and the only appearances of the mountain itself in the film come by way of what appears to be stock footage. The point of the title is that Mount Ararat in Eastern Turkey has always been the symbolic centre of Christian Armenia.

The film "Ararat" is the first attempt to document, by way of a major motion picture, the hideous genocide of Armenians in Turkey from 1914 to 1918. That genocide has been almost entirely ignored, in some degree because it occurred when the West was preoccupied with World War I. And the Nazi genocide of the Jews during the Second World War explains to some extent the lack of historical awareness of what the Turks did to the Armenians (the Jews have been much better propagandists than the Armenians in publicising their loss). But the blame for ignoring what was done to Christian Armenia lies especially with the Turkish nation, which has systematically denied that anything significant even took place!

In point of fact, the Turkish régime of the time effectively destroyed the Christian Armenian community by slaughtering vast numbers and forcing the emigration of the survivors to Europe (especially France ) and the Americas. Charles Aznavour's relations were among those *émigrés*, and he has contributed significantly to eleemosynary work among Armenians throughout his career.

The importance of the film "Ararat" for evangelical Christians is twofold. First, we are told every day, by everyone from Prime Minister Tony Blair (who, as a believing Christian, should know better) to the pundits and the media (who know next to nothing) that September 11 was the result of insane terrorism and *not* to any inherent viciousness in the Muslim religion. The history of Islam, of course, entirely belies such a judgment. Conversion by the sword was standard practice through much of the history of Islam, and the genocide of the Armenians (though also motivated, as the film shows, by economic considerations) is a further horrifying example of the consequences of bad religion. What one believes *makes all the difference in the world* as to what one *does*. Evangelical Christians – just about the only people left who maintain that religion is a matter of *truth,* not cosmic preference, can have their convictions and their concern to preach the Gospel to other faiths powerfully strengthened by way of this film.

Secondly (and this simply reinforces the first point), "Ararat," though scrupulously fair to the Turkish position and not at all religiously propagandistic, is based almost entirely on the account of the genocide written by an American evangelical missionary doctor! One Dr Clarence Ussher appears prominently in the film: his missionary clinic in the Armenian area of Van in Eastern Turkey provides extensive medical aid and Ussher attempts vainly to convince the fanatical Turkish military authorities not to exterminate the populace. In the credits at the end of the film, the statement is made that the film derives from a book by Dr Ussher.

No biographical information on Ussher is provided to the viewer, other than what can be gathered from the film itself. Having seen the film, I *had* to obtain such information – and, if possible, Ussher's book. I suspected that he must be an evangelical (was it Malcolm Muggeridge who said that he had yet to find a Unitarian leper colony?). On checking out-of-print book sources – and, as a bibliomaniac, I know a staggering number – I was unable to locate a copy of Ussher's book to purchase, but I did turn up a pamphlet, "Before Governors and Kings," by Clarence D. Ussher, M.D., published by Covenant House, Toronto, Canada. On obtaining this 14-page booklet, I read on its cover sheet: "With permission from a reprint by Howard A. Kelly, M.D., through the courtesy of Dr Ussher and the Houghton Mifflin Company." The pamphlet was clearly an extract from the book–and Kelly, to be sure, was the famous evangelical doctor and author! I then contacted the library of the Moody Bible Institute and was graciously provided with a photocopy of Ussher's 339-page book, titled, *An American Physician in Turkey,* published by Houghton Mifflin in 1917, and never reprinted. The Moody copy lacked the frontispiece photographs of Dr Ussher and his wife, but I was able to obtain a reproduction of these from a copy of Ussher's book at the University of Illinois.

Dr Clarence Ussher was, fascinatingly, a descendent of the Bishop Ussher celebrated (or notorious) for his biblical chronology and the dating of the creation at 4004 B.C. Clarence, a believing Episcopalian and licenced medical practitioner of Canadian origin, went to Turkey under the Congregationalist American Board of Commissioners for Foreign Missions. He had previously signed the Student Volunteer declaration, "I am willing and desirous, if God permits, to become a foreign missionary," and he went to Turkey out of a powerful evangelistic desire to bring the gospel to a land benighted by Islamic error. And there he was to recount, as an eyewitness, the horrors of the Turkish extermination of the Armenian Christian community.[1]

The events he recounts are not just moving; they are heartrending. For example, he describes the death of a young Armenian hero, Aram: "I had received word that he was coming, and met him at the operating-room door. He endeavored to reach for my hand, and smiling in my face he said: 'O Doctor, I am so glad I learned to know Jesus and am ready to go. But please, Doctor, let me die quickly.'"

In the final chapter of his book, appropriately titled, "Opportunity," Ussher writes: "They [Turkish Muslims] have had before their eyes unnumbered examples of fortitude and loyalty to Christ. Thousands of Armenians, after struggling footsore and starving along the road to exile for days, whipped along when exhausted, have been taken into Moslem villages and given their choice: 'Now accept Mohammed and you shall have a home and food and clothing and fields and implements and seed and a bonus from the Government – everything you need. Refuse and you shall have not a drop of water.' With hardly an exception these thousands have turned their backs on all thus offered and have gone into the desert to death, rather than deny Christ. So the hearts of the Turks are now open to Christian truth as never before in the history of Mohammedanism."

---

[1] "Nothing less than a plan of extermination was put into effect. Throughout the country, soldiers, state police, Kurds, and brigands fell upon the Armenians. The young men and the strong were exterminated, and the rest of the population deported under horrific conditions ... Of the 2,100,000 Armenians still in the Ottoman Empire, approximately one million perished from 1915 to 1918" (Jean-Pierre Alem, L'Arménie ("Que sais-je?," No.851; 2d ed., Paris: Presses Universitaires de France, 1963), pp. 58-59 (our translation). See also, H. L. Gates, *The Auction of Souls* (reprint ed.; London: Phoenix Press, 1968) [American title: *Ravished Armenia*], with references to Dr Clarence Ussher.

The "opportunity" of which Ussher spoke, was, of course, the privilege and responsibility of missionising that Muslim land. Let us today be especially vigilant not to allow irrational views of religious indifferentism blunt that evangelistic task, about which Ussher wrote so eloquently three-quarters of a century ago.

Clarence Ussher[2]

---

[2] Wikimedia / Clarence Ussher & Grace Knapp (1917), public domain.

## 27. Martin Scorsese's *Silence*

Film buffs appalled by Scorsese's *Last Temptation of Christ* may well have vowed to ignore anything else he does. But in the case of his latest epic film, *Silence,* this would be a mistake. It is clear that Scorsese, whatever bizarre personal take he has on the nature of the Christian gospel, has been bitten by the Hound of Heaven and understands well the difficulties Christian believers face in a secular, pluralistic world.

The film is the third adaptation of a novel by famed Japanese Christian writer Shûsaku Endô (1923-1996). Set in the 17$^{th}$ century, it tells the story of two Portuguese priests who persuade their superior to let them go to Japan to find their mentor, a missionary who is reported to have apostatized during the extreme wave of Buddhist and nationalist persecution of Christians taking place there. Once in Japan, they find the persecution far more extensive and terrible than imagined; one is killed, and the other discovers that their mentor has indeed left the faith and become a Buddhist scholar. The government Inquisitor has perceptively learned from experience that "martyrdom is the seed of the church" and now employs another method to stamp out Christianity: until a missionary recants, his flock are subjected, one by one, to horrible and excruciatingly painful deaths. The argument is presented: didn't your Jesus do everything to save you – so you must recant your faith to save the remaining members of your flock. The young priest apparently does so recant, but seems to have remained a secret Christian, since a tiny crucifix is hidden on him as his body is burned in Buddhist fashion.

The theme of the novel and the film is particularly relevant today, when Christians around the world are being persecuted as never before – particularly by Muslim fundamentalism.

We offer seven – the perfect number – of lessons from the film:

1) In the Western context today, Buddhism is presented – by way of the Dalai Lama, Christmas Humphreys, *et al.* – as a religion of sweetness and light, in stark contrast to supposedly persecutorial, imperialistic, missionizing western Christianity. The film illustrates the utter fallacy of such interpretations. Novelist Arthur Koestler, who flirted briefly with Eastern religions, rightly rejected Buddhism for its lack of any meaningful ethic (cf. the Buddhist kamikaze pilots in World War II).

2) The film should finish off any naïveté that "all religions teach the same thing." The horrible cruelties inflicted on the Christians by the Buddhist Inquisitor do not bother him at all. (The Roman Catholic inquisitions of the medieval period offer no analogy: they were contrary to the teachings and example of Jesus Christ and New Testament Christianity, whilst the Buddhist treatment of Christian missionaries could not be condemned by anything within that religious tradition.)

3) The arguments of the apostate mentor and former missionary against Christian truth show just how silly such arguments are. He denies any genuine Japanese conversions to Christianity – the martyrs are not dying for Christ but out of commitment to the missionaries. He even denies the possibility of translating biblical truth into Japanese (Francis Xavier is supposed to have accepted a Japanese translation of "Son of God" that was actually "Sun of God" – so instead of Christ's rising on the third day, he rises every morning).

4) The young priest correctly asserts that "truth is universal" – so Christianity is as true in Japan as in Europe or anywhere else. The reason for its lack of success in Japan is not the "soil" – the Japanese character and culture – but the fact that the soil has been "poisoned" – by Buddhist and other false religious teaching and by the persecution conducted by the opponents of the gospel.

5) Naturally, the Inquisitor sees the issues nationalistically and politically. He tells the story of a lord who had four mistresses who were continually fighting with each other – so he got rid of all of them and had peace. They represented European powers (Spain, Portugal, Netherlands, and England) wanting economic advantages in Japan. The young priest said: "We Christians are monogamous; the ruler should have just one wife." The Inquisitor replied, "The Portuguese?" The priest: "Christianity." The priest saw clearly that the problem – and the solution – was not political but religious.

6) The indifference to cruelty on the part of the Inquisitor and his minions reminds one of the Eastern theatre in World War II. A non-Christian culture has no foundation for or respect for human rights. The Burma railway and the Japanese prisoner camps of the Second World War should remind us that what one believes directly influences what one does. Did generations without Christ create an inherently dangerous Japanese personality, particularly in the political realm where totalitarianism could easily be justified?

7) The most difficult question posed in the film is surely the following: Is there ever a justification for apostasy – as here, where it was the

only way to save lives? God is not going to intervene; He is going to remain silent (note the film and book title) in a world where we sinners have corrupted everything. So what is to be done when facing such an ethical dilemma?

Note that the problem is not the Corrie Ten Boom "hiding place" dilemma: it is not a question of lying to the Nazis to protect Jewish lives. The issue is the priest's denying the faith publicly to save the lives of people who have already denied the faith or who must also deny it to survive.

As a lesser-of-evils situation, what is the greater evil – the loss of other people's lives through horrible torture, or the public denial of Christianity by its representative, thus telling the world that the faith is not worth dying for? Of course, the ideal is a heroic martyr's death on the part of all concerned, but suppose one simply does not have the personal strength to choose that route?

In general, the fundamental theological principle is that evangelism trumps all moral issues except right-to-life (the qualification is due to the fact that once people are dead neither evangelism nor moral values are relevant). Keeping the flock alive at least takes into account the possibility that the totalitarian Buddhist government may weaken and that returning to the faith may ultimately be possible.

More importantly, saving faith in Christ is a matter of one's inner commitment. The Reformation theologians insisted that saving faith is present only if one goes beyond *notitia* (doctrinal knowledge) and *assensus* (public affirmation) so as to arrive at *fiducia* (personal, heart commitment). If *assensus* is no longer possible, surely *fiducia* is still an option. This seems to be the film's lesson: In a world of sin, where believers do not always have the strength to withstand the individual and societal pressures of evil, outward conformity may sometimes be the lesser-of-evils. Faith in Christ should not properly exist only within the heart, but history has provided examples of such inner faith as the only humanly acceptable alternative.

## 28. Evangelical Chauvinism

A recent promotional e-mail from Jay Sekulow's American Center for Law and Justice informs us that "a Justice Souter replacement [on the U. S. Supreme Court] will more than likely maintain a strict view of church-state separation, *will apply international precedence to the U.S. Constitution,* and will be strongly in favor of abortion rights." This is no doubt an accurate assessment, but it is interesting to observe that among the future evils sure to accompany a liberal judicial appointment Sekulow includes the indictment we have italicized: the importation of international (i.e., non-American) legal notions into the American legal scene.

This is a common criticism among conservative American, and especially evangelical, jurisprudents. In line with traditional American isolationism, we are told in effect that American law is always best, and is invariably contaminated by notions deriving from other legal systems and especially by international law. "Stay away from the foreigners," is the byword. "Above all, do not ratify international conventions and treaties." "Do not allow foreign law to serve as precedents in American legislation or judicial decision-making." The justification? An assumption that American law is, by definition, more in line with revelational, i.e., biblical, law than is the law of any other nation – and certainly more so than any international law could be.

*May we go on record as opposing, root and branch, this philosophy?* Not because we live in Europe (or because we love French cuisine more than hominy grits) but on strictly scriptural and factual grounds.

No human legal system or constitution is divinely inspired; only Holy Writ offers an inerrant revelation of the Divine Will. The U. S. Constitution, though it reflects the morality of Scripture in many wonderful ways, never mentions Jesus Christ, atonement, redemption, the proper distinction between law and gospel, or the central, salvatory message of the Bible. The reason, of course, is that the leading "Founding Fathers" (Jefferson and Franklin, as egregious examples) were in no sense believing Christians: they represented the Deism of the 18$^{th}$ century, so-called "Enlightenment," which held that – in the words of Thomas Paine – the "Book of Scripture" needs to be replaced by the "Book of Nature" – both individually and societally. (Cf. Montgomery, *The Shaping of America* [Minneapolis: Bethany, 1976].)

It follows that there is no guarantee of infallibility for American law or the American legal system. Scriptural principles must stand in judgment over our legal activities in exactly the same way as they do over the legal actions of other countries operating nationally or internationally.

If the reader doubts the fallibility of American legal institutions, consider a couple of legislative examples which I cite in my book, *The Law Above the Law* (rev. ed.; Irvine, CA: NRP/1517.Legacy Project, 2015). "One thinks of a Kansas statute that changed the meaning of π from 3.1416 to an even 3, and another that declared: 'When two trains approach each other at a crossing, they shall both come to a full stop, and neither shall start up until the other has gone.'" Far less humorous and far more damnable is the U. S. Supreme Court decision in *Roe v. Wade*, which has created abortion-on-demand (cf. Montgomery, *Slaughter of the Innocents* [Westchester, IL: Crossway, 1981]; and "The Rights of Unborn Children," *Simon Greenleaf Law Review*, Vol. 5 [1985-1986] – reprinted in Montgomery, *Christ As Centre and Circumference* [Bonn: VKW, 2012], pp. 210 ff).

But is it possible that foreign legal systems or international law could ever improve on American law? *Certainly* – since original sin, being uniformly spread around ever since the Fall of Man, impacts the American legal scene, not just other geographical areas! Here are just a few thought-provoking examples:

*In the United Kingdom:* The Abortion Act 1967 requires, for an abortion to be legal and not subject to criminal penalties, that two physicians give their approval and that the abortion be performed in an approved hospital or facility (the approval of one physician suffices and the hospital requirement is waived only if the physician "is of the opinion, formed in good faith, that the termination is immediately necessary to save the life or to prevent grave permanent injury to the physical or mental health of the pregnant woman"). This is, to be sure, no bar to abortions in general, but it affords far more protection to the unborn than does American law, where, during the first trimester, abortion on demand is an absolute right of the pregnant woman.

*In France:* The French *Code pénal* (1994) includes severe criminal penalties for "non-assistance to a person in danger" Art. 223-6). This means that if I have the capacity to help another in such a situation and do not do so, my non-action is prosecutable criminally. The Anglo-American common law contains no such requirement. In 1964, thirty-eight New Yorkers watched for half an hour as one of their neighbours, Kitty Genovese, was being murdered in the street; no one called the police or did anything to help her; not a single one of these people were prosecuted, or could be prosecuted, for allowing the girl to die. If I watch a child drown and do nothing, I perform no illegal act under American common law. True, if I start to help and then walk away, I can be liable for my neglect; but only where statute has modified the common law am I guilty before the law if I simply do nothing at all. It should be all too obvious that the French law, unlike the Anglo-American common law, far better fulfills the biblical principle of being "my brother's keeper."

Moreover, the French Civil Code (art. 205), unlike American law, makes it a criminal offense for a child not to support his mother and father if they are incapable of supporting themselves. This principle is directly justified by the biblical command to honour father and mother. And Art. 909 of the *Code civil* prohibits physicians from receiving any gifts from terminal patients they are treating: a fine recognition of the potential effects of original sin on the medical profession!

Most important of all, the French Civil Code expressly prohibits judges from "making law" in the American fashion – as the U.S. Supreme Court did in its *Roe v. Wade* abortion decision. The Code states in no uncertain terms that no French magistrate may "make general, regulatory pronouncements" (art. 5) and that "a judicial decision is authoritative only for the specific matter being decided" (art. 1351). This is to stop judges in their tracks from substituting themselves for the elected members of the legislature – who alone have legitimate law-making power, since they, unlike judges, are the people's representatives.

Finally, *international law* (yes, international law!). Article 4 of the American Convention [i.e., Treaty] on Human Rights, ratified by most American nations (but not the U. S., for fear of being dragged before the Inter-American Court of Human Rights because of *Roe v. Wade*), protects human life "in general, from the moment of conception." This means that abortion on demand, as practiced in the United States, is contrary to the international law of the Americas. (See Montgomery, *Human Rights and Human Dignity* [Calgary, Alberta: Canadian Institute, 1995].)

But what about the current flap over children's rights? Is it not true that international conventions give rights to the child which could potentially fly in the face of parental rights (home schooling, etc.) as we understand them? It may well be that the interpretation of international law in the children's rights area goes too far. But the fundamental principle of chldren's rights – as concretized in England's Children Act 1989 through the efforts of former Lord Chancellor (and President of the Lawyers' Christian Fellowship!) Lord Mackay – has bright-line scriptural justification: "Of such little ones," declared our Lord, "is the Kingdom of heaven." Untrammeled and unrestricted parental rights over children can result in Jehovah's Witnesses' and Christian Scientists' refusing critical medical treatment to their children and Satanists' educating their children in the ways of damnation. The issue is not the alleged evils of international law, but *the de facto content of biblical standards*, which may – or may not – be better reflected in one legal system over against another, or in domestic law over against international legislation.

We are hardly arguing that foreign law or international law is always better than U. S. law. *But we are arguing that U. S. law is not always better than foreign or international law.* The point here is that Holy Scripture should be used as the judge of *all* human law – not just of law different from our own. Let's admit it, difficult as it may be for our chauvinistic nature as a nation: we, too, are sinners, and the revelation of our Lord needs to judge us as well as others. And it is always possible that we might learn something from legal systems elsewhere, if we would but exercise the humility to listen.

# 29. American Law and Freedom of Expression

As is well known, your author is an internationalist, and, in his capacity as an English barrister and member of the Paris bar, tends to defend the values of the great European legal systems – as well as classical French cuisine!

There are, however, times when it is important to stress the superiority of American law at its point of greatest strength: the defence of civil liberties. Our nation was founded very largely out of a concern that the citizen should be able to speak his or her mind and not be persecuted because of political, religious, or other opinions potentially or actually offensive to others. Interestingly enough, the separation of church and state, which occurred in France at the beginning of the 20th century, was based on the desire to keep the church out of the political realm; the American separation of church and state in the 18th century, by way of the Virginia Bill of Rights and the 1st Amendment to the Federal Constitution, had the reverse motivation: to keep the state from meddling in religious matters, especially in attempting to control the free expression and practice of believers.

In America, unless a belief or opinion poses an immediate danger – unless it is likely to cause a breach of the peace – it can receive public expression. (The breach-of-the-peace qualification parallels the adage, "Free speech does not give one the right to cry Fire! in a crowded theatre.") Even when the particular opinion or belief is obnoxious or patently false, the right to manifest it orally or in writing remains. Thus, in 1978, U.S. Federal Court upheld the right of a neo-Nazi organisation to express its beliefs by marching through Skokie, Illinois, even though that Chicago suburb was a predominantly Jewish area. The American principle is that a civilised populace should be mature enough to put up with what they find obnoxious, and the way to deal with false or absurd ideas is to show them to be such in the same public sphere where they are being presented. To repress such expressions of belief or opinion is merely to drive them underground and to suggest that they may, after all, have genuine credibility.

The European approach, however – at least following the racial atrocities of the Second World War – has been very different. In the contemporary law of most European countries, "incitement to hatred" statutes have criminalised a wide range of opinion statements that in the United States would be regarded as within the protected ambit of free speech. I limit myself to the French context, but close parallels can be found in most continental European legislation and practice.

In 1951, the great French Freedom of the Press Act of 29 July 1881 was amended to criminalise, with a penalty of 5 years imprisonment and a 45,000 Euro fine, any intentional publication of a defense or apology for "war crimes or crimes against humanity or serious criminal acts involving collaboration with the enemy." In 1972, a further revision was passed: Article 24 now also punishes with a year of imprisonment and/or a fine of 45,000 Euros "those who shall have provoked discrimination, hatred, or violence toward a person or a group owing to that person's or group's origin or to their connection or non-affiliation with a specific nation, race, or religion." At the end of December, 2004, a further clause was added to law, criminalising in the same terms any discrimination or provocation to hatred or violence directed against "a person or a group by reason of their sex, sexual orientation, or handicap." Even if the incitement to hatred is not published, but only uttered to the person himself or herself, it falls within the class of the most serious minor infractions (5th class contraventions), with a fine which can reach 1,500 Euros (double that if the offense is repeated).

To be sure, intent to harm must be shown, and vague allegations are not prosecutable. But since anti-discrimination organisations have standing to sue (as *parties civiles*) in these matters, there have been a fair number of cases against those who have allegedly incited anti-Jewish hatred by denying the Holocaust or the extent of it. Indeed, the 1951 addition to the law makes it a criminal act merely to attempt to justify "crimes against humanity" even if no provocation to racial hatred is involved.

Just a single example, occurring in our home area of the Alsace. In a news report of June 26, 2008, it was reported that the Court of Appeals in Colmar not only upheld a lower court conviction of a year's imprisonment but at the same time doubled the fine to 20,000 Euros in a case involving a Holocaust revisionist. The defendant, a Belgian resident, had written a pamphlet titled, *Holocauste? Ce que l'on vous cache* ("Holocaust? What They Are Hiding From You"), which was published in Saverne (an Alsatian city) and then throughout France.

Now, for the record, I am the last person to deny the existence or the horrors of the Holocaust. And I fully appreciate the fact that it occurred in Europe, so that Europeans have every right to be more incensed than Americans (or Australians or Chinese) by the cavalier treatment of it. But the answer to those who deny or minimize racial atrocities – or atrocities of any kind, for that matter – is to disprove their allegations in the public forum of ideas – not create martyrs to their cause by jailing them.

I have a dreadful time quoting Voltaire positively, since his deistic theology was and is an abomination – but he was right on target when he declared: "I disagree with what you say, but I shall defend to the death your right to say it."

## 30. Hate Speech

This author's appreciation of foreign law is well known (could it be otherwise for one who is not only an American lawyer but also an English barrister and *avocat à la cour, Barreau de Paris*?). Our view is that every legal system must be judged by the absolute standards of God's revealed word, the Holy Scriptures, and, if this is done, the result can be that principles in another legal system or in international law may turn out to be more in accord with the divine will than what can be found in American law. However, the reverse can also be the case, and a sad illustration thereof is the position of European legal systems on the matter of hate speech and "negationism" (denying historical facts such as genocide).

In American law, the Federal Constitution's First Amendment is the determining factor: freedom of speech, expression, and assembly are primary values. True, these are not unqualified. "Falsely shouting fire in a theatre and causing panic" is not protected and one will go to jail if he or she irresponsibly does such a thing (O. W. Holmes, Jr., in *Schenck v. United States*, 249 U.S. 47 [1919]). If there is a serious danger of riot and affray, public speech may be restrained. But where such limiting conditions do not exist, and when the defamation of another is not in question, one is legally allowed to express one's views – even when they are false, obnoxious, or hurtful to others. Thus, in a famous case ultimately decided by the U. S. Supreme Court, Nazis were allowed with impunity to parade through a predominately Jewish suburb of Chicago; though obnoxious and hurtful to the feelings of many, the philosophy of the marchers created no danger of insurrection (*National Socialist Party of America v. Village of Skokie*, 432 U.S. 43 [1977]). And in a recent case, an anti-gay congregation suffered no legal condemnation for expressing their opposition to homosexuality at the burial of soldiers who had died defending their country (*Snyder v. Phelps et al.*, 962 U.S. 443 [2011]). On balance, freedom of speech was more important than hurt feelings.

But in Europe, the perspective is very different. I recently attended a conference sponsored by the Criminal Law Institute of the Paris Bar on "Pénalisation de la Négation des Génocides." Why genocide? Because the French Parliament passed a law on 14 October 2016 criminalising the denial of the Turkish genocide of Armenians in 1915 to 1923. ("*How's that?*," you say. "Why are the French concerned with this item of ancient history?" Answer: a considerable number of Armenian refugees of the Turkish persecution settled in France – including the family of the archetypal

French singer Charles Aznavour – and the French president, Nicolas Sarkozy, is dead against Turkey's joining the European Union. On the Turkish genocide, see above, our chapter titled, "'Ararat,' the Armenians, and Missionary Doctor Clarence Ussher").

The French criminal law (like the legislation in most European countries) goes far beyond the Turkish-Armenian problem. The so-called Law Gayssot (No. 90-615 of 13 July 1990) criminalises any "contesting" of the crimes against humanity condemned by the Nuremberg War Crimes Tribunal at the end of World War II. Denial of the Nazi holocaust is thus a crime, as is questioning the extent of it. In Germany, it is still illegal to republish Hitler's *Mein Kampf*.[1] The justifications for such denials of free speech are various. It is argued that to deny acts of inhumanity is in effect to condone them, for only through collective memory are those acts able to be brought before subsequent generations. Not to do so is to defame the dead and to disregard the feelings of the survivors. And we are told that only through criminal penalties will the youth of today see the evils of the past and not repeat them.

The problem with such argumentation is that it confuses, on the one hand, the need to set forth and to teach the truth about past inhumanities of man to man, and, on the other, the desirability of *criminalizing critical speech about such acts*. To be sure, holocausts must be factually recorded and taught to subsequent generations; but it does not follow that sending to jail those misguided folk who deny them is a positive social act.

One of the most distinguished lawyers and statesmen in France, Robert Badinter (who was more responsible than anyone else in abolishing capital punishment in France) came out against this kind of legislation (*Huffington Post/Le Monde*, i5 and 25 Jan. 2012). His argument is that "Parliament is not a tribunal" and that such criminalization of free speech can well have a "boomerang" effect, since any politically incorrect speech could then become the object of similar legislation.

True, Europe in modern times has suffered far more than America from totalitarian evils. This may make the European legal denial of free speech more understandable, but it does not in any way justify it on principle. The answer to obnoxious viewpoints must not be that of a paternalistic society endeavouring to wall off its citizenry from falsehood through criminal

---

[1] The Bavarian government, which holds the copyright, has announced that it intends to publish an annotated edition in 2015 – just before *Mein Kampf* passes into the public domain (70 years after Hitler's death). One suspects that the government's motive is economic, not a sudden, laudable concern with freedom of speech.

penalties. To do so smacks of the very totalitarianism one desperately wants to eliminate. The answer to stupidity and falsehood is intelligence and truth: educating the populace is the solution, not repressing and jailing those who present obnoxious views. Those who maintain the flat earth theory need to be shown up as idiots in school and in the press, but they do not deserve to be jailed. The distance between stupidity and political incorrectness is hardly a bright line, and society needs to protect the right to be wrong and insensitive; otherwise, truth can be imprisoned as easily as falsehood.

Europeans often regard America as an adolescent, immature nation. But, in fact, it is the European approach to negationism that it immature: treating the populace as children, not letting anyone offend them. American law regards its subjects as potentially mature adults who need to be able to tolerate offensive speech and assembly – and insist on countering them with better reasons, better facts, and more adult corporate activity.

[Here are a few references to English discussions of the topic: Iganski, Paul (ed.), *The Hate Debate: Should Hate Be Punished As a Crime?* (London: Profile Books, 2002); Lipstadt, Deborah, *Denying the Holocaust: The Growing Assault on Truth and Memory* (New York: Free Press, 1993); Marshall, Peter and Shea, Nina, *Silenced: How Apostasy & Blasphemy Codes Are Choking Freedom Worldwide* (New York: Oxford University Press, 2011); Matsuda, Mari J. et al., *Words That Wound: Critical Race Theory, Assaultive Speech, and the First Amendment* (Boulder, Colorado, Westview Press, 1993).]

## 31. Check Your References

During my academic career, I have made students on both sides of the Atlantic miserable by insisting that (1) they never rely on unverified web references, and (2) they never copy a reference from an author without going to the cited source to make sure that the reference is accurate. This of course slows down the writing of research papers and debate preparation, but it is the only way to prevent the creation of "bibliographical ghosts": references to non-existent material or citations that actually lead nowhere.

Here is an example encountered serendipitously – and one that will warm the cockles of the heart of every conservative reader.

Go to the *Wikipedia* article on Chief Justice John Marshall (accessed 16 April 2012). There you will read: "Marshall himself was not religious and never joined a church; he did not believe Jesus was a divine being." The footnote (66) given as the authority for this assertion is "Smith, *John Marshall*, pp. 36, 406." This refers to Jean Edward Smith's acclaimed biography, *John Marshall: Definer of a Nation* (Henry Holt, 1996, 1998).

Smith is professor of political science at the University of Toronto. The book was listed as a *New York Times* Notable Book of 1996 and, typical of euphoric reviews, Gordon S. Wood wrote in the *New Republic*: "We are in Smith's debt for a richer, more accurate and more balanced view of Marshall and his achievements than we have ever had before ... The best single-volume biography of the Chief Justice that we have."

"More accurate and more balanced"? We go to page 406 and find the *Wikipedia* claim stated – but with no documentation. The claim also appears on page 36, in the following terms: Marshall was "unable to believe in the divinity of Christ." The authority for this assertion is given in a footnote as "Dillon, 3 *John Marshall: Life, Character, Judicial Services* 14-17." That three-volume collection of tributes to Marshall (Chicago, Callaghan, 1903) was edited by the distinguished jurist John F. Dillon and prepared as a centenary tribute to Marshall, who had been appointed chief justice by John Adams in 1801. Now go to Vol. 3, pp. 14-17: *you will find not a single word corroborating the claim that Marshall denied the deity of Christ, much less any comment about his religious views.*

But perhaps the page reference is just a typographical error? So we consult the detailed subject index at the end of the work (covering all three volumes) and what do we find? No reference *anywhere* in Dillon's work to such a view as held by Marshall. To the contrary, the following references are typical of those pertaining to Marshall's religious position:

> "Chief Justice Marshall was a steadfast believer in the truth of Christianity as revealed in the Bible. He was brought up in the Episcopal Church; and Bishop Meade, who knew him well, tells us that he was a constant and reverent worshipper in that church" (Justice Horace Gray, Volume 1, p. 88).
>
> "He [Marshall] was a sincere Christian and believed in and obeyed the commands of the Bible" (Simeon E. Baldwin, Vol. 1, p. 330).
>
> "Would you not call a man religious who said the Lord's Prayer every day? And the prayer he learned at his mother's knee went down with him to the grave. He was a constant and liberal contributor to the support of the Episcopal Church. He never doubted the fact of the Christian revelation, but he was not convinced of the fact of the divinity of Christ till late in life. Then, after refusing privately to commune, he expressed a desire to do so publicly, and was ready and willing to do so when opportunity should be had. The circumstances of his death only forbade it ... He was never professedly Unitarian, and he had no place in his heart for either an ancient or a modern agnosticism" (William Pinkney Whyte, Vol. 2, pp. 2-3).
>
> Marshall "was a Christian, believed in the gospel, and practiced its tenets" (Horace Binney, Vol. 3, p. 325).

To be sure, the above statements appear in eulogies and may not be regarded as primary sources (though Marshall's daughter is the source of the account of his late coming to faith in Christ's deity and consequent desire to commune). But suppose we hear from the Chief Justice himself? The following appears in Marshall's letter of 9 May 1833 to the Revd Jasper Adams:

> "No person, I believe, questions the importance of religion to the happiness of man even during his existence in this world. The American population is entirely Christian; and with us Christianity and religion are identical. It would be strange indeed if, with such a people, our institutions did not presuppose Christianity, and did not often refer to it and exhibit relations with it" (12 *The Papers of John Marshall*, ed. Charles Hobson [Chapel Hill: University of North Carolina Press, 2006], 278).[1]

To add insult to injury, Smith adds the following gratuitous comment to his entirely unfounded assertion as to Marshall's disbelief in Christ's deity:

---

[1] It is worth noting that this passage does not justify the notion that "America is a Christian nation" in the constitutional sense; no mention of the gospel or of Jesus Christ appears in the founding documents of the nation (see Montgomery, *The Shaping of America*, passim). But Marshall's statement is a reasonably accurate empirical description of the faith of most Americans in the 18th and 19th centuries.

"If Marshall needed reinforcement for that skepticism, it may have come from Pope. The *Essay on Man* is a ringing endorsement of the deist views of the Age of Reason, and although Pope was Catholic, his emphasis on man as a rational being inevitably diminished the role of Christianity" (Smith, p. 36).

But Marshall was no Unitarian-Deist, unlike Jefferson and Tom Paine. Smith here simply blows his cover in suggesting that rationality and Christianity are somehow incompatible. Years ago, when I was librarian of the Swift Library of Divinity and Philosophy at the University of Chicago, I compared the Swift book collection with that of the Trinity Evangelical Divinity School. The former had practically no conservative theological publications; the latter had both liberal and conservative materials. I wrote this up in an article that caused quite a ruckus: "Bibliographical Bigotry" (reprinted in my book, *Suicide of Christian Theology*). My conclusion was that liberals are often the illiberal ones. The lesson drawn from Smith's treatment of Marshall may suggest that they are often also very poor scholars – in spite of the accolades they receive in the press. And, sadly, those who do not check their references end up disseminating historical falsehoods in the guise of scholarship.

## 32. Beliefs Have Consequences – in Spades!

One of the very hottest shows in years played recently at the Noël Coward Theatre in London's West End. An indication of its popularity is the impossibility of getting tickets at my favourite location, the Half-Price Ticket Booth in Leicester Square. (People with Scottish chromosomes, such as I, are its best customers.)

Brilliant playwright Lucy Prebble's production is titled simply, "ENRON." By a combination of words, music, and lighting effects, it charts the rise and fall of that energy giant, which prior to its spectacular collapse on 2 December 2001, was America's seventh largest corporation.

The theoretician of ENRON's chimerical success was one Jeffrey Skilling, who would receive a 24-year prison sentence on multiple counts of fraud and conspiracy – but who remained defiant to the end, in spite of having effectively ruined the lives of more than twenty-thousand staff through the loss of $1.2 billion in pensions and investments.

What was Skilling's business philosophy? It had a number of elements, most of which were allied to a thoroughly rightist political and economic philosophy (both George Bush and George W. Bush were great supporters, sad to say). First, Skilling was against government intervention in the economic sphere – so as leave the field entirely open to his own brand of uncontrolled investment. ENRON was successful in getting the federal government to allow the deregulation of electricity; when California deregulated, ENRON caused appalling electrical power shortages in the State, thereby effectively blackmailing California into electric bills which rose by as much as 400 per cent. (Doctrinaire conservative readers may well want to ponder this.)

Secondly, Skilling shifted the focus from tangible assets (pipe and cable) to the brokerage of energy through the creation of a stock market for electricity and natural gas. This destabilization was accompanied by the realization of immediate profits on future activity – which created a smoke and mirrors operation. When debits rose, Skilling's CEO (who would later confess all and receive a considerably lighter sentence) came up with the idea of creating "special purpose entities" (in effect, sub-companies) for hiding ENRON's debt under the guise of assets.

In the play, Skilling justifies all this on Darwinian principle, specifically citing atheist Richard Dawkins' notion of the "selfish gene." He also argues that since the value of a company's stock is really based on the faith of the investment community in its intangible worth, this is comparable to religious faith – belief in the unseen.

One can of course draw lower-level lessons from ENRON's collapse and that of its famed accountancy firm Arthur Andersen. For example: the evils of bombastic, "old boy" Texans who make money their god (*Dallas redivivus*); or blame-shifting writ large – no-one willing to take responsibility (the lawyers blaming the accountants, the accountants blaming the directors, and the directors blaming everyone else; cf. Genesis 3:12-13); or the outworking of a classical Greek tragedy, eliciting pity and fear (Aristotle's *Poetics*), since this could happen to each of us as well. But let me suggest an even more compelling lesson: that *what one believes will inexorably impact what one does*.

In the film, *All the King's Men* (1949), based on Robert Penn Warren's novel, the leading character, a thinly disguised young and idealistic Huey Long, lets the end justify the means to become governor – after which, his philosophy of selfish compromise causes him to forgot his youthful ideals entirely. In ENRON, an atheistic belief in infinite human possibility leads to immense hurt. Dawkins' "selfish gene" reminds us of Ayn Rand – or of Robert J. Ringer's 1978 book, *Looking Out for Number One*. When absolute moral standards are regarded as nonsense, and the egotistic individual is all, as Skilling maintains in the play, chaos and destruction are just a matter of time, no matter how glitzy the present situation may appear.

What about Skilling's conviction that business success, as reflected in the stock market, is like religion – in the sense that both are founded not on tangible reality but on perceptions of worth? This is not a bad characterization of non-Christian faiths and the cults, but it certainly does not apply to historic Christianity. Genuine Christians don't have faith in faith ("the magic of believing") but faith in what God has concretely revealed. The Christian gospel is founded on reality itself: the demonstrable fact that God revealed himself in history, through the events and prophets of the Old Testament, and principally through the salvatory work of God's Son, our Lord Jesus Christ, by way of his incarnation, atoning death, and physical resurrection. Believing does not create reality; it makes the benefits of reality available to the believer.

The ENRON messes of this world – including, more recently, the staggering Ponzi schemes of Bernard Madoff – arise, not from an economic extension of biblical faith, but from the loss of it. (Madoff, allegedly a Jewish believer, first conned his fellow Jews out of their millions – "to the Jew first, then also to the Greek.") Christian faith, with its justifiable belief in moral absolutes and its demonstrable gospel that one is saved not by self-aggrandizement but by the grace of God in Jesus Christ, stands as the only effective counter to endemic ENRONism.

Be very careful what you believe. The consequences extend even beyond earthly economics: they impact eternity.

## 33. Why English Theology and Churchmanship Are Hopelessly Weak

Let me be perfectly clear at the outset: I have nothing against the grand tradition of Anglican worship. Indeed, whilst holding a professorship in an English university and practicing at the English bar, my wife and I (in the absence of satisfactory Lutheran church services) generally attended Morning Prayer at one of the churches maintained by the barristers' Inns of Court in London: the Temple Church or Lincoln's Inn Chapel.

But such solid, classical liturgy and biblical preaching were hard to find elsewhere. The general Anglican Church scene staggered between two extremes: flabby, broad-church liberalism and flabby, low-church charisma. The result of such national churchmanship has been no less than catastrophic. A generation ago, most high court judges (Denning, Diplock, MacKay) were serious, believing Christians, as were the most influential of British politicians (Mrs. Thatcher). Later, Prime Minister Tony Blair (I knew him personally) could not find any problem with the *Qur'an* and converted to Roman Catholicism, and his current successor at 10 Downing Street pushes for the recognition of same-sex unions. English high court judges now declare that Christian belief is irrelevant to a believer's conscience-based refusal to provide sex counseling to homosexual couples.

The standard historical explanation for this sad state of affairs is the Elizabethan Settlement, when Elizabeth I made a policy of theological "comprehension," i.e., allowing Anglican clergy of low, high, and broad persuasions to coexist within the same ecclesiastical body – thereby making the state church as comfortable as possible for all citizens. Subscription to the very fine (and in many respects Lutheran) Thirty-Nine Articles became, especially as biblical criticism appeared on the scene in the late 18$^{th}$ century, *quatenus* ("insofar as" the subscriber held that they represented revelatory truth), not necessarily *quia* (simply *because* they accorded with Holy Scripture). An important marker of Anglican inability to discipline deviant views was the Bishop Colenso controversy; of his views Charles Darwin wrote in a letter of 6 November 1862 to an American zoologist: "A book has appeared here which will, I suppose, make a noise, by Bishop Colenso, who judging from the extracts, smashes most of the Old Testament."

And thus we have the late Bishop James Pike (I debated him at McMaster University in Canada) who was never disciplined by the American Episcopal Church even though in a *Look* magazine article he had informed the general public that he had "jettisoned" the Incarnation, the Virgin Birth, and the Trinity, and who had famously declared, "I can sing the Creed but not say it." And thus also Bishop John A. T. Robinson in England and Bishop John Shelby Spong in the U. S. A.

Fully consistent with this approach is the remark of Prince Charles that though, on becoming King, he would be uncomfortable being "Defender of *the* Faith," he would not mind being "Defender of [undefined] faith." And it is not hard to see why the American Episcopal Church, in the course of less than a hundred years, could reach the point – over against clear and consistent biblical teaching – of ordaining practicing homosexual and lesbian clergy and bishops.

The "comprehension" explanation is quite correct, but it is not the whole story. There is a sociological factor to be taken into account – an interesting aspect to the English character. We noticed right away on moving to England how difficult it is for many English people to make a positive, unqualified statement on any subject. Assertions often end with "... isn't it?" – the speaker apparently wanting confirmation from the hearer that what he or she has just said is, after all, *really* so. Politics and religion make many English uncomfortable even in polite discussion – the weather is always a more palatable topic – and there are social clubs where religious and political discussions and prohibited by the by-laws.

This has resulted in flaccid theological teaching and writing, even among English evangelicals. Indeed, even the most conservative of them (F. F. Bruce, John Stott, Alistair McGrath) have not held to biblical inerrancy – such an "absolute" position presumably being incompatible with the English *via media*. It is generally agreed that C. S. Lewis (a Northern Irishman) never received a professorship at Oxford owing to the discomfort engendered among his colleagues by his uncompromising, orthodox Christian apologetic. There is the famous *Punch* cartoon of the two English horsemen meeting each other in the middle of a bridge too narrow for both to pass at the same time; they have turned to skeletons whilst repeating "After you!"

A recent illustration of the problem has surfaced in the writings of a former professor of medical law turned popular novelist, Alexander McCall Smith. Smith, who grew up in Zimbabwe, has created a wonderful series of books, "The No. 1 Ladies Detective Agency," whose leading character – Botswana's only female private detective – displays touching humanity in her relationships with others. Precious Ramotswe is a Christian believer, a member of the Anglican church, a regular attender at the Anglican Cathedral, and a friend of the Bishop. But her theological views are not dictated by a thoroughgoing commitment to the biblical text. Thus, she finds certain biblical miracles impossible to believe, contradicting, as they do, her ordinary experience.

In *Tea Time for the Traditionally Built,* Mma Ramotswe muses: "People believed in all manner of things, in the face of all the evidence, but if they did not, well, what then? ... We had to believe in something, she thought." And in a later novel in the series, *The Minor Adjustment Beauty Salon,* the question is raised as to whether one should reveal to a young man that he was born of an incestuous union. Mma Ramotswe's colleague, Mma Makutsi remarks: "That boy not knowing the truth ... not knowing who he really is." Mma Ramotswe replies, arguing that the boy should not be told about his real origins: "We need a story about ourselves, but does it really matter whether it is the true one or it has been made up?"

This very Anglican approach is made even more specific in Smith's non-fiction book, *What W. H. Auden Can Do for You* - a book, by the way, that tells you far more about Smith than about Auden. (Auden, though Anglican, stayed far more within the classical Christian theological tradition.) Significantly, Smith gives no clue as to Auden's dissatisfaction with his homosexual temperament and his conviction that such practices, even when he himself succumbed to them, were wrong.

In the final chapter of the book, Smith speaks of solutions for the "empty core at the heart of our existence," so trenchantly described by Auden in *The Age of Anxiety.* One solution presented - that of Auden - is "religious belief." But here, according to Smith, the issue is not the truth of that belief or the possibility of showing it to be a correct take on the universe. "Many people take that view, electing to believe in something that may wither under close scrutiny but that nonetheless represents an engaged response to evil and emptiness. And why should they not do this? ... That may amount to whistling in the dark, but if its effect is to give a sense of moral purpose and thus enable us to lead lives that have moral shape, then one might be justified in asking what is wrong with that." Smith continues:

> Not everybody is going to end up, as Auden did, in the Anglican Church or indeed in any church. The spiritual life can be cultivated in all sorts of ways: through music, through poetry, through the cherishing of others or, more broadly, the appreciation and understanding of nature ... Nor, I think, is it necessary to believe in a personal god of the sort that we find in Christian doctrine. Religions are full of myths and things that defy belief ... We can see them for what they are - expressions of value ... We can act, then, as if they

were true, although we know they are not, embracing the purpose and dignity they give to our lives, the example they set.

And there we have it: doctrine and truth are not really all that important. "We need a story about ourselves, but does it really matter whether it is the true one or it has been made up?" There could be no better description of why the Anglican Church is presiding over the death of a formerly Christian nation.

# 34. Parabolic Interpretation

## The Parabola in General

Linguistically, the biblical expression "parable" derives from the Ancient Greek παραβολή (*parabolḗ*), "parabola" – verbal source παραβάλλω (*parabállō*, "I set side by side"), from παρά (*pará*, "beside") + βάλλω (*bállō*, "I throw"). Incidentally, in the account appearing in all four Gospels of Jesus' cleansing of the Temple, our Lord "throws/heaves/casts" the money changers out of the sacred place – *ekbállō* – same root as the above and the source of our word "ballistics."[1] So much for the pacifist, non-violent Jesus ...

Geometrically, a parabola may be defined as as follows: for a given point, called the *focus*, and a given line not through the focus, called the *directrix*, a parabola is the locus of points such that the distance to the focus equals the distance to the directrix

A quadratic equation ($ax^2 + bx + c = 0$) is solvable by the formula

$$x = \frac{-b \pm \sqrt{b2 - 4ac}}{2a}$$

If a quadratic equation is plotted, the result is a parabola.
For example, the following equation produces the graph just below it:

$$y = \frac{1}{4}x^2 - \frac{3}{2}x + \frac{1}{4}$$

---

[1] Matt. 21:12-17; Mark 11:15-19; Luke 19:45-48; John 2:13-16.

Creating a computer graph of a parabola can be accomplished using the following program in the BASIC language:[2]

```
PLOTS
10  PRINT "INPUT THE NUMBER OF SPACES DESIRED TO THE LEFT OF
    ZERO";
20  INPUT M
30  PRINT
40  PRINT "       ";
50  FOR X=0 TO 50 STEP 10
60  PRINT " ";X;
70  NEXT X
80  PRINT
90  FOR X=1 TO 70
100 IF X/10=INT(X/10) THEN 130
110 PRINT "-";
120 GOTO 140
130 PRINT "+";
140 NEXT X
150 DEF FNQ(X)=(X-20)^2+3
160 FOR X=-3 TO 8
170 PRINT
180 FOR Y=M TO 70-M
190 IF Y <= 0 THEN 280
200 IF X=0 THEN 230
210 PRINT "!";
220 GOTO 240
230 PRINT "0";
240 IF FNQ(X)>0 THEN 310
250 REM IF FNQ(X) = 0 GO FIND WHERE IT IS
260 REM OTHERWISE GET THE NEXT VALUE OF X
270 GOTO 340
280 IF Y=FNQ(X) THEN 320
290 REM IF Y DOES NOT EQUAL FNQ(X) THEN PRINT A BLANK SPACE
300 PRINT " ";
310 NEXT Y
320 PRINT "*";
330 REM PLOT THE POINT AND GO TO NEXT X
340 NEXT X
350 END
    RUN
INPUT THE NUMBER OF SPACES DESIRED TO THE LEFT OF ZERO?0
       0    10   20   30   40   50
-------+----------+----------+----------+----------+----------+
!                                       *
!
!                              *
!                                    *
0  *
!    *
!       *
!             *
!
DONE
```

The essence of the parabola is that, in a single plane, its vertex will touch a line – the directrix – at right angles to its axis of symmetry *at but a single point*. The parabola starts in eternity, touches something else at just a single juncture, and returns to eternity in the other direction.

## Jesus' Parables

What has the above to do with biblical interpretation in general – or with the interpretation of New Testament parables in particular? A very great deal, since if one understands the fundamental nature of the parabola, one will necessarily conclude that *a biblical parable has but a single, central meaning, touching reality at a single point*. Biblical parables, then, will not be properly treated as allegories or moralistic narratives involving variegated sermonic lessons. Sadly, it is exactly the latter that seems to predominate

---

[2] BASIC has variations. We used TRS-80 BASIC but the program should compile in most BASIC dialects. See James A. Coan, *Basic Basic* (2d ed.; Rochelle Park, NJ: Hayden, 1978), pp. 125-31.

in the commentaries and the sermons purporting to explicate Jesus' parables.

Let us take classic and contemporary examples.

The $2^d/3^{rd}$ century church father Origen is known especially for his stress on the allegorical interpretation of Holy Writ – an approach heavily employed throughout the Middle Ages, particularly by way of the so-called "fourfold method" of interpreting Scripture (literal, tropological, analogical – and allegorical).[3] Thus Mount Zion was seen not just (or primarily) as a historical location (the literal meaning), but as an allegory of the church, a depiction of justice (tropological or moral), and as representing eternal life (analogical/futuristic). Such an approach made it all too easy to miss the straightforward, natural meaning of the text.

Luther's great contribution to biblical hermeneutics was to insist upon the primacy of the natural, literal meaning of Scripture. For him "metaphor was the devil's tool," the Bible needed to be viewed, by the "analogy of faith," as "about Christ alone, everywhere," and justification by grace through faith perceived as its overall teaching and the doctrine by which "the church stands or falls (*isto articulo stante stat Ecclesia, ruente ruit Ecclesia*)."[4]

Here is an example as to how Origen interprets our Lord's parables. In his *Commentary on Matthew*, he treats the Parable of the Sower in the following terms (Matthew 13:1-23):

> "After these things He answered and said to them, He that soweth the good seed is the Son of man" ... [Y]ou can otherwise take the good seed to be the children of the kingdom, because whatsoever good things are sown in the human soul, these are the offspring of the kingdom of God and have been sown by God the Word who was in the beginning with God, so that wholesome words about anything are children of the kingdom. But while men are asleep who do not act according to the command of Jesus, "Watch and pray that ye enter not into temptation," the devil on the watch sows what are called tares – that is, evil opinions – over and among what are called by some natural conceptions, even the good seeds which are from the Word. And according to this the whole world might be called a field, and not the Church of God only, for in the whole world the Son of man sowed the good seed, but

---

[3] Cf. Beryl Smalley, *The Study of the Bible in the Middle Ages* (Notre Dame, IN: University of Notre Dame Press, 1989).

[4] WA 40/3.352.3. See John Warwick Montgomery, "Luther's Hermeneutic vs. the New Hermeneutic," in his *In Defense of Martin Luther* (Milwaukee: Northwestern, 2017), pp. 40-85. Cf. Richard A. Muller and John L. Thompson (eds.), *Bible Interpretation in the Era of the Reformation* (Grand Rapids, MI: Eerdmans, 1996).

> the wicked one tares, – that is, evil words, – which, springing from wickedness, are children of the evil one. And at the end of things, which is called "the consummation of the age," there will of necessity be a harvest, in order that the angels of God who have been appointed for this work may gather up the bad opinions that have grown upon the soul, and overturning them may give them over to fire which is said to burn, that they may be consumed. And so the angels and servants of the Word will gather from all the kingdom of Christ all things that cause a stumbling-block to souls and reasonings that create iniquity, which they will scatter and cast into the burning furnace of fire. Then those who become conscious that they have received the seeds of the evil one in themselves, because of their having been asleep, shall wail and, as it were, be angry against themselves; for this is the "gnashing of teeth." Wherefore, also, in the Psalms it is said, "They gnashed upon me with their teeth." Then above all "shall the righteous shine," no longer differently as at the first, but all "as one sun in the kingdom of their Father."[5]

Observe that, in spite of Jesus' assertion that the sower of the good seed is himself, Origen interprets the sower as also "the children of the kingdom." The parable is allegorized, with the tares equaling "evil words" and "bad opinions that have grown upon the soul," leading to damnation.

The issue is not whether Origen states theological untruths here (he does not), but whether he has comprehended that the parable has but a single, central lesson, namely, that the Christ is uniquely the One who provides the Word of God to a race that very largely misuses and ignores it.[6]

Now a contemporary illustration: an explication of our Lord's parable of the Laborers in the Vineyard (Matt. 20:1-16).

> The master of the house would seem to be God and the vineyard is the place where those servants who have been called to work for the master as laborers will enter into the work. The laborers are those who have been called and saved by God. They enter into the work or their calling by God under the guidance of the master, which is Jesus Christ. In another place in the Scriptures, Jesus uses this symbolism of believers being used by God to labor for the Lord as in Matthew 9:37-38 where He says "The harvest is plentiful, but the laborers are few; therefore pray earnestly to the Lord of the harvest to send out laborers into his harvest." There is also another angle in this

---

[5] Origen, Commentary on Matthew, trans. John Patrick, Ante-Nicene Fathers, Original Supplement to the American Edition, 5th ed., Vol. X (Grand Rapids, MI: Eerdmans, 1980), pp. 414-15.

[6] An important thesis on Origen was successfully defended for the Diploma at the International Academy of Apologetics, Evangelism and Human Rights, Strasbourg, France, July, 2016: Tanner Christian Schmidt, "Patristic Apologetics: The Apologetic Approach of Origen of Alexandria."

parable. When vineyard laborers enter into the harvest, they are entering into a vineyard looking for those who bear fruit which Jesus says that those who are the children of God will be the only ones bearing fruit, showing those who are truly saved and those who are not (John 15). Jesus says in fact "You will recognize them by their fruits" (Matt 7:16) ...

No Christian has any right to feel jealous of what God has given to other believers, even if it's late in their life. God is generous to all who [sic] He saves and if others believe He is overpaying those who enter the kingdom's work later then that shows that they are questioning the master of the house ... or God Himself. The first being last and the last being first may be Jesus' way of saying that whatever time a person comes to saving faith, they all will receive the same wages ... since the wages of sin is death (Rom 6:23a), the wages of repentance and trust in the Savior is eternal life (Rom 6:23b). The thief on the cross will receive the same reward of eternal life as those who labored for the Lord most of their lives. This doesn't mean that they will receive the same rewards once they enter the kingdom since some will be given more responsibility and authority than others but all who trust in Christ will receive the same reward ... eternal life.[7]

Here we are told that the laborers in the vineyard are those "who have been called and saved by God." Moreover, "When vineyard laborers enter into the harvest, they are entering into a vineyard looking for those who bear fruit which Jesus says that those who are the children of God will be the only ones bearing fruit, showing those who are truly saved and those who are not."

Finally, we are informed that the message of the parable is that of heavenly rewards: "The thief on the cross will receive the same reward of eternal life as those who labored for the Lord most of their lives. This doesn't mean that they will receive the same rewards once they enter the kingdom since some will be given more responsibility and authority than others but all who trust in Christ will receive the same reward ... eternal life."

For a legal (but anything but legalistic) treatment of this parable, see this author's "Vineyard Salary Case." Our conclusion there:

> Here plaintiff servants – as typical fallen creatures – question the justice of their master (God). But His only "fault" lay in His generosity! The Jewish religious leaders of Jesus' day were offended by His open invitation to Gentiles to enter into the Kingdom at the close of the Old Testament age with no

---

[7] The author is one Jack Wellman, pastor of Mulvane Brethren Church, Kansas. His sermonic interpretation was posted on the Patheos "Christian Crier" website on 12 November 2014 (http://www.patheos.com/blogs/christiancrier/2014/11/12/parable-of-the-workers-in-the-vineyard-summary-meaning-and-commentary/).

fewer advantages than the Chosen People had enjoyed throughout the period of the Old Covenant. By the Jews' refusal to accept God's grace on His own terms the first would turn out to be the last, and the last, first. God himself went the second mile, and the Gentiles were grafted in: an "adoption of sons" occurred because of a loving God's desire that all men should be saved and come to a knowledge of the truth.[8]

In point of fact, instead of the parable being anthropocentric (telling us about ourselves or Christian believers) its focal message is *theocentric* – or, better, *Christocentric*: telling us what God in Christ has done for us. Specifically, his grace has exceeded all human legalisms, and in particular that of the orthodox Judaism of Jesus' day. God in Christ is far more generous than a fallen race; he has saved the gentiles at the end of time and they receive exactly the same salvatory benefits as the Jews who benefited from the oracles of God across the centuries of the Old Covenant and were the vehicle of salvation for all peoples. The Jewish people, sadly, rejected their Messiah, thereby making the first, last.

The inadequate treatment of Jesus' parables in many church circles impacts at the same time the treatment of our Lord's message in general. Thus – to take the most egregious example – the common interpretation of the Sermon on the Mount as a moralistic series of lessons for the improvement of human society. In point of fact, the Sermon has a single theme (cf. the single point-of-contact between a parable and its directrix): the state of a fallen race that cannot save itself and must come to Christ for salvation. The Sermon's theme is: "Be ye therefore perfect, as your heavenly Father is perfect" (Matt. 5:48). Any person honest with himself or herself will recognize that he/she is anything but such: we do not turn the other cheek or give our garments to those who have stolen from us – just the opposite. The Sermon was to point Jesus' hearers to *himself* and to the salvation that he would provide through his death on the Cross.

Hopefully, this little mathematical excursion can help us better to interpret portions of Scripture that have single, literal, natural meanings far from the realms of allegory and metaphor.

---

[8] John Warwick Montgomery, *Law & Gospel: A Study Integrating Faith and Practice* (Edmonton, Alberta: Canadian Institute for Law, Theology & Public Policy, 1994), pp. 14-15.

## 35. Two Mathematical Excursions

### I. A Slice of *Pi*

Pi ($\pi$) is a universally recognized mathematical symbol. It represents the ratio of the circumference of a circle to its diameter and was known to mathematicians as early as the Babylonian empire. Pi is an "irrational number," i.e., it cannot be expressed as a common fraction and its decimal representation never ends. It has no permanently repeating pattern and its digits seem to be randomly distributed (proof of which is still to be discovered). Pi is also a "transcendental number," signifying that it cannot be the root of a non-zero polynomial with rational coefficients. For practical purposes, Pi is generally expressed by the fraction 22/7 (=3.14159...). By the year 2013, Pi had been computer calculated to $10^{13}$ – over 12 trillion – digits.[1]

Here are three comments of theological import, offering both indigestible and digestible instances of Pi.

In the Old Testament (I Kings 7:23), the construction of King Solomon's palace is described in detail. We are informed that "He [Huram, Solomon's master craftsman] made a molten sea, ten cubits from the one brim to the other: it was round all about, and his height was five cubits: and a line of thirty cubits did compass it round about" (AV). The implication here is that Pi = approximately 3. Holy Scripture is not a mathematical or scientific text, but whatever it says – including its mathematical and scientific assertions – is in fact true. It is impossible epistemologically or theologically to separate the "secular" from the "religious" in biblical revelation, since Scripture records God's activity among human beings: he reveals himself in history, and ultimately enters the secular realm in the person of the incarnate Christ for our salvation.[2]

In 1897, Taylor I. Record of the Indiana House of Representatives presented "A Bill Introducing a New Mathematical Truth" as House Bill No. 246. This was the work of a medical doctor and eccentric amateur mathematician, one Edwin J. Goodwin. The purpose of the bill was to square the circle and indirectly to legislate the value of Pi (at 3.2), thereby simplifying

---

[1] Alfred S. Posamentier, *Pi: A Biography of the World's Most Mysterious Number* (Amherst, N.Y.: Prometheus Books, 2004); and cf. Petr Beckmann, *A History of Pi* (3d ed.; New York: St. Martin's Press, 1976).

[2] See Montgomery, *Tractatus Logico-Theologicus* (5th ed.; Bonn, Germany: Verlag für Kultur und Wissenschaft, 2012), proposition 4.6.

mathematical and engineering calculations throughout the State of Indiana. The Bill was unanimously passed by the House. Fortunately for Indiana, the Senate voted to postpone indefinitely further consideration of the Bill. This incident demonstrates (1) the noetic effect of original sin in increasing the extent of human stupidity, and (2) refutes the philosophy of Legal Positivism that regards true law as no more than "the decrees of the sovereign," refusing to critique legislation and court decisions by a higher standard (ultimately, by God's special revelation in Holy Scripture).

In his 1985 science fiction novel, *Contact,* the late atheistic astronomer Carl Sagan – famous for declaring again and again on television that the cosmos has been around for "billions and billions of years" – speculates that the digits of transcendental numbers like Pi may contain a hidden pattern constituting a message from advanced beings and perhaps from God: a message only discoverable by supercomputer. Typical of unbelievers, Sagan speculates concerning a divine message available by way of an irrational number – paying no attention to the *de facto* message offered by the historical life and ministry of Jesus Christ, attested as divine by fulfilled prophecy and by his resurrection from the dead, and offered through the biblical revelation on which the same Christ placed his divine stamp of approval. Unbelievers so often prefer unproved, and frequently unprovable, speculation to fact – the height of irony, since only the living Word, coming to us through the written Word, offers life and salvation.

## II. It Doesn't Compute

Once in a while, sadly, well-meaning but ill-conceived approaches to the defence of the faith appear. One of these is Marvin L. Bittinger's *The Faith Equation: Mathematical Evidence for Christianity* (2d ed., Advantage Inspirational).

Let me say first of all that (1) the author is a well-trained, competent mathematician, an honorary professor emeritus of mathematics education at Purdue University, where he obtained his Ph.D.; and (2) I have nothing against mathematics – having obtained, *inter alia,* the Open University's certificate in mathematics and computing. Indeed, in a paper chosen as the final chapter of David W. Baker's ETS volume, *Looking into the Future* (Baker Academic), I employed the statistician's Product Rule in arguing for the force of Old Testament prophecies in relation to our Lord's first coming; this has been reprinted in my book, *Christ Our Advocate* (Bonn, Germany: VKW).

And just so that the present commentary will not be seen as entirely negative, one must commend Professor Bittinger for refining the Product

Rule argument in respect to specific Old Testament prophecies of Christ's coming (pp. 90-106) – but he never acknowledges the prior work done in this area by your humble servant or by Wheaton professor Hawley O. Taylor (*Modern Science and Christian Faith,* ed. American Scientific Affiliation, 1st ed., Van Kampen Press).

There are two serious problems with the Bittinger book and, as we shall see, they both stem from the same cause. First, Bittinger is at pains throughout the book to argue mathematically for theological paradox; secondly, he provides some truly bizarre speculation as to the apocalyptic "new earth" based on the cosmological notions of wormholes and the "Big Crunch" (the alleged future reversal of the Big Bang).

Bittinger rightly recognises the existence of Christian doctrines, such as the Trinity and election/freewill, that constitute apparent logical contradiction. He sees these as illustrative of "paradox" throughout Christian experience, and argues that this should not bother us. Indeed, we should "embrace paradox in Christianity" (p. 49) – since paradox is fundamental to mathematics. He writes (p. 36):

> A form of paradox occurs to me every time I see or use proof by contradiction in mathematics. It amazes me that to prove $S$, I might first assume *not S* and try to find a sentence $P$ such that both $P$ and *not P* are true at the same time. We have seen how some truths and life and learning are the result of embracing paradox. Analogously, many truths in mathematics are the result of embracing paradox via truth by contradiction.

Toward the end of his book, Bittinger speculates on the end-time prophecies of the Bible and attempts to explain them scientifically. Here is the summary of his position (p. 219):

> God creates a wormhole, which is a passage from Earth's dimension as we know to a higher dimension, the New Jerusalem. String theorists hypothesize that with an extreme amount of energy, people can pass from one dimension to another. God is omnipotent; He has the energy. God then allow His followers to pass through the wormhole to the New Jerusalem ... Because of the energy that has been enacted [*sic*] by God, the six string dimensions are activated from their present inactive state. In what follows, a new physics prevails, the six string dimensions stay active, and there is no more night. The light of the New Jerusalem is Christ, and it shines forever. We might even construe these events to be God's grand resolution of a kind of paradox between the Big Bang and the Big Crunch.

What is the problem with these arguments?

Let us consider "paradox" first. As philosopher Gordon Clark rightly argued, even when one encounters apparent deviations from the law of non-contradiction (as with the Heisenberg indeterminacy principle), one must realise that the law of non-contradiction and the subject-object distinction were the route by which one discovered the problem; thus, "paradox" is never fundamental. Moreover, when, as in the case of the nature of light, one finds contradictory characteristics in nature (light is particulate *and* undulatory), one must go with the empirical data: thus the "photon," a "wave-particle." The Trinity and the election/freewill issue do not make paradox a fundamental element in Christian theology, any more than the photon makes paradox a basic characteristic of empirical science. The Trinity, election/freewill, and the like must be regarded, from a human standpoint, as logically irresolvable; but these truths are clearly set forth in demonstrable transcendent revelation (the Holy Scriptures), so we can confidently expect a resolution in eternity – and not before, whether on the basis of mathematics or an absolutising of a notion of paradox.

When Bittinger employs "proof by contradiction" as an analogy and justification of paradox, he misunderstands the very nature of mathematics. As Russell and Whitehead showed in their *Principia Mathematica,* pure mathematics is a strictly formal, deductive system based on the law of non-contradiction. Mathematics never tells you what the empirical world consists of; as Ludwig Wittgenstein sagely put it, mathematics does not represent the empirical world but is rather like the scaffolding around a building – telling you the *shape* of the world, not its nature. Being purely formal, mathematics is highly dangerous when used to create analogies with empirical reality (cf. the discussion in my *Tractatus Logico-theologicus* [Bonn, Germany: VKW], proposition 2).

Illustration: Atheists commonly argue that because of the mathematical notion of infinite regress, one needs no creator God to explain the existence of the real world. Such an argument confuses the purely formal notion of infinity in mathematics with the nature of empirical reality. As mathematicians Georg Cantor and David Hilbert have shown, an "actual infinite" is an irrational notion (cf. the celebrated model of "Hilbert's hotel"). In the real world, there are no actual infinities and one must not reason from mathematical infinity to a false empirical conclusion.

A reverse take on Bittinger's conceptual error is made by Donald E. Knuth, professor emeritus of the art of computer programming at Stanford University. In his book, *Things a Computer Scientist Rarely Talks About* (CSLI Publications). Knuth suggests that "infinity is not necessarily even one of God's attributes" (p. 172)! He continues: "But even [God's] ability to deal with finitely many numbers, on the order of Super K [= 10 $\uparrow\uparrow\uparrow\uparrow$ 3], is much more than enough to inspire awe." Such are the theological pitfalls into which one can readily plummet when one analogises from mathematical expressions to the nature of the empirical universe (or God).

As for the Big Crunch, wormholes and the Last Times, Bittinger makes the same mistake common to non-Christian cosmologists: he engages in speculative reasoning based on too little data. When I successfully debated atheistic cosmologist Sean M. Carroll at University College Dublin, Carroll offered exactly the same kind of speculation – but in support of a non-theistic universe. The concept of the "multiverse," recently embraced by Stephen Hawking, is of precisely the same nature – and similarly impossible to verify or disconfirm on principle (see my *Christ As Centre and Circumference* [Bonn, Germany: VKW], Pt. 1). When Christians engage in such reasoning, they reduce Christian faith to science fiction – on the level of the New Agers who, employing the Mayan calendar, tell us that the world was supposed to end (or be entirely transformed) in December, 2012.

Bittinger's fundamental problem is a common one today. He is a specialist in a particular field – mathematics. But he does not understand the nature of that discipline; he lacks an understanding of the *philosophy* of mathematics. He does not realise that it is a purely formal discipline, unable to say anything substantive about the empirical nature of the real world. Moreover, he is apparently unaware that mathematics entirely lacks the capacity to resolve cosmological issues. Early in the 20th century, Nathan R. Wood, a former president of Gordon College, produced a book (*The Secret of the Universe*) arguing that the universe in all its characteristics, including the atom, is tripartite, illustrating the Christian doctrine of the Trinity; sadly for the author, physics marched on, showing that the atom did not consist of but three irreducible entities. Apologists must be scrupulous in understanding the nature of the disciplines they wish to employ to support the faith – and avoid speculation like the plague. Otherwise, they are almost certain to postulate remedies that turn out to be worse than the secular disease they are endeavouring to treat.

# 36. Regeneration: Biological, Computational, Theological

Academic cross-fertilisation is rare in an age of hyperspecialisation. This is sad, since genius has sometimes been related to the jumping of the gaps between or among fields that have typically been seen as having no meaningful relationship to each other. In this concise paper, we shall deal with the notion of regeneration in three domains that normally do not interact at all: zoology, computing, and dogmatics.

## I. Biology: the Worms Turns

It is commonly known that if one cuts off a segment of a worm, the worm may be able to regenerate the lost portion of itself. Actually, the situation is a bit more complicated.

Distinguished zoologist G. E. Gates (1897-1987), a specialist in the morphology, physiology, taxonomy, and zoogeography of earthworms, devoted twenty years of his existence to the study of their regenerative possibilities. He tells us, sadly, that "little interest was shown" in his labours by his peers. He therefore published only a limited number of his findings, but these showed that it is at least theoretically possible in certain species of earthworms to grow two entire worms from a bisected specimen. Here are some of his results:[1]

> *Lumbricus terrestris* Linnaeus, 1758 replacing anterior segments from as far back as 13/14 and 16/17 but tail regeneration was never found.

> *Eisenia fetida* (Savigny, 1826) with head regeneration, in an anterior direction, possible at each intersegmental level back to and including 23/24, while tails were regenerated at any levels behind 20/21, i.e., two worms may grow from one.

> *Criodrilus lacuum* Hoffmeister, 1845 also has prodigious regenerative capacity with 'head' regeneration from as far back as 40/41.

---

[1] G. E. Gates, *Burmese earthworms: An introduction to the systematics and biology of megadrile oligochaetes with special reference to Southeast Asia* (Transactions of the American Philosophical Society, 1972).

*Lampito mauritii* Kinberg, 1867 with regeneration in anterior direction at all levels back to 25/26 and tail regeneration from 30/31; head regeneration was sometimes believed to be caused by internal amputation resulting from *Sarcophaga* sp. larval infestation.

*Perionyx excavatus* Perrier, 1872 readily regenerated lost parts of the body, in an anterior direction from as far back as 17/18, and in a posterior direction as far forward as 20/21.

It will be noted that the regeneration of worms entails two characteristics:

1) The same regeneration is not possible for all worms; the degree of regeneration depends on the particular worm in question.
2) The worm must suffer bisection for regeneration to take place.

## II. Computing: Earthworm Algebra

A fairly esoteric, out-of-the-way mathematical notion parallels in many ways the zoological phenomenon of regeneration.[2] Suppose one takes a two-digit positive number (the length of the worm), multiplies it by 2, and then truncates it so as to continue with only its last two digits (segments). One does the same with that result, and the iteration proceeds until the number (the worm) regenerates itself, or regeneration proves impossible – a funeral service for the worm then becoming the appropriate action.

Here is a standard Pascal program (developed by the author) to achieve computational worm regeneration:

---

[2] On this section of our paper, cf. Clifford A. Pickover, *Computers and the Imagination* (New York: St Martin's Press, 1991), pp. 237-39, and Donald E. Knuth, *The Art of Computer Programming*, Vol. 2 (2$^{nd}$ ed.; Boston: Addison-Wesley, 1981). (Not so incidentally: stay away from Knuth for theology. In his book, *Things a Computer Scientist Rarely Talks About* [CSLI Publications]. Knuth suggests that "infinity is not necessarily even one of God's attributes" [p. 172]! He continues: "But even [God's] ability to deal with finitely many numbers, on the order of Super K [= 10 ↑↑↑↑ 3], is much more than enough to inspire awe." Such are the theological pitfalls into which one can readily plummet when one analogises from mathematical expressions to the nature of the empirical universe – or God.) For instructions on running Pascal programs, see my website: http://www.jwm.christendom.co.uk (subsite: "Interactive Games"). In brief: using an Apple Mac with operating system 9x (or earlier OS), download a Pascal compiler from the net (we recommend THINK Pascal 4.5d4), copy the Earthworm program, and run it.

# Regeneration: Biological, Computational, Theological 375

```
program Earthworm (INPUT, OUTPUT);

var
x, a, b, c, d, e, f, g, h, i, j, k, l, m, n, o,
p, q, r, s, t: INTEGER;

begin

WRITELN ('Give a two-digit whole number as a
starting value representing the Worm's length;
note that to regenerate this must be a number
that is a multiple of 4 or of 20.');

{Odd numbers will never return; even numbers
other than multiples of 4 or 20 will loop indef-
initely - but try them to see our response!}

WRITELN;

READ(x);

a := (2 * x) mod 100;

{This truncates the starting value to its last
two digits - in effect cutting the worm so as to
leave only its last two segments.}

{In standard Pascal, the mod division operator
achieves the truncation by lopping off all but
the remainder; consider it the knife that severs
the worm!}

WRITELN;

WRITELN(a);

b := (2 * a) mod 100;
WRITELN(b);

c := (2 * b) mod 100;
WRITELN(c);
```

```
       d := (2 * c) mod 100;
       WRITELN(d);

       {At this point, the worm represented by a star-
       ting value equal to a multiple of 20 has regen-
       erated, so the program must stop. Otherwise, if
       the worm's length is a multiple of 4, the program
       must continue to the 20th iteration for regen-
       eration to be achieved.}

       if d <> x then
        begin

          e := (2 * d) mod 100;
          WRITELN(e);

          f := (2 * e) mod 100;
          WRITELN(f);

          g := (2 * f) mod 100;
          WRITELN(g);

          h := (2 * g) mod 100;
          WRITELN(h);

          i := (2 * h) mod 100;
          WRITELN(i);

          j := (2 * i) mod 100;
          WRITELN(j);

          k := (2 * j) mod 100;
          WRITELN(k);

          l := (2 * k) mod 100;
          WRITELN(l);

          m := (2 * l) mod 100;
          WRITELN(m);

          n := (2 * m) mod 100;
          WRITELN(n);
```

```
o := (2 * n) mod 100;
WRITELN(o);

p := (2 * o) mod 100;
WRITELN(p);

q := (2 * p) mod 100;
WRITELN(q);

r := (2 * q) mod 100;
WRITELN(r);

s := (2 * r) mod 100;
WRITELN(s);

t := (2 * s) mod 100;
WRITELN(t);
```

{The following series of statements prevents an infinite loop when an odd number – or an even number not a multiple of 4 or 20 – is initially entered.}

```
if t <> x then
  begin

    WRITELN;

    WRITE ('No regeneration is possible for this
poor worm! Only worms with an even number of
segments constituting a multiple of 4 or 20 will
regenerate.');

  end;

 end;

end.
```

\*   \*   \*   \*   \*   \*   \*   \*

Let us run this program with a worm of 80 segments (a multiple of 20), 16 segments (a multiple of 4), 17 segments (an odd number of segments), and 46 segments (an even number of segments, but not a multiple of either 4 or 20):

Give a two-digit whole number as a starting value representing the worm's length; note that to regenerate this must be a number that is a multiple of 4 or of 20.

**80**
60
20
40
**80**

Give a two-digit whole number as a starting value representing the worm's length; note that to regenerate this must be a number that is a multiple of 4 or of 20.

**16**
32
64
28
56
12
24
48
96
92
84
68
36
72
44
88
76
52
4
8
**16**

# Regeneration: Biological, Computational, Theological

Give a two-digit whole number as a starting value representing the worm's length; note that to regenerate this must be a number that is a multiple of 4 or of 20.

**17**
> 34
> 68
> 36
> 72
> 44
> 88
> 76
> 52
> 4
> 8
> 16
> 32
> 64
> 28
> 56
> 12
> 24
> 48
> 96
> 92

**No regeneration is possible for this poor worm! Only worms with an even number of segments constituting a multiple of 4 or 20 will regenerate.**

Give a two-digit whole number as a starting value representing the worm's length; note that to regenerate this must be a number that is a multiple of 4 or of 20.

**46**
> 92
> 84
> 68
> 36
> 72
> 44
> 88
> 76

```
        52
         4
         8
        16
        32
        64
        28
        56
        12
        24
        48
        96
```

**No regeneration is possible for this poor worm! Only worms with an even number of segments constituting a multiple of 4 or 20 will regenerate.**

Fascinatingly, if the starting number (the worm's length) is a multiple of 20, it will *always* regenerate in 4 iterations, and if it is a multiple of 4, regeneration will *always* occur in 20 iterations. In no other cases will regeneration occur.

It follows that – in parallel with zoological worm regeneration – mathematical-computational regeneration operates with two characteristics:

1) The same regeneration is not possible for all worms; the degree of regeneration depends on the particular worm in question.
2) The worm must suffer bisection for regeneration to take place.

## III. Theology: Regeneration Potentially Available for All

The word "regeneration" has etymological roots similar to those of the expression "being born again." Theologically, regeneration connects with baptism: Jesus teaches, "Except one is born of water and of the Spirit, he cannot enter the kingdom of God. ... You must be born again" (John 3: 5-7), and the Apostle Peter declares, "Baptism now saves us" (1 Peter 3:21).

The normative pattern in the historic church is, therefore, infant baptism with confirmation of one's faith in Christ on reaching an age of accountability.[3] In the case of an unbeliever who does not resist the Holy

---

[3] The justification of infant baptism proceeds as follows:
1) Our Lord's final (and therefore exceedingly important) command to the church was to "go baptise all nations" (Matt. 28:19). One becomes a member/citizen of a nation on birth. Therefore the command includes children.

Spirit, conversion normally occurs when baptism takes place; however, the reborn individual, though he need never be rebaptized or "re-regenerated," is not thereby exempted from later conversion experiences. Because of the constant presence of the "old man" in the Christian life, Luther considered conversion (a turning back to the God of baptism) as a proper daily activity on the part of the believer.[4]

The 17th-century dogmaticians were correct, therefore, in distinguishing between conversion in the case of the unregenerate person on the one hand, and conversion in the case of the regenerate but lapsed individual on the other. For example, Leonhard Hutter (1563-1616), professor of theology at Wittenberg, asserts that in the conversion of infidels a change occurs "from unregenerate to regenerate, from unbelievers to believers. But the condition of the lapsed in the Church is such that, although seduced by the devil, they have become subject to divine wrath and eternal damnation, nevertheless they have not yet altogether fallen from the covenant

---

2) "Without faith it is impossible to please God" (Hebrews 11:6), and faith is the gift of God (Ephesians 2:8-9). That gift of faith is provided through the word of God, which is available to adults by hearing it (Romans 10:13-17). But children before the age of accountability obviously cannot receive the word by hearing, since they are too young to understand it. Therefore, another means is also provided: water baptism – one is saved "through the washing of water by the word" (Ephesians 5:26).

3) "Baptism saves" (1 Peter 3:21). This does not mean, however, that one cannot subsequently fall away, since God's grace is resistible (Acts 7:51, 1 Thessalonians 5:19, Hebrews 6:4-6). Once the child reaches the age of accountability – that age of course varying from person to person – he/she must "confirm" by personal acceptance what was received in baptism – through entering into a conscious personal relationship with Christ. (Thus the place of Confirmation in the public life of the church.)

4) We do not know the state of unbaptised infants who die before reaching the age of accountability – though we know that God is love and does not want anyone to perish (1 Timothy 2:4). But we *do* know that baptised infants are saved – so a Christian parent will surely want that gift of grace for his/her child.
(See Uuras Saarnivaara, *Scriptural Baptism: A Dialog Between John Bapstead and Martin Childfont* (Eugene, OR: Wipf & Stock, 2003).

4  "Let everyone esteem his baptism as a daily dress in which he is to walk constantly, that he may ever be found in the faith and its fruits, that he suppress the old man and grow up in the new ... If any one fall away from it, let him again come into it. ... If therefore we have once in baptism obtained forgiveness of sin, it will remain every day, as long as we live, that is, as long as we carry the old man about our neck" (*Large Catechism*). Cf. Montgomery, "The Place of Conversion in the Life of the Christian," *Global Journal of Classical Theology*, 2/3 (August, 2001): www.globaljournalct.com.

itself and from the right of adoption of the sons of God, so far as God is concerned; nor do they absolutely fall away from that, unless they persevere to the end in sin."[5] They are in the same position as the prodigal son: though in his self-centredness he departs from his Father's house and squanders his gifts, the lights in the Father's house continue to burn and he may always return if he will repent and "come to himself," saying "I have sinned against heaven and before thee" (Luke 15: 11-32).

Theological regeneration, then, differs considerably from both biological and computational regenerations. It does not require scission (since it applies to the whole person) and it is not limited in its effects to only certain classes of people:

1) The same regeneration is possible for every person, since Christ died for all; regeneration is not a matter of degree, and the particular characteristics of the person are irrelevant for its efficacy – regeneration depending, as it does, solely on one's willingness to acknowledge one's selfcentredness and to trust in Christ alone for forgiveness and salvation.[6]
2) The person need suffer no truncation for regeneration to take place; indeed, true wholeness arrives only through such regeneration: "If anyone is in Christ, he is a new creature: old things are passed away; behold, all things are become new" (2 Corinthians 5: 17).

The appropriate connection between natural and supernatural regeneration discussed in this paper was classically made by hymn writer Isaac Watts:

> **Alas! and did my Savior bleed**
> **And did my Sovereign die?**
> **Would He devote that sacred head**
> **For such a worm as I?**

---

[5] *Loci communes theologici* (1619), quoted in Schmid, *Doctrinal Theology*, trans. Hay and Jacobs (5th ed.; Philadelphia: United Lutheran Publishing House, 1899), p. 473.
[6] And the faith itself is the product not of human ability, since every member of our fallen race is "dead in trespasses and sins" (Ephesians 2:1; cf. Rom. 3:23), but is entirely the product of divine grace – the gift of God, "not of works, lest any person should boast" (Ephesians 2:8-9).

# Index of Names

Abraham .................................... 174
Adams, Douglas ..................... 157
Adams, Jasper ........................ 350
Adams, John ........................... 349
Adler, Mortimer ....................... 55
Ahab ........................................ 113
Aland, Barbara ....................... 248
Aland, Kurt ........ 228, 236, 248, 250, 268
Albright ................................... 118
Al-Bukhaari ............................ 290
Alem, Jean Pierre .................. 331
al-Gaddafi .............................. 291
Ali, Shabir .............................. 271
Allbeck, W. D. ....................... 210
Al-Sha'rawi, Mitwalli ............. 173
Althamer, Andreas ................ 204
Althaus, Paul ........................ 197
Amos, the Prophet ................ 113
Ananias .................................. 294
Andersen, Arthur ................... 354
Andreae, Jakob ..................... 212
Andreae, Johann Valentin ..... 203
Aquinas, Thomas ........ 47, 95, 135, 183, 203, 209
Archbold .................................. 35
Archer, Gleason L. .......... 110, 111
Archimedes ............... 139, 150, 181
Arden ...................................... 191
Aristotle ........ 47, 97, 135, 160, 236, 354
Aslerougii, M. ........................ 173
Atta, Muhammed ................... 286
Aubin, Emmanuel .................. 283
Auden, W. H. ................... 93, 359

Augustine ...... 33, 47, 122, 123, 124, 144, 322
Aulén, Gustav ............ 191, 192, 206
Austin, John ......................... 94, 130
Averroës ................................ 199
Aznavour, Charles ............ 329, 346
Bacon, Francis ...................... 74, 78
Badinter, Robert .................... 346
Baier ................................ 193, 204
Baker, David. W. .......... 26, 175, 368
Bakker, Jim ........................... 294
Baldwin, Simeon E. ............... 350
Ball, V. C. ................................ 48
Bankowski, Z. K. .................. 96, 97
Barbour, Ian G. ..................... 155
Barnum, P. T. ........................ 321
Barth, Karl ...................... 100, 257
Bartholomew, David J. .......... 166
Bauckham, Richard ........ 188, 230, 272
Baumann, M. .......................... 17
Behe, Michael ....................... 167
Beherens, Achim .............. 252, 262
Bell, John .......................... 73, 75
Benchley, Robert .................. 156
Bentham, Jeremy ........ 57, 130, 135
Bentley, Richard ................... 242
Berger, Peter ......................... 224
Berkeley ................................ 158
Berkouwer, G. C. .................... 100
Best, Arthur ............................ 56
Binney, Horace ...................... 350
Bittinger, Marvin L. ......... 368, 369, 370, 371
Black, David Alan ................. 247

Blackstone, William ............ 99, 135
Blair, Tony ................. 287, 330, 357
Bligh, Gur .................................... 285
Bloesch, Donald ......................... 100
Boda, Mark J. ............................. 248
Bohr, Niels .......................... 155, 156
Bonappetit, M. Saveur .............. 282
Bonhoeffer, Dietrich ......... 107, 126
Boom, Corrie ten ............... 315, 335
Borchert, Donald M. ..................... 61
Bork, Robert ........................... 75, 76
Bouman, H. J. A. ......................... 214
Brahe, Tycho .............................. 202
Briden, John ................................. 43
Bridge, J. W. ................................ 101
Bronner, Ethan ............................. 76
Broom, Herbert ............................ 73
Broughton, William P. ................. 15
Brown, Peter .............................. 122
Bruce, F. F. .............. 49, 53, 240, 358
Brunner, Emil ............................. 100
Bruns, Peter .................................. 26
Buckland, William ..................... 296
Bull, Peter and Hazel Mary ...... 275
Bultmann, Rudolf ................ 70, 194
Burrows, Roland .......................... 74
Bush, George H. W. ................... 353
Bush, George W. ........................ 353
Byrne, W. J. .................................. 73
Caesar, Julius ............................... 29
Caesar, Tiberius ........................... 86
Calov ................................... 193, 204
Calvin, John ......... 99, 100, 123, 278, 322
Campbell, L. ................................. 44
Campbell, Robert ................. 69, 184
Campbell, William F. .................. 31
Campbell-Jack, C. ........................ 17
Camus .......................................... 149
Cantor, Georg ............................. 370
Capell, Edward .......................... 248

Caplan, H. ..................................... 85
Carpzov, Johann Benedict ........ 216
Carroll, Sean M. ......................... 371
Carson, Clayborne ..................... 327
Chadbourn, James H. .................. 23
Chandler, H. P. ............................. 48
Chaplin, Shirley ......................... 275
Charles, Prince ........................... 358
Chemnitz, Martin .... 193, 203, 211, 212, 266
Chytraeus, David ...... 192, 204, 211, 215
Cicero ................................. 160, 196
Clark, Gordon H. ........ 207, 213, 243, 244, 254, 370
Clark, H. B. ................................. 102
Clement ....................................... 296
Clifford, Ross ................................ 15
Coan, James A. ........................... 362
Cohn, Norman ........................... 319
Colenso ....................................... 357
Colson, Charles .......................... 109
Coppola, Francis Ford .............. 287
Cotton ......................................... 119
Coulson, N. J. ............................... 52
Countess, Robert H. ................... 224
Covington, R. N. .......................... 48
Cowan, Stephen ........................... 65
Craig, William Lane ..................... 65
Cranfield, C. E. B. ....................... 277
Crehan, J. H. ............................... 203
Cressey, Donald ......................... 297
Cross, Rupert ......................... 25, 73
Cullmann, Oscar ........ 238, 240, 252
Dalai Lama ................................. 333
Daniel, the Prophet ... 90, 113, 114, 121, 124
Dannhauer .................................. 204
Dante ........................................... 149
Darwin, Charles .......... 71, 167, 185, 357

# Index of Names

Dau, W. H. T. .......................... 77, 104
Daube, D. ...................................... 50
Davenport, E. H. ....................... 296
David, H. T. ................................ 152
Davies, O. ........................... 147, 152
Davis, J. E. .................................. 282
Davis, William C. ........................ 22
Dawkins, Richard ...... 243, 321, 353, 354
Demarest, Bruce A. ................... 100
Dennett, Daniel ......................... 158
Denning, L. J. ......... 28, 279, 321, 357
Derrett, J. D. M. ............................ 52
Desmond, Adrian ........................ 71
Detmold, M. J. ............................. 95
Diamond, H. A. ........................... 38
Diamond, Paul ................... 273, 280
Dickens, A. G. ........................... 179
Dillon, John F. ........................... 349
Dio, Cassius ................................ 86
Diplock ........................ 279, 321, 357
Döllinger, Ignaz von .......... 178, 179
Dooyeweerd ............................. 224
Dudley ...................................... 119
Dunning, H. C. .......................... 107
Dworkin, Ronald .................. 75, 95
Earman, John .......... 27, 61, 164, 172
Edwards, W. J. Gabel ................ 171
Eekelaar, John ............................ 75
Ehrman, Bart D. ........ 236, 245, 248, 249, 250, 254, 269
Einstein ... 27, 28, 61, 155, 156, 166, 172
Ekelöf, Per Olof ........................... 71
Elert, Werner ..... 193, 194, 199, 202, 203, 204
Elijah, the Prophet .................... 114
Eliot, T. S. .................................. 177
Elizabeth I ................................. 357
Elizabeth, mother of John the Baptist .... 228, 250, 261, 268, 308

Elliott, J. Keith .......... 227, 228, 232, 245, 246, 247, 250, 251, 255, 256
Ellul, Jaques .............................. 100
Elwes, Sylvia ............................... 44
Elwork, Amiram ......................... 39
Emerline, G. D. ......................... 296
Endicott .................................... 119
Endô, Shûsaku .......................... 333
Engle, George ............................. 73
Epp, E. J. .......................... 246, 248
Erasmus ................... 185, 219, 231
Erickson, Erick ......................... 178
Erlandsson, Seth ................. 18, 211
Euclid ....................................... 233
Evans, Jim ................................... 76
Falwell, Jerry ..................... 275, 278
Fee, G. D. ................................. 246
Feldkeller, Andreas .................... 17
Feuerbach, Ludwig .................. 194
Finnis, John ............. 95, 96, 97, 111
Fischer, Robert H. ............. 197, 198
Fitzpatrick, Peter ........................ 74
Flacius, Matthew .............. 193, 222
Fletcher, Joseph ........ 107, 108, 316
Flew, Antony ......................... 24, 27
Forell, George W. ............. 177, 199
Fosdick, Harry Emerson ........... 306
Fraenkel, Peter ......................... 100
Francisco, A. S. ........................... 18
Frank, Fr. .................................. 237
Franklin .................................... 337
Frederick the Wise ................... 296
Friedrich, Carl Joachim ...... 93, 101
Fuller, Charles .......................... 257
Fuller, Daniel ........................... 257
Funk, Robert W. ......................... 87
Gadamer .................................... 70
Gallio ....................................... 118
Galpin, Brian .............................. 73
Garrison, William N. ........... 93, 117
Gaskin, Richard H. ..................... 23

Gates, G. E. ...373
Gates, H. L. ...331
Gauquelin ...163
Gavin, Antoine ...296
Geehan, E. R. ...213
Geisler, Norman L. ...65, 106, 242, 315, 316
Genovese, Kitty ...338
Gerhard, Johann ...193, 203, 237
Gerrish, B. A. ...197
Gewirth ...97
Gibson, Peter ...89
Gluckman, Max ...50
Goddard ...35
Goethe ...88
Good, Irving John ...18, 27, 161ff
Goodwin, Edwin J. ...367
Gordon, Cyrus ...85
Gordon, Elizabeth Oke ...296
Graham, Billy ...69, 187
Gray, John Chipman ...35, 94
Greenleaf, Simon ...49, 54, 56, 93, 106, 279, 321, 338
Greenlee, Harold ...256
Greenstein, Daniel I. ...88, 247
Gregory, Brad S. ...177, 180, 181, 182, 183, 184, 185
Grotius, Hugo ...203
Gundry, S. N. ...78, 86
Habel, Norman C. ...230
Habermas, Gary R. ...65, 84
Hacker ...75
Hafenreffer ...203
Hahn, H. F. ...90
Hailsham ...279, 321
Haines, C. G. ...95
Haines-Eitzen, Kim ...247
Hall, D. ...17
Hallaq, Wael B. ...288
Hammerstein, Oscar ...158
Hansen, Walter A. ...193

Harris, J. W. ...75, 94
Hart, H. L. A. ...75, 77, 94, 131, 132, 323
Hassig, Ross ...282
Hastie, R. ...38
Hawking, Stephen ...156, 371
Hay ...382
Haynes, Stephen R. ...70
Hazlitt, W. C. ...282
Heerbrand ...203
Hegel ...70
Heisenberg ...155, 156, 370
Hernandez, Juan ...247
Herod ...118
Hiatt, Alfred ...296
Hick, John ...32
Hickman, Bert ...294
Hilbert, David ...370
Hinsley, F. H. ...161
Hirschl, S. D. ...48
Hitler ...29, 110, 131, 134, 161, 319, 346
Hobbes, Thomas ...97, 140, 149, 179
Hobson, Charles ...350
Hollande ...322
Hollaz, David ...193, 204
Holmes, Michael W. ...245, 248, 268
Holmes, O. W. ...284, 345
Holmes, Sherlock ...58, 85, 165
Homer ...85, 236
Hooper, W. ...54
Hopkins, Tighe ...295
Hort ...241
Horton, Rich ...158
Hosmer, F. E. ...171
Hospers, John ...171, 172, 173, 174
Hospinian ...210
Howard, Roy J. ...70

# Index of Names

Huelsemann .................................. 204
Hume, David .... 27, 47, 61, 164, 171, 172
Hunnius, A. ................................... 203
Hunt, Alan ...................................... 74
Huram ............................................ 367
Hussein, Saddam ......................... 328
Hutter, Leonhard ............... 210, 381
Idi Amin ............................... 134, 319
Iganski, Paul ................................. 347
Irenaeus ....................... 228, 250, 262
Isaiah, the Prophet ............. 90, 112
Isham, C. J. .................................... 156
Jackson, Robert H. ............. 133, 134
Jacob .............................................. 200
Jacobs ............................................. 382
Janik, Allan ..................................... 56
Jastrow, Robert .......................... 147
Jefferson ............................... 337, 351
Jezebel ........................... 113, 114, 197
John, the Apostle ......... 88, 89, 256, 259, 262, 269, 319
John, the Baptist ....... 102, 225, 229, 270
Johnson, Alan F. .......................... 100
Johnson, Paul .............................. 122
Johnson, Samuel ........................ 248
Jolowicz, H. F. ................................ 51
Jones, J. ......................................... 163
Jordan, Jeff ..................................... 30
Joseph .................................. 121, 124
Jowett, Benjamin .......................... 44
Judas, the Apostle ...................... 265
Jude ..................................... 245, 246
Julliard, Jaques ................... 327, 328
Kadane, Joseph B. ........................ 82
Kafka .............................................. 149
Kagehiro, D. K. ............................... 38
Kant, Immanuel ........... 47, 137, 203
Kantonen, T. A. ............................. 235
Kantzer, Kenneth S. .............. 17, 78

Käsemann, Ernst ........................ 194
Katz, Stanley N. ............................. 99
Kelly, Howard A. .......................... 330
Kelly, J. N. D. ................................. 209
Kelman, Mark ................................ 74
Kelsen, Hans ............... 95, 131, 132
Kennedy, Duncan .......................... 74
Kent, James ................................. 284
Kenyon, Frederick G. ......... 240, 241
Kepler, Johann ................... 193, 202
Kerr, N. L. ............................ 38, 39, 41
Khan, Genghis .................... 138, 143
Kierkegaard, Søren .......... 149, 186, 192, 193, 196
Kilgour, David .............................. 277
King, Martin Luther .................. 327
Kiralfy, Albert ................................ 28
Kloha, Jeffrey .......... 18, 227ff, 307ff
Klug, Eugene F. A. ................. 69, 70
Knox, John .................................. 123
Knox, Ronald ...................... 85, 158
Knuth, Donald E. ............... 370, 374
Kochan, M. ................................... 288
Koehneke, P. F. ............................ 214
Koestler, Arthur ......................... 333
Kubrick, Sranley ......................... 161
Kuenen ........................................... 89
Küng, Hans .................................. 184
Kurzweil, R. ......................... 148, 152
Kuyper, Abraham ............. 100, 123
Ladele ........................................... 275
Laden, Osama ben ..................... 286
Lakatos, Imre ................................ 57
Landon, Charles ................ 245, 246
Lasok, D. ....................................... 101
Lazarus ................................ 62, 174, 175
Lehmann, Hartmut ................... 177
Lehmann, Paul ........................... 107
Lelouch, Claude ......................... 129
Lenzen .......................................... 156
León-Portilla, Miguel ............... 282

Lessing, Gotthold E. .........26, 47, 65, 199
Lewis, Bernard ............................286
Lewis, C. S. .......33, 54, 85, 102, 106, 162, 258, 358
Lienhard, Marc ....................99, 101
Lincoln ............................................29
Lindsay, Matthew J. ...................284
Linnemann, E. ...............................87
Lipstadt, Deborah ......................347
Lissner, Jorgen .............................99
Littell, F. H. ...................................197
Littman, D. ...................................288
Livingstone, David........................71
Luedemann, Gerd ........................87
Luke ....... 49, 88, 228, 229, 230, 232, 250, 258
Lull, Ramón ..................................184
Luther, Martin ..... 21, 77, 99, 103ff, 123, 177ff, 210ff, 222, 231, 232, 233, 234, 235, 238, 253, 254, 269, 271, 277, 296, 317, 322, 363, 381
Maas, K. D. .....................................18
MacGregor............................87, 88
Machiavelli ...................97, 149, 150
MacKay...................................339, 357
Madoff, Bernard ................293, 354
Magruder, Jeb .............................109
Mah, Harold................................179
Maier, G..........................................87
Maitland, Frederic William........72
Makutsi ........................................359
Malcolm, Norman......................139
Mark ............................49, 229, 247
Marquart, Kurt E. .......................258
Marshall, John.......73, 75, 251, 349, 350, 351
Marshall, Peter ...........................347
Martin, Elizabeth A. ....................73
Martin, R. ..............................149, 152
Martin, Walter R. .........................31

Marx, Karl .....................................194
Mary, mother of Jesus....... 26, 228, 229, 250, 261, 268, 308
Masius, H. G. ...............................204
Matsuda, Mari J. .........................347
Matthew, the Apostle... 49, 88, 235
Maxwell, W. D...............................73
Mba, Celestine ............................274
Mbuyi, Sarah................................274
McClintock, Andrew.................275
McCloskey ...............................52, 53
McCormick, C. T. ............. 22, 36, 49
McFarlane, Gary ............... 274, 279
McGarth, G. J. ...............................17
McGlone, Patrick........................81
McGrath, Alistair .......................358
McKenzie, Steven L. .....................70
McKerrow, Ronald B.................248
McLaughlin...................................48
McNeile ..........................................85
Meade ..........................................350
Melanchthon, Philipp ..... 193, 204, 211, 220, 223
Mendel, A. ........................... 147, 152
Mendelsohn, S.............................51
Menuge, Angus J. L. .......... 276, 284
Metzger, Bruce ................. 242, 319
Miles, Sara....................................71
Mohammed........ 132, 173, 290, 331
Monnier, Jean-Frédéric ...........189
Montaigne, Michel de ..............282
Montefiore, Hugh ......................161
Moore, G. E. ............................71, 97
Morgan, Edmund ........................56
Morgenstern..................................90
Morton..................................87, 88
Moses .......... 89, 107, 113, 132, 174, 204, 235
Mueller, J. Theodore. 191, 192, 206
Mueller, S. P...................................18
Mueller-Vollmer, Kurt................70

# Index of Names

Mugabe .................................................. 319
Muggeridge, Malcolm, ............... 330
Muhammad, Shaykh ................. 173
Muller, Richard A. ....................... 363
Myshrall ..................................... 248
Napoleon ...................... 29, 177, 229
Nash, Ronald H. .......................... 213
Nation, C. R. I. ............................. 262
Nebuchadnezzar ......................... 114
Nehushtan, Yossi ....... 323, 325, 326
Nero ............................................ 113
Nestle .......... 228, 236, 248, 250, 268
Newman, Jon O. ............................ 44
Nietzsche ..................................... 194
Noah ...................... 78, 110, 111, 329
Noland, Martin R. ...... 239, 262, 263, 268
Noll, Mark ..................................... 71
Oark, T. F. ................................... 100
Odgers, Charles E. ......................... 73
Oesch, Wilhelm .......................... 235
Ogden, S. M. ........................... 73, 74
Olearius, Gottfried ..................... 221
Olearius, Johann ......................... 216
Origen .......... 228, 250, 262, 363, 364
Orwell, George .................... 129, 303
Osborne ........................................ 86
Osteyee, D. B. ............................. 162
Overd, M. ................................... 274
Paine, Thomas .......... 182, 185, 337, 351
Parker, David C. ......................... 248
Pascal ........................................... 30
Paterculus, Velleius ...................... 86
Patrick, John .............................. 364
Patterson, Richard North ........... 37
Paul, the Apostle ....... 22, 24, 49, 62, 87, 105, 118, 119, 124, 125, 187, 188, 200, 205, 216, 233, 240, 249, 254, 260, 264, 272
Payne, J. Barton ................. 231, 265
Pelikan, Jaroslav ....... 192, 193, 195, 196, 199, 203, 204
Penrose, Roger .................. 155, 156
Penzel, K. .................................... 199
Pepper .......................................... 77
Perelman, Ch. ............................... 95
Perrott, D. L. .............................. 101
Peter, the Apostle ...... 47, 115, 118, 119, 240, 264, 269, 294, 295, 380
Philip, the Apostle ..................... 265
Phillips, J. B. ................................. 53
Pickover, Clifford A. ................... 374
Pieper, Francis ............ 236, 263, 266
Piepkorn, Arthur Carl ...... 234, 253
Pike, James A. ....... 79, 108, 307, 357
Pilate .......................................... 118
Pitts, Andrew W. ................ 245, 246
Plass, E. M. ................................. 196
Plato ..................................... 47, 168
Plautus ......................................... 54
Plummer, Christopher .............. 329
Ponzi, Charles ............................ 283
Popper, Karl ................................. 76
Porter, Stanley E. ....... 245, 246, 248
Posamentier, Alfred S. .............. 367
Pot, Pol ............................... 134, 319
Prebble, Lucy ............................. 353
Preus, Robert D. ........ 159, 216, 266
Pusey, E. B. .................................. 90
Quenstedt ........................... 204, 236
Ramotswe .................................. 359
Rand, Ayn .................................. 354
Rawls, John ......... 97, 137, 147, 149, 152
Raymond, Ibrahim .................... 286
Raz ............................................... 75
Reagan, Ronald .......................... 261
Record, Taylor I. ........................ 367
Reich, Charles A. ....................... 108
Reid, Thomas ............................... 22
Reidy, D. ............................. 149, 152

Reimann, Henry W. ................... 222
Reumann, John .......................... 258
Reymond, Robert L. ................... 224
Reynolds, Alastair ...................... 158
Rieke, Richard .............................. 56
Ringer, Robert J. ........149, 150, 152, 354
Roady, T. G. .................................. 48
Robertson, Geoffrey ................... 288
Robertson, Pat ............................ 280
Robespierre ................................. 126
Robin, Jean .................................. 286
Robinson, Alan ............................. 44
Robinson, J. A. T. .................. 49, 358
Rodgers, Richard ........................ 158
Rodwell, Daniel ............................ 40
Röhl, Katharina ........................... 283
Rörer ............................................ 197
Rosalia ......................................... 296
Rose, H. J. .................................... 85
Rosenbaum, Alan S. ............... 94, 95
Rousseau, Jean-Jaques .............. 140
Russell ......................................... 370
Saarnivaara, Uuras ..................... 381
Sagan, Carl ........27, 28, 162, 166, 368
Salzmann, Jorg Christian ........ 252, 262
Sand, P. H. ................................... 106
Sanday, Peggy Reeves ................ 282
Sapphira ...................................... 294
Sarkozy, Nicolas ........280, 322, 346
Sartre ........................................... 149
Sasse, Hermann .........210, 237, 266, 322
Sayers, Dorothy ............................ 86
Scarman ........................................ 36
Schaeffer, Francis ....................... 321
Scharlemann, Robert ........ 194, 203
Schiaparelli .................................. 156
Schirrmacher, Christine ........... 287, 288, 324
Schlink, Edmund ....... 212, 214, 217, 218, 219, 220
Schmid ........................................ 382
Schmidt, Alvin J. ........ 151, 152, 243, 290, 325, 327
Schmidt, Christian ..................... 364
Schmidt, J. M. ............................. 147
Schmidt, Sebastian ..................... 221
Schoenberg ............................ 52, 53
Schrödinger, Erwin .......... 155, 157
Schultz, Robert C. ...................... 193
Schum, David ........................ 55, 57
Scorsese, Martin ......... 18, 274, 333
Sealy, A. P. ....................... 38, 39, 41
Searle, John ....................... 148, 152
Seidman, R. B. ............................ 107
Sekulow, Jay ...................... 280, 337
Shain, M. ....................................... 49
Shakespeare ....................... 247, 248
Shapiro, B. J. ................................. 35
Sharp, G. Granville ...................... 73
Shea, Nina ................................... 347
Sherlock, Thomas ............... 29, 172
Sherwin-White, A. N. ................... 86
Silva, Moises ................................. 72
Simpson, A. W. B. ......................... 56
Sittler, Joseph ............................. 234
Skilling, Jeffrey .................. 353, 354
Smalley, Beryl ............................. 363
Smith, Alexander McCall ......... 358, 359
Smith, Jean Edward ......... 349, 350, 351
Smith, Joseph ............... 29, 272, 290
Smith, Michael ........................... 161
Solomon ..................................... 367
Sourdel, Dominique and Janine ....................................... 288
Sovik, Arne ................................... 99
Spencer, Robert .......................... 288
Spong, John Shelby ................... 358

# Index of Names

Sproul, R. C. ............................ 65, 211
Stewart, H. F. ............................... 30
Stott, John ................................. 358
Stripp, Alan ............................... 161
Strong, John William .................. 22
Stump, Joseph .......................... 103
Suetonius .................................... 86
Swinburne, Richard .................... 61
Switzer, Cal ............................... 294
Tacitus ................................. 86, 230
Talleyrand ......................... 141, 151
Tallis, R. ............................. 148, 153
Tawney ..................................... 178
Taylor, Charles .......................... 180
Taylor, Hawley O. ..................... 369
Teetotalus, A. ........................... 262
Terry, Richard R. ......................... 69
Tertullian .................................. 209
Thatcher ................................... 357
Thayer ........................................ 48
Tholuck ..................................... 194
Thomas, the Apostle ......... 62, 233, 254, 264
Thompson, John L. .................... 363
Thucydides ............................... 258
Timothy ............................ 119, 269
Tipler, F. ................................... 156
Tolkien, J. R. R. .......................... 257
Tonkin, John M. ........................ 179
Torrance, T. F. ........................... 100
Toulmin, Stephen ...... 47, 48, 55, 56
Toynbee, A. ....................... 151, 153
Tribe, Laurence ..................... 75, 76
Troeltsch, Ernst ................. 193, 199
Truzzi, Marcello ... 27, 28, 162, 164, 166
Tsarnaïev, Djokhar .................... 291
Tucker, George Fox .................. 283
Turing, Alan ...................... 152, 161
Turow, Scott ..................... 315, 317
Twining, William L. .... 56, 57, 58, 64

Unger, Roberto ........................... 74
Ussher, Clarence D. ......... 289, 329ff
Valla, Lorenzo .................... 201, 296
Van der Heyden, Ulrich .............. 17
Van Til, Cornelius .... 100, 207, 213, 224, 259
Veatch, Henry B. .................... 96, 97
Voegelin, Eric ........................... 106
Voelz, James W. ........ 227, 229, 250, 255
Voltaire ............................. 163, 343
Vulpius, Melchior ..................... 189
Wachtel, Klaus .......................... 268
Wahlstrom ................................ 191
Walch, Johann Georg ................ 209
Wall, James M. .......................... 117
Walters ....................................... 35
Walther, C. F. W. ........ 77, 104, 263, 322
Warfield, B. B. .................... 242, 322
Warraq, Ibn .............................. 286
Warren, Robert Penn ................ 354
Wasserman, Tommy ......... 245, 250
Wasteney, Victoria ................... 274
Watson, Philip S. ........ 99, 196, 197, 206
Watts, Isaac .............................. 382
Weber ....................................... 178
Wegner, Paul D. ........................ 243
Weichman, Gordon ................... 161
Weisberg, Frederick H. ............... 83
Wellhausen ................................. 89
Wellman, Jack ........................... 365
Wesley, John ...................... 21, 315
Whitehead ................................ 370
Whyte, William Pinkney ........... 350
Wieser, Maguerite .................... 100
Wigmore, John Henry ... 23, 55, 56, 57, 58, 61, 66, 67, 164
Wilberforce .............................. 125
Willard, Dallas ............................ 18

Williams, Andrea Minichiello...85, 273, 275
Wilson, George Grafton............283
Winch, Peter................................70
Winkworth, Catherine..............189
Winthrop....................................119
Wittgenstein, Ludwig.........76, 138, 139, 142, 143, 150, 153, 168, 181, 221, 370
Wolfe, Christopher....................276
Wood, Gordon S.........................349
Wood, Nathan R.........................371
Worrall, John................................57
Wright, G. H. ...............................70
Wright, N. T. ................................86
Wyon, Olive...............................199
Xavier, Francis ..........................334
Yamauchi, E. ...............................85
Ye'or, Bat....................................288
Zabotec, Judas Iscariote............282
Zahar, Elia ...................................57
Zöckler........................................194
Zwingli........201, 202, 210, 212, 219

www.ingramcontent.com/pod-product-compliance
Lightning Source LLC
Chambersburg PA
CBHW071143300426
44113CB00009B/1066